Donald Charrett has written a must-read primer for anyone in construction law, considering the current reality in the construction industry worldwide. The new *FIDIC Contracts in the Americas* is undoubtedly a delightful guide full of important information for those who want to manage contracts in different jurisdictions and realities. By far, this book will set trends for future project execution in Latin America.

Rodrigo Hernández Riquelme, BSc, MSc, LLM, PgD, Associate Director JS HELD [Chile], Board Member of the Chilean Society of Construction Law

Donald Charrett is a multifaceted professional – barrister, arbitrator, mediator, expert and dispute board member – and a prolific author of important articles and books on International Construction Law. In this his most recent work, Donald presents us with the coordination of a comprehensive guide on the use of FIDIC contracts in the Americas, with the participation of renowned lawyers, engineers and architects. The book *FIDIC Contracts in the Americas: A Practical Guide to Application* is necessary work for professionals and students, as well as for everyone who seeks to understand the increasing importance of FIDIC contracts in the Americas and the rest of the world.

Júlio César Bueno, Partner Pinheiro Neto Advogados Brazil

For decades FIDIC Contracts have been the gold standard for international construction agreements. As such, a comprehensive guide to FIDIC contracts in the Americas is greatly welcomed. This addition to the series is accessible and practical and should immediately become an indispensable part of every construction practitioner's library.

Chris Fladgate FCIArb, Managing Partner, Garson, Ségal, Steinmetz, Fladgate LLP

FIDIC CONTRACTS IN THE AMERICAS

FIDIC contracts are the most widely used contracts for international construction around the world and are used in many different jurisdictions, both common law and civil law. For any construction project, the General Conditions of Contract published by FIDIC may need to be supplemented by Particular Conditions that specify the specific requirements of that project and jurisdiction.

FIDIC Contracts in the Americas: A Practical Guide to Application provides readers with an overview of the legal environment, the construction industry and features of contract law applying to construction contracts in a number of jurisdictions in the Americas. It provides detailed guidance for the preparation of the Particular Conditions for FIDIC contracts that will comply with the requirements of the applicable laws that apply to the site where the work is carried out, and for the governing law of the contract. This book also details the impact of COVID-19 on both the execution of construction projects and the operation of construction contracts in each jurisdiction.

This book is essential reading for construction professionals, lawyers and students of construction law.

Dr Donald Charrett is a barrister, arbitrator, mediator, expert and dispute board member practising in technology, engineering and construction (TEC) disputes. He is a member of the FIDIC President's List of Adjudicators and a Fellow of the Chartered Institute of Arbitrators. He was named Best Construction Law Practitioner, Australia 2016 by *Business Worldwide Magazine*, and a Thought Leader – Construction by Who's Who Legal in 2019, 2020 and 2021, saying 'Donald is an excellent and knowledgeable lawyer'. His legal publications include articles on expert evidence, FIDIC contracts, dispute boards, dispute avoidance and resolution, contract risk, forensic engineering, contractual lessons from past projects, design and construct contracts, quantum meruit and solidary liability. He is the author, co-author or editor of ten books on construction law.

PRACTICAL LEGAL GUIDES FOR CONSTRUCTION AND TECHNOLOGY PROJECTS

Series Editor: Donald Charrett

The books in this series provide lawyers and construction professionals with the relevant knowledge, resources and practical guidance to understand the contemporary construction industry and the law necessary to achieve successful outcomes for construction projects. The topics covered include front-end issues such as project procurement, the production, negotiation and administration of contracts, and the avoidance of disputes, as well as backend issues such as taking part in, managing or resolving disputes. The series aims to keep abreast of the technologies that have increasing impact in changing traditional ways of working, contracting and resolving disputes.

FIDIC CONTRACTS IN ASIA PACIFIC
A Practical Guide to Application
Donald Charrett (ed)

CONTRACTS FOR CONSTRUCTION AND ENGINEERING PROJECTS
Second Edition
Donald Charrett

CONTRACTS FOR INFRASTRUCTURE PROJECTS
An International Guide to Application
Philip Loots and Donald Charrett

FIDIC CONTRACTS IN EUROPE
A Practical Guide to Application
Donald Charrett (ed)

FIDIC CONTRACTS IN THE AMERICAS
A Practical Guide to Application
Donald Charrett (ed)

For more information, please visit: www.routledge.com/Practical-Legal-Guides-for-Construction-and-Technology-Projects/book-series/PLGCTP

FIDIC CONTRACTS IN THE AMERICAS

A PRACTICAL GUIDE TO APPLICATION

EDITED BY DONALD CHARRETT

informa law
from Routledge

Designed cover image: © Donald Charrett

First published 2024
by Informa Law from Routledge
4 Park Square, Milton Park, Abingdon, Oxon OX14 4RN

and by Informa Law from Routledge
605 Third Avenue, New York, NY 10158

Informa Law from Routledge is an imprint of the Taylor & Francis Group, an informa business

British Library Cataloguing-in-Publication Data
A catalogue record for this book is available from the British Library

ISBN: 978-1-032-06225-9 (hbk)
ISBN: 978-1-032-06224-2 (pbk)
ISBN: 978-1-003-20125-0 (ebk)

DOI: 10.4324/9781003201250

Typeset in Times New Roman
by Deanta Global Publishing Services, Chennai, India

This book is dedicated with grateful thanks to my wife, Jeyami, without whose continuing understanding of and tolerance for the time-consuming demands entailed by my writing activities, this book would not have been possible.

CONTENTS

List of figures xi
List of tables xii
About the editor xiii
Table of cases xiv
Table of legislation xvi
Contributors xxvi
Acknowledgements xxxiii
Foreword xxxv

CHAPTER 1 INTRODUCTION 1
Dr Donald Charrett

CHAPTER 2 THE FIDIC GOLDEN PRINCIPLES 44
Dr Donald Charrett

CHAPTER 3 PREPARATION OF PARTICULAR CONDITIONS 54
Dr Donald Charrett

CHAPTER 4 APPLYING FIDIC CONTRACTS IN THE PLURINATIONAL STATE OF BOLIVIA 74
Claudia Andrea Lopez Monterrey and Polina Chtchelok

CHAPTER 5 APPLYING FIDIC CONTRACTS IN BRAZIL 105
Thiago Fernandes Moreira and Caio Gabra

CHAPTER 6 APPLYING FIDIC CONTRACTS IN CANADA 129
Sharon C Vogel

CHAPTER 7 APPLYING FIDIC CONTRACTS IN CHILE 162
Dr Elina Mereminskaya, Alex Wagemann and Fernando Landeros

CHAPTER 8 APPLYING FIDIC CONTRACTS IN ECUADOR 186
Dr Mario Alejandro Flor, Juan Carlos Herrera-Quenguan and Alejandro Pérez

CHAPTER 9 APPLYING FIDIC CONTRACTS IN MEXICO 207
Roberto Hernández García and Juan Pablo Sandoval García

CHAPTER 10 APPLYING FIDIC CONTRACTS IN PERU 231
Jaime Gray, Jonnathan Bravo and Guillermo Alarcón

CHAPTER 11 APPLYING FIDIC CONTRACTS IN THE UNITED STATES OF AMERICA 257
Joseph F Moore

CHAPTER 12 APPLYING FIDIC CONTRACTS IN URUGUAY 274
Dr José Luis Echevarría Petit

Glossary 305
Index 323

FIGURES

1.1 Oxford Stringency Index – Bolivia, Brazil, Canada and Chile 28
1.2 Oxford Stringency Index – Ecuador, Mexico, Peru and USA 29
4.1 Structure and priority order of legal norms at State level 78
4.2 Structure and priority order of legal norms at Departmental level 78
4.3 Structure and priority order of legal norms at Municipal level 79
4.4 Structure and priority order of legal norms at Indigenous level 79
9.1 The multi-tier dispute prevention and resolution mechanisms in the 2017 FIDIC rainbow suite 217

TABLES

1.1	FIDIC Conditions of Contract for contracts between Employer and Contractor	16
1.2	Order of precedence of Contract documents in the FIDIC rainbow suite	19
1.3	Country accessions to international conventions and agreements	36
1.4	Editions of FIDIC Conditions of Contract for contracts between Employer and Contractor	43
3.1	Contract Data in 2017 Yellow Book, annotated with default provisions	70

ABOUT THE EDITOR

Dr Donald Charrett BE(Hons), LLB(Hons), MConstLaw, PhD, ProfCertArb, Dip International Arbitration, FIEAust, FCIArb

Dr Charrett is a barrister, arbitrator, mediator, expert and dispute board member practising in technology, engineering and construction (TEC) disputes. Prior to joining the Victorian Bar, he worked as a solicitor at a large Australian law firm. His construction law briefs have included litigation, mediation, expert determination, facilitation of experts' conferences, arbitration and membership of dispute boards. He is a Fellow of the Chartered Institute of Arbitrators and a member of the FIDIC President's List of Adjudicators. He was named Best Construction Law Practitioner, Australia 2016 by *Business Worldwide Magazine*. In 2019, 2020 and 2021, Who's Who Legal included him on their list of *Thought Leaders: Construction*, saying 'Donald Charrett is looked on with enormous favour by sources for his vast experience in construction and engineering disputes' and 'Donald is an excellent and knowledgeable lawyer'.

Prior to becoming a lawyer, he worked as an engineer for over 30 years, including 12 years as a director of a consulting engineering firm. Dr Charrett's engineering experience included computer applications, structural design, managing engineering projects, acting as an expert witness and management roles in contract negotiation and administration, insurance, international joint ventures and corporate restructuring. From 2012 to 2014 he was the non-executive chairman of the consulting engineering company AMOG.

Dr Charrett has published widely on legal and engineering subjects and has presented conference papers, workshops and training courses in Australia and internationally. He is a Senior Fellow at the University of Melbourne, teaching a Master of Construction Law subject on international construction law.

His legal publications include articles on expert evidence, FIDIC contracts, dispute boards, dispute avoidance and resolution, contract risk, forensic engineering, contractual lessons from past projects, design and construct contracts, quantum meruit, solidary liability, construction insurance, professional indemnity insurance and reinsurance. He is the author of *Contracts for Construction and Engineering Projects*; a joint author of *Contracts for Infrastructure Projects: An International Guide*, *The Application of Contracts in Developing Oil and Gas Projects* and *Practical Guide to Engineering and Construction Contracts*; and the editor of *FIDIC Contracts in Europe*, *FIDIC Contracts in Asia Pacific*, *The International Application of FIDIC Contracts: A Practical Guide* and *Global Challenges, Shared Solutions*.

TABLE OF CASES

Australia

Akai Pty Ltd *v.* The People's Insurance Co Ltd (1996) 188 CLR 418 10
Attorney-General of Botswana *v.* Aussie Diamond Products Pty Ltd (No 3) [2010] WASC 14 10
Bonython *v.* the Commonwealth of Australia (1950) 81 CLR 486 10
Bonython *v.* Commonwealth of Australia [1951] AC 201 10
Garsec *v.* His Majesty the Sultan of Brunei [2008] NSWCA 211 [128] 10
John Pfeiffer *v.* Rogerson (2000) 203 CLR 503 10
Mendelsohn-Zeller Inc *v.* T&C Providores Pty Ltd [1981] NSWLR 366 10
Vita Food Products Inc *v.* Unus Shipping Co Ltd [1939] AC 277 10

Brazil

Court of Appeals of the State of Goiás, Appeal no. 0151633-54.2015.8.09.0051 121
Court of Appeals of the State of Paraná, Appeal no. 1.292.381-0 127
Court of Appeals of the State of São Paulo, Appeal no. 21099854520158260000 127
Superior Court of Justice, Interim Special Appeal no. 16121 SP 2018/0155547-5 120
Superior Court of Justice, Interim Special Appeal no. 979663/MG 126
Superior Court of Justice. Special Appeal no. 1.569.422/RJ 122

Canada

Bhasin *v.* Hrynew, 2014 SCC 71 152
Buttcon Ltd *v.* Toronto Electric Commissioners, 2003 CanLII 9258 (ON SC) 146
C.M. Callow Inc *v.* Zollinger, 2020 SCC 45 152
Crosslinx *v.* Ontario Infrastructure 2022 ONCA 187 151
Hengyun International Investment Commerce Inc *v.* 9368-7614 Quebec Inc 2020 QCCS 2251 151
The Queen (Ont.) *v.* Ron Engineering, [1981] 1 SCR 111 145
Sattva Capital Corp *v.* Creston Moly Corp, 2014 SCC 53 159
Uber Technologies Inc *v.* Heller, 2020 SCC 16 152
Wastech Services Ltd *v.* Greater Vancouver Sewerage and Drainage District, 2021 SCC 17 152

Chile

Supreme Court Case No 3965-2011, 2 May 2012, Chile 177
Supreme Court 22 May 2019, Case No 38.506-2017, Chile 180

Malaysia

Ooi Boon Long *v.* Citibank NA [1984] 1 M.L.J. 222 7

Mexico

Rosendo Radilla Pacheco *v.* Mexico Varios 912/2010 210

Philippines

Lambert *v.* Fox 26 Phil 588 8

United Kingdom

Eco World – Ballymore Embassy Gardens Company Limited *v.* Dobler UK Limited [2021] EWHC 2207 (TCC) 178
Enka Insaat Ve Sanayi AS *v.* OOO Insurance Company (Enka Insaat) [2020] UKSC 38 59
Fiona Trust & Holding Corp *v.* Privalov [2007] UKHL 40; [2007] All ER 951 26
Nelson v Nelson [1995] HCA 25; (1995) 184 CLR 538 8
Power Curber International Ltd *v.* National Bank of Kuwait [1981] 1 WLR 1233 10
Printing and Numeral Registering Co. *v.* Sampson (1875) L. R. 19 Eq., 462 7

TABLE OF LEGISLATION

International Instruments

Agreement on Government Agreement (WTO GPA) ... 36
- Annex 4 ... 35
- Annex 5 ... 35
- Annex 6 ... 35

CNICA Arbitration Rules ... 57
- Art. 2 ... 57
- Art. 3 ... 57

European Contracts Convention (Rome I) ... 58

European Convention on Human Rights ... 6

Hague Principles ... 56
- Art. 2 ... 56
- Art. 3 ... 56
- Art. 11 ... 56

Inter-American Convention on International Commercial Arbitration (Panama 1975) ... 301

Inter-American Convention on the Extraterritorial Validity of Foreign Judgments and Arbitral Awards (Montevideo, 1979) ... 302

Inter-American Convention on the Law Applicable to International Contracts ... 58

International Centre for Settlement Investment Disputes Convention (ICSID Convention) ... 89

International Conventions on Human Rights and Community Law ... 78

New York Convention on the Recognition and Enforcement of Foreign Arbitral Awards ... 15, 34–36, 272, 301

Protocol on Cooperation and Jurisdictional Assistance in Civil, Commercial, Labor and Administrative Matters (Mercosur, Las Leñas, Argentina) ... 302

Safety and Health in Construction Convention, 1988 (No. 167) 2014 ... 85

UNCITRAL Model Law on International Commercial Arbitration ... 36, 184, 272, 288
- Art. 16(1) ... 26

UNIDROIT Principles of International Commercial Contracts 2016 ... 8, 14, 26, 36, 58
- Art. 1.3 ... 9

United Nations Provisional Central Product Classification
- Div 51 ... 35

Austria

Austrian Bürgerliches Gesetzbuch, 1811 ... 5

Bolivia

Código Civil 1975 [Civil Code]
- Art. 350 ... 95
- Art. 380 ... 95, 100
- Art. 382 ... 95, 100
- Art. 391 ... 101
- Art. 399 ... 95
- Art. 450 ... 100
- Art. 451 ... 100
- Art. 454 ... 87, 93
- Art. 511 ... 99
- Art. 518 ... 99
- Art. 519 ... 99
- Art. 520 ... 99
- Art. 524 ... 99
- Art. 532 ... 99
- Art. 533 ... 99
- Art. 568 ... 96
- Art. 569 ... 96
- Art. 577 ... 96, 100
- Art. 578 ... 96, 100
- Art. 581 ... 100
- Art. 732–749 ... 100

Art. 733 93
Art. 735 93
Art. 737 .... 93, 95
Art. 738 93
Art. 740 93
Art. 741 93
Art. 742 .... 93, 95
Art. 744 95
Art. 745 .... 93, 95
Art. 748 93
Art. 992 101
Art. 998 101
Art. 1507 99
Art. 1508 99
Código de Comercio de Bolivia 1977 [Bolivian Commercial Code] 101
Art. 801 98
Art. 802 100
Art. 804 99
Art. 806 100
Art. 810 100
Art. 818 101
Art. 820 101
Art. 1447 100
Art. 1509 100
Art. 1513 100
Art. 1585 101
Art. 1593 100
Código de Salud 1978 [Health Code] 102
Código de Seguridad Social 1956 [Social Security Code] 83
Código Procesal Civil 2013 [Civil Procedure Code] 88, 100
Código Tributario 1992 [Tributary Code] 101
Constitución Política del Estado 2009 (CPE) [State Constitution] 77
Art. 320 89
Art. 410 78
Convenio sobre seguridad y salud en la construcción 2014 [Convention on safety and health in construction] 102
Diferimiento y facilidades de pago del impuesto sobre las utilidades de las empresas 2020 (DS 4198) [Deferral and payment facilities of the tax on corporate profits] 92
DS 2195 (2014) 101
DS 2298 (2015) 101
DS 3946 (2019) 94
DS 4058 (2019) 87
DS 4199 (2020) 90
DS 4200 [2020] 90
DS 4206 92
DS 4214 (2020) 90
DS 4216 92
DS 4229 (2020) 90
DS 4248 (2020) 92
DS 4298 (2020) 92
DS 4409 (2020) 92
DS 4430 (2021) 91
DS 4443 (2021) 91
DS4464 (2021) 91
DS 29033 (2007) 101
DS 29124 (2007) 101
Ley 25 Art 45 80
Ley 73 80
Ley 439 88
Ley 545 (2014) 85
Ley 620 80
Ley 708 (2015) 89, 97
Art. 4 89
Art. 5 no. 3 87
Art. 40 96
Art. 45 88
Transitory Article 4 87
Ley 1178 Art 47 97
Ley 1883 88
Ley de Administración y Control Gubernamentales 1990 [Government Administration and Control Act] 97
Ley de Conciliación y Arbitraje 2015 [Conciliation and Arbitration Law] 89, 97, 100, 103
Ley de Conservación del Patrimonio Natural 2015 [Natural Heritage Conservation Law] 77
Ley de Derecho de Autor 1992 [Copyright Law] 101
Ley de Deslinde Jurisdiccional 2010 [Jurisdictional Demarcation Law] 80
Ley de Electricidad 1994 (Ley 1604) [Electricity Law] 86
Ley de gestión integral de residuos 2015 [Comprehensive waste management law] 101
Ley de Hidrocarburos 2005 (Ley 3058) [Hydrocarbons Law] 86
Ley de la Empresa Pública 2013 (Ley 466) [Public Company Law] Art 6 86

Ley del Ejercicio Profesional de la Ingeniería 1993 [Law of the Professional Practice of Engineering] 100
Ley del Ejercicio Profesional del Arquitecto 1992 [Law of the Professional Practice of the Architect] 100
Ley del Medio Ambiente 1992 [Environmental Law] 101
Ley del Organo Judicial 2010 [Law of the Judicial Branch] 79–80
Ley del Presupuesto General del Estado 2020 (Ley 1356) [Law of the General State Budget] 90
Ley del Sistema de Planificación Integral del Estado de Bolivia 2016 [Law of the Comprehensive Planning System of the State of Bolivia] 101
Ley de Minería y Metalurgia 2014 (Ley 535) [Mining and Metallurgy Law] 86
Ley de Pensiones 2010 [Pension Law] 83
Ley de Promoción de Inversiones 2014 [Investment Promotion Law] 89
Ley de Seguro Obligatorio de Accidentes de la Trabajadora y el Trabajador en el Ámbito de la Construcción 2019 (Ley 1155) [Law on Compulsory Accident Insurance for Workers in the Construction Field] 87, 88
Ley de Seguros de la República de Bolivia 1998 [Insurance Law of the Republic of Bolivia] 88, 102
Ley excepcional de diferimiento de pagos de créditos y reducción temporal del pago de servicios básicos 2020 (Ley 1294) [Exceptional law for the deferral of credit payments and temporary reduction in the payment of basic services] 92
Ley Forestal 1996 [Forest Law] 101
Ley General de Higiene, Seguridad Ocupacional y Bienestar 1979 [General Law of Hygiene, Occupational Safety and Wellbeing] 84, 102
Ley General del Trabajo 1942 [General Labour Law] 83, 101
Ley General de Telecomunicaciones, Tecnologías de Información y Comunicación 2011 (Ley 164) [General Law on Telecommunications, Information and Communication Technologies] 86, 94
Ley transitoria para la tramitación de los procesos contenciosos y contencioso administrativo 2014 [Transitory Law for the processing of contentious and administrative litigation processes] 80
Los preceptos y el contenido mínimo de los Contratos de Alianzas Estratégicas de Inversión Conjunta 2018 (DS 3469) [The precepts and minimum content of the Joint Investment Strategic Alliance Contracts] 86, 101
Norma Básica del Sistema de Administración de Bienes y Servicios 2009 (DS 181) [Basic Standard of the Goods and Services Administration System] 87, 89, 94
  Art. 20 100
  Art. 30 87
  Art. 46 88
  Art. 76 88
  Art. 86 88
  Art. 87 88
  Art. 88 94
  Art. 89 87
Obligatorio de Empleadores – ROE [Required for Employers] 101
Programa Especial de Apoyo a la Micro, Pequeña y Mediana Empresa, y el Plan de Emergencia de Apoyo al Empleo y Estabilidad Laboral a las empresas legalmente constituidas 2020 (DS 4216) [Special Program to Support Micro, Small and Medium Enterprises, and the Emergency Plan to Support Employment and Labor Stability for legally constituted companies] 92
Protección de Fauna Silvestre 2021 (DS 4489) [Wildlife Protection] 101
Reglamento de Autorizaciones para Actividades Arqueológicas, Resolución Ministerial Nº

349/2012 (2012) [Regulation of Authorizations for Archaeological Activities, Ministerial Resolution No. 349/2012] Art 4 ... 98
Reglamento de Diferimiento de Pagos de Créditos y Reducción Temporal del Pago de Servicios Básicos 2020 (DS 4206) [Regulation of Deferral of Payments of Credits and Temporary Reduction of the Payment of Basic Services] ... 92
Reglamento de higiene, seguridad y medicina del trabajo 1982 (DS18886) [Occupational hygiene, safety and medicine regulations] ... 102
Reglamento de la Ley 545 2016 [Regulation of Law 545] ... 85
Reglamento de la Ley de Derecho de Autor 1994 (DS 23907) [Regulation of the Copyright Law] ... 101
Reglamento de la Ley General del Trabajo (DS 224) 1943 [Regulation of the General Labor Law] ... 101
Reglamento del saneamiento del medio ambiente 1982 (DS 18886) [Environmental Sanitation Regulation] ... 101
Reglamento general de gestión Ambiental 1995 (DS 24176) [General Environmental Management Regulations] ... 101
Reglamento para actividades con sustancias peligrosas 1995 (DS 24176) [Regulations for activities with dangerous substances] ... 101
Reglamento para diseño, construcción, operación y abandono de ductos en Bolivia 1997 (DS24721) [Regulations for the design, construction, operation and abandonment of pipelines in Bolivia] ... 101
Reglamento para el Desarrollo de Actividades Económicas del Sector de Construcción [Regulation for the Development of Economic Activities of the Construction Sector] ... 91
Reglamento para la Construcción y Operación de Refinerías, Plantas, Petroquímicas y Unidades de Proceso 1999 (DS 25502) [Regulations for the Construction and Operation of Refineries, Plants, Petrochemicals and Process Units] ... 101
RM 105/18 (Ministerio de Trabajo) Registro [(Ministry of Labour) Registration] ... 101
RM 186/14 (Ministerio de Obras Publicas) Guía Boliviana de Construcción de Edificaciones [(Ministry of Public Works) Bolivian Guide to Construction of Buildings] ... 102
RM 388/17 (Ministerio de Medioambiente) Aprobación de las normas técnicas de seguridad en la construcción [(Ministry of the Environment) Approval of technical safety standards in construction] ... 102
Subasta Electrónica y Mercado Virtual Estatal 2021 (DS 4453) [Electronic Auction and State Virtual Market] ... 87, 101
Trabajadora y el Trabajador en el Ámbito de la Construcción 2019 [Worker and Worker in the Construction Field] ... 102
Tramitación de la licencia ambiental 2011 (DS 902) [Processing of the environmental license] ... 101
Tribunal Supremo de Justicia Sala Civil [Supreme Court of Justice Civil Chamber]
- AS 190/2013 ... 87
- AS 281/2012 ... 87
- AS 286/2012 ... 87

Brazil

Bankruptcy Law (Federal Law No. 11,101/2005) ... 124, 125, 127
Brazilian Arbitration Law (Federal Law No. 9,307/1996) ... 114, 119, 124, 126
- Art. 2 ... 119
- Art. 31 ... 121
- Art. 34 ... 115

Civil Code
- Art. 209 ... 120
- Art. 317 ... 117
- Art. 393 ... 117

Art. 403 .... 120, 123
Art. 424 120
Art. 425 119
Art. 478 .... 127, 128
Art. 479 127
Art. 480 127
Art. 618 121
Art. 619 126
Art. 623 123
Art. 625 .... 117, 128
Code of Civil Procedure (Federal Law No. 13,105/2015) 126
Art. 25 114
Comissão Interna de Prevenção de Acidentes (CIPA) [Internal Accident Prevention Commission] 111
Consolidação das Leis Trabalhistas [Consolidation of Labour Laws] (Labour Code) 110
Decree No. 46,973 issued on 16 March 2020 116
Decree No. 47,209 issued in August 2020 116
Environmental Crimes Law (No. 9,605/1998) 125
Environmental Policy (No. 6,938/1981) 125
Federal Constitution
Art. 7 110
Art. 24 116
Art. 37 112–113
Federal Decree No. 10,306/2020 issued on 2 April 2020 112
Law No. 4,657/1942 (Decree of Introduction to Brazilian Law)
Art. 4 107
Law No. 5,194/1966 .... 109, 124
Art. 6 110
Law No. 6,001/1973 124
Law No. 6,453/1977 125
Law No. 8,666/1993 (Public Procurement Law) 112, 123, 125
Law No. 9,472 of 16 July 1997 112
Law No. 9,478 of 6 August 1997 112
Law No. 9,610/1998 124
Law No. 10,406/2002 .... 123–125, 126
Law No. 12,378 of 31 December 2010 109
Law No. 12,598 of 21 March 2012 113
Law No. 12,651/2012 125
Law No. 13,105/2015 124
Law No. 13,303 of 30 June 2016 112
Law No. 14,010/2020 issued on 10 June 2020 .... 118, 119
Art. 3 119
Law No. 14,133/2021 (New Public Procurement Law) 112
Law No. 16,873/2018 .... 114, 122
Mediation Law (Federal Law No. 13,140/2015) 126
Mineral Exploration Act (No. 7,805/1989) 125
Municipality Decree 1,405 issued on 8 May 2020 116
New Public Procurement Law 125
Art. 5 113
Art. 28 113
Art. 32 113
Norma Regulamentadora No. 2 – Inspeção Prévia [Normative Resolution No. 2 – Prior Inspection] 111
Norma Regulamentadora No. 4 – Serviços Especializados em Engenharia de Segurança e em Medicina do Trabalho [Normative Resolution No. 4 – Specialized Services in Safety Engineering and Work Medicine] 111
Norma Regulamentadora No. 5 – Comissão Interna de Prevenção de Acidentes [Normative Resolution No. 5 – Internal Accident Prevention Commission] 111
Norma Regulamentadora No. 6 – Equipamentos de Proteção Individual [Normative Resolution No. 6 – Individual Protection Equipment] 111
Normative Ruling No. 79 of the Company Registration Department, dated 14 April 2020 119
Normative Ruling No. 622, dated 17 April 2020 119
Ordinance No. 3,214 of 8 June 1978 111
Pesticides Law (No. 7,802/1989) 125
Private Insurance Law (Federal Decree No. 73/1966) 125
Public Procurement Law
Art. 3 113
Art. 22 113
Regional Council of Engineering, Architecture and Agronomy) (CREA)

Resolution No. 1,025 of 30 October 2009 ... 109
Resolution No. 1,121 of 19 December 2019 ... 109
Resolution No. 1,125 of 19 December 2019, Article 11 ... 109
Water Resources Act (No. 7,805/1989) ... 125

Canada

Arbitration Act, 1991 S.O. 1991, c. 17 (Ontario) ... 149, 157, 159
Architects Act R.S.O. 1990, c. A.26 (Ontario) ... 140, 157
Assignment and Preferences Act R.S.O. 1990, c. A. 33 (Ontario) ... 157
Bankruptcy and Insolvency Act R.S.C., 1985, c. B-3 ... 157, 158
Builders' Lien Act RSNS 1989, c. 277 (Nova Scotia) ... 134
Builders' Lien Act SS 1984-85-86, c. B-7.1 (Saskatchewan) ... 134
Builders' Lien Amendment Regulations, 2020 (Saskatchewan) ... 134
Builders' Lien (Prompt Payment) Amendment Act, 2019 SS 2019, c. 2 (Saskatchewan) ... 134
Builders' Lien (Prompt Payment) Amendment Act, 2020 (Alberta) ... 134
Building Code Act, 1992 S.O. 1992, c. 23 (Ontario) ... 153, 158
Building Code (Ontario) ... 142
Building Opportunities in the Skilled Trades Act, 2021 (Ontario) ... 140
s 2(b) ... 140
S.O. 2021, c. 28 ... 157
S.O. 2021, c. 28 at s 2(c) ... 140
Civil Code (Quebec)
s 1470 ... 151
s 1693 ... 31, 151
s 1694 ... 31, 151
s 2100 ... 151
Commercial Arbitration Act R.S.C., 1985, c. 17 (2nd Supp.) ... 157, 159
Commercial Mediation Act, 2010 S.O. 2010, c. 16 (Ontario) Sched. 3 ... 159
Companies' Creditors Arrangement Act R.S.C., 1985, c. C-36 ... 158
Competition Act R.S.C., 1985, c. C-34 ... 146
s 47 ... 146
s 47(2) ... 146
Constitution Act, 1867 ... 131
s 91(24) ... 132
s 92(13) ... 131
Constitution Act, 1982 ... 131
s 5(1) ... 134
s 35 ... 132
Construction Act R.S.O. 1990, c. C. 30 (Ontario) ... 133, 157, 158, 159
s 6.4(1) ... 154
s 6.4(2) ... 154
s 6.5 ... 154, 155
s 6.6 ... 154
s 13.2 ... 148
s 13.5 ... 155
s 13.5(1) ... 148
s 13.5(5) ... 155
s 13.13 ... 155
Consumer Protection Act, 2002 S.O. 2002, c. 30, Sched. A ... 157
Copyright Act R.S.C., 1985, c. C-42 ... 158
Corruption of Foreign Public Officials Act S.C. 1998, c. 34 ... 146
Courts of Justice Act R.S.O. 1990, c. C. 43 (Ontario) ... 158
R.R.O. 1990, Reg. 194 Rules of Civil Procedure ... 149, 158
Criminal Code R.S.C., 1985, c. C-46 ... 146
s 121 ... 146
s 121(1)(a) ... 146
Emergency Management and Civil Protection Act (Ontario) ... 149
O. Reg. 82/20 ... 149
Employment Standards Act 2000 S.O. 2000, c. 41 (Ontario) ... 142, 158
O. Reg. 288/01 ... 142
Environmental Protection Act R.S.O. 1990, c. E. 19 (Ontario) ... 142, 153, 158
Evidence Act R.S.C. 1985, c. C. 5 ... 158
Evidence Act R.S.O. 1990, c. E.23 (Ontario) ... 158
Fairness in Procurement Act, 2018 S.O. 2018, c. 4 (Ontario) ... 158
Federal Courts Act R.S.C., 1985, c. F-7
s 28(1) ... 136
s 28(1) ... 136
Federal Prompt Payment for Construction Work Act S.C. 2019, c. 29 ... 135
s 4 ... 135
s 387 ... 135

First Nations Land Management Act S.C. 1999, c. 24 .... 132, 158
Frustrated Contracts Act R.S.O. 1990, c. F. 34 (Ontario) 157
Heritage Act R.S.O. 1990, c. O. 18 (Ontario) 158
Human Rights Code R.S.O. 1990, c. H. 19 (Ontario) 143, 158
s 5(1) 143
s 5(2) 143
Indian Act R.S.C., 1985, c. I-5 132
Insurance Act R.S.O. 1990, c. I. 8 (Ontario) 158
International Commercial Arbitration Act, 2017 S.O. 2017, c. 2, Sched. 5 .... 157, 159
Labour Code R.S.C., 1985, c. L-2 158
Labour Relations Act, 1995 S.O. 1995, c. 1 (Ontario) 142
Sched. A 142, 158
Limitations Act, 2002 S.O. 2002, c. 24 (Ontario)
Sched. B 157, 158, 159
Mechanics Lien Act of 1873 (Ontario) 133
Negligence Act R.S.O. 1990, c. N.1 (Ontario) 157, 158
New Home Warranties Plan Act R.S.O. 1990, c. O. 31 (Ontario) 158
Occupational Health and Safety Act R.S.O. 1990, c. O.1 (Ontario) 143, 153, 158
O. Reg. 213/91 143
s 23 143
s 30 143
s 54 143
s 66 144
Personal Property Security Act R.S.O. 1990, c. P. 10 (Ontario) 157
Planning Act R.S.O. 1990, c. P. 13 (Ontario) 142, 153, 158
Professional Engineers Act R.S.O. 1990, c. P.28 (Ontario) 140, 157
Prompt Payment for Construction Act (Manitoba) 135
Sale of Goods Act R.S.O. 1990, c. s 1 (Ontario) 157
Supreme Court Act R.S.C., 1985, c. S-26
s 40(1) 136
Surveyors Act R.S.O. 1990, c. S.29 (Ontario) 140, 157
Workplace Safety and Insurance Act, 1997 S.O. 1997, c. 16 (Ontario) 144
Sched. A 144, 158

Chile
Civil Code 164
Art. 14 175
Art. 16 175
Art. 45 173
Art. 1462 164
Art. 1478 180
Art. 1489 179
Art. 1542 178
Art. 1543 178
Art. 1544 178
Art. 1545 .... 164, 176, 184
Art. 1546 .... 176, 177
Art. 1560 177
Art. 1682 164
Art. 1996 181
Art. 2000 181
Commercial Code 169
Decree with the Power of Law No 458 179
Decree with the Power of Law No 164 171
Employment Protection Law No 21.227 172
General Law of Urbanism and Constructions 179
Labour Code 1931 167
Art. 183-A 167
Art. 183-B 167
Law No 16,744 167
Law No 19,880 168
Law No 19,971 on International Commercial Arbitration 184
Art. 28 175
Law No 21,044 170
Law No 21,227 173
Law No 458 179
Law No 4055 167
Organic Law No 3170 of 1916 167
Public Works Concessions Law 170
Art. 22 174
Art. 36 170
Resolution No 160 of 2015 169
Supreme Decree No 75 of 2004 .... 168, 171
Art. 89 175
Supreme Decree No 108 of 2009 168
Supreme Decree No 236 169

Ecuador **203–206**
Arbitration and Mediation Act
Art. 31 .... 189, 197
Civil Code
Art. 1453 200

Art. 1461 200
Art. 1477 ....200, 201, 202
Art. 1937 196
Company Law
Art. 6 195
Construction Standard 190
Disabilities Organic Act 193
Ecuadorian Constitution 2008
Art. 1 188
Art. 88 189
Art. 94 189
Art. 190 ....189, 197
Art. 217 188
Art. 336 202
Art. 429 188
General Organic Code of Procedures
Art. 363 189
Art. 363(2) 189
Art. 363(3) 189
General Regulation to the Arbitration and Mediation Act 197
Humanitarian Support Act 199–200
Labour Code 192
Art. 434 194
Art. 469 para 6 200
Law of the National Registry of Machinery and Equipment 190
Law of the Professional Practice of Civil Engineering 190–191
Law of the Professional Practice of Engineering 190–191
Law on the Professional Practice of Architecture 190–191
Organic Code of Territorial Organisation
Art. 32 202
Art. 54 202
Organic Code of the Judiciary
Art. 170 189
Organic Law of Public Service 192
Organic Law on Incentives for Public–Private Partnerships 197, 202
Public Procurement Law 195, 197, 202

European Union
Regulation (EC) number 593/2008
Art. 3.1 8
Art. 21 8

France
Napoleonic Civil Code 1804 .... 5, 164, 188

Germany
German Bürgerliches Gesetzbuch, 1896 5
German Civil Code 12

India
Contracts Act 1972 (India) 7

Italy
Italian Codice Civile, 1942 5

Japan
Japanese Minpo, 1896 5

Malaysia
Contracts Act 1950 (Malaysia) 8
s 1(2) 7

Mexico
Bankruptcy Law 224, 227
Commercial Code 222, 229
Federal Act for Bond and Insurances Institutions 215
Federal Civil Code 222
Art. 1794 220
Art. 1795 220
Art. 1796 220–221
Art. 1949 ....226, 228
Art. 2111 223
Federal Labour Law 213
General Law for the Equilibrium and Protection of the Environment 226
Law of the Insurance Contract 215
Local Civil Code
Art. 1796 223
Obligatory Rules of Social Security for the Construction Workers by Work or Time 213
Public Works and Related Services Law 215, 220, 221, 222, 223

Peru
Arbitration Act 234
Art. 5 246
Civil Code 234, 244
Art. 1314–1332 255
Art. 1328 251
Art. 1341 ....250, 256
Art. 1351–1528 252
Art. 1362 252
Art. 1428 252

Art. 1429 252
Art. 1430 252
Art. 1440 252
Art. 1771 .... 247, 249
Art. 1771–1789 .... 252, 254
Art. 1784 .... 250, 251, 255
Art. 1785 255
Art. 2001 255
Art. 2004 248
Art. 2095 246
Constitution 233
Criminal Code
Art. 226–231 254
Art. 304–314D 254
Directorial Resolution 009-2020-EF/63.01 241
Emergency Decree No 021-2020 .... 241, 245
General Administrative Procedure Law 234
General Law for Companies 234
General Law of Health (Law No 26842)
Art. 105 254
Law No 16053 237
Law No 17752 243
Law No 28611 243
Law No 28858 237
Law No 29338 243
Law No 29783 237
Law No 30225 245
Law No 30884 242
Legislative Decree No 1071 241
Legislative Decree No 1224 245
Ley de los Recursos Hídricos [Water Resources Law] 243
Ley de Seguridad y Salud en el Trabajo [Occupational Health and Safety Law] 237
Ley General de Aguas [General Water Law] 243
Ley General del Ambiente [General Environmental Law] 243
Ley que Aprueba Procedimiento para la Contratación del Servicio de Asistencia Técnica Especializada para la Gestión de Inversiones [Law that Approves the Procedure for Hiring the Specialized Technical Assistance Service for Investment Management] 236
Ley que Autoriza a los Colegios de Arquitectos del Perú y al Colegio de Ingenieros del Perú para Supervisar a los Profesionales de Arquitectura e Ingeniería [Law that Authorizes the College of Architects of Peru and the College of Engineers of Peru to Supervise Architecture and Engineering Professionals]
Art. 3 236
Ley que Complementa la Ley No 16053 [Law that Complements Law No 16053]
Art. 1 237
Ley que Regula el Plástico de un Solo Uso y los Recipientes o Envases Descartables [Law Regulating Single-Use Plastics and Disposable Containers] 242
Public–Private Partnership Law 233, 234
Public Procurement Law 233, 234, 241, 245, 247
Art. 40 .... 250, 251
Urgency Decree No 021-2020 239
Works for Taxes Law 233

Philippines
Civil Code of the Philippines
Art. 1306 8

Switzerland
Swiss Zivilgesetzbuch, 1907 5

United Kingdom
Bribery Act 2010 (UK) 25
Housing Grants, Construction and Regeneration Act 1996 (UK) 6
Human Rights Act 1998 (UK) 6

United States of America
False Claims Act 271
Federal Arbitration Act 272
Foreign Corrupt Practices Act 271
OSHA Regulations 262
Second Restatement of Contracts 270
Statute of Frauds 269
Uniform Acts 271
Uniform Arbitration Act 271, 272
Uniform Commercial Code 271

Uruguay
Civil Code 278, 288, 292, 293
Art. 1216..296
Art. 1844.............................293, 296, 297
Commercial Code 289
Constitution..277
Art. 6..289
Decree 65/998 (10 March 1998)...............286
Decree 500/991 (27 September 1991)......286
Decree No 276/2013 (9 September 2013).... 286
General Procedure Code................. 288, 289, 298, 300
Art. 372–376 300
Art. 472 297
Art. 477 299
Industrial Promotion Law.........................289
Law No 15,637...279
Law No 16,002 286
Law No 16,736...286
Law No 17,008 (25 September 1998).......279
Law No 18,600 286
Law of Insolvency...................................295
Public–Private Partnerships Law 289
Texto Ordenado de Contabilidad y Administración Financiera [Ordered Text of Financial and Accounting Administration]
Art. 33 285

CONTRIBUTORS

Mr Guillermo Alarcón (Peru) is a Senior Associate of NPG Abogados and holds an LLB from Pontificia Universidad Católica del Perú, a Postgraduate Diploma in International Arbitration and Investment from Universidad del Pacífico and a Postgraduate Diploma in Construction Law from UPC. He also holds a Master of Construction Law from the University of Melbourne. He has experience advising contractors and public entities in several public and private infrastructure projects from mining, highways, ports, airports, power plants and industrial buildings to educational, cultural exposition and sports infrastructure under traditional and design-build contracts. He lectures in construction law and dispute avoidance and in international engineering and construction contract forms such as FIDIC 99/2017 rainbow suite and ECC NEC 3/NEC4 main options (a to f).

Contact: galarcon@npg.pe

Mr Jonnathan Bravo (Peru) is an Of-Counsel of NPG Abogados. He holds an LLB from Pontificia Universidad Católica del Perú, a Postgraduate Diploma in International Arbitration and Investment from Universidad del Pacífico and an MSc in Construction Law and Dispute Resolution from King's College London as a Chevening Scholar awarded by the UK Government. He is a Fellow of the Chartered Institute of Arbitrators (FCIArb), Fellow of the Arbitrators' and Mediators' Institute of New Zealand (AMINZ Arb) and Fellow of the Malaysian Institute of Arbitrators (FMIArb). He is a co-founder and member of the Board of Directors of the Infrastructure and Investment Research Institute – Perú and a member of the UK Society of Construction Law, the Peruvian Society of Construction Law, the Adjudication Society, the King's College Construction Law Association, the Dispute Resolution Board Foundation (DRBF) and the YIAG of the London Court of International Arbitration (LCIA).

Jonnathan is the Director of the Postgraduate Programme in Construction Law and Dispute Resolution at UPC, a professor of undergraduate and postgraduate courses, and the author of academic papers on topics regarding construction law, public procurement, dispute resolution and Public–Private Partnerships. He has experience in the management of concession contracts; EPC and EPCM contracts; tailor-made construction and engineering contracts; design, negotiation and interpretation of standard forms of contracts (FIDIC, NEC, JCT, PPC 2000, FAC-1) and collaborative schemes with BIM. He has been involved in a number of local and international arbitrations.

Contact: jbravo@npg.pe

Ms Polina Chtchelok (Bolivia) is a lawyer and a mechanical engineer practising in construction law, commercial law and contract law.

She has extensive experience in delivering multi-million-dollar construction projects in Asia, Africa and Latin America. She started her career as a mechanical engineer and transitioned into a legal role upon admission as a legal practitioner to the Supreme Court of Queensland. She managed contract negotiations for a number of mega oil and gas construction projects. She was a lead negotiator for several projects closing contractual claims in relation to construction change orders, variations and time issues.

Polina has an Executive MBA, a Juris Doctor and a Bachelor of Mechanical Engineering (Hons). She has published several papers in legal journals and presented papers at international conferences. She was an editor of the *Construction Law International* journal published by IBA and a co-chair of the Project Establishment Subcommittee of IBA.

Contact: polina.chtchelok@espcsconsulting.com

Dr Mario Alejandro Flor (Ecuador) is a Senior Partner in Flor Bustamante Pizarro & Hurtado Law firm. His Doctorate of Law degree was conferred by the Catholic University of Quito, Ecuador in 1995. His doctoral thesis was entitled 'Promotion and Protection of Foreign Investment Under International Guarantee Programs and Double Taxation Treaties'.

Dr Flor's main areas of work are civil and administrative procedures, project finance, mergers and acquisitions, corporate law, mining, oil and gas, arbitration, telecommunications and electricity. During his professional career, Dr Flor has held different positions, such as General Manager of Duke Energy International del Ecuador Cia. Ltda. in 1999; General Manager of Gillette del Ecuador S.A. from December 2000 to June 2002; Legal Representative of Eli Lilly Interamerica Inc. (Quito branch) since 2001; General Attorney-in-Fact of Reuters Limited since 2002; and Mediator of the Ecuadorian-American Chamber of Commerce of Quito since 2000. His professional background includes teaching as a Professor of Civil and Roman Law at the Catholic University of Quito from 1995 to 1996, and as a Professor of Negotiations at the School of Law of the same university in 1999. Dr Flor is a member of the Quito Bar Association, the Inter-American Bar Association, the Chamber of Commerce of Quito and the Ecuadorian-American Chamber of Commerce.

Contact: mario.flor@fbphlaw.com

Mr Caio Lucas Gabra (Brazil) is an associate at the energy and infrastructure practice of Mattos Filho Advogados, specialising in project development transactions and project-related dispute resolution. Caio constantly represents clients in structuring and negotiating contracts for the development of energy and infrastructure assets in Brazil and Latin America. He also applies his expertise in infrastructure projects in representing clients in related disputes and arbitrations and was a foreign associate at Freshfields Bruckhaus Deringer's Global Project's Disputes team in Dubai. Caio holds a bachelor's degree from the Federal University of Rio de Janeiro and is an LLM Candidate in International Economic Law, Business and Policy at Stanford University. He is a former Vice President of the Brazilian Arbitration Student Association and a founding member of the Brazilian Chapter of the Energy Related Arbitration Practitioners Association. He lectures on International Contract Law at the Executive Education Program at Alumni COPPEAD in Rio de Janeiro.

Contact: caio.gabra@mattosfilho.com.br

Mr Roberto Hernández García (Mexico) is an international construction lawyer based in Mexico City. He is a Partner Director of COMAD, a law firm specialising in international construction law, public procurement and international anticorruption measures for the E&C industry. He acts as counsel in international construction contracts and as counsel, arbitrator, Dispute Board and mediator in international construction disputes. He has worked on construction projects in seven countries in Latin America in different capacities. He is a certified FIDIC Adjudicator included in the President's List. He is registered in five centres across Latin America as a Dispute Board. He is a panel member of the International Center of Dispute Resolution of the American Arbitration Association. He acts as an Arbitrator under ICC, LCIA and ICSID rules. He has served as the Co-Chair of the International Construction Projects Committee of the IBA and Chair of the Construction Disputes of ICC México and is a board member of Division 4 (Latin America) of the Dispute Resolution Board Foundation. He has acted as a consultant for the Interamerican Development Bank and the Central American Bank of Economic Integration (BCIE) in connection with international construction contracts and dispute resolution mechanisms for their procurement specialists. He is a Fellow of the American College of Construction Lawyers and a Fellow of the International Academy of Construction Lawyers. He is the co-author of five books and author of three books: *Construction Law in Mexico, Covid-19 and Construction* and *Dispute Boards: Theory and Practice*. He has been recognised for 14 consecutive years in Chambers and Partners as a leading lawyer in the project section and he is considered a Thought Leader in Construction in the Who's Who Legal international publication.

Contact: rhernandez@comad.com.mx

Mr Juan Pablo Sandoval Garcia (Mexico) got his law degree from Universidad Iberoamericana, Mexico City, obtaining the Excellency Award for his score obtained in the official national test, as well as the San Ignacio de Loyola Medal, recognition received by the Director of Universidad Iberoamericana. Juan Pablo has a postgraduate degree in arbitration from Escuela Libre de Derecho and the International Chamber of Commerce and attended the Construction Law Summer School in 2020.

He has a long experience in civil, commercial, administrative and constitutional litigation representing both national and foreign companies. He also has long experience in domestic and international arbitration of high global impact such as the arbitration of the New International Airport of Mexico City in which Juan Pablo participated as co-counsel of the Project Manager.

Juan Pablo's practice is also specialised in construction law having advised several companies (both domestic and foreign) in private contracts negotiation processes, as well as in public procurement. Juan Pablo has participated in several webinars as an invited speaker by the Latin American Association of Construction Law (ALDEC), and his recent article was published in the e-booklet of FIDIC Future Leaders. Additionally, Juan Pablo is an active member of 'The Dispute Resolver', a blog from Division 1 (Litigation and Dispute Resolution) of the American Bar Association.

Mr Sandoval is a key member of the litigation and dispute resolution team in COMAD, SC.

Contact: jpsandoval@comad.com.mx

Mr Jaime Gray (Peru) is a Founding Partner of NPG Abogados; he holds an LLB from the Universidad San Martín de Porres and an LLM in Corporate Law from the Universidad Peruana de Ciencias Aplicadas (UPC). He is President of the Dispute Resolution Board Foundation's Region 4 – Latin America and DRBF's Peruvian Representative, and he was Co-Chair of the International Construction Projects Committee of the International

Bar Association (IBA). He is also a Fellow of the International Academy of Construction Lawyers (IACL), a member of the American Bar Association (ABA) and a member of the Capacity Building Committee of the International Federation of Consulting Engineers (FIDIC). He was the first President of the Peruvian Society of Construction Law and has been recommended as an expert in construction law in various legal publications and rankings such as Who's Who Legal and Chambers and Partners.

Jaime is a professor, lecturer and author of academic papers on topics regarding construction law, public procurement, dispute resolution and Public–Private Partnerships. He has been involved in the most important projects in Peru including, most recently, the New Terminal of the International Jorge Chavez Airport and the New Infrastructures for the 2019 Pan American and Parapan American Games held in Lima, Peru. He is also an arbitrator and dispute board member of local and international projects.

Contact: jgray@npg.pe

Mr Juan Carlos Herrera-Quenguan (Ecuador) obtained his law degree (LLB) from the Universidad de las Américas in Quito, Ecuador, and his master's degree (LLM) in International Dispute Resolution from the Université de Genève and the Institut de Hautes Études Internationales et du Développement in Geneva, Switzerland. In addition, he holds a Certificate in Witness Examination in International Arbitration Proceedings from the Foundation for International Arbitration Advocacy (FIAA) and a Certificate in Public International Law from the Académie de Droit International de La Haye in the Netherlands. His practice focuses on energy and natural resources, investment protection, and dispute resolution. He frequently writes, lectures and speaks about public international law, international economic law and international dispute resolution issues. He is a co-founder of the Ecuadorian Society of International Law (SEDI).

Contact: juan.herrera@fbphlaw.com

Mr Fernando Landeros (Chile) is a partner of WAGEMANN Lawyers & Engineers. He is an architect with more than 12 years of experience in the fields of architecture, infrastructure construction, contract management and engineering and construction claim analysis. Before joining WAGEMANN, he was the head of the division of the Faculty of Engineering of the University of Chile charged with carrying out technical surveys and analysis in court and arbitration proceedings.

He has participated in more than 60 disputes between Owners and Contractors, both in public and private sectors, on construction, mining, energy and infrastructure projects, providing technical and strategic support to Owners, Contractors, courts and arbitral tribunals. He has performed technical surveys required by ordinary and arbitration courts and Concession Commissions (PPP).

Contact: flanderos@wycia.com

Dr Elina Mereminskaya (Chile) is a lawyer and partner of WAGEMANN Lawyers & Engineers. She has focused her professional practice on providing consultancy services to Chilean, Latin-American and European companies in construction, infrastructure, mining and energy projects, in both public and private sectors. She is experienced in the field of dispute prevention and claim management in construction contracts, excelling also as a specialist in arbitration.

Elina holds an LLM and PhD from the University of Göttingen, Germany. She acts as an arbitrator and is a member of the arbitration rosters of CAM Santiago, the Lima Chamber of Commerce and the ICDR, among others.

Contact: emereminskaya@wycia.com

Ms Claudia Andrea Lopez Monterrey (Bolivia) is a lawyer with extensive experience supporting project management for large-scale construction projects in the energy sector in Bolivia and is an expert in corporate governance, business negotiations and insurance matters.

She was a member of the Board of Directors for a number of energy sector companies specialising in exploration, exploitation, construction and transportation in Bolivia. She has held positions from Legal Manager and Legal Counsel to General Manager. In these roles, she was a lead negotiator for international and construction contracts, managed various due diligence processes and conducted multiple assets as well as supported the financial team during capital increase.

She has a law degree from Bolivian Catholic University's 'San Pablo' campus (La Paz, Bolivia) and an LLM in Economic Law.

She has published articles on construction and HSE matters and energy sector exploration in specialised magazines and newspapers and presented papers at international conferences.

Contact: claudia.lopez@espcsconsulting.com

Mr Thiago Fernandes Moreira (Brazil) concentrates his practice on construction and complex contracts, including onshore and offshore contracts, equipment supply contracts, contracts typical to the oil and gas industry (e.g. charter agreements, operation and maintenance agreements, floating production storage and offloading units, drilling package units and platform construction contracts and gas supply contracts), take-or-pay contracts and contracts related to the hotel industry (e.g. construction of hotels, built to suit, hotel management agreements and franchising), as well as project development and infrastructure-related transactions.

His experience includes advice to owners and contractors on preparation, negotiation, pre-litigation and arbitration involving complex contracts. He has substantial experience in sectors such as energy, ports, airports, subways, railways, shipbuilding and oil and gas. Prior to joining Mattos Filho, Thiago worked for the Inter-American Investment Corporation in Washington, DC. He is a member of the Society of Construction Law in London and is currently the co-chair of the Project Execution Subcommittee of the International Construction Projects Committee of the International Bar Association.

Contact: thiago.moreira@mattosfilho.com.br

Mr Joseph F Moore (USA) is dual-qualified as a civil engineer and a lawyer. He has over 30 years of professional experience in the construction industry. Over his career, he has worked as a design engineer, owner's representative, contractor and counsel. His experience includes power generation and transmission, rail, bridges, transit, clean water, wastewater, highways, manufacturing, processing facilities and building facilities. He has also developed expertise in innovative building technologies and routinely advises and lectures internationally on Building Information Modeling and the automation of the construction industry. Joseph currently maintains an active law practice focused on the resolution of international and domestic construction disputes in which he acts as an advocate and counsel. He also maintains a noncontentious practice that includes the negotiation and drafting of complex construction agreements and provisions of project counsel services aimed at resolving disputes as part of the construction process. He serves as a mediator and arbitrator on technically challenging disputes. He holds a Bachelor of Science degree from the University of California at Davis and a Juris Doctorate degree from the University of San Francisco. He sits as the current co-chair of the International Projects Committee of the International Bar Association.

Contact: joe@jfmoore.net

Mr Alejandro Pérez (Ecuador) is a lawyer from Universidad de las Américas (UDLA). He has a postgraduate degree in public management from the Instituto de Altos Estudios Nacionales (IAEN). He holds a Master's degree in finance with a minor in securities markets and banking from UDLA. He has wide experience in project finance, energy, M&A and PPP. The portfolio of projects advised includes energy, ports, mobility, water and sanitation, infrastructure and retail. He has actively participated in several legal and regulatory reform processes, providing inputs to improve the bankability of projects. He is a member of the World Association of PPP Units and Professionals (WAPPP) based in Geneva, Switzerland, and of the Ibero-American Institute of Law and Finance, based in Madrid, Spain. He is the author of several articles, a lecturer and a guest professor at several national and international universities.

Contact: alejandro.perez@fbphlaw.com

Dr José Luis Echevarría Petit (Uruguay) is a Doctor of Law and Social Sciences (University of the Republic of Uruguay) and has a Master's degree in Corporate Law (University of Montevideo) and a Master's degree in Administrative Law (University of Montevideo). He is Partner in Charge of Echevarría Leunda & Echevarría Petit Abogados, Director of the Master in Administrative Law of the University of Montevideo, Professor of Administrative Contracts in the Master of Administrative Law, former Vice President of the Uruguay Chamber of Commerce, Member of the Direction Council of the Centre of Arbitration of the Chamber of Commerce of Uruguay and Arbitrator of the Centre of Arbitration of the Chamber of Commerce of Uruguay and of the Inter American Centre of Arbitration (CIAC). He is a consultant to the Uruguayan State on Public–Private Partnership finance, contracted by IDB, and to the Uruguay Construction Chamber on Construction and PPP. He is the author of *Best Practices in Construction Procurement* (University of Montevideo, 2020), co-author of various books and author of diverse papers and publications.

Contact details: jlep@echevarriaabogados.com

Ms Sharon C Vogel (Canada) is a named Partner and Co-Chair of the Construction and Infrastructure Law group at Singleton Urquhart Reynolds Vogel LLP, based out of the Toronto, Canada office. She handles the negotiation, mediation, arbitration and litigation of construction disputes and has appeared at all levels of court. She has been involved with public policy mandates, including acting as co-counsel retained by the Ontario government and federal government to prepare reports and make recommendations on prompt payment and adjudication. Sharon is a Senior Fellow at the University of Melbourne where she teaches international construction law. She is a Certified Specialist in Construction Law and a Fellow of the Chartered Institute of Arbitrators, Canadian College of Construction Lawyers and American College of Construction Lawyers. She is ranked Band 1 by Chambers, was named as one of the 25 most influential lawyers in Canada by *Canadian Lawyer*, is listed as one of 12 Global Thought Leaders in Construction in North America by Who's Who Legal, and was named Canadian construction lawyer of the year in 2021 as well as 2022 and has been consistently named as one of the top women litigators in Canada by *Benchmark*.

Contact: SVogel@singleton.com

Mr Alex Wagemann (Chile) is a lawyer and founding partner of WAGEMANN Lawyers & Engineers. He has focused his professional career on providing consultancy services to large companies in engineering, construction and services contracts covering such areas as mining, power generation, manufacturing, public works and concessions. He holds both a broad legal knowledge and an encompassing technical outlook.

He has more than 20 years of experience leading several planning, tendering and contracting proceedings, risk analysis, contract and claims management, expert opinions, surveys and arbitration proceedings. Most recently, he has concentrated on providing expert support and guidance to multidisciplinary teams with expertise in the aforementioned areas, participating in high-level task forces and with the aim of improving the Owner–Contractor relationship.

Contact: awagemann@wycia.com

ACKNOWLEDGEMENTS

FIDIC Contracts in the Americas: A Practical Guide to Application was inspired by the success of the book *The International Application of FIDIC Contracts: A Practical Guide*, published by Routledge in 2020. One of the reviewers of that book opined:

> In time and if its contents were allowed to spread to other jurisdictions in which FIDIC contracts are commonly used, it will develop into a vital encyclopaedia for all those tasked with the production, amendment and finalisation of a FIDIC construction contract.[1]

The first outcome of that challenge was the publication of *FIDIC Contracts in Asia Pacific: A Practical Guide to Application* in late 2021, followed by *FIDIC Contracts in Europe: A Practical Guide to Application* in late 2022. This book is the third in the series, comprising chapters on a number of the major jurisdictions in North and South America. The contents covered in each jurisdiction chapter in *FIDIC Contracts in the Americas* follow the original format of *The International Application of FIDIC Contracts* but have also been expanded to include a section on the construction industry and sections on the impacts of COVID-19 on the execution of construction projects and the operation of construction contracts.

This book has the ambitious aim of addressing the specific legal requirements of the applicable construction law in a number of jurisdictions in the Americas. Each of these jurisdictions has its own particular legal landscape that impacts the application of FIDIC (and other) construction contracts. Articulating the breadth and complexity of construction law in each of these jurisdictions required the skill and knowledge of expert local construction law practitioners. The chapter authors and their profiles and affiliations are identified in the Contributors section. Each of those profiles demonstrates a deep well of legal and practical experience in local construction law in general and the requirements of FIDIC contracts in particular. The authors are all eminent professionals who have had to fit the writing for their chapters into their busy schedules, in circumstances where normal professional life in every country was severely impacted by the ravages of COVID-19 and the new ways of working it entailed. I am very grateful to each of them for their commitment and hard work. The exigencies of busy professional lives and the COVID-19 pandemic have inevitably delayed chapter delivery times, and the book has taken longer to complete than originally planned.

The authors of the jurisdiction chapters closely followed a template that I provided; accordingly, any deficiencies in the scope of topics covered by the jurisdiction chapters are my responsibility, not those of the chapter authors. To state the obvious, this book

1 Nick Longley, 'Book Review: The International Application of FIDIC Contracts: A Practical Guide' [2020] 1 *International Construction Law Review* 96, 98.

could not have been written without the skill and expertise of the authors of the jurisdiction chapters.

I also sincerely thank Juan Eduardo Figueroa Valdés, Professor of Construction Law at the Los Andes University in Santiago, for writing the Foreword.

In addition to those named here, I acknowledge and thank the many colleagues I have met at international FIDIC conferences and training courses who have contributed to my knowledge and interest in the international application of FIDIC contracts.

I also thank Guy Loft and Amelia Bashford of Routledge, who have been unfailingly encouraging and helpful in publishing this book. Deanta Global has done an excellent job of the difficult task of copyediting the manuscript and ensuring consistency of style and presentation, for which I am most grateful.

FOREWORD

This book provides a lucid comparative study of the main nine jurisdictions in the Americas in which FIDIC contracts are or can be used, the applicable law that may impact the operation of the Contract, the execution of the Works and the determination of disputes arising under or in connection with the Contract. Each of those jurisdiction chapters gives a brief overview of the legal landscape and the construction industry, the impact of the COVID-19 pandemic on the operation of construction contracts and on the execution of construction projects, a discussion of any Special Provisions required for that jurisdiction and a listing of the applicable law for the jurisdiction. It also identifies issues that a court or arbitral tribunal may construe differently than expected from the words of the Contract because of local law or custom.

The book clearly demonstrates that the use of FIDIC contracts across jurisdictions is of particular interest in considering the extent to which there is a 'common law of construction contracts' or a '*lex constructionis*', despite the differences in legal systems and jurisdictions, that can promote best practice for successful projects in which the constructing parties' legitimate expectations can be realised.

This book is a great source for a Contract Administrator or lawyer unfamiliar with the requirements of the Conditions of a FIDIC Contract or operation with a FIDIC Contract in a jurisdiction they are unfamiliar with. It is logically structured, written with clarity and geared to the needs of the practitioner in the twenty-first century. A related issue is the involvement of practitioners in major international construction projects of parties from different jurisdictions with different cultural approaches, and indeed with different legal systems. The information gathered in this book will be very useful when parties may choose to use a standard form, typically making amendments to tailor the form to the project in question, or they may use the standard form as the starting point for drafting a bespoke contract.

On the other hand, the book gives a clear explanation of the importance of the FIDIC Golden Principles that promote a fair and balanced risk/reward allocation and a clear definition of scope, duties, roles, rights and responsibilities and contract documents that constitute a contract management manual for best practice in international project execution.

I highly recommend this book for practitioners in the construction industry because it helps to understand construction law issues from a variety of different perspectives – the employers', the contractors', the designers', the expert witnesses' and the dispute resolvers' – and how they should act in different jurisdictions in the Americas. It also confirms that many constructors and clients have applied the wrong approach where they have applied the same system of law to all of their projects irrespective of the place of execution, in order to achieve uniformity in the assessment and evaluation of risks and administration of the contracts.

Juan Eduardo Figueroa Valdés
Professor of Construction Law
Los Andes University
Santiago, Chile
September 2022

CHAPTER 1

Introduction

Dr Donald Charrett

CONTENTS

1.1	Construction contracts	3
	1.1.1 Overview	3
	1.1.2 Legal systems	5
	1.1.3 Contract law	6
	1.1.4 Freedom of contract	6
	1.1.5 Pacta sunt servanda	9
	1.1.6 Proper law of the contract	9
	1.1.7 International construction contracts	11
1.2	*Lex constructionis*	11
	1.2.1 What is it?	11
	1.2.2 Promotion of best practice for successful projects	12
	1.2.3 Proposed principles of lex constructionis	13
	1.2.4 Discussion	14
1.3	FIDIC contracts	15
	1.3.1 Overview	15
	1.3.2 MDB use of FIDIC contracts	17
	1.3.3 FIDIC contract documents	18
	1.3.4 Contract agreement	18
	1.3.5 Particular Conditions	19
	1.3.6 Particular Conditions Part A – Contract Data	19
	1.3.7 Particular Conditions Part B – Special Provisions	19
	1.3.8 General Conditions	20
1.4	The FIDIC Golden Principles	20
1.5	Applicable laws	21
	1.5.1 Laws	21
	1.5.2 Governing law of the contract	24
	1.5.3 Intersection of local laws with the governing law of the contract	25
	1.5.4 Laws with extra-territorial reach	25
	1.5.5 Laws applicable to the execution of a construction project	25
	1.5.6 Laws applicable to arbitration of a dispute	26

DOI: 10.4324/9781003201250-1

1.6 COVID-19 26
1.6.1 Government responses to COVID-19 26
1.6.2 The impact of COVID-19 on construction 28
1.6.3 Execution of construction projects impacted by COVID-19 29
1.6.4 Operation of construction contracts 30
1.6.5 Economic measures 31
1.6.6 Claims arising from COVID-19 under FIDIC contracts 31
1.6.7 Dispute resolution 33
1.7 Impact of the applicable laws 33
1.8 Country accessions to international conventions and agreements 34
1.8.1 New York Convention 34
1.8.2 WTO Agreement on Government Procurement 35
1.8.3 ICSID Convention 38
1.9 Aims of the book 38
1.10 References 39
1.10.1 *Books on construction law* *39*
1.10.2 References on dispute resolution 40
1.10.3 Books on FIDIC contracts – 2017 Editions 41
1.10.4 Books on FIDIC contracts – 1999 Editions 41
1.10.5 Guides on FIDIC contracts 42
1.10.6 Internet resources 42
1.10.7 Case law 42
Annexure 43

1.1 Construction contracts

1.1.1 Overview

Construction contracts can be defined in various ways. The following definition is used for the purposes of this book:

> any contract where one person [this includes a corporation] agrees for valuable consideration to carry out construction works, which may include building or engineering works, for another.[1]

A contract for design does not involve 'construction' as such, and for the purposes of this book is not considered to be a construction contract. A design and construct contract includes design, but it also involves construction and therefore falls within the definition adopted here. Moreover, a subcontract in which a Subcontractor undertakes construction work for a Contractor is a species of construction contract and may be 'back-to-back' with the Head Contract between the Employer and the Contractor.[2]

In this book, the **Contract** means the construction contract being referred to. In general terms, the parties to a construction contract are the **Employer** for whom the work is done and the **Contractor** who carries out the work. In the case of a subcontract, the Contractor under the **Head Contract** functions as the Employer, and the Subcontractor functions as the Contractor.

Construction contracts have a number of specific features that give them some unique characteristics that distinguish them from other commercial contracts. The following issues arise by operation of law, or because of specific terms that are incorporated in most construction contracts, or because of the nature of construction work. The unique distinguishing features of construction law can be conveniently considered under the following headings that address issues generally relevant to all construction projects.

Scope

- The subject matter of the contract relates to construction of a unique facility that will be affixed to the land at a specific location over a specific period of time
- The constructed facility becomes part of the real property of the landowner when attached
- The required design, scope, time, cost and quality requirements of the Works and the finished project are usually defined by extensive and complex technical documentation
- The Employer (generally) has the right to increase or decrease the originally agreed scope of work by the issue of Variations, and the Contractor is obliged to carry out or omit the varied work
- The execution of the construction work and/or the performance of the Contract may be supervised by an 'independent' Engineer who is not a party to the Contract

1 Stephen Furst & the Hon Sir Vivian Ramsey, *Keating on Construction Contracts* (8th edn, Sweet & Maxwell, 2006) 1.

2 Capitalised terms not specifically defined in this book are defined in the relevant FIDIC Conditions of Contract. The Glossary contains definitions of terms specifically defined in this book.

- The Contract may be an entire contract
- There are many different types of construction contract: e.g. construct only, design and construct, engineer procure and construct (**EPC**), engineer procure and construction management (**EPCM**)

Risk

- There are many risks in a construction project – known knowns, known unknowns and unknown unknowns
- Ground conditions are never completely known, including geotechnical conditions, groundwater, contamination or heritage items
- Weather conditions can have a significant impact on construction activities and delay completion
- Freedom of contract may be constrained, e.g. *Security of Payment* legislation that mandates payment obligations and makes some provisions illegal, such as pay-when-paid clauses
- Many aspects of a construction project are subject to Government laws and regulations
- There are usually a series of independent and interrelated contracts between a number of different parties: e.g. Employer/Designer, Employer/Engineer, Employer/Contractor/DAAB or DAB Member, Employer/Contractor, Contractor/Subcontractor, Subcontractor/Sub-Subcontractor, Employer/Insurer, Contractor/Insurer
- Construction activities are potentially dangerous, e.g. heavy machinery, working at heights, confined spaces, etc.
- Construction involves significant environmental impacts: noise, dust, smells, vibration, nuisance, water run-off, sediment and erosion
- Construction may adversely impact adjacent property
- Insurance of the works is usually mandatory and is a significant risk transfer mechanism
- Insolvency of parties to interrelated contracts may impact performance

Time

- The time for contractual performance may extend over a number of years, including a period after completion of construction (and when the Employer is in possession of the Site) during which the Contractor is liable to rectify defects
- There are usually significant financial consequences for late contract completion

Cost

- The contract sum and cash flow are typically substantial – cash flow is the lifeblood of construction
- The Contractor is usually required to provide security for its performance

Quality

- A construction contract may involve the assumption of obligations that are very long-term, e.g. maintenance or liability for defects arising many years after construction was completed
- Construction works apparently completed in accordance with contractual requirements may contain latent defects which only manifest themselves many years after construction was completed

Disputes

- Disputes are common and frequently involve complex technical issues and large volumes of documents

Every construction contract is unique: the Site is a unique location in the Country, constructed by a particular Contractor for a particular Employer over a particular period of time for a specific purpose.

1.1.2 Legal systems

There are a number of 'families' or systems of law, the most widespread being the systems considered in this book: common law and civil law. Other legal systems include Shari'a law and socialist law.

Common law is the body of law developed by judges from around the 11th century in England and later exported to its various colonies such as Canada, the USA, Australia, Singapore and India. The basic principle is that earlier judicial decisions, usually of the higher courts, made in a similar case should be followed in subsequent cases. The principle that precedents should be respected is known as ***stare decisis*** and although it has never been legislated, courts regard it as binding. However, superior courts can decide that a previous case was wrongly decided and modify the law accordingly. In addition to the law made by judges in decided cases, common law is also based on statutes, which judges interpret by discerning the intention of Parliament and apply accordingly.

Civil law is a system of law in which the laws are codified in a large number of general rules and principals. Pejovic describes civil law in the following terms:

> Civil law has its origin in Roman law, as codified in the Corpus Iuris Civilis of Justinian. Under this influence, in the ensuing period the civil law has been developed in Continental Europe and in many other parts of the world. The main feature of civil law is that it is contained in civil codes, which are described as a 'systematic, authoritative, and guiding statute of broad coverage, breathing the spirit of reform and marking a new start in the legal life of an entire nation'. Most civil codes were adopted in the nineteenth and twentieth centuries: French Code Civil, 1804, Austrian Bürgerliches Gesetzbuch, 1811, German Bürgerliches Gesetzbuch, 1896, Japanese Minpo, 1896, Swiss Zivilgesetzbuch, 1907, Italian Codice Civile, 1942. Between these codes there are some important differences, and they are often grouped in the Romanic and the Germanic families. Even though the civil codes of different countries are not homogenous, there are certain features of all civil codes which bind them together and 'sets them apart from those who practice under different systems'.
>
> Civil law is largely classified and structured and contains a great number of general rules and principles, often lacking details. One of the basic characteristics of the civil law is that

> the courts main task is to apply and interpret the law contained in a code, or a statute to case facts. The assumption is that the code regulates all cases that could occur in practice, and when certain cases are not regulated by the code, the courts should apply some of the general principles used to fill the gaps.[3]

Notwithstanding the differences between common law and civil law systems, and the differences between jurisdictions within either of these systems, construction contracts can be executed in the knowledge that, notwithstanding local law differences, there are appropriate methods of dispute resolution, broad agreement on what constitutes a just outcome in most situations and international norms that ensure remedies can be realised.

The differences between common law and civil law have become much fewer in recent years:

- The volume of legislation in common law countries has increased substantially over recent decades. Increasingly, more of the law is explicitly stated in legislation, which either codifies or amends the previous common law or forms new 'social legislation' which achieves legislatively desirable social outcomes not addressed by the common law, e.g. the *Human Rights Act 1998* (UK), which incorporates the rights and freedoms of the *European Convention on Human Rights* into British law, and the *Housing Grants, Construction and Regeneration Act 1996* (UK), which introduced a statutory right to adjudication of construction disputes
- Because the answer to a legal issue may not be found in the *Codes* (which may not have been updated recently), the courts in civil law countries are relying to a much greater extent than previously on the precedential value of court judgments on a similar issue, e.g. in a book on FIDIC contracts, the authors list a significant number of cases from the French and German civil law jurisdictions, as well as cases from various common law jurisdictions[4]

1.1.3 Contract law

Contract law around the world is based on the two fundamental principles of freedom of contract and *pacta sunt servanda.* These principles are universal in jurisdictions subject to the rule of law, the necessary precondition for the exercise of the parties' autonomy and the enforcement of their rights and obligations. Freedom of contract sets the 'ground rules' which govern the parties' rights to enter into the contract of their choice. *Pacta sunt servanda* governs the performance of a contract after it has been entered into. These two principles of law apply to the entry into, execution and termination of contracts.

1.1.4 Freedom of contract

Freedom of contract is the ability of legal persons to enter into a binding agreement to do anything, providing it is not contrary to the law or public policy (and in some jurisdictions,

3 Casalev Pejovic, 'Civil Law and Common Law: Two Different Paths Leading to the Same Goal' (2001) 32(3) *Victoria University of Wellington Law Review* 817. www.victoria.ac.nz/__data/assets/pdf_file/0008/830780/Pejovic (accessed 12 November 2021).

4 Axel-Volkmar Jaeger & Götz-Sebastian Hök, *FIDIC – A Guide for Practitioners* (Springer, 2010) xix–xxx.

morals). Subject to these qualifications, courts generally uphold freedom of contract, even if one of the parties has accepted risks that it cannot manage or insure for.

This freedom to contract about anything has a long history in English common law. Well over 100 years ago Sir George Jessell MR stated that freedom of contract was the paramount public policy in English common law:

> if there is one thing which more than another public policy requires it is that men of full age and competent understanding shall have the utmost liberty of contracting, and that their contracts when entered into freely and voluntarily shall be held sacred and shall be enforced by courts of justice.[5]

India is a common law country, but for over 100 years it has had a detailed statute that effectively constitutes a default contract code. The *Contracts Act 1972* (India) provides for freedom of contract in the following terms:

> 10 All agreements are contracts if they are made by the free consent of parties competent to contract, for a lawful consideration and with a lawful object, and are not hereby expressly declared to be void. Nothing herein contained shall affect any law in force in India and not hereby expressly repealed by which any contract is required to be made in writing or in the presence of witnesses, or any law relating to the registration of documents.

Malaysia is also a common law country with a *Contracts Act*. The *Contracts Act 1950* (Malaysia) enshrines freedom of contract in statute in the following terms:

> s1(2) Nothing herein contained shall affect any written law or any usage or custom of trade, or any incident of any contract, not inconsistent with this Act.
>
> 10. (1) All agreements are contracts if they are made by the free consent of parties competent to contract, for a lawful consideration and with a lawful object, and are not hereby expressly declared to be void.
>
> (2) Nothing herein contained shall affect any law by which any contract is required to be made in writing or in the presence of witnesses, or any law relating to the registration of documents.
>
> s24 The consideration or object of an agreement is lawful, unless–
>
> (a) it is forbidden by a law;
> (b) it is of such a nature that, if permitted, it would defeat any law;
> (c) it is fraudulent;
> (d) it involves or implies injury to the person or property of another; or
> (e) the court regards it as immoral, or opposed to public policy.
>
> In each of the above cases, the consideration or object of an agreement is said to be unlawful. Every agreement of which the object or consideration is unlawful is void.

However, the very freedom of contract provided in the *Contracts Act 1950* (Malaysia) gives the parties the freedom to derogate from its provisions. In *Ooi Boon Long v Citibank NA*,[6] Lord Brightman held that s1(2) of the *Contracts Act 1950*

> does not say that the contracting parties are unable by agreement to vary the legal consequences spelt out by the Act. Section 1 (2) has no effect on the freedom of contracting parties to decide upon what terms they desire to contract.

5 *Printing and Numeral Registering Co. v Sampson* (1875) L. R. 19 Eq., 462, 465 per Sir George Jessel MR.
6 [1984] 1 M.L.J. 222 (Malaysian Privy Council).

Therefore, if parties desire to oust the application of a certain provision of the *Contracts Act 1950*, their intention should be made clear expressly.

Freedom of contract is also a fundamental principle under civil law systems, e.g.:

> In this jurisdiction [Philippines] contracts are enforced as they are read, and parties who are competent to contract may make such agreements within the limitations of the law and public policy as they desire, and the courts will enforce them according to their terms.[7]

In this case, the principle is enshrined in statute – Article 1306 of the *Civil Code of the Philippines* states:

> The contracting parties may establish such stipulations, clauses, terms and conditions as they may deem convenient, provided they are not contrary to law, morals, good customs, public order or public policy.

Public policy is largely concerned with the potential for manifest unfairness or injustice in a given situation. Thus, the courts may disregard or refuse to give effect to contractual obligations which, whilst not directly contrary to any express or implied statutory prohibition, nevertheless contravene 'the policy of the law' as discerned from a consideration of the scope and purpose of the particular statute.[8]

Public policy has a very powerful reach in civil law systems. In the European community, most of whose member states have civil law legal systems, parties have a similar freedom of contract to that applying under common law systems and are free to choose (within certain limits) the law which is to apply to their contract. *Regulation (EC) number 593/2008* of the European Parliament (***Rome I***) provides in Article 3.1 that 'A contract shall be governed by the law chosen by the parties'. However, it also provides in Article 21 that:

> The application of a provision of the law of any country specified by this Regulation may be refused only if such application is manifestly incompatible with the public policy (*ordre public*) of the forum.

The universal application of freedom of contract is reinforced by its statement in principles that may be regarded as private codifications or restatements of international contract law (modern statements of the *lex mercatoria*):

> *UNIDROIT Principles of International Commercial Contracts 2016*:[9]
>
> 1.1 The parties are free to enter into a contract and to determine its content.
>
> *Trans-Lex Principles*:[10]
>
> IV.1.1 The parties are free to enter into contracts and to determine their contents (principle of party autonomy).

---

7 *Lambert v Fox* 26 Phil 588 [Philippines], cited in Edgardo L Paras, *Civil Code of the Philippines Annotated Volume Four* (14th edn, 2000) 332.

8 *Nelson v Nelson* [1995] HCA 25; (1995) 184 CLR 538, 552, 611.

9 The UNIDROIT Principles and their application to construction contracts are discussed in: Donald Charrett, *Contracts for Construction and Engineering Projects* (2nd edn, Informa Law from Routledge, 2022) Chapter 36.

10 www.trans-lex.org/principles/of-transnational-law- (accessed 30 October 2020).

Thus, one of the consequences of freedom of contract is that, subject to the applicable mandatory law and public policy, parties generally have the freedom to make an explicit choice of the proper or governing law of their contract, irrespective of the laws of the Country.

Governments legislate to restrain freedom of contract in various ways, including:

- Illegality/unenforceability of certain contractual terms
- Implying terms into all contracts of a particular type
- Creating statutory rights that coexist with contractual rights
- Mandating the way in which a court or tribunal is to settle disputes or determine contractual rights

1.1.5 Pacta sunt servanda

The obverse of the principle of freedom of contract is articulated by the doctrine of ***pacta sunt servanda***, a Latin phrase which means that agreements are to be kept. It is a fundamental principle of international law that the provisions of treaties concluded properly are to be observed. The principle means that once parties have exercised their freedom to enter into a contract, they have the legal rights and obligations they have agreed to, and these will be enforced by a court or an arbitrator. Thus, for instance, if the contracting parties have agreed that any disputes will be settled by arbitration, the courts will generally stay any court proceedings commenced in breach of the agreement to arbitrate, on the principle that the parties should be kept to their agreement.

Article 1.3 (Binding character of contract) of the *UNIDROIT Principles of International Commercial Contracts 2016* gives effect to the principal of *pacta sunt servanda* in the following terms:

> A contract validly entered into is binding upon the parties. It can only be modified or terminated in accordance with its terms or by agreement or as otherwise provided in these Principles.

The universal nature of this principle has been stated as: 'All the world's legal systems focus on the sanctity of contracts, and damages as the remedy for breach of contract'.[11] The consequences are rather reassuring in the context of construction law:

> the principle of *pacta sunt servanda* ... is universal to all legal systems. This means that the vast majority of construction disputes are fought and won or lost primarily over the wording of the contract (and alleged facts).[12]

Thus, the contract language will generally govern the parties' rights most of the time.

1.1.6 Proper law of the contract

One important aspect of freedom of contract is that parties are generally free to choose the law that governs their contractual relations, known as the **governing law of the contract**

11 Robert Knutson (ed), *FIDIC: An Analysis of International Construction Contracts* (Wolters Kluwer, 2005) xiv.

12 *Ibid.* xvi.

or the **proper law of the contract**. In *Garsec v His Majesty the Sultan of Brunei* [2008] NSWCA 211 [128], Campbell JA noted an Australian court's analysis of the factors to be considered if the parties have not made an explicit choice of the proper law:

> An important feature of the proper law of an international contract is that, subject to questions of public policy and bona fides, the parties are free to choose what the proper law will be: *Vita Food Products Inc v. Unus Shipping Co Ltd* [1939] AC 277. If, on construing the contract, the court is unable to conclude that the parties intended that contract to be governed by reference to a particular system of law, the court identifies a proper law by ascertaining the system of law with which the transaction has its closest and most real connection: *Bonython v Commonwealth of Australia* [1951] AC 201; *Akai Pty Ltd v. People's Insurance Co Limited* [1996] HCA 39; 91996) 188 CLR 418 at 440-1. But whether the proper law is ascertained from the intention of the parties, or under the *Bonython* test, makes no difference to those aspects of the contract – which might, on some accounts of the law, extend to its formation, validity, interpretation, and the rights and obligations of the parties under it – that are decided in accordance with the proper law of the contract. Other systems of law besides that of the forum and the proper law can sometimes come to bear upon the contract – as when its performance is illegal under the law of the place where it is to be performed. However it can be seen that one of the purposes of recognising a proper law of contract is to allow the parties to have freedom of choice about the system of law that will govern their relations, to the extent that other systems of law do not impose themselves upon the formation, performance or enforcement of the contract. That purpose is also advanced by applying the substantive/procedural distinction articulated in *John Pfeiffer v. Rogerson* (2000) 203 CLR 503 to litigation concerning international contracts.

In *Attorney-General of Botswana v Aussie Diamond Products Pty Ltd (No 3)* [2010] WASC 14, in dealing with the factors relevant to the ascertainment of the proper law of the contract in Australia, Murphy J noted in paragraphs 207 and 208:

> In my view, the law of Western Australia is the system of law with which the contract is most directly connected, and hence is the proper law of the contract: see *Bonython v. the Commonwealth of Australia* (1950) 81 CLR 486, 498: *Akai Pty Ltd v. The People's Insurance Co Ltd* (1996) 188 CLR 418, 434. The following features are relevant. The offer, in the quotation dated 13 May 2003, and all subsequent contractual communications, was in English. The consideration provided by the Department was in Australian dollars. It was to be paid by a confirming bank in Australia upon the presentation of documents. The goods were to be supplied from Australia and c.i.f obligations were to be undertaken by the defendant in Australia. Although commissioning was to occur in Botswana, that fact alone does not outweigh the other considerations to which I have referred, which point to the law of the contract being the law of Western Australia.
>
> Whilst the question of the proper law is, in each case, dependent on the particular nature and terms of the contract and its surrounding circumstances, the conclusion which I have reached here derives some support, I think, from *Mendelsohn-Zeller Inc v T&C Providores Pty Ltd* [1981] NSWLR 366 and *Power Curber International Ltd v. National Bank of Kuwait* [1981] 1 WLR 1233 and the factors considered relevant in those cases.

Where the parties have not made an explicit choice of the governing law of the contract, and there is more than one legal jurisdiction whose laws govern the Contract, there is a conflict of laws. A judge or arbitrator adjudicating a dispute must determine the governing law of the contract by the appropriate conflict of laws rules. The application of conflict of laws rules may involve a complicated interaction between the facts of the case and the procedural law and substantive law of different legal jurisdictions, where there is no unanimity of conflict of laws rules.

In this writer's view, it is highly desirable to make an explicit choice of the governing law of the contract in the Contract Data, to avoid the possibility of subsequent dispute over what it is. As noted in section 1.5.1, the default position in the FIDIC rainbow suite of contracts is that the law of the Country will be the governing law of the contract, excluding any conflict of law rules.

1.1.7 International construction contracts

The main focus of the book is on international contracts. An **international construction contract** is a contract for the provision of goods and services in which:

(a) The parties to the Contract have, at the time of the conclusion of their agreement, their places of business in different legal jurisdictions; or
(b) One of the following places is situated outside the legal jurisdiction in which the parties have their places of business:
  (i) the Site; or
  (ii) any place where a substantial part of the obligations for the Works is to be performed.

Although building work is a species of construction, domestic building work is outside the scope of this book, and accordingly, there is no reference to any legislation or other provisions that regulate domestic building contracts or work in any jurisdiction.

1.2 *Lex constructionis*[13]

1.2.1 What is it?

The use of FIDIC contracts across jurisdictions is of particular interest in considering the extent to which there is a 'common law of construction contracts' or a '*lex constructionis*', despite the differences in legal systems and jurisdictions. The book by Jaeger and Hök[14] is especially valuable for its commentary on different philosophical approaches to drafting international contracts, and how the FIDIC contracts are applied in civil law jurisdictions. The book edited by Knutson[15] contains chapters on the use of FIDIC contracts in 13 different countries – four common law,[16] eight civil law[17] and one Shari'a law.[18] The commentaries in Knutson's book clearly underscore the differences between legal jurisdictions in the use of FIDIC contracts, leading one to question whether there could be any such concept as *lex constructionis*.

13 This topic is discussed in more detail in: Donald Charrett, '*Lex constructionis* – or My Country's Rules?' [2021] *International Construction Law Review* 61; and Donald Charrett, *Contracts for Construction and Engineering Projects* (2nd edn, Informa Law from Routledge, 2022) Chapter 35.

14 Axel-Volkmar Jaeger & Götz-Sebastian Hök, *FIDIC – A Guide for Practitioners* (Springer, 2010).

15 Robert Knutson (ed), *FIDIC: An Analysis of International Construction Contracts* (Kluwer Law International, 2005).

16 England, India, Malaysia and the USA.

17 Brazil, Egypt, France, Germany, Japan, the Netherlands, Sweden and Switzerland.

18 Saudi Arabia.

However, notwithstanding the common law genesis of FIDIC contracts, and the significant differences in a number of legal theories, the following observation from the perspective of German law suggests there may be substantive common ground:

> The legal background of the 'Werkvertrag' as contained in the German Civil Code does not lead to a completely different structure of a construction contract compared to the FIDIC-new series model forms, however some features of the FIDIC-new series, which stem from English construction law, are either unknown (eg the Engineer) or differently regulated (eg provisional and final acceptance of the works) in German construction law. Apart from these two major differences both the structure and the system of a construction contract of CONS [red book] and P & DB [yellow book] seem to lead to both in similar legal principles and sometimes even the same results (eg *force majeure*, risk and responsibility, damages and compensation.[19]

Perhaps the clearest pointer to what there is of a *lex constructionis* is the following statement on the fundamental importance of the words of the contract itself, vindicating the twin principles of freedom of contract and *pacta sunt servanda*:

> Finally, deep in the night, with no one else around, most lawyers in their heart of hearts will admit – the Contract usually decides the issues, despite what the law is.[20]

1.2.2 Promotion of best practice for successful projects

It is suggested that *lex constructionis* can promote best practice for successful projects in which the contracting parties' legitimate expectations can be realised. In this writer's view, those legitimate expectations are typically along the following lines:

Employer

- Completion of the project on time, for the Contract Price and to the agreed standard of quality
- Timely and adequate communication from the Contractor of any departures from the original scope of Works, the materialisation of risks and any claims

Contractor

- Prompt payment of all amounts due under the Contract
- Freedom to carry out the construction in accordance with the Contract without hindrance by the Employer
- Timely and adequate communication from the Employer of the materialisation of any risks, communication of instructions and assessment of claims

It is submitted that the principles proposed here, if followed, would fulfil those expectations. The proposed principles have been formulated taking into account the unique features of construction projects and construction contracts discussed earlier, the Abrahamson principles of balanced risk allocation,[21] the FIDIC General Conditions in the

19 Wolfgang Rosener & Gerhard Dorner, 'Germany' in Robert Knutson (ed), *FIDIC: An Analysis of International Construction Contracts* (Kluwer Law International, 2005) 87, 125.

20 Robert Knutson (ed), *FIDIC: An Analysis of International Construction Contracts* (Kluwer Law International, 2005) xix.

21 Max W Abrahamson, 'Risk Management' (1983) *International Construction Law Review* 241, 244.

rainbow suite, the FIDIC Golden Principles[22] and 'social obligations' owed to third parties. They are also influenced by Molyneaux's paper on this topic in which he formulated a 'modest Mosaic ten' principles.[23]

One of the criticisms that could be directed to the proposed (or any) principles of *lex constructionis* is that they cannot cover all situations, nor can they necessarily be applied in their entirety in many situations. The following discussion of principles in the context of *lex mercatoria* is equally applicable to the proposed principles of *lex constructionis*:

> General principles do not necessarily have pre-set conditions for application. Instead they merely constitute 'rules of optimal application' which means that they may be complied with in varying degrees. The required degree of compliance depends not only on the actual but also on the legal options open to the target group. Application of general principles therefore requires a substantial process of weighing up contradictory principles and rules. General principles are therefore always subject to a continual discussion about the effectiveness and scope.[24] (citations omitted)

1.2.3 Proposed principles of lex constructionis

Overarching principles

1. *Pacta sunt servanda*
2. ***Rebus sic stantibus*** – doctrines or rules relating to changed conditions
3. The parties must act in accordance with good faith and fair dealing in construction contracts

Scope

4. The contract defines, in writing, the original scope of Works and the known conditions at the Site
5. The Employer has the right to instruct Variations consistent with the original scope of the Contract, and the Contractor has the obligation to carry out all such Variations
6. Construction Works must be carried out so as to protect the health and safety of workers
7. Construction Works must not adversely affect the environment or the interests of third parties
8. Subject to any contractual requirements, the Contractor selects the methods and timing of the Works

Risk

9. Each risk is allocated to the Party best able to manage and control it and the consequences if it eventuates, or to the Party who will derive any benefit or suffer the least consequences if the risk eventuates

22 See Chapter 2.

23 Charles Molineaux, 'Moving toward a construction *lex mercatoria*: A *lex constructionis*' (1997) 1 *JIntArb* 55.

24 Klaus Peter Berger, *The Creeping Codification of the New Lex Mercatoria* (Wolters Kluwer The Netherlands, 2010), 201 (citations omitted).

10. A Party is not allocated risks that it cannot insure for or has insufficient financial resources to bear
11. The Contractor is responsible for the Works whilst it is in possession of the Site

Time

12. The parties have a reasonable time to perform their obligations and exercise their rights
13. The Contractor provides the Employer with prompt and adequate notice of any unexpected conditions that affect its performance, the occurrence of any risk events and any Claims
14. The Employer provides the Contractor with prompt and adequate notice of the occurrence of any risk events that affect the Contractor, instructions and responses to Claims
15. The Contractor is liable to pay damages if it does not complete the Works by the contractually agreed date

Cost

16. The Employer has adequate financial resources to complete the Contract
17. The Contractor provides security for its performance
18. The Employer pays the Contractor its contractual entitlements promptly

Quality

19. The Contractor either rectifies defects in its Works or pays damages to reinstate the Works to the contractually specified quality

Disputes

20. Unresolved disputes are finally determined by arbitration

1.2.4 Discussion

Space does not permit a detailed exposition of each of these principles. Some would probably be accepted as implied terms that go without saying. Others may be more controversial.

The overarching principles are contained in statements of the *lex mercatoria*, such as the UNIDROIT Principles. In this writer's view, they are important for the successful execution of construction projects that frequently take place over a long time and involve changed circumstances. In particular, the requirements of honesty, fairness and reasonableness inherent in the good faith principle will necessarily be relied upon to resolve amicably (where possible) many of the expected and unexpected issues that can arise during the execution of a construction contract.

The principles on scope acknowledge the complexity of construction projects and the possibility that the scope may need to change and that the Works impact third parties and the environment. Risks are inherent in any construction project, and their appropriate allocation is often critical to achieving a successful project.[25]

The principles related to time reiterate the requirement of reasonableness and emphasise the importance of adequate and timely communication from Contractor to Employer and vice versa. Damages for late completion are appropriate to compensate the Employer for its inability to make commercial use of the constructed facility from the agreed date.

Certainty and promptness of payment are usually of great importance to the Contractor and may be critical to its solvency. The requirement for a Contractor to rectify or pay for defect rectification is merely a construction-specific implementation of *pacta sunt servanda.*

The near-universal implementation of the *New York Convention*, the norms of international arbitration and the finality and enforcement of awards are the basis for arbitration to generally be the most appropriate method for resolving international construction disputes. However, litigation in the international commercial courts recently established in a number of jurisdictions may provide a viable alternative to arbitration for some international construction disputes.[26]

1.3 FIDIC contracts

1.3.1 Overview

The Fédération Internationale des Ingénieurs-Conseils (**FIDIC**) (known by its English name of the International Federation of Consulting Engineers) publishes standard form Conditions of Contract that are used in many countries and are probably the most widely used international construction contracts in the world. Although they have a common law pedigree, they are intended to be used in any legal jurisdiction whether common law, civil law or any other type of law.

FIDIC publishes the standard forms of construction contract between Employer and Contractor shown in Table 1.1.[27]

The various editions of the FIDIC Conditions of Contract for contracts between Employer and Contractor are tabulated in Table 1.4 in the Annexure to this chapter.

In March 2021 FIDIC announced that the Contracts Committee would set up task groups to develop three new FIDIC contract forms: Public Private Partnerships (**PPP** or **3Ps**), Engineering, Procurement and Construction Management (EPCM) and alliancing.

25 For a discussion of the consequences of inappropriately allocating risk, see: Japan International Cooperation Agency, 'Check List for One Sided Contracts' (2011), 1. www.jica.go.jp/english/our_work/types_of_assistance/oda_loans/oda_op_info/guide/c8h0vm0000aoeprl-att/guide02.pdf (accessed 4 April 2022).

26 International commercial courts, including the enforcement of international court judgments are discussed in Philip Loots & Donald Charrett, *Contracts for Infrastructure Projects: An International Guide to Application* (Informa Law from Routledge, 2022) ¶28.13.2.

27 These FIDIC contracts were listed on the FIDIC website (www.fidic.org/bookshop) on 4 November 2020.

Table 1.1 FIDIC Conditions of Contract for contracts between Employer and Contractor

1977 Red Book	Conditions of Contract for Works of Civil Engineering Construction – Third Edition 1977
1987 Red Book	Conditions of Contract for Works of Civil Engineering Construction Fourth Edition 1987
1987 Yellow Book	Conditions of Contract for Electrical and Mechanical Works – Third Edition 1987
1995 Orange Book	Conditions of Contract for Design-Build and Turnkey – First Edition 1995
1999 Red Book	Conditions of Contract for Construction – First Edition 1999
1999 Yellow Book	Conditions of Contract for Plant and Design-Build – First Edition 1999
1999 Silver Book	Conditions of Contract for EPC/Turnkey Projects – First Edition 1999
2017 Red Book	Conditions of Contract for Construction – Second Edition 2017
2017 Yellow Book	Conditions of Contract for Plant and Design-Build – Second Edition 2017
2017 Silver Book	Conditions of Contract for EPC/Turnkey Projects – Second Edition 2017
Green Book	Short Form of Contract – First Edition 1999, Second Edition 2021
Pink Book	Conditions of Contract for Construction – Multilateral Development Bank Harmonised Edition for Building and Engineering Works Designed by the Employer – Version 1: 2005, Version 2: March 2005, Version 3: 2010
Gold Book	Conditions of Contract for Design, Build and Operate Projects – First Edition, 2008
Blue-Green Book	Form of Contract for Dredging and Reclamation Works – First Edition 2006, Second Edition 2016
Emerald Book	Conditions of Contract for Underground Works First Edition 2019

FIDIC publishes the following standard forms of subcontract between Contractor and Subcontractor:[28]

- Conditions of Subcontract for Work of Civil Engineering Construction – First Edition 1994
- Conditions of Subcontract for Construction – First Edition 2011
- Conditions of Subcontract for Plant and Design (Yellow Book 1999) – First Edition 2019

The **Red Book**,[29] **Yellow Book**[30] and **Silver Book**[31] (as well as the Pink Book) are commonly referred to as the **rainbow suite**. The focus of this book is mainly on the rainbow suite, and sub-clause references refer to the Second Edition 2017 Red, Yellow and Silver Books unless otherwise noted. However, the principles outlined are generally applicable to all the FIDIC standard form contracts.

A number of guides to the use of FIDIC contracts are listed in section 1.10.5.

28 These FIDIC contracts were listed on the FIDIC website (www.fidic.org/bookshop) on 24 February 2022.

29 References to the Red Book without a year preface refer to the 1999 Red Book and the 2017 Red Book.

30 References to the Yellow Book without a year preface refer to the 1999 Yellow Book and the 2017 Yellow Book.

31 References to the Silver Book without a year preface refer to the 1999 Silver Book and the 2017 Silver Book.

The FIDIC rainbow suite standard forms generally comprise:

- Acknowledgements
- Notes
- General Conditions
- Guidance for the Preparation of Particular Conditions
- Annexes: Forms of Securities
- Forms of Letter of Tender, Letter of Acceptance, Contract Agreement and Dispute Avoidance/Adjudication Agreement

The Acknowledgements list the numerous groups and individuals that contribute to the rigorous process of developing, reviewing, refining and approval of FIDIC standard form contracts. These contributors include the Contracts Committee that drafts the documents, the Task Groups that provide input to the Contracts Committee, special advisors and friendly reviewers. The large number of individuals involved from many countries with extensive contract, construction, engineering and legal skills highlights FIDIC's comprehensive process of drafting contracts that acknowledge the importance of the many stakeholders and their endeavours to produce balanced contracts that represent best international practice.

1.3.2 MDB use of FIDIC contracts

A number of multilateral development banks (**MDBs**) use FIDIC General Conditions in their Standard Bidding Documents (**SBDs**). MDBs that have embraced FIDIC General Conditions include the World Bank, Asian Development Bank, Black Sea Trade and Development Bank, European Bank for Reconstruction and Development, Caribbean Development Bank and Inter-American Development Bank.

The use of FIDIC General Conditions by MDBs in their SBDs led to the promulgation of the Pink Book in 2005. This was based on the 1999 Red Book, with the addition of a number of provisions required by MDBs to further their development goals of enhancing living standards and to protect the MDBs' interests in probity and proper use of loan funds. In particular the Pink Book contains the following additional 12 sub-clauses in the Red Book clause 6 Staff and Labour:

6.12 Foreign personnel
6.13 Supply of foodstuffs
6.14 Supply of water
6.15 Measures against insect and pest nuisance
6.16 Alcoholic liquor and drugs
6.17 Arms and ammunition
6.18 Festivals and religious customs
6.19 Funeral arrangements
6.20 Forced labour
6.21 Child labour
6.22 Employee records of workers
6.23 Workers' organisations

These 'social provisions' in the Pink Book provide protections for labour, local communities and the environment that may not be adequately covered by legislation in less developed countries. The Pink Book also contains draconian MDB-specific provisions on the consequences of corrupt or fraudulent practices by the Contractor or any of its employees.[32]

The extensive international input into the drafting of FIDIC General Conditions and its acceptance as an appropriate contract for international contracts is evidenced by the World Bank's implementation of the 2017 Red Book in its 2019 Standard Procurement Document.[33] The Particular Conditions of Contract in the World Bank Standard Procurement Document does not change the balanced risk/reward allocation in the General Conditions and mainly comprises 'social provisions' such as those outlined for the Pink Book.

Japan International Cooperation Agency (JICA) is one of the world's largest bilateral aid agencies supporting socioeconomic development in developing countries in different regions of the world. It is in charge of administering Japan's Official Development Assistance and uses FIDIC General Conditions in some of its SBDs. JICA's rationale for its strong support of FIDIC contracts and its continued use of the Pink Book is explained elsewhere.[34]

1.3.3 FIDIC contract documents

A 'FIDIC Contract' comprises a number of documents that are to be taken as mutually explanatory of one another, in the order of precedence in the event of inconsistency between them shown in Table 1.2.[35]

1.3.4 Contract agreement

The Contract Agreement form is a two-page pro forma document that requires the essential details of the Contract to be filled in and formally executed by the Parties. As this document is the highest in priority of the Contract documents, it is essential that it be accurate and comprehensive and executed in accordance with the governing law of the contract. Appropriate legal advice should be sought to ensure that the resulting Contract complies with all of the relevant legal requirements. Particular jurisdictions may require specific formalities for the Contract to be legally binding, such as payment of stamp duty. Specific jurisdiction requirements are discussed in the later chapters.

---

32 Sub-clause 15.6.

33 http://pubdocs.worldbank.org/en/865231562944956956/SPD-Request-for-Bids-WORKS-after-prequalification.docx (accessed 28 August 2020).

34 Takashi Ito & Michino Yamaguchi, 'JICA's Perspectives on the use of FIDIC Contracts' in Donald Charrett (ed), *The Application of FIDIC Contracts in Asia Pacific: A Practical Guide to Application* (Informa Law from Routledge, 2022) Chapter 5.

35 Rainbow suite sub-clause 1.5.

Table 1.2 Order of precedence of Contract documents in the FIDIC rainbow suite

	2017 Red Book	2017 Yellow Book	2017 Silver Book
(a)	The Contract Agreement	The Contract Agreement	The Contract Agreement
(b)	The Letter of Acceptance	The Letter of Acceptance	The Particular Conditions Part A – Contract Data
(c)	The Letter of Tender	The Letter of Tender	The Particular Conditions Part B – Special Provisions
(d)	The Particular Conditions Part A – Contract Data	The Particular Conditions Part A – Contract Data	The General Conditions
(e)	The Particular Conditions Part B – Special Provisions	The Particular Conditions Part B – Special Provisions	The Employer's Requirements
(f)	The General Conditions	The General Conditions	The Schedules
(g)	The Specification	The Employer's Requirements	The Tender
(h)	The drawings	The Schedules	The JV Undertaking (if the Contractor is a JV)
(i)	The Schedules	The Contractor's Proposal	Any other documents forming part of the Contract
(j)	The JV Undertaking (if the Contractor is a JV)	The JV Undertaking (if the Contractor is a JV)	
(k)	Any other documents forming part of the Contract	Any other documents forming part of the Contract	

1.3.5 Particular Conditions

The table of Contract documents in Table 1.2 highlights that the Particular Conditions (those Conditions of Contract that are specific to the unique Contract) comprise two parts:

- Part A – Contract Data
- Part B – Special Provisions

1.3.6 Particular Conditions Part A – Contract Data

The Contract Data, as its name implies, contains the data that is required to define all the unique characteristics of the particular Contract, e.g. the Parties, the Site, the Time for Completion, the governing law of the contract, Contract Price, liability, securities, Defects Notification Period etc. It is pro forma consisting of five pages of items referring to sub-clauses of the General Conditions which require insertion of data by the Employer (before calling Tenders) or the Contractor (in its Tender). The Annexure to Chapter 3 shows the Contract Data in the 2017 Yellow Book, annotated with default provisions.

1.3.7 Particular Conditions Part B – Special Provisions

Special Provisions necessary for the particular requirements of the Works may comprise either modifications to the General Conditions or additional provisions. Such modifications may be necessary or desirable:

- To comply or align with applicable law
- For the specific requirements of the Site or the Works, or
- For the Employer's preferences

Each of these topics is dealt with in more detail in the following.

1.3.8 General Conditions

The General Conditions as printed are FIDIC copyright and accordingly cannot legally be reproduced or amended without FIDIC permission. In particular, this includes scanning to produce a soft copy that is then modified. As noted earlier, whilst the FIDIC General Conditions have been drafted to be applicable to a wide range of international construction contracts in various jurisdictions, the unique requirements of a particular Contract may mean that the FIDIC General Conditions require modification. The use of a single Conditions of Contract document incorporating both Particular Conditions and General Conditions is discussed in section 3.5.

1.4 The FIDIC Golden Principles

The Guidance for the Preparation of Particular Conditions in the Emerald Book contains the following recommendation:

> FIDIC strongly recommends that the Employer, the Contractor and all drafters of the Special Provisions take all due regard of the five FIDIC Golden Principles:
>
> GP1: The duties, rights, obligations, roles and responsibilities of all the Contract Participants must be generally as implied in the General Conditions, and appropriate to the requirements of the project.
> GP2: The Particular Conditions must be drafted clearly and unambiguously.
> GP3: The Particular Conditions must not change the balance of risk/reward allocation provided for in the General Conditions.
> GP4: All time periods specified in the Contract for Contract Participants to perform their obligations must be of reasonable duration.
> GP5: Unless there is a conflict with the governing law of the Contract, all formal disputes must be referred to a Dispute Avoidance/Adjudication Board (or a Dispute Adjudication Board, if applicable) for a provisionally binding decision as a condition precedent to arbitration.[36]

These FIDIC Golden Principles are described and explained in the publication FIDIC's Golden Principles (http://fidic.org/bookshop) and are necessary to ensure that modifications to the General Conditions:

- Are limited to those necessary for the particular features of the Site and the project, and necessary to comply with the applicable law
- Do not change the essential fair and balanced character of a FIDIC contract, and
- The Contract remains recognisable as a FIDIC contract.[37]

---

36 Since publication of the 2017 editions of the rainbow suite, GP5 has been amended by the addition of the prefatory words: 'Unless there is a conflict with the governing law of the Contract'.

37 Emerald Book Guidance for the Preparation of Particular Conditions, 8. The 2017 Red Book, 2017 Yellow Book and the 2017 Silver Book contain a similar recommendation.

A more detailed explanation of the Golden Principles is in Chapter 2. That chapter includes some general guidance on preparing Particular Conditions to comply with the Golden Principles. The overarching justification for the Golden Principles is to enable a contract to be recognised as a 'FIDIC Contract' that complies with widely accepted international norms and promotes best practice in contract execution and administration.

For another view on the FIDIC Golden Principles, see the article in *Construction Law International* by Graeme Christie.[38]

1.5 Applicable laws

Applicable laws can be mandatory or non-mandatory:

- **Mandatory law** is based on public policy, and as it cannot be excluded by the parties, it will prevail over any Conditions of Contract
- **Non-mandatory law** will apply to the extent that the parties have not agreed otherwise

Distinguishing between mandatory and non-mandatory law can generally only be determined by construction of the relevant law itself.

Irrespective of the wording of the Conditions of Contract and notwithstanding freedom of contract, if the General Conditions are incompatible with mandatory law, mandatory law will apply. Applicable mandatory law that may be inconsistent with the General Conditions could be, *inter alia*, Laws relating to execution of work at the Site or any other location and/or the governing law of the contract.

As Site personnel and Contract Administrators may not be familiar with all of the applicable law, in this writer's view it is desirable that Special Provisions are included in the Particular Conditions Part B that articulate all the changes to the General Conditions that are necessary to comply with mandatory law. As discussed further in section 3.1, it may also be desirable for Particular Conditions to incorporate provisions that are not incompatible with the General Conditions but refer to issues within the scope of the mandatory law that are not referred to in the General Conditions. Such Particular Conditions will ensure that the Conditions of Contract are an accurate and comprehensive contract management manual that can safely be followed.

Each of the jurisdiction Chapters 4–12 address Special Provisions both necessary for consistency with mandatory law and desirable to articulate issues within the scope of the mandatory law which are not referred to in the General Conditions.

1.5.1 Laws

The 2017 Yellow Book has the following relevant provisions referring to Laws:

> **1.1 Definitions**
>
> 1.1.49 '**Laws**' means all national (or state or provincial) legislation, statutes, acts, decrees, rules, ordinances, orders, treaties, international law and other laws, and regulations and by-laws of any legally constituted public authority.

38 Graeme Christie, 'The Golden Principles – FIDIC's Shiny Christmas Present' (2018) 13.2 *Construction Law International* 10.

1.13 Compliance with Laws:

The Contractor and the Employer shall, in performing the Contract, comply with all applicable Laws.

The definition of Laws includes laws of the Country as well as the governing law of the contract. Compliance with Laws is referred to in a number of other subclauses in the Yellow Book:

3.5 Engineer's Instructions

... If ... the Contractor considers that the instruction: ...

(b) does not comply with applicable Laws ...

The Contractor shall immediately ... give a Notice to the Engineer with reasons.

4.8 Health and Safety Obligations

The Contractor shall:

(a) comply with all applicable health and safety regulations and Laws; ...

The Contractor shall ... maintain records and make reports (in compliance with the applicable health and safety regulations and Laws) concerning the health and safety of persons and any damage to property.

4.10 Use of Site Data

... the Contractor shall be deemed ... to have been satisfied before submitting the Tender as to all matters relevant to the execution of the Works, including:

(d) the Laws, procedures and labour practices of the Country; ...

4.18 Protection of the Environment

... The Contractor shall ensure that emissions, surface discharges, effluent and any other pollutants from the Contractor's activities shall exceed neither the values indicated in the Employer's Requirements nor those prescribed by applicable Laws.

5.1 General Design Obligations

The Contractor shall carry out, and be responsible for, the design of the Works. Design shall be prepared by designers who: ...

(c) are qualified and entitled under applicable Laws to design the Works. ...

5.3 Contractor's Undertaking

The Contractor undertakes that the design, the Contractor's Documents, the execution of the Works and the completed Works will be in accordance with:

(a) the Laws of the Country; ...

5.4 Technical Standards and Regulations

The Contractor's Documents, the execution of the Works and the completed Works (including defects remedied by the Contractor) shall comply with the Country's technical standards, building, construction and environmental Laws, Laws applicable to the product being produced from the Works, and other standards specified in the Employer's Requirements, applicable to the Works, or defined by applicable Laws. ...

6.2 Rates of Wages and Conditions of Labour

The Contractor shall pay rates of wages, and observe conditions of labour, which comply with all applicable Laws …

6.4 Labour Laws

The Contractor shall comply with all the relevant labour Laws applicable to the Contractor's Personnel, including Laws relating to their employment (including wages and working hours), health, safety, welfare, immigration and emigration, and shall allow them all their legal rights.

The Contractor shall require the Contractor's Personnel to obey all applicable Laws, including those concerning health and safety at work.

7.4 Testing by the Contractor

… The Contractor shall provide all apparatus, assistance, documents and other information, temporary supplies of electricity and water, equipment, fuel, consumables, instruments, labour, materials, and suitably qualified, experienced and competent staff, as are necessary to carry out the specified tests efficiently and properly. All apparatus, equipment and instruments shall be calibrated in accordance with the standards specified in the Employer's Requirements or defined by applicable Laws and, if requested by the Engineer, the Contractor shall submit calibration certificates before carrying out testing. …

7.7 Ownership of Plant and Materials

Each item of Plant and Materials shall, to the extent consistent with the mandatory requirements of the Laws of the Country, become the property of the Employer at whichever is the earlier of the following times, free from liens and other encumbrances: …

11.11 Clearance of Site

… If the Contractor fails to comply with sub-paragraphs (a), (b) and/or (c) above within 28 days after the issue of the Performance Certificate, the Employer may sell (to the extent permitted by applicable Laws) or otherwise dispose of any remaining items and/or may reinstate and clean the Site (as may be necessary) at the Contractor's cost. …

15.2 Termination for Contractor's Default

15.2.1 Notice
The Employer shall be entitled to give a Notice … to the Contractor of the Employer's intention to terminate the Contract or, in the case of sub-paragraph (f), (g) or (h) below a Notice of termination, if the Contractor: …

(g) becomes bankrupt or insolvent; goes into liquidation, administration, reorganisation, winding-up or dissolution; becomes subject to the appointment of a liquidator, receiver, administrator, manager or trustee; enters into a composition or arrangement with the Contractor's creditors; or any act is done or any event occurs which is analogous to or has a similar effect to any of these acts or events under applicable Laws; …

16.2 Termination by Contractor

16.2.1 Notice
The Contractor shall be entitled to give a Notice … to the Employer of the Contractor's intention to terminate the Contract or, in the case of sub-paragraph (g)(ii), (h), (i) or (j) below, a Notice of termination, if:

(i) the Employer becomes bankrupt or insolvent; goes into liquidation, administration, reorganisation, winding-up or dissolution; becomes subject to the appointment of a liquidator, receiver, administrator, manager or trustee; enters into a composition or arrangement with the Employer's creditors; or any act is done or any event occurs which is analogous to or has a similar effect to any of these acts or events under applicable Laws; or …

19.2 Insurance to be provided by the Contractor

19.2.6 Other insurances required by Laws and by local practice
The Contractor shall provide all other insurance as required by the Laws of the countries where (any part of) the Works are being carried out, at the Contractor's own cost.

These provisions refer explicitly or implicitly to the Laws of the Country where the Site is located, with the exception of sub-clause 5.1 (General Design Obligations) and 19.2 (Insurance to be provided by the Contractor) where the relevant Works may be executed in a country other than the Country where the Site is located.

1.5.2 Governing law of the contract

The 2017 Yellow Book refers to the governing law of the contract as follows:

1.4 Law and Language

The Contract shall be governed by the law of the country (or other jurisdiction) stated in the Contract Data (if not stated, the law of the Country), excluding any conflict of law rules.

The governing law is referred to in the following additional sub-clauses of the Yellow Book:

1.16 Contract Termination

Subject to any mandatory requirements under the governing law of the contract, termination of the Contract under any Sub-Clause of these Conditions shall require no action of whatsoever kind by either Party other than as stated in the Sub-Clause.

18.6 Release from Performance under the Law

In addition to any other provision of this Clause, if any event arises outside the control of the Parties (including, but not limited to, an Exceptional Event) which: (a) makes it impossible or unlawful for either Party or both Parties to fulfil their contractual obligations; or (b) under the law governing the Contract, entitles the Parties to be released from further performance of the Contract, …

21.2 Failure to Appoint DAAB Member(s)

… Thereafter, the Parties and the member(s) so appointed shall be deemed to have signed and be bound by a DAAB Agreement under which: … (ii) the law governing the DAAB Agreement shall be the governing law of the contract defined in Sub-Clause 1.4 *[Law and Language]*.

The governing law is referred to in the following sub-clauses of the Appendix General Conditions of Dispute Avoidance/Adjudication Agreement:

10 Resignation and Termination

10.9 Subject to any mandatory requirements under the governing law of the DAA's Agreement, termination of the DAA Agreement under this Clause shall require no action of whatsoever kind by the Parties or the DAAB Member (as the case may be) other than as stated in this clause.

1.5.3 Intersection of local laws with the governing law of the contract

The following are a few examples of issues in which the governing law may be inconsistent with applicable and mandatory Laws of the Country:

- Decennial liability and liability generally for the total or partial collapse of structures[39]
- Use of liens[40]
- Local procurement[41]
- Adjudication of disputes[42]
- Termination for reorganisation[43]

These issues are covered in more detail in Chapter 3.

1.5.4 Laws with extra-territorial reach

In addition to obligations that arise under the governing law of the contract, or the Laws applicable to the Site and the Country, there may be laws applying to legal persons in particular jurisdictions that apply irrespective of the jurisdiction of the Site or Country. For example, no matter what jurisdiction they are operating in, anti-trust/corruption laws apply to US companies, and human rights laws apply to European companies. Not only does the *Bribery Act 2010* (UK) apply to the UK and UK companies, but the UK courts have jurisdiction if an offence is committed by someone with a close connection with the UK, or by a corporation which does business in the UK, regardless of where the alleged offence was carried out.

1.5.5 Laws applicable to the execution of a construction project

Applicable Laws relevant to the execution of a construction project may include:

- The law governing the parties' capacity to enter into a contract
- The governing or proper law of the contract
- Laws relating to the Site where the Works are carried out (referred to in the FIDIC General Conditions as discussed in section 1.5.1) (***lex loci rei sitae***)
- The law relating to the disposition of property (***in rem* claims**)
- Procedural law that applies to any court proceedings, including the coercive power of the court in support of arbitration proceedings (**law of the forum** or ***lex fori***)
- Laws applying to a corporation which does business in a country (e.g. the *Bribery Act 2010* [UK])

---

39 E.g. see sections 9.9.2.2 and 12.5.1.1.
40 E.g. see section 6.1.5.
41 E.g. see section 12.8.1.
42 E.g. see section 6.1.5.
43 E.g. see section 5.10.2.

1.5.6 Laws applicable to arbitration of a dispute

The following laws may apply to arbitration of a dispute arising from a construction project:

- The law governing the parties' capacity to enter into an arbitration agreement
- The law governing the substance of the dispute, generally the governing law of the contract
- The law governing the arbitration agreement and the performance of that agreement
- The law governing the existence and operation of the arbitral tribunal (***lex arbitrii***, sometimes referred to as the **curial law**), generally the law of the 'seat' of arbitration
- The law (or laws) governing the recognition and enforcement of an arbitral award

The arbitration agreement is usually incorporated in the Contract but is treated for legal purposes as a separate and independent agreement for the purpose of determining its validity or enforceability. This **doctrine of separability** is a generally recognised principle of the law of international arbitration.[44] It is specifically recognised in the *UNCITRAL Model Law on International Commercial Arbitration* (***UNCITRAL Model Law***),[45] the basis of the arbitration law in 118 jurisdictions and 85 States.[46] In providing the arbitral tribunal competence to rule on its own jurisdiction, Article 16(1) of the *UNCITRAL Model Law* provides:

> The arbitral tribunal may rule on its own jurisdiction, including any objections with respect to the existence or validity of the arbitration agreement. For that purpose, an arbitration clause which forms part of a contract shall be treated as an agreement independent of the other terms of the contract. A decision by the arbitral tribunal that the contract is null and void shall not entail *ipso jure* the invalidity of the arbitration clause.

The doctrine of separability raises the possibility that the governing law of the contract may not be the same as the governing law of the arbitration agreement, i.e. the law governing the existence and performance of the arbitration agreement. This issue is discussed further in section 3.2.3.

1.6 COVID-19

1.6.1 Government responses to COVID-19

The worldwide advent of the COVID-19 pandemic in 2020 and 2021 had tragic impacts on the lives of many people and resulted in enormous disruption to the economic fabric of countries around the world. Governments responded with legislation that implemented unprecedented policies in containment and border closure, economic assistance and health measures. The Blavatnik School of Government at the University of Oxford collected data

44 E.g. *Fiona Trust & Holding Corp v Privalov* [2007] UKHL 40; [2007] All ER 951.

45 **UNCITRAL** is the United Nations Commission on International Trade Law.

46 https://uncitral.un.org/en/texts/arbitration/modellaw/commercial_arbitration/status (accessed 19 November 2021).

from 186 countries and regions on the measures governments took to respond to the pandemic, and presented their findings in the Coronavirus Government Response Tracker (**Response Tracker**). The dataset in the Response Tracker contains 23 indicators organised into four groups:

- **Containment and closure policies** (indicators C1–C8) record information on containment and closure policies, such as school closures and restrictions in movement.
- **Economic policies** (indicators E1–E4) record economic policies, such as income support to citizens or provision of foreign aid.
- **Health system policies** (indicators H1–H8) record health system policies such as the COVID-19 testing regime, emergency investments into healthcare and most recently, vaccination policies.
- **Vaccine policies** (indicators V1–3) record vaccination policies: a country's prioritisation list, eligible groups, and the cost of vaccination to the individual. [47]

In addition to the 23 individual policy indicators, the Response Tracker calculates several indices to give an overall impression of government activity. The **stringency index** provides a single index combining all of the eight containment and closure policies, thereby providing one comparative measure of the impact of the pandemic on economic life.[48] The eight containment and closure policies recorded numerical measures for the following:

- C1 – closings of schools and universities
- C2 – closing of workplaces
- C3 – cancelling public events
- C4 – limits on gatherings
- C5 – closing of public transport
- C6 – orders to 'shelter in place' and otherwise confine to the home
- C7 – restrictions on internal movement between cities/regions
- C8 – restrictions on international travel for foreign travelers[49]

These indices have been plotted for some of the countries covered in this book for the period 1 January 2020 to 4 November 2021 in the following two figures for clarity: Figure 1.1 (Bolivia, Brazil, Canada and Chile) and Figure 1.2 (Ecuador, Mexico, Peru and the USA).

These figures show how most governments reacted rapidly and strongly to the pandemic in February or March 2020. Countries were able to gradually reduce the level of stringency over the following months; however, further waves in 2020 and 2021 required the reintroduction of greater stringency. The maximum stringency recorded for the 12 countries in

47 Thomas Hale et al. 'Oxford COVID-19 Government Response Tracker' (2020) *Blavatnik School of Government.* www.bsg.ox.ac.uk/research/research-projects/coronavirus-government-response-tracker#data (accessed 22 November 2021).

48 https://github.com/OxCGRT/covid-policy-tracker/blob/master/documentation/index_methodology.md (accessed 23 November 2021).

49 https://github.com/OxCGRT/covid-policy-tracker/blob/master/documentation/codebook.md (accessed 24 February 2022).

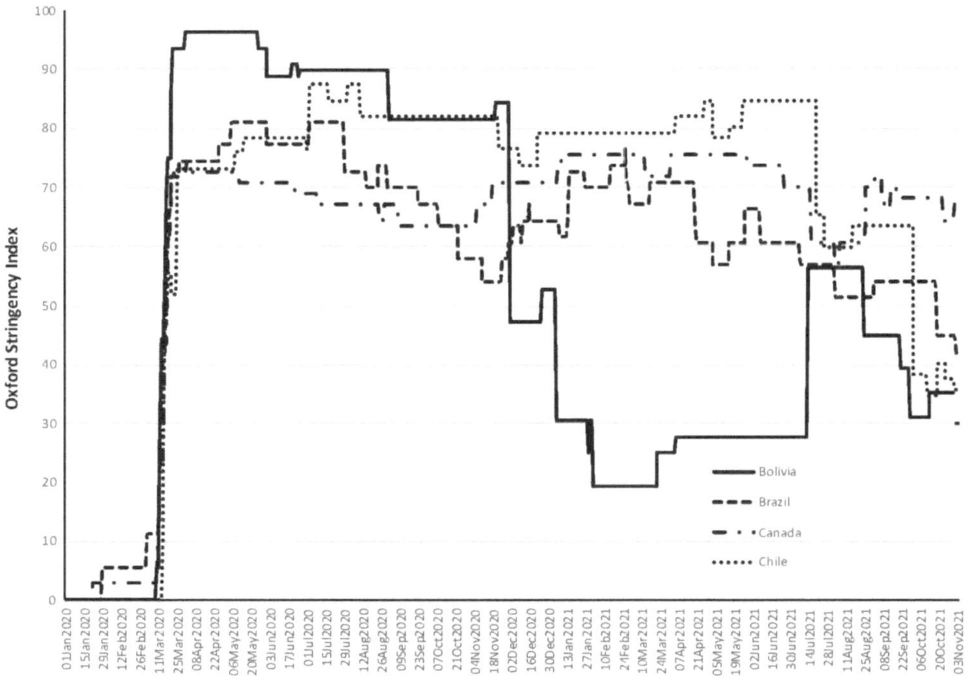

Figure 1.1 Oxford Stringency Index – Bolivia, Brazil, Canada and Chile.

March–June 2020 was typically between 70 and 95. Whilst some countries had reduced their level of stringency to below 40 by November 2021, some were still above 50, indicating the persistent impact of significant government containment measures.

1.6.2 The impact of COVID-19 on construction

The closure of borders, shutdown of businesses, restrictions on movement, physical distancing, wearing masks and new health and safety protocols all impacted construction projects, resulting in increased costs and delays. Such impacts have inevitably resulted in claims for time and cost under construction contracts. Some of those claims will no doubt be rejected and result in disputes.

FIDIC responded rapidly to the COVID-19 challenges by running a series of webinars addressing some of the issues that may arise under FIDIC contracts. FIDIC also provided resources to assist contracting parties, including the 'FIDIC COVID-19 Guidance Memorandum to Users of FIDIC Standard Forms of Works Contract', prepared by the Contracts Committee.[50] This Guidance Memorandum is discussed in section 1.6.6.

The unprecedented array of legislation to deal with the health and economic impacts of COVID-19 significantly constrained freedom of contract in many situations, not least

50 https://fidic.org/sites/default/files/COVID%2019%20Guidance%20Memorandum%20-%20PDF.pdf (accessed 4 April 2022).

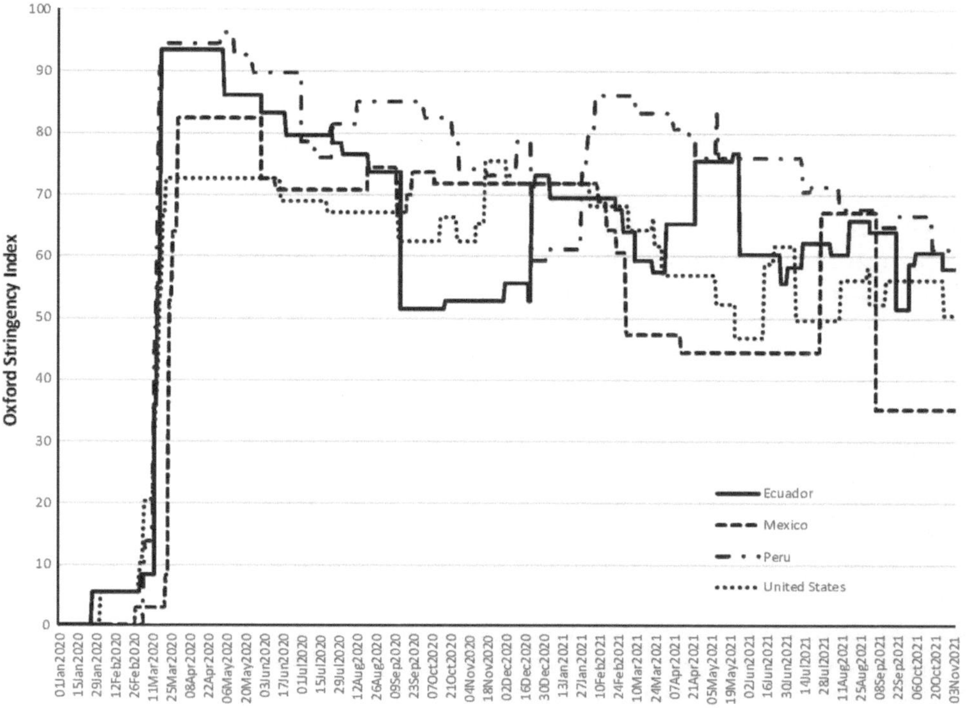

Figure 1.2 Oxford Stringency Index – Ecuador, Mexico, Peru and USA.

of which were those laws and regulations that impacted construction projects and construction contracts. The legislative interventions that are relevant to construction were measures that constrained:

- The execution of construction projects
- The operation of construction contracts
- Resolution of disputes arising out of COVID-19

In some jurisdictions, the impacts were a result of legislation specifically addressing the construction industry, and others were part of more general government actions to control the spread of COVID-19 or to provide economic support. The following are some examples of the COVID-19-specific measures introduced in various jurisdictions. Each individual jurisdiction chapter following provides details of the measures adopted in that jurisdiction.

1.6.3 Execution of construction projects impacted by COVID-19

Restrictions on travel – some countries and regions closed their borders to non-residents.

Shut down of construction sites – some countries shut down construction sites after the onset of infection; others only permitted essential services to operate during certain periods.

Constraints on working on construction sites – the operation of some construction projects was significantly restricted by limiting the number of personnel on construction sites.

Increased hours of working – some jurisdictions permitted construction sites to operate on weekends and public holidays irrespective of what consents might otherwise allow.

Physical distancing was the primary method of protection mandated in many countries, requiring all persons outside their homes (and including construction sites) to be separated by a distance of 1.0, 1.5, 1.8 or 2 metres.

Additional OHS precautions – many jurisdictions required additional health precautions to be implemented, e.g. wearing face masks outside the home or temperature checks prior to entering workplaces.

Stringent cleaning protocols were required, including frequent hand washing and sanitising by regularly and frequently disinfecting contact surfaces in an endeavour to prevent infection and deep cleaning of premises where infection had occurred.

Enhanced documentation of employees such as mandatory daily declarations and updating by employers of work permits in the construction sector on stay-home notices, or enhanced record keeping to ensure that persons who had been in close contact with an infected person could be identified, advised and tested.

Isolation of infected personnel – personnel diagnosed with COVID-19 were required to isolate from others, typically for a period of 14 days.

Quarantine – many countries required incoming travellers to be quarantined for 14 days. Some countries required particular areas of high risk to be quarantined from outside contact.

Labour laws – some constraints on the employment of labour were temporarily put in abeyance, such as the introduction of flexible work schedules to use unused working hours to offset overtime hours or the reduction of work hours and/or workdays per week, and rotation of workers and forced leave were permitted.

Labour payments – some countries introduced new requirements to protect the income of infected persons, such as payment of the salary of a documented infected worker, or payment of full wages to a worker categorised as a suspected COVID-19 infection during the quarantine/isolation period.

1.6.4 Operation of construction contracts

Governments in various jurisdictions passed specific laws in respect of the impacts of COVID-19 on general commercial activities, such as financial compensation for reduced turnover, deferment of taxes and charges and insolvency provisions. Several of the jurisdictions covered in this book passed COVID-specific legislation that impacted the operation of construction contracts; e.g. in Ecuador, the government enacted a law that enabled modification of normal labour relationships and bankruptcy rules.[51]

51 See section 8.3.2.

The provisions of the general law on the operation of a construction contract that may be engaged by the impact of COVID-19 include *force majeure*, *vis major*, hardship, frustration and impossibility. The operation of any of these doctrines in any specific case will depend on the wording of the contract and the governing law of the contract.

In common law jurisdictions, *force majeure* is entirely a creature of contract and will only apply if the factual circumstances of the COVID-19 impact fall within the contractual definition. Some *Civil Codes* have *force majeure* provisions that may provide for an extension of time for delays as a result of COVID-19, e.g. the *Brazilian Civil Code*,[52] the *Quebec Civil Code*[53] and the *Chile Civil Code*.[54]

Hardship provisions in *Civil Codes* may provide for a rebalancing of contractual relationships in the event of an unforeseeable and inevitable event that results in the contract becoming materially disproportionate for one party, e.g. Brazil.[55]

In the event that the impact of COVID-19 makes the performance of the Contract impossible, the common law doctrine of frustration may apply. Impossibility of performance is a similar doctrine under *Civil Codes*, e.g. Quebec.[56]

As discussed by several authors in the jurisdiction chapters to follow, the contractual consequences of the impact of COVID-19 are uncharted waters with little guidance from existing case law. Negotiation between Employer and Contractor in good faith (an integral aspect of *Civil Codes*) will generally be the most desirable means of resolving the most appropriate contractual outcome. Section 1.6.6 discusses the type of claims that may arise under FIDIC contracts.

1.6.5 Economic measures

In addition to the measures outlined that directly impact the execution of construction projects and the operation of construction contracts, governments provided financial assistance to individuals and businesses that indirectly assisted the construction industry.

1.6.6 Claims arising from COVID-19 under FIDIC contracts

Construction projects were significantly delayed, postponed or terminated as a result of COVID-19; those that continued were subject to increased costs as a result of the health measures required to keep workers safe – stringent cleaning and disinfection, physical distancing and increased use of personal protective equipment (**PPE**) among other economic impacts. Contractors will inevitably seek costs and EOTs and a substantial number of claims can therefore be expected. At the time of writing (June 2022) the COVID-19 pandemic is far from over, and there is already anecdotal evidence of claims on many construction projects.

52 See section 5.3.2.
53 See section 6.3.2.
54 See section 7.3.2.
55 See section 5.3.2.2.
56 *Quebec Civil Code* ss1693, 1694.

Early in the pandemic (April 2020) FIDIC issued the 'FIDIC COVID-19 Guidance Memorandum to Users of FIDIC Standard Forms of Works Contract'.[57] That Memorandum contains an outline of the provisions in FIDIC's standard forms of contract for works relevant to likely scenarios arising as a consequence of COVID-19:

> FIDIC's core purpose of drafting this Guidance Memorandum is to help Parties to a FIDIC contract to consider mutually satisfactory solutions and avoid disputes arising between them. COVID-19 pandemic is a unique broad scale and extraordinary event which should be recognized as such.

The Guidance Memorandum does not refer to any specific legal system or jurisdiction and cautions that the legal interpretation of the contract will depend upon matters such as the precise wording of the various documents in the Contract and the governing law. The Memorandum takes the approach of outlining a number of possible scenarios and suggests likely relevant responses by reference to relevant provisions of FIDIC contracts.

FIDIC's list of scenarios identifies the following circumstances that are expected to give rise to claims unique to the impact of COVID-19: [58]

1. The local authorities/government do not promulgate any new piece of legislation or regulation banning construction activity or works on Site. However, the Contractor is facing difficulties in mobilizing personnel, who fear for their safety, and in obtaining Goods due to issues in the supply chain.
2. The Contractor is under the same circumstances as scenario No. 1 above. However, instead of facing difficulties in mobilizing personnel or obtaining Goods, the Contractor is suffering delays caused by the authorities (for example making repeated health and safety inspections on the Site).
3. The local authorities or government have promulgated changes to the Laws restricting construction activities and works on the Site. The Contractor is still able to proceed with the Works, however it is suffering delay and or incurring additional Cost as a result of those changes.
4. The local authorities/government have issued an order(s)/decree(s) preventing construction activities (including lockdown, curfew, inaccessible quarantined areas, etc), and execution of the Works on Site has now become impossible. Consequently, the Contractor and/or the Employer is prevented from performing obligations under the Contract.
5. Under scenario No. 4 above, can the Contractor subject this scenario to Clause 17 [*Risk and Responsibility/Care of the Works and Indemnities*]? Under Clause 17 the Contractor is entitled to a financial compensation in addition to an EOT, rather than only an EOT, when a natural Force Majeure or Exceptional Event occurs.
6. Under scenarios Nos. 1, 2, or 3, above, can the Employer or the Contractor resort to Clause 19 [*Force Majeure*], Clause 18 [*Exceptional Events*], or Clause 18 [*Exceptional Risks*] (in the relevant FIDIC contract as the case may be), to address such scenarios?

---

57 https://fidic.org/sites/default/files/COVID%2019%20Guidance%20Memorandum%20-%20PDF.pdf (accessed 4 April 2022).

58 *Ibid.*

7. There has been no change in Laws of the Country nor real impact on the availability of personnel or on the supply chain so far. However, the personnel of the Employer (including the Engineer or the Employer's Representative, as the case may be) are, as a precaution, working remotely and hence are most of the time away from Site. As a consequence, the Contractor suffers delay and/or incurred additional Cost due to slow decision making.

1.6.7 Dispute resolution

The spread of COVID-19 prompted government, judicial and other bodies around the globe to adopt measures responding to the need for greater flexibility and remote connectivity in the operation of courts and dispute resolution practice. The IBA documented the impact of COVID-19 on court operations and litigation practice in 37 countries.[59] The Chartered Institute of Arbitrators issued guidance for remote proceedings,[60] as did other arbitral institutions such as HKIAC[61] and AAA-ICDR.[62] The Dispute Resolution Board Foundation recognised the restrictions on in-person meetings during the pandemic and published best practice guidelines and a checklist for virtual Dispute Board proceedings.[63]

1.7 Impact of the applicable laws

In summary, the applicable law can impact the operation of a contract in various ways:

- The provisions of mandatory law will override any contractual provisions
- A construction contract must be executed in accordance with the applicable Laws irrespective of the contract wording
- Non-mandatory law may provide default options if they are not covered or explicitly derogated from by the specific terms of the Contract

It is apparent that in any jurisdiction there is potentially a substantial number of laws that impact: the entry into, operation of and termination of a contract; the design and execution of the Works; and the resolution of any disputes that arise from or in connection with the Contract. Subject to the desirability of the Conditions of Contract comprising an accurate contract management manual, it is not the place of contract documents to constitute a complete definition of the parties' legal rights and obligations or a project management

59 'The Impact of COVID-19 on Court Operations and Litigation Practice' (June 2020), *International Bar Association.* www.ibanet.org/Covid-19/Home.aspx (accessed 25 February 2021).

60 'Guidance Note on Remote Dispute Resolution Proceedings' (2020) *Chartered Institute of Arbitrators.* www.ciarb.org/media/9013/remote-hearings-guidance-note_final_140420.pdf (accessed 23 November 2021).

61 'HKIAC Guidelines for Virtual Hearings' (2020) *HKIAC.*

62 'AAA-ICDR Virtual Hearing Guide for Arbitrators and Parties' (2020) *AAA-ICDR.* https://go.adr.org/rs/294-SFS-516/images/AAA268_AAA%20Virtual%20Hearing%20Guide%20for%20Arbitrators%20and%20Parties.pdf (accessed 23 November 2021).

63 'Best Practice Guidelines for Virtual Dispute Board Proceedings' (2020) *Dispute Resolution Board Foundation.* www.disputeboard.org/wp-content/uploads/2020/07/Best-Practice-Guidelines-for-Virtual-Dispute-Board-Proceedings-5-August-2020.pdf (accessed 23 November 2021); 'Checklist for Dispute Board Members in Preparation for Virtual Dispute Board Proceedings' (2020) *Dispute Resolution Board Foundation* www.disputeboard.org/wp-content/uploads/2020/07/DRBF-Checklist-for-Virtual-DB-Proceedings-5-August-2020.pdf (accessed 23 November 2021).

manual (nor would it be feasible). Accordingly, the Conditions of Contract, even in a well-written and comprehensive FIDIC Contract, can never identify all the applicable laws that may define the parties' rights and obligations in all circumstances.

Construction of any significant infrastructure or facility in the modern world is a complex undertaking in which the interests of many stakeholders must be considered, and a myriad of legal obligations complied with. Those involved at the 'coalface' of a construction project administering the Contract as Engineer, Employer or Contractor need to be generally aware of their legal obligations under the applicable Laws so that they can make the appropriate enquiries as to their specific obligations in particular circumstances. Complex or unusual situations will undoubtedly require input from competent construction lawyers experienced in the relevant jurisdiction.

However, except in exceptional circumstances, it is unlikely that such legal advice will be available on a day-to-day basis on the construction Site. The personnel administering the Contract may be engineers or other construction professionals with a general understanding of contract and other law, but they are unlikely to have the depth of knowledge of an experienced construction lawyer. The challenge for such Contract Administrators is to have sufficient knowledge of their obligations to know when and where to seek further information and advice on a specific issue. This problem may be particularly acute in a situation where the Contract Administrator is operating in a jurisdiction in which she/he is unfamiliar.

1.8 Country accessions to international conventions and agreements

Each of the countries considered in this book has acceded to certain international conventions and agreements and incorporated their principles into their domestic law. Table 1.3 identifies, for each country, whether they have a civil law or common law system and whether they have acceded to various international conventions, agreements or principles of relevance to construction law.

1.8.1 New York Convention

Perhaps the most important international convention for international users of FIDIC contracts is the *1958 New York Arbitration Convention on the Recognition and Enforcement of Foreign Arbitral Awards* (***New York Convention***). This convention ensures that commercial arbitration is an effective means of finally resolving international commercial disputes by means of an award that can be enforced by a court judgment in any state that is a party to the *New York Convention*. It is significant that all the countries covered in this book are party to the *New York Convention*.

The *New York Convention* gives practical effect to the principle of *pacta sunt servanda* by providing a mechanism to hold parties to the consequences of the bargain they have made. If a dispute arises out of or in connection with a contract, the appointed arbitral tribunal will determine the appropriate remedy in the light of the terms of the contract and the applicable law. Their award is final and binding, and not subject to appeal on findings of fact or law. A court in a Convention State can only set aside or refuse to enforce an award on very narrow jurisdictional grounds.

The *New York Convention* is perhaps the single most important agreement that facilitates international commercial commerce in general and international construction in particular. International arbitration removes a dispute from the jurisdiction of the courts of either party's home jurisdiction that may be perceived as giving one of them an advantage. The arbitration award can be enforced by normal court processes in any jurisdiction that is party to the *New York Convention*, typically in a jurisdiction where the debtor has assets. It is therefore unsurprising that FIDIC General Conditions require international arbitration to finally settle any disputes that have not been avoided or resolved by the decision of a Dispute Avoidance/Adjudication Board or Dispute Adjudication Board.

1.8.2 WTO Agreement on Government Procurement

Purchases of goods and services by government agencies with public resources for public purposes are generally referred to as government/public procurement.

Achieving 'value for money' is a primary aim of most procurement regimes. Open, transparent and non-discriminatory procurement is generally considered to be the best tool to achieve this goal as it optimises competition among suppliers. The liberalisation of government procurement markets holds the potential to generate benefits both in terms of procurement efficiency and commercial interests. One of the ways the World Trade Organisation (**WTO**) promotes the liberalisation of government is through the Agreement on Government Agreement (**WTO GPA**).

The WTO describes the WTO GPA as follows:

> The GPA is a plurilateral agreement within the framework of the WTO, meaning that not all WTO members are parties to the Agreement. At present, the Agreement has 20 parties comprising 48 WTO members. 36 WTO members/observers participate in the GPA Committee as observers. Out of these, 12 members are in the process of acceding to the Agreement.
>
> The fundamental aim of the GPA is to mutually open government procurement markets among its parties. As a result of several rounds of negotiations, the GPA parties have opened procurement activities worth an estimated US$ 1.7 trillion annually to international competition (i.e. to suppliers from GPA parties offering goods, services or construction services).
>
> The GPA is composed mainly of two parts: the text of the Agreement and parties' market access schedules of commitments.
>
> The text of the Agreement establishes rules requiring that open, fair and transparent conditions of competition be ensured in government procurement. However, these rules do not automatically apply to all procurement activities of each party. Rather, the coverage schedules play a critical role in determining whether a procurement activity is covered by the Agreement or not. Only those procurement activities that are carried out by covered entities purchasing listed goods, services or construction services of a value exceeding specified threshold values are covered by the Agreement.[64]

Under the WTO GPA, the coverage schedule of each party contains seven annexes, including Annex 4 goods, Annex 5 services and Annex 6 construction services. The two countries listed in Table 1.3 that have acceded to the WTO GPA have defined their coverage of construction services as all construction services in Division 51 of the United Nations Provisional Central Product Classification (except dredging services and construction services procured by or on behalf of the federal Department of Transport [Canada]) and

64 www.wto.org/english/tratop_e/gproc_e/gp_gpa_e.htm (accessed 9 November 2020).

Table 1.3 Country accessions to international conventions and agreements

Country	Civil or common law	*New York Arbitration Convention on the Recognition and Enforcement of Foreign Arbitral Awards, 1958*[a]	*United Nations Convention on International Settlement Agreements Resulting from Mediation (2018) (the 'Singapore Convention on Mediation')*[b]	*Hague Convention of 30 June 2005 on Choice of Court Agreements*[c]	*UNCITRAL Model Law on International Commercial Arbitration* (1985 with amendments as adopted in 2006)[d]	*United Nations Convention of Contracts for the International Sale of Goods* (CISG)[e]	Member State of UNIDROIT[f]	WTO Agreement on Government Procurement[g]	*UNCITRAL Model Law on Cross-Border Insolvency* (1997)[h]	ICSID Member State[i]
Bolivia	civil law	YES					YES			
Brazil	civil law	YES	Signature			YES	YES		YES	
Canada	common law	YES			YES	YES	YES	YES	YES	YES
Chile	civil law	YES	Signature		YES	YES	YES		YES	YES
Ecuador	civil law	YES	YES			YES				YES
Mexico	civil law	YES		YES	YES	YES	YES		YES	YES
Peru	civil law	YES			YES	YES				YES
USA	common law	YES	Signature	Signature	8 States	YES	YES	YES	YES	YES
Uruguay	civil law	YES	Signature		YES	YES	YES			YES

[a] http://www.newyorkconvention.org/countries (accessed 10 September 2021).
[b] https://uncitral.un.org/en/texts/mediation/conventions/international_settlement_agreements/status (accessed 10 September 2021).
[c] https://www.hcch.net/en/instruments/conventions/status-table/?cid=98 (accessed 10 September 2021).
[d] https://uncitral.un.org/en/texts/arbitration/modellaw/commercial_arbitration/status (accessed 10 September 2021).
[e] https://uncitral.un.org/en/texts/salegoods/conventions/sale_of_goods/cisg/status accessed 10 September 2021).
[f] https://www.unidroit.org/about-unidroit/membership (accessed 10 September 2021).
[g] https://www.wto.org/english/tratop_e/gproc_e/memobs_e.htm (accessed 10 September 2021).
[h] https://uncitral.un.org/en/texts/insolvency/modellaw/cross-border_insolvency/status (accessed 10 September 2021).
[i] https://icsid.worldbank.org/about/member-states/database-of-member-states (accessed 10 September 2021).

procured by the entities in Annexes 1 (central government entities), 2 (sub-central government entities) and 3 (other entities).

1.8.3 ICSID Convention

ICSID is the International Centre for the Settlement of Investment Disputes:

> ICSID is the world's leading institution devoted to international investment dispute settlement. It has extensive experience in this field, having administered the majority of all international investment cases. States have agreed on ICSID as a forum for investor-State dispute settlement in most international investment treaties and in numerous investment laws and contracts.[65]

ICSID publishes the *Convention on the Settlement of Investment Disputes between States and Nationals of Other States*.[66] The ***ICSID Convention*** is a treaty ratified by 155 Contracting States which, *inter alia*:

- Establishes ICSID's jurisdiction
- Authorises conciliation
- Authorises arbitration
- Addresses replacement and disqualification of Conciliators and Arbitrators
- Discusses the cost of proceedings
- Deals with the place of proceedings
- Provides for disputes between Contracting States[67]

The significance of other individual conventions is discussed in the later chapters.

1.9 Aims of the book

One of the aims of this book is to identify, for a range of jurisdictions in the Americas in which FIDIC contracts are or can be used, the applicable laws that may impact the operation of the Contract, the execution of the Works or the determination of disputes arising under or in connection with the Contract. It does not purport to provide guidance on FIDIC Contracts *per se*; there are a number of texts which provide an in-depth discussion of FIDIC Contracts, including general commentary on what modifications may be required for use in particular jurisdictions. The following section contains a list of references on FIDIC contracts.

This book is intended to be a sourcebook for a Contract Administrator or lawyer unfamiliar with the requirements for the Particular Conditions of a FIDIC Contract or operating with a FIDIC Contract in a jurisdiction they are unfamiliar with. It does not provide specific guidance on what Particular Conditions clauses might be necessary or desirable for any jurisdiction; such guidance would always need to be specific to the requirements

65 https://icsid.worldbank.org/about (accessed 14 February 2022).

66 https://icsid.worldbank.org/sites/default/files/ICSID%20Convention%20English.pdf (accessed 14 February 2022).

67 https://icsid.worldbank.org/resources/rules-and-regulations/convention/overview (accessed 14 February 2022).

of the particular project at the particular point in time and require input from a competent construction lawyer. It should also be noted that, although the laws identified are believed to be correct as of July 2022, legislation and case law are constantly changing, another reason why competent advice needs to be sought when necessary.

Chapter 2 provides further details of the FIDIC Golden Principles, which FIDIC recommend should be complied with in preparing Particular Conditions. Chapter 3 provides more specific details of what should be in the Particular Conditions, choosing the governing law of the contract and guidance on the preparation of Particular Conditions necessary or desirable for particular purposes, without attempting to address the differences between jurisdictions.

Each of the remaining chapters in the book deals with a specific jurisdiction, prepared by one or more construction lawyers and/or engineers, experienced in the application of FIDIC contracts in that jurisdiction. Each of those jurisdiction-specific chapters provides a brief overview of the legal landscape and the construction industry, the impact of the COVID-19 pandemic on construction contracts and construction projects, a discussion of any Special Provisions required if the governing law is that jurisdiction and a listing of the applicable law if the Site is in the jurisdiction. Each chapter also identifies issues that a court or arbitrator may construe differently from that expected from the words of the Contract because of local law or custom.

1.10 References

1.10.1 Books on construction law

Andrew Burr (ed), *Delay and Disruption in Construction Contracts* (Informa Law from Routledge, 2016)

Anthony Edwards & Roger Gibson, *A Practical Guide to Disruption and Productivity Loss on Construction and Engineering Projects* (Wiley, 2015)

Arent van Wassenaer, *A Practical Guide to Successful Construction Projects* (Informa Law from Routledge, 2017)

Charles O'Neill, *Global Construction Success* (Wiley Blackwell, 2019)

Charles O'Neill, *Human Dynamics* (Contract Dynamics Sdn Bhd, 2014)

David Chappell, Michael Cowlin & Michael Dunn *Building Law Encyclopedia* (Wiley Blackwell, 2009)

David Mosey, *Collaborative Construction Procurement and Improved Value* (John Wiley & Sons, 2019)

David Mosey, *Early Contractor Involvement in Building Procurement* (Wiley-Blackwell, 2009)

Donald Charrett (ed), *Global Challenges Shared Solutions* (Society of Construction Law Australia, 2013)

Donald Charrett, *Contracts for Construction and Engineering Projects* (2nd edn, Informa Law from Routledge, 2022)

Edward W Merrow, *Industrial Megaprojects Concepts, Strategies and Practices for Success* (Wiley, 2011)

Furmston, *Powell-Smith and Furmston's Building Contract Case Book* (4th edn, Blackwell, 2006)

John R Cooke, *Architects, Engineers and the Law* (Federation Press, 2010)

John Scriven & Nigel Pritchard, *EPC Contracts and Major Projects* (Sweet & Maxwell, 2011)

John Uff, *Construction Law: Law and Practice Relating to the Construction Industry* (12th edn, Sweet & Maxwell/Thomson Reuters, 2017)

Julian Bailey, *Construction Law (Volumes 1–3)* (3rd edn, London Publishing Partnership, 2020)
Julian Bailey, *Construction Law, Costs and Contemporary Developments: Drawing the Threads Together: A Festschrift for Lord Justice Jackson* (Hart Publishing, 2018)
Justin Sweet, Mark Schneier *Legal Aspects of Architecture, Engineering and the Construction Process* (Cengage Learning, 2009)
Keith Pickavance, *Construction Law and Management* (Informa Law from Routledge, 2016)
Lukas Klee, *International Construction Contract Law* (2nd edn, John Wiley & Sons Inc, 2018).
Michael Sergeant & Max Wieliczko, *Construction Contract Variations* (Informa Law from Routledge, 2014)
Monika Chao-Duivis, *Studies in European Construction Law* (Den Haag: Instituut voor Bouwrecht, 2015)
Nicholas Dennys & Robert Clay, *Hudson's Building and Engineering Contracts* (14th edn, Sweet & Maxwell, 2020)
Paul Reed QC, *Construction All Risks Insurance* (Sweet & Maxwell, 2016)
Peter Edwards, Michael Edwards & Paulo Vaz Serra, *Managing Project Risks* (Wiley-Blackwell, 2019)
Philip Bryan, *Successful Delivery of Resources Projects* (Clayton Utz, 2013)
Philip Loots & Donald Charrett, *Contracts for Infrastructure Projects: An International Guide for Application* (Informa Law from Routledge, 2022)
Philip Loots & Donald Charrett, *The Application of Contracts in Developing Offshore Oil and Gas Contracts* (Informa Law from Routledge, 2019).
Phillip Greenham (ed), *The International Compendium of Construction Contracts* (Society of Construction Law Australia & De Gruyter, 2021)
PJ Keane, Anthony F Caletka, *Delay Analysis in Construction Contracts* (Wiley-Blackwell, 2015)
Richard Moorwood, Deborah Scott & Ian Pitcher, *Alliancing: A Participant's Guide: Real Life Experiences for Constructors, Desoigners, Facilitators and Clients* (Maunsell AECOM, 2008)
Robert Hogarth, Alexandra Anderson & Simon Goldring (eds) *Insurance Law for the Construction Industry* (2nd edn, Oxford University Press, 2013)
Robert J Gemmell, *Quantification of delay and disruption in construction and engineering projects* (2nd edn, Thomson Reuters, 2021)
Roger ter Haar QC & Camilla ter Haar, *Remedies in Construction Law* (2nd edn, Informa Law from Routledge, 2017)
Sarah Lupton, *Cornes and Lupton's Design Liability in the Construction Industry* (Wiley, 2013)
Simon Tolson, *Dictionary of Construction Terms* (Informa Law from Routledge, 2012)
Stephen Furst & Vivian Ramsey, *Keating on Construction Contracts* (11th edn, Sweet & Maxwell/ Thomson Reuters, 2020)
Tim Read, *International Comparative Legal Guide to Construction and Engineering Law 2015* (Ashurst, 2015)
Tom Kendrick, *Identifying and Managing Project Risk* (AMACOM, 2009)
Will Hughes, Ronan Champion & John Murdoch, *Construction Contracts Law and Management* (5th edn, Routledge, 2015)

1.10.2 References on dispute resolution

Cyril Chern, *Chern on Dispute Boards* (4th edn, Informa Law from Routledge, 2021)
Cyril Chern, *The Law of Construction Disputes* (3rd edn, Informa Law from Routledge, 2020)
Darryl Royce, *Adjudication in Construction Law* (Informa Law from Routledge, 2016)
Dimitar Kondev, *Multi-Party and Multi-Contract Arbitration in the Construction Industry* (John Wiley & Sons Inc, 2017)

Dispute Resolution Board Foundation, *Dispute Board Manual* (Dispute Resolution Board Foundation, 2019)
Dr Paula Gerber & Brennan Ong, *Best Practice in Construction Disputes* (Lexis Nexis Butterworths, 2013)
James Pickavance, *A Practical Guide to Construction Adjudication* (Wiley, 2015)
Rashda Rana & Michelle Sanson, *International Commercial Arbitration* (Lawbook Co, 2011)
Redfern & Hunter, *Law & Practice of International Commercial Arbitration* (6th edn, Thomson/ Sweet & Maxwell, 2014)
Renato Nazzini, *Transnational Construction Arbitration: Key Themes in the Resolution of Construction Disputes* (Informa Law from Routledge, 2017)

1.10.3 Books on FIDIC contracts – 2017 Editions

Corbett & Co, *FIDIC 2017 A Practical Legal Guide* (Corbett & Co International Construction Lawyers Ltd, 2020)
Donald Charrett (ed), *FIDIC Contracts in Asia Pacific A Practical Guide to Application* (Informa Law from Routledge, 2022)[68]
Donald Charrett (ed), *FIDIC Contracts in Europe A Practical Guide to Application* (Informa Law from Routledge, 2022)[69]
Donald Charrett (ed), *The International Application of FIDIC Contracts A Practical Guide* (Informa Law from Routledge, 2020)[70]
Jakob B Sørensen, *FIDIC Silver Book - A companion to the 2017 EPC/Turnkey Contract* (Institution of Civil Engineers, 2019)
Jeremy Glover & Simon Hughes, *Understanding the FIDIC Red and Yellow Books: A Clause-by-Clause Commentary* (4th edn, Sweet & Maxwell, 2018)
Leo Grutters & Brian Barr, *FIDIC Red, Yellow and Silver Books: A Practical Guide to the 2017 Editions* (Sweet & Maxwell, 2018)
Nicholas Alexander Brown, *FIDIC 2017: A Definitive Guide to Claims and Disputes* (Thomas Telford Ltd, 2022)
William Godwin QC, *The 2017 FIDIC Contracts: The Second Editions of the Red, Yellow and Silver Books* (Wiley Blackwell, 2020)

1.10.4 Books on FIDIC contracts – 1999 Editions

A Hewitt, *The FIDIC Contracts: Obligations of the Parties* (Wiley, 2014)
Axel-Volkmar Jaeger & Götz-Sebastian Hök, *FIDIC – A Guide for Practitioners* (Springer, 2010)
Brian Totterdill, *FIDIC Users' Guide: A Practical Guide to the 1999 Red and Yellow Books* (Thomas Telford, 2006)
Ellis Baker, Ben Mellors, Scott Chalmers & Anthony Lavers, *FIDIC Contracts: Law and Practice* (Informa Law, 2009)
Jeremy Glover & Simon Hughes, *Understanding the FIDIC Red Book: A Clause-by-Clause Commentary* (3rd edn, Sweet & Maxwell, 2011)
M Robinson, *A Contractor's Guide to the FIDIC Conditions of Contract* (Wiley Blackwell, 2013)

68 This book has chapters on the application of FIDIC contracts in 16 jurisdictions in Asia Pacific and a chapter on the application of the Emerald Book for Underground Works.

69 This book has chapters on the application of FIDIC contracts in 16 jurisdictions in Europe.

70 This book has chapters on the application of FIDIC contracts in the following jurisdictions not included in this book: Australia, China, Czech Republic, Fiji, France, Germany, Ghana, Hong Kong, Italy, Malaysia, Papua New Guinea, Romania, South Africa, Sri Lanka, Switzerland and United Arab Emirates.

M Robinson, *An Employer's and Engineer's Guide to the FIDIC Conditions of Contract* (Wiley Blackwell, 2013)
Nael G Bunni, *The FIDIC Forms of Contract* (Blackwell, 2005)
Raveed Khalani & Mahdi Saadat Fard, *FIDIC Plant and Design-Build Forms of Contract Illustrated* (Wiley, 2015)
Robert Knutson (ed), *FIDIC: An Analysis of International Contracts* (Kluwer Law International, 2005)

1.10.5 Guides on FIDIC contracts[71]

Standard Letters and Notices. For use with the FIDIC Conditions of Contract for Works of Civil Engineering Construction, 4th ed, 1987 Red Book.
Electrical and Mechanical Works Guide (1st ed, 1988). Guide to the Use of the FIDIC Conditions of Contract for Electrical and Mechanical Works 3rd ed. 1987 Yellow Book. Includes Yellow Book 3rd ed 1987 conditions.
Red Book Guide (1st ed, 1989). Guide to the Use of FIDIC Conditions of Contract for Works of Civil Engineering Construction 4th ed, 1987 Red Book. Includes Red Book Conditions.
FIDIC 4th - A Practical Legal Guide (1991). A commentary on the Red Book 4th ed, 1987 by E.C. Corbett.
Design-Build and Turnkey Guide (1st ed. 1996). Guide to the Use of FIDIC Conditions of Contract for Design-Build and Turnkey. A clause by clause commentary on the provisions contained in Part 1 of the 1995 Orange Book.
FIDIC Contracts Guide to the Construction, Plant and Design-Build and EPC/Turnkey Contracts (1st Edition, 2000).
The New EIC Red Book Guide, 2001. European International Contractors (EIC) Contractors Guide to the FIDIC Conditions of Contract for Construction.
The New EIC Yellow Book Guide, 2003. European International Contractors (EIC) Contractors Guide to the FIDIC Conditions of Contract for Plant and Design-Build.
The EIC Silver Book Guide, 2nd Edition, 2003. European International Contractors (EIC) Contractors Guide to the FIDIC Conditions of Contract for EPC/Turnkey Projects.
FIDIC Contracts Guide Supplement: MDB Harmonised Construction Contract (2006). Guide to the March 2006 release of the MDB Harmonised Construction Contract.
DBO (2008 Gold Book) Contract Guide 1st ed, 2011.

1.10.6 Internet resources

Construction & Engineering Laws and Regulations 2018 https://iclg.com/practice-areas/construction-and-engineering-law-laws-and-regulations (accessed 8 June 2022)

1.10.7 Case law

A list of cases and publicly available arbitration awards is available at: http://corbett.co.uk/wp-content/uploads/Table-of-FIDIC-Cases.pdf

71 'Contract advice' www.fidic.org/bookshop (accessed 24 February 2022).

Annexure

Table 1.4 Editions of FIDIC Conditions of Contract for contracts between Employer and Contractor

Short Form of Contract (Green Book)	**Construction (Red Book)**	**Construction (MDB edition) (Pink Book)**	**Plant and Design Build (Yellow Book)**	**EPC/Turnkey (Silver Book)**	**Design, Build and Operate (Gold Book)**	**Underground Works (Emerald Book)**	**Dredging and Reclamation Works (Blue-Green Book)**
	First ed. 1957		First ed. 1963				
	Second ed. 1969						
	Third ed. 1977		Second ed. 1980				
	Fourth ed. 1987		Third ed. 1987				
	1992 Revised ed.	2005 ed.					
	1996 DAB Supplement	2006 Revised ed.		1995 Orange Book			
Short Form of Contract First ed. 1999	Conditions of Contract for Construction First ed. 1999	Conditions of Contract for Construction MDB Harmonised Edition 2010	Conditions of Contract for Plant and Design Build First ed. 1999	Conditions of Contract for EPC/Turnkey Projects First ed. 1999	Conditions of Contract for Design, Build and Operate Projects First ed. 2008		Form of Contract for Dredging and Reclamation Works First ed. 2006
Short Form of Contract Second ed. 2021	Conditions of Contract for Construction Second ed. 2017		Conditions of Contract for Plant and Design Build Second ed. 2017	Conditions of Contract for EPC/Turnkey Projects Second ed. 2017		Conditions of Contract for Underground Works First ed. 2019	Form of Contract for Dredging and Reclamation Works Second ed. 2016

CHAPTER 2

The FIDIC Golden Principles[1]

Dr Donald Charrett[2]

CONTENTS

2.1	Introduction	45
2.2	Fair and balanced contracts	45
2.3	The FIDIC Golden Principles	47
2.4	Reasons for Golden Principles	49
2.5	Guidance for drafting contract documents for consistency with the Golden Principles	51
2.6	Conclusion	53

1 This chapter was first published in (2018) *Construction Law International* 13(2), and is reproduced by kind permission of the International Bar Association, London, UK © International Bar Association.

2 Principal Drafter, FIDIC Working Group TG15.

 DOI: 10.4324/9781003201250-2

2.1 Introduction

FIDIC publishes General Conditions of Contract that are widely used for international construction contracts. They are intended to be used in any legal jurisdiction. FIDIC General Conditions are explicitly based on a fair and equitable risk allocation between Employer and Contractor and are widely recognised as striking an appropriate balance between the reasonable expectations of the contracting Parties.

Arguably, a contract recognised as a fair and balanced 'FIDIC contract' has real commercial value to both Employer and Contractor, both at the tendering stage and while the Works are being performed.

General Conditions prepared for use in a wide range of projects and jurisdictions inevitably require supplementation with Particular Conditions that address the particular requirements of the Site and the unique features of the specific project. Particular Conditions may also be necessary to amend the General Conditions to comply with mandatory law that applies to the Site or the legal jurisdiction.

Provided that such modifications are limited to those necessary for the particular features of the Site and the project and do not change the essential fair and balanced character of a FIDIC Contract, the contract is recognisable as a FIDIC contract.

The essential features of a FIDIC Contract that make the risk/reward allocation fair and balanced are referred to as the **FIDIC Golden Principles (GPs)**.

This chapter outlines the development of the GPs, the reasons for them and their application in drafting Particular Conditions.

2.2 Fair and balanced contracts

Contract risks refer to the chance that contractual objectives will not be fulfilled. The Contract defines who bears the liability for the contract risks. The form and terms of the Contract can increase or decrease those risks from the norm. Thus, use of the appropriate form and terms of a construction contract can play a major role in minimising the risk that the contractual objectives will not be fulfilled. Conversely, use of an inappropriate form or terms of a construction contract can significantly increase the risk that the contractual objectives will not be fulfilled.

Strictly, it is incorrect to refer to contracts as 'allocating' risk, as contracts allocate obligations and confer rights.[3] A risk, being the chance of an event happening, is not 'allocated' to either Party by the Contract. A risk event may exist separate from and independent of the obligations and rights of the Parties, or the risk event may be under the 'control' of one of the Parties. Whether or not one of the Parties has 'control' over a risk event, it is the obligations and rights arising as a consequence of the risk event happening that are 'allocated' by the Contract, and this is the commonly accepted usage of the term 'risk allocation'.

3 Report by NPWC/NBCC Joint Working Party, 'No Dispute Strategies for Improvement in the Australian Building and Construction Industry' (May 1990) 7.

Many standard form contracts are based on the explicitly stated principle of balanced or fair risk allocation, e.g., the Australian Standard 4000 series,[4] the US ConsensusDocs,[5] the UK New Engineering Contract,[6] contracts promoted by the European Engineering Industries Association,[7] the International Chamber of Commerce,[8] the Baltic and International Marine Council[9] and the UK offshore oil and gas industry.[10] The principle is also espoused by government procurement agencies in the UK,[11] Australia[12] and the USA.[13]

Many writers suggest that adherence to the principle of balanced risk allocation enhances the prospect of successful contracts, by encouraging contractual performance that minimises adverse outcomes and thereby reduces disputation.[14] In a survey of ten case studies of Australian projects to determine project-related factors critical to project success, Sidwell et al. found that equitable risk allocation was one of the top four factors found to be critical in explaining overall project performance and was the most significant factor related to the conditions of contract.[15]

'Non-standard' contract terms (in the sense of altering the 'normal' balanced risk allocation in standard form contracts) in either standard form contracts or bespoke contracts are usually put forward by one party to alter the risk allocation to be more favourable to it. As Employers generally put forward proposed conditions of contract with the tender documents, it is likely that non-standard terms in these contracts will involve the Contractor in accepting more risk than 'normal'.

The conditions of contract based on a standard form contract typically comprise General Conditions and Particular Conditions (or amendments to the General Conditions). The General Conditions are typically drafted by a committee representing a wide range of interests and represent a consensus of contract terms appropriate to many 'typical'

---

4 'Standard Conditions of Contract' (2001) 4 *BDPS News* 1, 4.

5 www.consensusdocs.org/FooterSection_About/FooterSection_WhyConsensusDocs (accessed 18 March 2018).

6 Brian Eggleston, *The New Engineering Contract: A Commentary* (Blackwell Publishing 1996) 7.

7 Orgalime Turnkey Contract for Industrial Works.

8 International Chamber of Commerce Model Turnkey Contract for Major Projects (2007). www.iccbooks.com/Product/ProductInfo.aspx?id=488 (accessed 18 March 2018).

9 www.bimco.org/about-us-and-our-members/about-us/our-history (accessed 18 March 2018).

10 Leading Oil and Gas Industry Competitiveness (LOGIC) www.logic-oil.com (accessed 18 March 2018).

11 HM Treasury, *The Green Book Appraisal and Evaluation in Central Government* http://greenbook.treasury.gov.uk/annex04.htm (accessed 26 August 2008): 'The governing principle is that risk should be allocated to whichever party from the public or private sector is best placed to manage it. The optimal allocation of risk, rather than maximising risk transfer, is the objective, and is vital to ensuring that the best solution is found.'

12 Department of Treasury and Finance Victorian Government, *Partnerships Victoria Updated Standard Commercial Principles* (2008) 99: 'Both the government and the private party should seek to ensure that cost and adequate risk transfer are balanced as far as possible to achieve the best value for money on a particular project.'

13 US Department of Transportation Federal Highway Administration, *Risk Assessment and Allocation for Highway Construction Management* (2006) § 6.1.1. www.international.fhwa.dot.gov/riskassess/risk_hcm06_06.cfm (accessed 26 August 2008): 'A fundamental tenet of risk management is to allocate the risks to the party best able to manage them. The party assuming the risk should be able to best evaluate, control, bear the risk of, and benefit from its assumption.'

14 NPWC/NBCC Joint Working Party, 'No Dispute Strategies for Improvement in the Australian Building and Construction Industry' (May 1990) 6–7; Sir Michael Latham, 'Constructing the Team' (July 1994) Final Report 37.

15 AC Sidwell, RJ Kennedy & APC Chan, 'Re-Engineering the Construction Delivery Process' (2002) *Construction Industry Institute Australia Report* 34.

projects and locations. However, these General Conditions cannot take account of the specific requirements of a particular project, or perhaps the requirements for a particular location. General Conditions typically require modification for the project.

Every project has unique circumstances, and there are many legitimate reasons for Particular Conditions that alter standard-form General Conditions to suit these circumstances. For example, provisions in the General Conditions may be inconsistent with the mandatory law of the Site.

Typically, there is no formal constraint on the extent of risk transfer to the Contractor via the Particular Conditions, other than the requirements of mandatory law. However, arguably, Particular Conditions that alter the fundamental balanced risk allocation in the General Conditions change the character of the contract so that it is no longer recognisable as a contract of the type understood by the name of the General Conditions.

The consequences of inappropriately allocating excessive risk to the Contractor can actually have the opposite effect to that desired, by increasing the Employer's risks. The Japan International Cooperation Agency (JICA) commissioned the Association of Japanese Consulting Engineers to prepare a 'Check List for One Sided Contracts', to be used for the preparation of reasonable bidding documents. JICA noted that if modifications for a particular project alter the originally contemplated risk distribution in a FIDIC Red Book Contract to a large extent and the risks allocated to the Contractor become excessively high, the following problems may occur:

- Higher bid price
- Bid failure and disruption of project implementation
- Non-participation in the bid by conscientious and capable contractors
- Contract award to a bidder who failed to or was not capable of estimating the risks properly
- Poor construction quality and delay to the progress of the work due to lack of risk contingency
- Undermining the relationship of mutual trust and respect between the Employer and the Contractor
- Repetition of groundless claims from the Contractor
- Frequent disputes between the Employer and the Contractor, and
- In an extreme case, termination of the contract[16]

2.3 The FIDIC Golden Principles

The Golden Principles were developed by FIDIC Task Group 15 (**TG15**),[17] which reported to the FIDIC Contracts Committee. Consistent with FIDIC's structured approach to developing consensus documents, drafts of TG15's report were reviewed by the Contracts Committee and a number of friendly reviewers. As noted in section 1.4, the Emerald Book

16 Checklist for One Sided Contracts (Japan International Cooperation Agency 2011), 1.

17 The author was the Principal Drafter for TG15. The other members were Husni Madi (Jordan) – Team Leader, Axel Jaeger (Germany) and Dr Rafal Morek (Poland).

and the Second Editions of the FIDIC Red, Yellow and Silver Books recommend that the drafters of Particular Conditions take all due regard to the Golden Principles.[18]

The Golden Principles have been articulated for Works Contracts and not Services Contracts. FIDIC has confined its attention to Particular Conditions (**PCs**) that change the General Conditions (**GCs**) to the extent that they do not comply with the GPs. It has not considered misuse of unamended GCs.

In order to promote understanding, the GPs have been formulated at a conceptual level to encapsulate the essence of a FIDIC contract. Each GP expresses a single readily understood and generally accepted concept. The GPs have been limited to the minimum number necessary for completeness. Except for GP5, the GPs are stated in broad terms, without reference to specific clauses of the GCs.

GPs function as constraints on modifications to the GCs made in the PCs. They cannot prevent misapplication of existing unamended GCs. By definition, unamended GCs are an application of the GPs.

The following overarching considerations underpin the GPs:

- The terms of the contract are comprehensive and fair to both contracting Parties
- The legitimate interests of both contracting Parties are appropriately considered and balanced. The legitimate interests of each Party include the right to enjoy the benefits of the contractual relationship generally recognised as implicit in the GCs. For example, the Employer's legitimate interests include the right to a facility constructed to the contractually specified quality, within the time and for the price in the Contract. The Contractor's legitimate interests include the right to execute the Works in the manner contracted for, within a reasonable time and for a commercial price paid on time
- Best practice principles of fair and balanced risk allocation between the Employer and the Contractor are put into effect in accordance with the provisions of the GCs
- No Party shall take undue advantage of its bargaining power
- Payments to the Contractor or Subcontractor in accordance with the Contract are adequate to maintain its cash flow
- The Employer obtains the best value for money
- To the extent possible, cooperation and trust between the contracting Parties are promoted, and adversarial attitudes are to be discouraged and should be avoided
- The contract provisions can be practically put into effect
- Disputes are avoided to the extent achievable, minimised when they do arise, and resolved efficiently

The Golden Principles are as follows:

GP1: The duties, rights, obligations, roles and responsibilities of all the Contract Participants must be generally as implied in the General Conditions and appropriate to the requirements of the project.

GP2: The Particular Conditions must be drafted clearly and unambiguously.

18 Guidance for the Preparation of Particular Conditions, 8.

GP3: The Particular Conditions must not change the balance of risk/reward allocation provided for in the General Conditions.

GP4: All time periods specified in the Contract for Contract Participants to perform their obligations must be of reasonable duration.

GP5: Unless there is a conflict with the governing law of the Contract, all formal disputes must be referred to a Dispute Avoidance/Adjudication Board (or a Dispute Adjudication Board, if applicable) for a provisionally binding decision as a condition precedent to arbitration.

2.4 Reasons for Golden Principles

GP1: The duties, rights, obligations, roles and responsibilities of all the Contract Participants must be generally as implied in the General Conditions and appropriate to the requirements of the project.

As with most construction contracts, FIDIC Contracts refer to a number of other persons (such as the Engineer, DAAB/DAB and Subcontractors), in addition to the contracting Parties (Employer and Contractor). All the persons referred to in a FIDIC Contract (**Contract Participants**) have clearly defined roles, duties and obligations important to the efficient administration and proper functioning of the Contract. Concomitant with those roles are rights defined in the Contract.

The allocation of specific roles, duties and obligations to the various Contract Participants in FIDIC Contracts has evolved over a long period and has stood the test of time. Experience has shown that this allocation is consistent with widely accepted and understood international usage. Further, it is submitted that it provides the best opportunity for the Contract Participants to deliver a project that satisfies the Parties' reasonable performance expectations.

The delivery of a large construction project involves a complex interaction between all the Contract Participants. Each has its own roles, duties and obligations, which interface with the roles, duties and obligations of the other Contract Participants. The roles, duties and obligations defined in a FIDIC Contract have been determined to be those most appropriate to the efficient delivery of the contractual objectives and best suited to the skills and expertise normally expected of and exercised by the Contract Participants.

A FIDIC contract is based on the Employer and the Contractor undertaking their roles, duties and obligations, and having their rights as implicit in the General Conditions. For the Employer this involves, for example, providing access to the Site at the time contracted for and paying the Contractor. For the Contractor it involves, for example, executing and completing the Works in accordance with the Contract and rectifying defects during the Defects Notification Period.

The roles, duties and obligations of other Contract Participants as defined in the GCs are equally important for efficiently delivering the contractual objectives (notwithstanding that, not being Parties, they are not bound by the terms of the Contract). Thus, for the Red, Pink and Yellow Books, this requires that an Engineer be appointed with appropriate authority, competence and resources to carry out the role and that they fulfil their duties and obligations as defined in the Contract. Further, the Engineer must exercise its contractual authority and make fair determinations in accordance with the Contract, taking due regard of all relevant circumstances. This means that it must not make determinations that only suit the Employer's interests without having due regard to the Contractor's rights under the Contract.

Similarly, for the Silver Book, the Employer's Representative must have appropriate authority to carry out the role and must carry out that role to enable the Contractor to enjoy its contractual rights.

GP2: The Particular Conditions must be drafted clearly and unambiguously.

FIDIC GCs undergo a comprehensive drafting and independent review process to ensure that they are clear and unambiguous. Clear and unambiguous drafting is fundamental to all Contract Participants understanding their roles and duties so they can fulfil their obligations and exercise their rights.

The conditions of a FIDIC Contract comprise the GCs and the PCs, which incorporate any additions or changes to the GCs. A 'FIDIC contract' will only be clearly and unambiguously drafted if the Particular Conditions are clearly and unambiguously drafted, and interface harmoniously with the GCs and the Appendix to Tender/Contract Data.

GP3: The Particular Conditions must not change the balance of risk/reward allocation provided for in the GCs.

Fair and balanced risk allocation is widely accepted as the most appropriate basis for drafting of construction contracts to minimise the prospects of disputes and enhance the likelihood of achieving successful project outcomes. It is a fundamental principle on which FIDIC contracts are based.

The **Abrahamson Principles**, well known to construction lawyers, are widely regarded as the basis of 'balanced' or 'fair' risk allocation.[19] These principles, as refined by Nael Bunni, stipulate that risks should be allocated by considering:

- Which Party can best control the risk and the associated consequences?
- Which Party can best foresee the risk?
- Which Party can best bear the risk?
- Which Party ultimately most benefits or suffers when the risk eventuates?[20]

GP4: All time periods specified in the Contract for Contract Participants to perform their obligations must be of reasonable duration.

Time periods specified in the GCs have evolved as a consensus among the international construction community as an appropriate balance between the interests of a Contract Participant required to perform a duty and the interests of the Party whose rights are dependent on the execution of that duty. FIDIC considers they are reasonable time periods, sufficient to carry out the required duties, but without undue delay.

The consequences of reducing the time periods provided for in the GCs may result in a Contract Participant having insufficient time to perform their required duties properly or

19 Max W Abrahamson, 'Risk Management' [1983] *International Construction Law Review* 241, 244.

20 Nael Bunni, 'The Four Criteria of Risk Allocation in Construction Contracts' (2009) 26 *International Construction Law Review* 4, 9.

to exercise their rights. An earlier trigger of a time bar than is contemplated in the GCs is one potential consequence of reducing time periods.

Conversely, significantly extending those time periods may adversely affect the rights and entitlements of the Party for whose benefit the duties are being performed. For example, a longer period for issuing a Payment Certificate will result in the Contractor's cash flow being adversely affected.

In many provisions of the GCs, the Parties are invited to amend the 'default' time periods by agreement, using words such as 'unless otherwise agreed'. Such time periods are recognised as being determined by negotiation if appropriate, whilst providing a default option considered to be a reasonable time period.

> *GP5: Unless there is a conflict with the governing law of the Contract, all formal disputes must be referred to a Dispute Avoidance/Adjudication Board (or a Dispute Adjudication Board, if applicable) for a provisionally binding decision as a condition precedent to arbitration.*

The Dispute Avoidance/Adjudication Board (**DAAB**) in the 2017 Red, Yellow and Silver Books, the Dispute Adjudication Board (**DAB**) in the 1999 Red Book and the Dispute Board (**DB**) in the 2010 Pink Book have evolved as important entities to help the Parties avoid disputes and as a procedure for resolving disputes (at least provisionally) at much lower cost and in much less time than required for arbitration. The DAAB/DAB procedure provides an independent third party that assists in maintaining appropriate communication between the contracting Parties and promotes early resolution of disputes to enable the project to proceed without unnecessary disruption. The 1999 Yellow Book and the 1999 Silver Book provide for an 'ad hoc' DAB, implemented when a dispute has arisen. A DAAB or DAB resolves the conflicts of interest that formerly occurred, where the Engineer (engaged and paid by the Employer) not only certified the Contractor's entitlements under the Contract but also had the authority to resolve disputes.

If one of the Parties is not satisfied with a DAAB/DAB decision, it can issue a Notice of Dissatisfaction and trigger the arbitration process. However, arbitration can be delayed until the project is complete, helping to prevent project personnel from becoming distracted. In the meantime, the Parties have a decision that provides a provisional resolution of the dispute.

FIDIC considers the availability of an independent and impartial DAAB/DAB to (provisionally) resolve disputes fundamental to a fair and balanced contract. A DAAB/DAB can resolve disputes in real time, and thereby enable the Parties to plan their future activities based on the reasoned decision of experienced, independent and impartial persons who are familiar with the execution of projects and administration of construction contracts.

2.5 Guidance for drafting contract documents for consistency with the Golden Principles

Minor additions or grammatical changes to the wording of a GC sub-clause that do not alter the intent are not a breach of the GPs. However, such cosmetic changes should only be made for good reason.

In the PCs, changes to the GCs required to comply with local law are consistent with GC sub-clause 1.13 and are necessary and appropriate for the Contract to express the Parties' legal and contractual obligations properly. Such changes do not constitute a breach of the GPs.

One of the following terms in a GC generally indicates that it may be amended by the PCs without being in conflict with the GPs:

- 'or as otherwise agreed'
- 'except as otherwise agreed'
- 'unless otherwise agreed'
- 'unless otherwise agreed by both Parties'
- 'unless otherwise stated in the Particular Conditions'
- 'except as otherwise stated in these Conditions' or
- 'unless otherwise stated in the Contract' (however, this is ambiguous as it does not necessarily refer to the Particular Conditions)

It is important that the technical documents do not redefine the duties, rights, obligations, roles or responsibilities of any Contract Participants in a manner that is inconsistent with the GCs as modified by the PCs. For example, the Engineer has a clearly defined role in the Red and Yellow Books to make determinations as required by the Contract, after consulting both Parties. It would be a breach of GP1 for a Contract to require the Engineer to seek approval from the Employer before issuing any determination under sub-clause 3.5 (1999 editions) or sub-clause 3.7 (2017 editions).

The requirements of the project include the Laws applicable to execution of the Works, as well as the applicable Laws relevant to the rights and obligations of the Contract Participants. Changes in the PCs to make the Contract compliant with the relevant legal regimes are appropriate and necessary, and not in conflict with GP1.

Compliance with GP2 requires, amongst other things, that each of the documents comprising the Contract provide a cohesive and comprehensive whole, without overlap or inconsistencies. The contents of each Contract document should be confined to its scope as generally understood. The appropriate document to amend the GCs is the PCs; the 'contractual' issues detailed in the GCs should not be amended in other documents such as the Employer's Requirements or the Specification.

The content of 'technical' documents such as the Employer's Requirements, drawings or Specifications should be confined to technical issues, consistent with the provisions of the GCs as modified by the PCs.

GP3 is a fundamental principle that should be considered in any PC amendment to the GCs. The yardstick to apply in drafting any provision that amends the roles, duties or obligations as defined in the GCs is to enquire whether risks are being allocated to the Party that is in the best position to control them and bear the consequences of a potential risk becoming a reality. If so, the amendment is compliant with GP3.

There are two alternative considerations involved in complying with GP4 in respect of providing the Contract Participants with a reasonable time to perform their obligations and exercise their rights:

- 'Fixed' timeframes (i.e., those that are not qualified by a phrase such as 'unless the parties agree otherwise') should not be significantly changed from their value in the GCs
- 'Default' timeframes (i.e., those that are qualified by a phrase such as 'unless the parties agree otherwise') when amended should not provide unreasonably short or unreasonably long timeframes. A timeframe would be unreasonably short if it did not provide sufficient time for the Contract Participant to perform its duties properly or exercise its rights; a time frame would be unreasonably long if it significantly affects a Party's enjoyment of its rights, such as the Contractor's right to suspend or terminate the Works

GP5 requires that the Contract provide for a DAAB or DAB to give a provisionally binding decision on any formal dispute, as a condition precedent to referring a dispute to arbitration. Compliance with GP5 (and GP1) entails retention of the GC clauses referring to the role and operation of the DAAB/DAB and not significantly changing its role, duties, obligations and rights as defined in the GCs.

2.6 Conclusion

FIDIC's initiative in promoting the recognition and application of the GPs is intended to encourage the use of FIDIC GCs as they have always been intended: fair and balanced risk/reward allocation, clear definition of scope, duties, roles, rights and responsibilities and contract documents that constitute a contract management manual for best practice international project execution.

The use of the GPs is endorsed in the 2017 Editions of the Red, Yellow and Silver Books and the Emerald Book in the following terms:

> FIDIC strongly recommends that the Employer, the Contractor and all drafters of the Special Provisions take all due regard of the five FIDIC Golden Principles.[21]

21 Guidance for the Preparation of Particular Conditions, 8.

CHAPTER 3

Preparation of Particular Conditions

Dr Donald Charrett

CONTENTS

3.1 What should be in the Particular Conditions? 55
3.1.1 Particular Conditions Part A – Contract Data 55
3.1.2 Particular Conditions Part B – Special Provisions 55
3.2 Governing law 56
3.2.1 Governing law of the contract 56
3.2.2 Choosing the governing law of the contract 58
3.2.3 The law governing the agreement to arbitrate 58
3.3 Special Provisions for consistency with applicable law 59
3.4 Guidance for the Preparation of Particular Conditions 61
3.4.1 Special Provisions necessary or desirable for consistency with the governing law of the contract 62
3.4.2 Special Provisions necessary or desirable for consistency with applicable laws 63
3.4.3 Special Provisions necessary or desirable for the project requirements 64
3.4.4 Special Provisions necessary or desirable for the Employer's preferences 66
3.5 Format of Conditions of Contract 69
3.6 References 70
Annexure 70

DOI: 10.4324/9781003201250-3

3.1 What should be in the Particular Conditions?

As noted in section 1.3.5, the Particular Conditions in the 2017 rainbow suite comprise Part A – Contract Data and Part B – Special Provisions.

3.1.1 Particular Conditions Part A – Contract Data

The Contract Data provides the specific information referred to in the General Conditions required to define the unique characteristics of the particular Contract. Most of this information will be provided by the Employer to define its requirements in the Tender documents, including the time and cost parameters of the Contract, certain risk allocation parameters and a number of contract administration matters. The 'legal' data required is confined to the governing law of the contract; if this is not specified, the governing law of the contract will be the law of the Country. Certain parts of the Contract Data may be provided by the Contractor in its Tender.

Not all of the data items will require completion, as some refer to options in the General Conditions that may not be applicable, e.g., the data for the proportions of local and foreign currency (sub-clause 14.15(a)(i)) does not need to be completed if payment is to be made in one currency only. Many of the data items have default provisions specified in the relevant sub-clause that will apply if the item is not completed in the Contract Data. The Annexure to this chapter comprises the Contract Data from the 2017 Yellow Book, annotated with the default provisions in the General Conditions.

If data is not provided for some items, the data may be provided by the applicable law; e.g. if the number of days for the Time for Completion is not defined for sub-clause 1.1.86, the law would generally imply that the time period be reasonable.

It is strongly recommended that, to avoid ambiguity, all the items in the Contract Data be filled in, with the project-specific data, reference to the default in the sub-clause if that is appropriate or Not Applicable if the sub-clause provision does not apply. This will materially assist in the subsequent administration of the Contract, by providing all the relevant information in one location.

3.1.2 Particular Conditions Part B – Special Provisions

Particular Conditions Part B – Special Provisions is the contract document where any changes or additions to the General Conditions are documented. All references in the following sections to Particular Conditions refer to Part B – Special Provisions in the 2017 rainbow suite.

Special Provisions necessary for the particular requirements of the Works may comprise either modifications to the General Conditions or additional provisions that supplement the General Conditions. Such modifications may be necessary or desirable so that:

- The Contract wording is consistent with applicable law
- The Contract wording draws attention to relevant applicable law that must be complied with
- Specific requirements for the Site or the Works are documented
- The Employer's preferences are defined

As noted in the table of contract document hierarchy in Table 1.2, the Particular Conditions have precedence over the General Conditions in the event of any ambiguity. Thus, any Special Provisions that modify the General Conditions supersede the relevant parts of the General Conditions.

For clarity, the Special Provisions should comply with the following:

- A Special Provision modification to a sub-clause of the General Conditions should use the same sub-clause numbering as in the General Conditions
- Additional Special Provisions should use sub-clause numbers that are not used in the General Conditions
- Special Provisions may provide additional provisions to the General Conditions or may change provisions in the General Conditions

Skilled legal advice is required to determine whether the contractual provisions of the General Conditions are incompatible with the applicable mandatory law and to make the necessary amendments in the Special Provisions. Legal review should also determine whether it is appropriate to add Special Provisions to modify non-mandatory law that would otherwise apply. The following chapters provide guidance on the applicable law in a range of jurisdictions where FIDIC contracts are or can be used.

3.2 Governing law

3.2.1 Governing law of the contract

The principle of freedom of contract means that, subject to any mandatory law, the Parties are free to choose the governing law of their Contract, even if this is in a different jurisdiction to where the work is carried out or to the domicile of the contracting Parties. This principle of party autonomy in selecting the governing law of a contract is widely recognised. For example, the following articles of the *2015 Principles on Choice of Law in International Commercial Contracts*[1] of the Hague Conference on Private International Law (**Hague Principles**) provide:

> **Article 2 Freedom of choice**
> 1. A contract is governed by the law chosen by the parties.
>
> [...]
>
> 4. No connections required between the law chosen and the parties for their transaction.
>
> **Article 3 Rules of law**
>
> The law chosen by the parties may be rules of law that are generally accepted on an international, supranational or regional level as a neutral and balanced set of rules, unless the law of the forum provides otherwise.
>
> **Article 11 Overriding mandatory rules and public policy (*ordre public*)**
>
> 1. These Principles shall not prevent a court from applying overriding mandatory provisions of the law of the forum which apply irrespective of the law chosen by the parties.

1 https://assets.hcch.net/docs/5da3ed47-f54d-4c43-aaef-5eafc7c1f2a1.pdf (accessed 23 February 2021).

2. The law of the forum determines when a court may or must apply or take into account overriding mandatory provisions of another law.
3. A court may exclude application of a provision of the law chosen by the parties only if and to the extent that the result of such application would be manifestly incompatible with fundamental notions of public policy (*ordre public*) of the forum.
4. The law of the forum determines when a court may or must apply or take into account the public policy (*ordre public*) of a State the law of which would be applicable in the absence of a choice of law.
5. These Principles shall not prevent an arbitral tribunal from applying or taking into account public policy (*ordre public*), or from applying or taking into account overriding mandatory provisions of a law other than the law chosen by the parties, if the arbitral tribunal is required or entitled to do so.

The nature of the Hague Principles are as follows:

> **I.8** As their title suggests, the Principles do not constitute a formally binding instrument such as a Convention that States are obliged to directly apply or incorporate into their domestic law. Nor is this instrument a model law that States are encouraged to enact. Rather, it is a non-binding set of principles, which the Hague Conference encourages States to incorporate into their domestic choice of law regimes in a manner appropriate for the circumstances of each State. In this way, the Principles can guide the reform of domestic law on choice of law and operate alongside existing instruments on the subject (see Rome I Regulation and Mexico City Convention both of which embrace and apply the concept of party autonomy).[2]

The Hague Principles have so far only been implemented in legislation in Paraguay[3] and Uruguay.[4] However, a number of arbitration centres either have incorporated the Principles into their own institutional rules or are advertising or facilitating their use in other ways compatible with the Hague Principles. For example, in respect of the Council for National and International Commercial Arbitration in India (**CNICA**):

- The CNICA Arbitration Rules are consistent with the Hague Principles
- The CNICA Arbitration Rules allow parties to select the applicable law (Article 2)
- Tribunals constituted under the CNICA Arbitration Rules respect the law chosen by the parties
- Parties are free to select a non-state law under the CNICA Arbitration Rules (Article 3)
- Tribunals constituted under the CNICA Arbitration Rules respect the parties' choice of a non-state law (Article 3)[5]

The law of the forum (or *lex fori* as it is sometimes known) is the law of the place in which court or arbitral proceedings are conducted. Thus, under the Hague Principles and more generally, if the Parties have not selected the governing law of the contract, it will be determined by a judge in the jurisdiction where legal proceedings are initiated, or by an arbitral tribunal. Due to differences in conflicts of law rules, the outcome may be unpredictable.

2 https://www.hcch.net/en/instruments/conventions/full-text/?cid=135 (accessed 23 February 2021).
3 *Paraguayan Law 5393 of 2015* regarding the applicable law to international contracts: https://assets.hcch.net/upload/contractslaw_py.pdf (accessed 23 February 2021).
4 www.diputados.gub.uy/wp-content/uploads/2020/11/00130.pdf (accessed 23 February 2021).
5 https://assets.hcch.net/docs/b9627fbb-eac1-4aae-a23c-ef059e24849e.pdf (accessed 8 June 2022).

It should be noted that the Hague Principles do not require the rules of law to be laws of a country. The UNIDROIT Principles of International Commercial Contracts would be regarded as 'an international neutral and balanced set of rules'. Such anational rules of law are also permitted by the *European Contracts Convention* (*Rome I*),[6] and the *Inter-American Convention on the Law Applicable to International Contracts*.[7]

3.2.2 Choosing the governing law of the contract

As noted in the Annexure to this chapter, if the Parties do not nominate the governing law of the contract in the Contract Data for sub-clause 1.4 in the 2017 rainbow suite, the default position in the General Conditions is that the governing law of the contract will be the law of the Country.

Issues to consider in choosing the governing law if it is not to be the law of the Country:

- Are there any legal constraints on selecting the governing law in the Country or the domiciles of the contracting Parties?[8]
- Is the proposed law well known?
- Is legal advice on the proposed law readily available?
- Is the proposed law familiar to the contracting Parties, the DAAB/DAB and arbitrators?
- Is the governing law predictable?
- Are there any potential inconsistencies with the Laws of the Country?
- What is the extent of modification of FIDIC General Conditions necessary for consistency with the governing law?
- The preferences of the contracting Parties
- Availability of reference materials (e.g. books, legislation, case law) in the language for communication

3.2.3 The law governing the agreement to arbitrate

In respect of sub-clause 21.6 Arbitration, the Notes on the Preparation of Special Provisions in the 2017 rainbow suite recommend careful selection of the place or '**seat**' of arbitration in a jurisdiction other than the Country:

> For major projects tendered internationally, it is desirable that the place of arbitration be situated in a country other than that of the Employer or Contractor. This country should have a modern and liberal arbitration law and should have ratified a bilateral or multilateral convention (such as the *1958 New York Convention on the Recognition and Enforcement of Foreign Arbitral Awards*), or both, that would facilitate the enforcement of an arbitral award in the states of the Parties.

The consequence of nominating the seat of arbitration is the selection of that jurisdiction's law as the *lex arbitrii* – the law governing the arbitration process. The intent of FIDIC's

6 *Regulation (EC) No 593/2008* of the European Parliament and of the Council of 17 June 2008 on the law applicable to contractual obligations.

7 www.oas.org/juridico/english/treaties/b-56.html (accessed 8 June 2022).

8 For example, Article 869 of the *Colombian Commercial Code* states that Contracts that are performed in Colombia will be governed by Colombian Law.

recommendation is to ensure that neither Party will have a 'home country' advantage in the dispute resolution process.

As discussed in section 1.5.6, the law governing the arbitration process (*lex arbitrii*) is not necessarily the same as the governing law of the contract, or the law governing the agreement to arbitrate. Where the governing law of the contract is different to the *lex arbitrii*, there may be a question of what the governing law of the arbitration is, that is, the law governing the validity and scope of the arbitration agreement. Where the Parties have not made an explicit choice of the governing law of the contract, there are arguments (and case law) in support of the law governing the arbitration agreement being either the governing law of the contract or the *lex arbitrii*.

The finely balanced arguments for either possibility were canvassed in the case of *Enka Insaat Ve Sanayi AS v OOO Insurance Company* (*Enka Insaat*).[9] In this case, the central issue concerned which system of national law governed the validity and scope of the arbitration agreement when the governing law of the contract containing it differed from the law of the seat of the arbitration. The Parties had not made an explicit choice of the governing law of the contract but had selected London as the seat of arbitration. The majority (Lord Hamblen and Lord Leggatt, Lord Kerr agreeing) applied English common law rules for resolving conflicts of laws and held that in the absence of the parties' choice, the law applicable to the arbitration agreement is the system of law with which the arbitration agreement is most closely connected. Where the parties have chosen a seat of arbitration, the governing law of the arbitration agreement will generally be the law of the seat, even if this differs from the governing law of the contract.[10] In dissent, Lord Burrows (with whom Lord Sales agreed) held that the 'main contract' approach should be preferred to the 'seat' approach in determining the governing law of the arbitration agreement.

Where the Parties have made a choice of governing law of the contract, the majorities' summary in *Enka Insaat* noted that under English law:

> iv) Where the law applicable to the arbitration agreement is not specified, a choice of governing law for the contract will generally apply to an arbitration agreement which forms part of the contract.
> v) The choice of a different country as the seat of the arbitration is not, without more, sufficient to negate an inference that a choice of law to govern the contract was intended to apply to the arbitration agreement.[11]

As the FIDIC Conditions of Contract specify the governing law of the contract either by explicit nomination or in default as the law of the Country, the issue of a different law governing the agreement to arbitrate is probably unlikely to arise except in unusual circumstances.

3.3 Special Provisions for consistency with applicable law

Irrespective of the wording of the Conditions of Contract, mandatory law will always apply, and the Parties are required to comply with it both as a matter of law and to comply with the Contract. Such mandatory law may comprise either

9 [2020] UKSC 38.
10 *Ibid.* [170].
11 *Ibid.*

(a) Provisions that are incompatible with the General Conditions, or
(b) Provisions that are not incompatible with the General Conditions, but the General Conditions do not refer to the issue within the scope of the mandatory law

In the case of (a), it is highly desirable that Special Provisions are written to modify the General Conditions and make them consistent with the mandatory law. In addition, it is also desirable to prepare Special Provisions to incorporate mandatory law provisions of type (b), to draw attention to these obligations in a document that (hopefully) is used as a contract management manual.

Special Provisions that incorporate mandatory law of type (a) will ensure that the contract wording is accurate and not misleading; Special Provisions that incorporate mandatory law of type (b) will significantly enhance the usefulness of the Conditions of Contract as a comprehensive contract management manual.

As discussed in section 1.5, statute law may be either mandatory or non-mandatory. If a law is not mandatory, contracting Parties may choose not to follow it by incorporating specific terms in the Contract. However, unless there are such contract terms 'otherwise' the law will apply as a default option, whether or not the Parties are aware of it. In the circumstances where the Parties do not wish to apply the default law, Special Provisions will be necessary to define the contractual alternative.

Thus, the General Conditions may require modification, or it may be desirable to modify them where the governing law of the contract is that of a particular jurisdiction. The following are some examples of issues where it may be necessary or desirable to prepare Special Provisions that align the Conditions of Contract with the provisions of the governing law:

- Changed conditions:
  - Laws of economic disequilibrium, e.g. France, former French colonies and Turkey
  - Rules about commercial impracticability, e.g. USA
- Limitation period for liability, e.g. Brazil
- Delay damages (liquidated damages)/proof of loss:
  - May be lowered if the actual damage is less in a civil law jurisdiction, e.g. Switzerland
  - May be nullified if it is not a genuine pre-estimate of loss in a common law jurisdiction, e.g. Australia, England
- Termination, e.g. Australia, Brazil, France
- *Force majeure*, e.g. China, the Philippines, Indonesia, United Arab Emirates
- Obligation to complete with a certain result, e.g. Peru
- Subcontractors, e.g. China, France
- Provisions relating to the extinguishing of liability will not apply in jurisdictions that do not allow contractual waiver of liability in the case of gross negligence or fraud, e.g. California
- Disputes relating to non-contractual claims may not be arbitrable, e.g. fraud in Pakistan
- Rights of 'set off', 'abatement' or similar rights that are inconsistent with the payment provisions in the General Conditions, e.g. under the common law, a right of set-off is difficult to exclude by contract language

- Valuation of Variations, e.g. France
- Burdensome obligations on the Contractor in the EPC Silver Book are unlikely to be upheld in France and Francophone and other countries of French civil law tradition
- The responsibility of Contractors to implement Variations instructed by the Employer, e.g. Germany
- The corresponding duty of Employers to pay for Variations, e.g. Brazil, Italy
- Principles relating to the obligations to produce a result versus the obligation to apply the means, e.g. Peru
- Good faith, e.g. Brazil, Peru
- Time bars may not be allowed under the governing law as a breach of good faith in civil law jurisdictions, e.g. Peru, United Arab Emirates
- Legislation dealing with unfair contract conditions, e.g. Germany, Holland, Sweden, England, France
- Allocation of ground risk, e.g. Brazil, Germany

Each of the following chapters of this book provides guidance on the application of FIDIC contracts in a particular jurisdiction and addresses the aforementioned issues where they are relevant to the jurisdiction.

3.4 Guidance for the Preparation of Particular Conditions

The Guidance for the Preparation of Particular Conditions in the 2017 rainbow suite contains detailed Notes on the preparation of Special Provisions in the section titled Particular Conditions Part B – Special Provisions. The Introduction to this section includes a strong recommendation 'that the Employer, the Contractor and all drafters of the Special Provisions take all due regard of the five FIDIC Golden Principles' enumerated in bold (see section 1.4). The FIDIC Golden Principles are listed and discussed in detail in Chapter 2.

Some direct warnings on amending sub-clauses then follow:

> Before incorporating any new or changed sub-clauses, the wording must be carefully checked to ensure that it is wholly suitable for the particular circumstances. Unless it is considered suitable, example wording should be amended before use.
>
> Where any amendments or additions are made to the General Conditions, great care must be taken to ensure that the wording does not unintentionally alter the meaning of other clauses in the Conditions of Contract, does not inadvertently change the obligations assigned to the Parties or the balance of risks shared between them and/or does not create any new ambiguity or misunderstanding in the rest of the Contract documents.

The Notes on the Preparation of Special Provisions are prefaced with the following caution prior to providing detailed suggestions for specific clauses:

> It is very important that all Employers (and all drafters of the Special Provisions) work with their professional advisers to review specific terminology in the General Conditions for compliance and consistency with accepted practice in the legal jurisdiction they are operating in.
>
> [...]
>
> The following references and examples show some of the Sub-Clauses in the General Conditions which may need amending to suit the needs of the project or the requirements of the Employer. The selected Sub-Clauses and the example wording are included as examples

only. They also include, as an aide memoire, references to other documents such as the Specification and/or Drawings and the Contract Data, where particular issues may need to be addressed.

The selected Sub-Clauses do not necessarily require changing and the example wording may not suit the needs of a particular project or Employer. It is the responsibility of the drafter of the Special Provisions to ensure that the selection of the Sub-Clauses and the choice of wording is appropriate to the project concerned.

Furthermore, there may be other Sub-Clauses, not mentioned below, which need to be amended. Great care must be taken when amending the wording of Sub-Clauses from the General Conditions, or adding new provisions, to ensure that the balance of obligations and rights of the Parties are not unintentionally compromised.

The following sections identify four distinct types of modifications that may be required to the clauses in the General Conditions, as identified in the 2017 rainbow suite:

- Special Provisions necessary or desirable for consistency with the governing law of the contract
- Special Provisions necessary or desirable for consistency with applicable laws
- Special Provisions necessary or desirable for the Project requirements
- Special Provisions necessary or desirable for the Employer's Preferences

The following sections are intended as a brief introduction to some of the more common and well-recognised General Conditions clauses that may require modification. Although extracted from the Notes in the 2017 rainbow suite, they are not intended to provide detailed guidance, nor to suggest specific wording for particular sub-clauses – those are covered in considerable detail in the FIDIC rainbow suite.

The following tables do not provide any indication of which modifications may be necessary or desirable for a particular jurisdiction – those are covered in the following chapters, each of which addresses the requirements of a particular jurisdiction.

3.4.1 Special Provisions necessary or desirable for consistency with the governing law of the contract

Some of the following Special Provisions are also included in the table in section 3.4.2, as the Laws in the Country may be applicable in some circumstances.

Yellow Book sub-clause	Special Provision	Page[a]
1.1.XX[b] Additional Definitions	Add definition of Gross Negligence	15
1.6 Contract Agreement	Contract Agreement: If entry into a formal Contract Agreement is mandatory, delete the words 'unless they agree otherwise.'	15
4.2 Performance Security	The provisions in sub-clause 4.2 in respect of Performance Securities may have to be amended to comply with applicable law.	22
8.XX Additional sub-clause for Concurrent Delay	Add a Special Provision 8.XX to define the rules and procedures applicable to concurrent delay under the governing law of the contract.	35

Yellow Book sub-clause	Special Provision	Page[a]
11.10 Unfulfilled Obligations	It may be necessary to review the effect of sub-clause 11.10 in relation to the period of liability imposed by the applicable law, and in particular the second paragraph may require amending.	36
15.2 Termination for Contractor's Default	Sub-clause 15.2 may require amendment for consistency with the governing law of the contract.	47
15.5 Termination for Employer's Convenience	Amend the wording of sub-clause 15.5 if it is not permissible under the governing law of the contract for the Employer to terminate the Contract for convenience.	48
16.2 Termination by Contractor	Amend the wording of sub-clause 16.2 if the General Condition provision for termination by the Contractor is not compatible with the governing law of the contract.	48

[a] Page numbers are the page numbers in the Guidance for the Preparation of Particular Conditions in the 2017 Yellow Book.

[b] XX denotes a new number distinct from the numbering in the General Conditions. See section 3.1.2.

3.4.2 Special Provisions necessary or desirable for consistency with applicable laws

The following Special Provisions generally refer to applicable laws of the Site and in the Country.

Yellow Book sub-clause	Special Provision	Page[a]
1.6 Contract Agreement	Contract Agreement: If entry into a formal Contract Agreement is mandatory, delete the word 'unless they agree otherwise.'	15
1.13 Compliance with Laws	Special Provision in sub-clause 1.13 in respect of the Goods for a plant contract.	16
3.5 Engineer's Instructions	Amend sub-clause 3.5 if the applicable law prevents the Contractor from complying with any Engineer's instruction that may have an adverse effect on the health and safety of the Contractor's Personnel.	21
4.2 Performance Security	The provisions in sub-clause 4.2 in respect of Performance Securities may have to be amended to comply with applicable law.	22
4.16 Transport of Goods	Add a Special Provision to sub-clause 4.16 if the Contractor is required to obtain permission prior to the delivery of Goods to the Site.	25
5.2.2 Contractor's Documents – Review by Engineer	Amend sub-clause 5.2.2 if there is a requirement under the applicable law for the mandatory review/checking of certain elements of design (by an authorised professional or other legally recognised individual) and/or verification that such design is in accordance with the applicable law, before such design can be implemented in the Works.	29

(*Continued*)

(Continued)

Yellow Book sub-clause	Special Provision	Page[a]
6.3 Recruitment of Persons	Amend or delete sub-clause 6.3 if the relevant labour Laws applicable to the Contractor's Personnel and/or the Employer's Personnel do not permit any restriction on the right of any worker to seek other positions.	30
11.10 Unfulfilled Obligations	It may be necessary to review the effect of sub-clause 11.10 in relation to the period of liability imposed by the applicable law, and in particular the second paragraph may require amending.	36
14.1 The Contract Price 14.XX Additional sub-clause for Import Duties	Amend sub-clause 14.1 and add an additional sub-clause 14.XX if the Contractor is not required to pay import duties on Goods imported by the Contractor into the Country.	40
14.1 The Contract Price 14.XX Additional sub-clause for Expatriate Staff Income Tax	Amend sub-clause 14.1 and add an additional sub-clause 14.XX if expatriate staff are exempted from paying local income tax.	40

[a] Page numbers are the page numbers in the Guidance for the Preparation of Particular Conditions in the 2017 Yellow Book.

3.4.3 Special Provisions necessary or desirable for the project requirements

Yellow Book sub-clause	Special Provision	Page[a]
1.1 Definitions	Amend definitions of Country, Local Currency, add new definitions.	14
Various	Consider increasing the timescales for Notices in the General Conditions if Notices are only to be given in paper format by post. The following sub-clauses in the Yellow Book provide for specific periods of time for submitting a Notice: 1.9; 3.4; 3.5; 3.7.3; 3.7.4; 3.7.5; 4.2.2; 4.3; 4.4; 4.5.1; (4.7.2); 4.9.1; 4.12.2; 4.16; 4.17; 5.2.2; 6.12; 7.5; 8.1; 8.3; 8.12; 9.1; 9.2; 10.1; 10.3; 11.6; 11.7; 11.9; 12.1; 15.2.2; 16.1; 16.2.1; 16.2.2; 17.3; 18.2; 20.2.1; 20.2.2; 20.2.4; 21.4.4. The following sub-clauses in the Yellow Book Dispute Adjudication Agreement provide for specific periods of time for submitting a Notice: 2.2; 9.1. Rule 10 in the Yellow Book DAAB Procedural Rules provides for specific periods of time for submitting a Notice.	15
1.5(g) Priority of Documents	If the Employer's Requirements are to comprise a number of documents, consider amending sub-clause 1.5(g) by adding an order of precedence for the various documents in the Employer's Requirements.	15

Yellow Book sub-clause	Special Provision	Page[a]
1.14 Joint and Several Liability	Special Provisions in sub-clause 1.14 if the Contractor is a Joint Venture.	16
2.1 Right of Access to the Site	Amendments to sub-clause 2.1 it right of access to, and possession of, the Site cannot be granted by the Employer in the normal way.	18
3.4 Delegation by the Engineer	Amendments to sub-clause 3.4 if it is anticipated that the Engineer's Assistants may not all be fluent in the language for communication is defined in 1.4.	20
3.5 Engineer's Instructions	Special Provision to sub-clause 3.5 to allow for the giving of oral instructions by the Engineer.	21
4.2.1 Performance Security – Contractor's Obligations	If the sample forms for Performance Securities are not used, consider adding to sub-clause 4.2.1 a Special Provision to reduce the amount of the Performance Security following issue of the Taking-Over Certificate for the whole of the Works.	22
4.3 Contractor's Representative	Special Provisions to sub-clause 4.3 if it is necessary to stipulate that the Contractor's Representative shall be qualified, experienced and competent in a particular engineering discipline in relation to the Works, be fluent in a particular language other than the language for communications or is not required to be fluent in the language for communications.	22
4.8 Health and Safety Obligations	Amend sub-clause 4.8 if the Contractor is sharing occupation of the Site with others.	24
4.21 Security of the Site 4.22 Contractor's Operations on Site	Amend sub-clauses 4.21 and 4.22 if the Contractor is sharing occupation of the Site with others.	26
6.8 Contractor's Superintendence	Amend sub-clause 6.8 if it is permissible that the Contractor's superintending staff are not all fluent in the language for communications.	30
6.8 Contractor's Superintendence	Special Provision to sub-clause 6.8 if it is necessary to stipulate that the Contractor's superintending staff shall be fluent in a particular language.	31
6.12 Key Personnel	Special Provision to sub-clause 6.12 if it is permissible that all Key Personnel are not fluent in the language for communications.	31
6.XX Additional sub-clauses for circumstances of the Site	It may be necessary, appropriate and/or desirable to include additional Special Provisions to clause 6 to take account of the circumstances and locality of the Site: Foreign personnel Supply of foodstuffs Supply of water Measures against insect and pest nuisance Alcoholic liquor or drugs Arms and ammunition Festivals and religious customs	

(Continued)

(Continued)

Yellow Book sub-clause	Special Provision	Page[a]
	Funeral arrangements Forced labour Child labour Employment records of workers Workers organisations Non-discrimination and equal opportunity	
8.3(a) – (k) Programme	For less complex projects, considered simplifying the requirements for the Contractor's programme in sub-clause 8.3(a) – (k).	34

Page numbers are the page numbers in the Guidance for the Preparation of Particular Conditions in the 2017 Yellow Book.

3.4.4 Special Provisions necessary or desirable for the Employer's preferences

Yellow Book sub-clause	Special Provision	Page
1.5 Priority of Documents	Amend sub-clause 1.5 if no order of precedence of documents is to be prescribed in the Contract. In the event of an ambiguity or discrepancy, the priority will be determined by the governing law of the contract.	15
1.10 Employer's Use of Contractor's Documents	Special Provisions to sub-clause 1.10 may be required if all rights to particular items of eg computer software are to be assigned to the Employer.	15
1.15 Limitation of Liability	Replace sub-clause 1.15 if it is required that the limitation of each Party's liability to the other Party is to include certain 'indirect or consequential loss or damage' and is also to take into account liabilities to be insured under 19.	16
2.6 Employer-Supplied Materials and Employer's Equipment	Special Provisions to sub-clause 2.6 if Employer Supplied Materials or Employer's Equipment are listed in the Employer's Requirements.	18
3.2 Engineer's Duties and Authority	Any requirements for the Engineer to obtain the Employer's consent should be added to sub-clause 3.2.	20
4.4 Subcontractors	Special Provision to sub-clause 4.4 if it is appropriate or desirable to encourage the Contractor to employ local subcontractors.	23
4.4 Subcontractors	Delete the last three paragraphs of sub-clause 4.4 if no consent by the Engineer to Subcontractors is required.	23
4.4 Subcontractors	Amend sub-clause 4.4 if the Engineer's consent is required to the suppliers of certain Materials, or subcontracts should provide for assignment of the subcontractor to the Employer pursuant to sub-clause 15.2 or after the expiry of the DNP.	23

Yellow Book sub-clause	Special Provision	Page
4.4 Subcontractors	Amend sub-clause 4.4 if it is anticipated that a Subcontractor that is not a Nominated Subcontractor is to be instructed under sub-clause 13.3.	24
4.12 Unforeseeable Physical Conditions	If the risk of Unforeseeable physical conditions is to be shared between the Parties, amend sub-clause 4.12.	25
4.17 Contractor's Equipment	Add a Special Provision to sub-clause 4.17 if vesting of the Contractor's Equipment to the Employer is required (and consistent with the Laws of the Country).	26
4.XX Additional sub-clause for completion of certain parts of the Works	Special Provision 4.XX if the Employer wishes to have certain parts of the Works completed within certain times but does not wish to take over such parts when completed (Milestones).	27
14.4 Schedule of Payments	Amend sub-clause 14.4 if certain payments to the Contractor to be made on completion of each Milestone.	28
7.7 Ownership of Plant and Materials	Add a Special Provision to sub-clause 7.7 if the Contractor is to provide high-value items of Plant and/or Materials.	33
7.XX Additional sub-clause for financing institution rules	Add a Special Provision 7.XX if the Contract is being financed by an institution whose rules or policies require a restriction on the use of its funds.	34
8.1 Commencement of Works	Amend sub-clause 8.1 if the Commencement Date is not to be within 42 days after the Contractor receives the letter of Acceptance.	
8.XX Additional sub-clause for early completion incentives	Add a Special Provision 8.XX if the Contract provides incentives for early completion.	35
9.1 Contractor's Obligations	Amend sub-clause 9.1 if the product produced by the Tests on Completion is to be retained by the Contractor and not the Employer.	36
11.3 Extension of Defects Notification Period	Amend the period of two years in sub-clause 11.3 if the Employer requires a longer or shorter period.	36
11.XX Additional sub-clause for new or innovative technology	Add a Special Provision 11.XX if the Works comprise new or innovative technology in the Country and the Employer requires its permanent operating personnel to be given supervisory assistance in the operation and maintenance of the Plant during the DNP.	37
12.1 Procedure for Tests after Completion	Amend sub-clause 12.1 if the provisions for Tests after Completion are to be different to those in the General Conditions.	37
13.2 Value Engineering	Add Special Provisions for sharing of the benefit, costs and/or delay between the Parties applying to a Value Engineering Variation instructed by the Engineer.	

(*Continued*)

(Continued)

Yellow Book sub-clause	Special Provision	Page
13.7 Adjustments for Changes in Cost	Amend sub-clause 13.7 if it would be unreasonable for the Contractor to bear the risk of escalating costs due to inflation.	38
14.XX Additional sub-clauses for exceptions to payment provisions	Add Special Provisions 14.XX to cover any exceptions to the provisions in sub-clause 14.1 and if sub-clause 14.1(a) (lump sum) is not to apply.	40
14.2 Advance Payment	Amend sub-clause 14.2 if the Employer wishes to provide the advance payment in instalments.	42
14.XX Additional sub-clause for interim payments	Add a Special Provision 14.XX if interim payments are to be paid other than on the basis of a Schedule of Payments.	43
14.XX Additional sub-clause for simple measurement for interim valuations	If the Works consist of only a few different types of operations, a simple measurement type of approach for interim valuations may be detailed in a Special Provision 14.XX.	44
14.8 Delayed Payment	Amend sub-clause 14.8 if payment is to be on the basis of the Contractor's actual financing Costs.	45
14.XX Additional sub-clause for guarantee instead of Retention Money	Add a Special Provision 14.XX if part of the Retention Money is to be released and substituted by an appropriate guarantee.	45
14.15 Currencies of Payment	Replace sub-clause 14.15 if all payments are to be made in Local Currency.	45
14.XX Additional sub-clause for requirements of financing entities	Add Special Provisions 14.XX to cover the requirements of financing entities such as aid agencies, development banks, export credit agencies, or other international financing institutions.	46
14.XX Additional sub-clause for Contractor finance	Add a Special Provision 14.XX for Contractor finance.	47
15.XX Additional sub-clause for Employer-Supplied Materials	A Special Provision 15.XX may be appropriate if the Employer has made available any Employer-Supplied Materials and/or Employer's Equipment.	47
16.3 Contractor's Obligations after Termination	Amendment of sub-clause 16.3 may be desirable if the Employer has made available any Employer Supplied Materials and/or Employer's Equipment.	48
17.XX Additional sub-clause for Contractor's use of Employer's facilities	Add a Special Provision 17.XX if the Contractor is to be allowed to use and/or occupy any of the Employer's facilities and/or accommodation temporarily during the Contract.	49
19 Insurance	Amend sub-clause 19 if the Employer wishes to change the insurance provisions in the General Conditions.	49
20.1 Claims	Consider replacing the words 'within a reasonable time' in the last paragraph of sub-clause 20.1 by a specified time period.	50

Yellow Book sub-clause	Special Provision	Page
1.1.22 Definition of DAAB 1.1.23 Definition of DAAB Agreement 21.1 Constitution of the DAAB 21.3 Avoidance of Disputes 21.4 Obtaining DAAB's Decision	Amendments to sub-clauses 1.1.22, 1.1.23, 21.1 and 21.4 and deletion of sub-clause 21.3 will be required if an ad-hoc Dispute Adjudication board (DAB) is to be appointed instead of a DAAB.	52
21.5 Amicable Settlement	A longer period than 28 days may be desirable under sub-clause 21.5 to give the Parties an opportunity to arrive at an amicable settlement procedure.	53
Various	If Building Information Modelling (BIM) is to be adopted, a number of sub-clauses need to be thoroughly reviewed when drafting the Special Provisions.	58

3.5 Format of Conditions of Contract

As noted earlier, there are a number of legitimate reasons why the General Conditions may need to be modified and/or supplemented by Special Provisions.

In an endeavour to discourage users from changing the General Conditions excessively, FIDIC currently insists on the use of the General Conditions in their original form, irrespective of the extent to which Particular Conditions might change them.

Before a Contract has been entered into, a tenderer needs to assess the Conditions of Contract to determine, amongst other things, the risks that are to be undertaken by the Contractor. A tenderer familiar with FIDIC General Conditions needs to assess, in particular, those Particular Conditions that alter the risk allocation under the General Conditions. From the practical perspective of assessing how far a Contract deviates from a 'FIDIC contract', a redlined markup of the FIDIC General Conditions is the most user-friendly. It avoids a reviewer spending any time on assessing unaltered sub-clauses, and it draws specific attention to those sub-clauses that have been altered, and the specific way in which they have been altered. This is not necessarily straightforward if the alterations are in a separate Particular Conditions document, as this requires a close comparison of the corresponding General Conditions sub-clauses.

However, once a contract has been executed, for the purpose of complying with and administering the Contract, users generally prefer a single 'clean' document of the Conditions of Contract that incorporates the General Conditions, plus the Particular Conditions, Contract Data, the General Conditions of the Dispute Adjudication Agreement, Dispute Adjudication Agreement and Procedural Rules all using the FIDIC sub-clause numbering.

Under current arrangements, users can obtain the benefits of a single Conditions of Contract document by negotiating a licence for an electronic copy with FIDIC. This avoids the inconvenience of referring to a separate Particular Conditions document in addition to the General Conditions to understand the Contract Conditions.

Under existing arrangements FIDIC may negotiate an electronic licence on an exceptional basis as follows:

- FIDIC provides a soft copy of the General Conditions
- The licensee may alter the text of the General Conditions
- The final issued version of the Contract must append a markup of the amended FIDIC General Conditions that identifies the changes by redlining
- The amended General Conditions may only be used for a single Project
- **The resulting Contract will no longer be a 'FIDIC contract' and must not be represented as one**

Thus, those preparing Conditions of Contract must weigh up the cost and convenience of having a single user-friendly document (and a red-lined version showing changes to the General Conditions), with the traditional approach of having a separate document for Particular Conditions that must be read in conjunction with the printed General Conditions to understand the Conditions of Contract.

3.6 References

- Conditions of Contract for Construction (2nd edn, 2017) Guidance Notes for the Preparation of Particular Conditions
- Conditions of Contract for Plant and Design-Build (2nd edn, 2017) Guidance Notes for the Preparation of Particular Conditions
- Conditions of Contract for EPC/Turnkey Projects (2nd edn, 2017) Guidance Notes for the Preparation of Particular Conditions

Annexure

Table 3.1 Contract Data in 2017 Yellow Book, annotated with default provisions

Sub-clause	Data to be given	Default data
1.1.20	Where the Contract allows for Cost Plus Profit, percentage profit to be added to the Cost:	5%
1.1.27	Defects Notification Period (DNP):	One year.
1.1.30	Employer's name and address:	
1.1.35	Engineer's name and address:	
1.1.86	Time for Completion:	
1.3 (a) (ii)	Agreed methods of electronic transmission:	System(s) acceptable to the Engineer.
1.3 (d)	Address of Employer for communications:	
1.3 (d)	Address of Engineer for communications:	
1.3 (d)	Address of Contractor for communications:	

Sub-clause	Data to be given	Default data
1.4	Contract shall be governed by the law of:	The law of the Country.
1.4	Ruling language:	The language of these Conditions.
1.4	Language for communications:	The ruling language of the Contract.
1.8	Number of additional paper copies of Contractor's Documents:	0
1.9	Period for notification of errors, faults or other defects in the Employer's Requirements:	42 days.
1.15	Total liability of the Contractor to the Employer under or in connection with the Contract:	The Accepted Contract Amount.
2.1	After receiving the Letter of Acceptance, the Contractor shall be given right of access to all or part of the Site within:	Within such times as may be required to enable the Contractor to proceed in accordance with the Programme or, if there is no Programme at that time, the initial programme submitted under Clause 8.3 [Program].
2.4	Employer's financial arrangements:	
4.2	Performance Security (as percentages of the Accepted Contract Amount in Currencies): percent: currency: percent: currency:	Sub-clause 4.2 does not apply.
4.4 (a)	Maximum allowable accumulated value of work subcontracted (as a percentage of the Accepted Contract Amount):	The whole of the Works.
4.4 (b)	Parts of the Works for which subcontracting is not permitted:	
4.7.2	Period for notification of errors in the items of reference:	28 days.
4.19	Period of payment for temporary utilities:	Each month.
4.20	Number of additional paper copies of progress reports:	0
6.5	Normal working hours on the Site:	
8.3	Number of additional paper copies of programmes:	0
8.8	Delay Damages payable for each day of delay:	
8.8	Maximum amount of Delay Damages:	No limit.
13.4 (b) (ii)	Percentage rate to be applied to Provisional Sums for overhead charges and profit:	

(Continued)

(Continued)

Sub-clause	Data to be given	Default data
14.2	Total amount of Advance Payment (as a percentage of Accepted Contract Amount):	Sub-clause 14.2 does not apply.
14.2	Currency or currencies of Advance Payment:	
14.2.3	Percentage deductions for the repayment of the Advance Payment:	25%
14.3	Period of payment:	After the end of each month.
14.3 (b)	Number of additional paper copies of Statements:	0
14.3 (iii)	Percentage of retention:	
14.3 (iii)	Limit of Retention Money (as a percentage of Accepted Contract Amount):	
14.5 (b) (i)	Plant and Materials for payment when shipped:	
14.5 (c) (i)	Plant and Materials for payment when delivered to the Site:	
14.6.2	Minimum amount of Interim Payment Certificate (IPC):	
14.7 (a)	Period for payment of Advance Payment to the Contractor:	21 days.
14.7 (b) (i)	Period for the Employer to make interim payments to the Contractor under Sub- Clause 14.6 [*Interim Payment*]:	56 days.
14.7 (b) (ii)	Period for the Employer to make final payment to the Contractor under sub-clause 14.13 [*Final Payment*]:	28 days.
14.7 (c)	Period for the Employer to make final payment to the Contractor:	56 days.
14.8	Financing charges for delayed payment (percentage points above the average bank short–term lending rate as referred to under sub-paragraph (a))	3% above benchmark specified in sub-clause 14.8.
14.11.1 (b)	Number of additional paper copies of draft Final Statement:	0
14.15	Currencies for payment of Contract Price:	
14.15 (a) (i)	Proportions or amounts of Local and Foreign Currencies are: Local: Foreign :	
1415 (c)	Currencies and proportions for payment of Delay Damages:	
14.15 (g)	Rates of exchange	Those prevailing on the Base Date.

Sub-clause	Data to be given	Default data
17.2 (d)	Forces of nature, the risks of which are allocated to the Contractor:	
19.1	Permitted deductible limits: Insurance required for the Works: Insurance required for Goods: Insurance required for liability for breach of professional duty: Insurance required against liability for fitness for purpose (if any is required): Insurance required for injury to persons and damage to property: insurance required for injury to employees Other insurances required by Laws and by local practice:	
19.2 (1) (b)	Additional amount to be insured (as a percentage of the replacement value, if less or more than 15%):	
19.2 (1) (iv)	List of Exceptional Risks which shall not be excluded from the insurance cover for the Works:	
19.2.2	Extent of insurance required for Goods:	
19.2.3 (a)	Amount of insurance required for liability for breach of professional duty:	The amount agreed with the Employer.
19.2.3 (b)	Insurance required against liability for fitness for purpose:	No insurance required against liability for fitness for purpose.
19.2.3	Period of insurance required for liability for breach of professional duty:	
19.2.4	Amount of insurance required for injury to persons and damage to property:	The amount agreed with the Employer.
19.2.6	Other insurances required by Laws and by local practice (give details):	
21.1	Time for appointment of DAAB:	28 days.
21.1	The DAAB shall comprise	Three members.
21.1	List of proposed members of DAAB: - proposed by Employer: - proposed by Contractor:	
21.2	Appointing entity (official) for DAAB members:	

CHAPTER 4

Applying FIDIC Contracts in the Plurinational State of Bolivia

Claudia Andrea Lopez Monterrey and Polina Chtchelok

CONTENTS

4.1	Outline of the Bolivian's legal environment	77
	4.1.1 The constitutional structure of Bolivia	77
	4.1.2 The legal system in Bolivia	78
	4.1.3 The court system in Bolivia	79
4.2	The construction industry in Bolivia	80
	4.2.1 Overview	80
	4.2.2 Size of Bolivian contractors, extent of subcontracting and international contractors	82
	4.2.3 Licensing/registration in the construction industry in Bolivia	82
	4.2.4 Labour relations	83
	4.2.5 Safety culture	84
	4.2.6 Modular construction using factory-fabricated components	85
	4.2.7 Technology/innovation/BIM	85
	4.2.8 Government/private sector procurement	86
	4.2.9 Insurance requirements	87
	4.2.10 Common forms of contract	88
	4.2.11 Dispute resolution	88
	4.2.12 Current challenges	90
	4.2.13 Unique features of the construction industry in Bolivia	90
4.3	The impact of COVID-19 in Bolivia	90
	4.3.1 The impact of COVID-19 on the execution of construction projects in Bolivia	90
	4.3.2 The impact of COVID-19 on the operation of construction contracts in Bolivia	91
4.4	Bolivian governing law of the contract	93
	4.4.1 Constraints on the governing law of a construction contract	93
	4.4.2 Formal requirements for a construction contract	94
4.5	What Special Provisions in the Particular Conditions are necessary for consistency with applicable laws in Bolivia?	94
	4.5.1 FIDIC General Conditions are incompatible or inconsistent with Bolivian governing law of the contract	94

 DOI: 10.4324/9781003201250-4

4.5.1.1 Illegality/unenforceability of certain contractual terms 95
4.5.1.2 Allocation of ground risk 95
4.5.1.3 Burdensome obligations on the Contractor in the EPC Silver Book 95
4.5.1.4 Principles relating to a lump sum contract 95
4.5.1.5 Proving entitlements to extension of time 95
4.5.1.6 Payment for Variations 95
4.5.1.7 Termination 96
4.5.1.8 Force majeure 96
4.5.2 FIDIC General Conditions are incompatible or inconsistent with the law of the Site/Country 96
4.5.2.1 Health and safety (sub-clause 4.8) 96
4.5.2.2 Environment (sub-clauses 4.18, 5.4) 97
4.5.2.3 Subcontractors (sub-clause 4.4) 97
4.5.2.4 Design (sub-clauses 5.1, 5.2, 5.3) 97
4.5.2.5 Ownership of Plant and Materials (sub-clause 7.7) 97
4.5.2.6 Employer's sale of Contractor's Equipment, surplus material, wreckage and Temporary Works (sub-clause 11.11) 97
4.5.2.7 Bankruptcy, insolvency, liquidation (sub-clauses 15.2, 16.2) 97
4.5.2.8 Insurance (sub-clause 19.2) 97
4.5.3 FIDIC General Conditions are incompatible or inconsistent with the relevant laws on dispute determination in Bolivia 97
4.5.3.1 Mandating the way in which a court or tribunal is to settle disputes or determine contractual rights 97
4.5.3.2 Disputes relating to non-contractual claims may not be arbitrable 98
4.6 What Special Provisions in the Particular Conditions are desirable for consistency with applicable laws in Bolivia? 98
4.6.1 Outsourcing 98
4.6.2 Archeological discovery 98
4.6.3 Penalty clause 98
4.6.4 Applicable law 99
4.6.5 Good faith 99
4.6.6 Implying terms in all contracts of a particular type 99
4.6.7 Delay damages/penalties 99
4.6.8 Limitation period for liability 99
4.7 Summary of applicable legislation for Bolivia governing law of the contract 100
4.7.1 Entry into a construction contract 100
4.7.2 Operation of a construction contract 100
4.7.3 Termination of a construction contract 100
4.7.4 Dispute resolution 100

4.8 Summary of applicable legislation if the Site/Country is in Bolivia 100
4.8.1 Operation of a construction contract 100
4.8.2 Termination of a construction contract 102
4.8.3 Dispute resolution 102
4.9 Summary of applicable legislation if the 'seat' of the dispute determination is Bolivia 103
4.10 Additional references for Bolivia 103
4.10.1 Books 103
4.10.2 Internet 103
4.10.2.1 Online publications 103
4.10.2.2 Legislation 103
4.10.2.3 Court decisions 103
4.10.3 Websites for the Ministries and other government entities 104

4.1 Outline of the Bolivian's legal environment

4.1.1 The constitutional structure of Bolivia

The Plurinational State of Bolivia (**Bolivia**) is a representative democratic State; the President is head of the Government and is directly elected for a five-year term by popular vote.

Since 2009 Bolivia has had a new *Constitución Política del Estado 2009*[1] (***CPE***) defining constitutional reform in the country and establishing fundamental bases, rights and duties of citizens, structure and organisation of the State and the territories within the State. There are three powers established under the *CPE*: Executive Power headed by the President, Legislative Power (Parliament) and Judiciary Power (Courts). There is a fourth power (Electoral System); however, its independence and impartiality are widely questioned because of the Presidential electoral process in 2019.

The Bolivian Parliament is formed by 36 senators and 130 deputies, with seven seats reserved explicitly for representatives of the indigenous groups. The members of the Parliament are elected by proportional representation from the current parties' lists and indigenous people's communities with the Electoral Authority responsible for the methodology for the distribution of seats based on the population count in each Department during the last census; the Departments with lesser population and lesser grade of economic development have a minimum number of seats assigned automatically.

In the country, there are two capitals: the State's political capital in La Paz (base for the Executive and the Legislative Power) and the historic capital in Sucre (base for the Judicial Power).

Bolivia is divided into nine Departments, 112 Provinces, 314 Municipalities and 1,384 Cantons[2] that had territorial autonomy granted initially in 1995 and confirmed in 2009 under the new *CPE*. Each Department, including its Prefecture, is administrated by the Governor and Departmental Council. In the case of Municipalities, these are headed by a Mayor and Municipal Council. The overall government system is level-based: State, Department, Municipal and the autonomous indigenous territories. The *CPE* establishes the right to autonomous and indigenous self-government. It vests the indigenous communities with exclusive property rights to the forest resources of their territory.

The *CPE* defines a hierarchy of competencies between these governmental levels,[3] but at the same time, this creates conflict between State, Departmental and Municipal Governments as the hierarchy of competencies vests each level of the government system with parallel and shared competencies.

For example, as part of the State Government, the *Ministerio de Medio Ambiente y Agua* has exclusive competency to supervise and control environmental matters in the strategic sectors, such as hydrocarbons or mining. The State exclusively regulates the strategic sectors; however, this competency can be delegated or transferred to other governmental entities through an express authorisation. To illustrate, in 2015 the Department of Santa Cruz passed the *Ley de Conservación del Patrimonio Natural 2015*[4] within the framework of its competency at the departmental level to protect the environment, which defined the departmental function in overseeing and monitoring the environmental impact of activities of

1 Promulgated 7 February 2009.
2 www.familysearch.org/wiki/es/Geograf%C3%ADa_actual_de_Bolivia (accessed 23 August 2021).
3 *CPE* Art 297.
4 *Ley 98*.

hydrocarbons projects within the boundary of the Santa Cruz Department. Even though this law encroaches over State control of strategic activities, the law was not declared unconstitutional and consequently imposes additional legal requirements upon commercial entities.

4.1.2 The legal system in Bolivia

The Bolivian legal system is based on civil law; the priority of the applicable legislation is based on the principle of the hierarchy of norms: governance of the state framework legislation and autonomy of the competency of each level of government.

The *CPE* and the *International Conventions on Human Rights and Community Law* are defined as the supreme law and take precedence over any other law or legal norm. All other *Conventions* ratified by the Bolivian Government have the status of special laws and can prevail over other laws but not at the level of the *CPE*. The structure and priority order of legal norms in Bolivia are shown in Figures 4.1–4.4.[5]

Figure 4.1 Structure and priority order of legal norms at State level.

Figure 4.2 Structure and priority order of legal norms at Departmental level.

5 *CPE* Art 410.

Figure 4.3 Structure and priority order of legal norms at Municipal level.

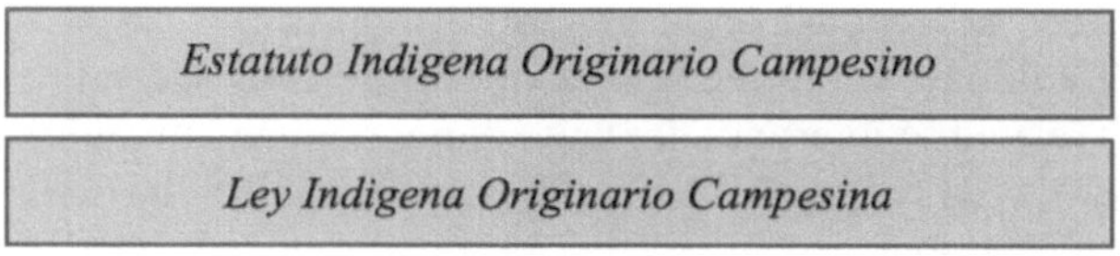

Figure 4.4 Structure and priority order of legal norms at Indigenous level.

4.1.3 The court system in Bolivia

The structure and organisation of the Bolivian court system are established by the *Ley del Organo Judicial 2010*:[6] the court system consists of the Plurinational Constitutional Court (based in Sucre), the Supreme Court of Justice (based in Sucre), the Departmental Courts of Justice, the Sentencing Tribunal and Courts, the Agriculture and Environmental Courts and, finally, the Indigenous Jurisdiction – exercised by indigenous authorities. The judges are elected by the population whereas, before the constitutional reform in 2009, they were elected by the parliament from a list.

The Plurinational Constitutional Court ensures the supremacy of the *Constitution*, exercises control of constitutionality and safeguards the respect and validity of constitutional rights and guarantees.

In Bolivia, the court proceedings are in the first instance heard by the Sentencing Tribunal or a specific public court and in the second instance appeals are heard by the Departmental Courts. The Supreme Court has the competency to hear cassation appeals but is limited to review only questions regarding application of the law. The Supreme Court also presides over matters in relation to conflicts of jurisdiction, extradition proceedings and crimes of the President and Vice-President during the corresponding mandate.

6 *Ley 25.*

The Departmental Courts (Tribunals of second instance) are divided into specialised Chambers that preside over cases and appeals in relation to civil, commercial, family, children and domestic violence, labour and social security matters as well as in relation to criminal offences. These Chambers are composed of 32 magistrates in La Paz, 28 in Santa Cruz, 24 in Cochabamba, 16 in Chuquisaca, Oruro and Potosi, 12 in Tarija, 11 in Beni and seven in Pando.[7]

Each Sentencing Tribunal is composed of two technical judges and three citizens that are competent to hear and resolve actionable offences. The number of Tribunals is defined based on the size of the territory and the nature of matters heard in each Province or Municipality.

The judges of the public courts hear civil, criminal, commercial, family, labour and social security matters. Like the Sentencing Tribunals, the number of public courts is defined based on the size of the territory and the nature of matters heard in each Province or Municipality.

The autonomous indigenous territories are regulated by the *Ley de Deslinde Jurisdiccional 2010*,[8] which allows the indigenous people to administer justice in accordance with their own customs and traditions within the framework of the *CPE*. However, the law excludes criminal offences related to international law, crimes against humanity, tax and customs crimes, human, arms and drug trafficking, civil lawsuits against the State and all lawsuits in relation to labour law, social security law, administrative law, mining law, hydrocarbons law, forestry law, public and private international law and agriculture law.

The Higher Council of Judges is responsible for the disciplinary regime of the ordinary justices and justices in the specialised jurisdictions, as well as control and supervision of its administrative and financial management of the judicial system and formulation of its management policies.

The *CPE* does not mention how contentious administrative processes shall be addressed and the *Ley de Órgano Judicial 2010* only states, in a transitory provision, that the courts hearing administrative, tax, coercive and fiscal matters will continue exercising their powers until a specific law is issued. In 2014, the Bolivian Government passed the *Ley transitoria para la tramitación de los procesos contenciosos y contencioso administrativo 2014*[9] which aimed at creating Chambers in Contentious and Contentious Administrative Matters within the structure of the Supreme Court and Departmental Courts. These Chambers are to be in charge of cases in relation to contractual matters with the state and state-owned entities.

4.2 The construction industry in Bolivia

4.2.1 Overview

The construction industry in Bolivia generates a considerable amount of employment through construction companies, professionals in the area, manufacturers and suppliers

7 *Ley 25* Art 45.
8 *Ley 73.*
9 *Ley 620.*

of materials and labour, as well as the auxiliary services necessary for the construction industry to function, such as logistics, catering for staff and others. As of the first quarter of 2021, there are 360,000 persons over the age of 14 who are engaged in the construction industry, representing 9.2% of the total employed population.[10]

Many Bolivian suppliers are implicated in construction activities: aggregates, cement, fuels and others. In addition, services are also making a significant contribution, such as insurance, transport, equipment rentals, essential services, professionals and others. Finally, there are the construction clients: State or State-owned entities, followed by the housing and oil and gas sectors.

The construction sector in Bolivia enjoyed healthy performance and growth from 2006 until 2018, with the gross domestic product of construction (**GDPC**) consistently being higher than the gross domestic product (**GDP**). In 2018, GDP reached 4.22%, whereas the activity of the construction sector fell to 3.54% and continued to decline. This decline is attributable to political instability, increased bureaucracy, State deficit, inflation and COVID-19. At the same time, the construction sector performance is also impacted by the government's investment policy focusing predominately on agriculture and hydrocarbons, with the private sector not having sufficient capacity to attract more significant investments.[11] As a result, the construction surface area in 2020 reached 1,867,797 m^2, representing 61% of the surface area of the permits granted in 2019.[12] The further decline in the construction industry is illustrated by the closure and non-renovation of business registration by the construction companies: out of 340,634 construction companies existing in Bolivia, as of March 2021, 753 have chosen to close their registration, and only 21.48% have updated their company registration.[13] This translated into a 2.9% employment loss in the construction sector, which equates to a loss of 155,907 jobs.[14]

The construction industry in Bolivia is predominately focused on four broad areas of activity:

- Major infrastructure: roads, dams, public transportation, domestic gas and electricity
- Natural resources: mining and oil and gas
- Non-residential buildings: hospitals, offices, shops, hotels and industrial zones, and
- Residential building: apartment buildings and individual houses

10 www.economiayfinanzas.gob.bo/el-presidente-luis-arce-presenta-el-seguro-obligatorio-contra-accidentes-para-trabajadores-de-la-construccion.html (accessed 5 August 2021).

11 https://eldeber.com.bo/economia/sector-de-la-construccion-registra-su-menor-crecimiento-en-13-anos_146081 (accessed 5 August 2021).

12 www.caboco.org/normativa/datos-estadisticos-2021 (accessed 5 August 2021).

13 *Ibid.*

14 https://fundacion-milenio.org/coy-469-la-perdida-de-empleo-en-bolivia-por-el-covid-19-una-aproximacion-al-tema/ (accessed 5 August 2021).

4.2.2 Size of Bolivian contractors, extent of subcontracting and international contractors

Local construction companies are small and typically act as subcontractors to larger international companies when bidding for projects of significant size and importance, especially in the infrastructure sector. In the infrastructure sector, the construction companies are predominately Brazilian or Chinese. In the oil and gas sector, the construction companies are predominately European, Argentinian or Chinese. Either local or Spanish companies carry out building construction. Depending on the location of the offices of the construction company it may choose to become a member of *Cámara Boliviana de la Construcción* (**CABOCO**)[15] or *Cámara de la Construcción de Santa Cruz* (**CADECOCRUZ**).[16]

4.2.3 Licensing/registration in the construction industry in Bolivia

The construction industry in Bolivia is highly regulated, especially in relation to environmental protection. At the same time, various regulatory texts are not uniform and can contain contradictory provisions. As State, Department or Municipal governments can issue legislation and regulations governing construction activity, these can be contradictory. The construction industry's licensing and registration of commercial entities fall under the same rules that apply to any commercial entity registration. On the other hand, some complications can arise if a company would like to engage in an activity not yet existing in the country and thus not covered by the regulation – for example, recycling facilities for various materials. For a commercial entity to start its activities in Bolivia, it must first obtain a tax identification number (*Número de Identificación Tributaria*) from the *Servicio de Impuestos Nacionales*,[17] then it must register with the *Fundación para el Desarrollo Empresarial* (**FUNDEMPRESA**)[18] in order to obtain legal capacity in the form of *Matricula de Comercio* and finally apply for a municipal *licencia de funcionamiento* (operating license based on the activity the company plans to exercise), *padrón municipal* and *licencia ambiental* at the Municipality where the business is located. Depending on the company's construction activity, it might need to apply for additional licenses from the relevant authority (handling, storage and use of chemicals or dangerous substances, disposal of waste, use of blasting explosives, etc.). Unfortunately, in Bolivia, no central government service provides information about the licenses, regulations and approvals applicable to any given activity in the construction or any other sector.

The engineering profession and classification of engineers in Bolivia are controlled and regulated by *Sociedad de Ingenieros de Bolivia*,[19] whose website permits checking the qualifications of all registered engineers in Bolivia. The same applies to the profession of architects through the *Colegio de Arquitectos de Bolivia*.[20] The professionals and technicians in hygiene, occupational safety and occupational medicine are registered with the *Ministerio de Trabajo*. There are also the National Register for Refrigeration and Air-Conditioning Work (**RENTRAA**) and the National Register for Environmental

15 www.caboco.org (accessed 5 August 2021) – La Paz, Cochabamba, Oruro, Tarija, Beni and Pando.
16 www.cadecocruz.org.bo/index.php?op=2 (accessed 5 August 2021).
17 www.impuestos.gob.bo (accessed 5 August 2021).
18 https://miempresa.gob.bo (accessed 5 August 2021).
19 www.sib.org.bo/institucion/ambito-juridico.html (accessed 5 August 2021).
20 www.cab.org.bo (accessed 5 August 2021).

Consultants (**RENCA**).[21] The skilled labour certification is not centralised and is done through courses and certifications run by such entities as the *Instituto Boliviano de Normalización y Calidad* (IBNORCA),[22] *Instituto Boliviano del Cemento y el Hormigón* (IBCH)[23] and *Unidad de Educación Continua* (CENACE).[24] Even though various certifications are readily available, the cost of these certifications is high compared to the level of salaries in the construction industry. As such, smaller construction companies often employ uncertified labour or run informal apprentice arrangements, consequently impacting the construction quality.

4.2.4 Labour relations

Bolivia's workplace relations system is governed by the *Ley General del Trabajo 1942*, *Código de Seguridad Social 1956*, *Ley de Pensiones 2010*[25] and the decrees that regulate these laws and other specific regulations and ministerial resolutions that cover both State and private sector employees in Bolivia. These laws, codes and decrees are lengthy and cover in-depth the labour relations framework; their practical application is overseen, as applicable, by the *Ministerio de Trabajo*[26] and labour courts. The *Ministerio de Trabajo* oversees the implementation of mechanisms for the resolution of individual and collective disputes on employment matters, declarations on the legality or illegality of strikes, compliance inspections of labour regulations and mechanisms for collective negotiations and registration of resulting collective agreements. The labour courts have a much broader scope in overseeing:

- Matters that have not reached conciliation
- Approval of minutes of conciliation labour and social security proceedings
- Preparatory and precautionary matters
- Individual and collective actions regarding labour rights and social benefits, severance, compensation, reinstatement, infraction of labour laws and health and safety laws and other labour-related conflicts
- Proceedings for collecting contributions by social security entities, and
- Proceedings for recovery of trade union assets

All employers in Bolivia must register with the *Ministerio de Trabajo*, the *Administradoras de Fondos de Pensiones*[27] and the *Caja Nacional de Salud*.[28] It is important to note that foreign nationals cannot represent more than 15%[29] of an employer's total workforce.

21 http://snia.mmaya.gob.bo/web/modulos/RENCA/ (accessed 5 August 2021).
22 www.ibnorca.org/es/nosotros (accessed 5 August 2021).
23 www.ibch.com/index.php?option=com_content&view=article&id=1&Itemid=3 (accessed 5 August 2021).
24 https://cenace.upsa.edu.bo/portafolio-de-cursos (accessed 5 August 2021).
25 *Ley 65*.
26 www.mintrabajo.gob.bo (accessed 5 August 2021).
27 www.afp-futuro.com/siswww/es/ab2/bienvenida/bienvenida.html (accessed 5 August 2021); www.prevision.com.bo (accessed 5 August 2021).
28 www.cns.gob.bo (accessed 5 August 2021).
29 *Ley General del Trabajo 1942* Art 3.

The employer acts as a retention agent and pays contributions to the Integrated Pensions System for Bolivian and foreign nationals.

Salaries are negotiated between the employer and employee but cannot be below the national minimum wage; however, the salaries can be fixed in any foreign currency or bolivianos (local currency in Bolivia). An enforceable employment contract must be in writing, generally for an indefinite period of employment, and approved by the *Ministerio de Trabajo*. Collective agreements are recognised under the Bolivian labour law. One particularity of Bolivian labour law is that work hours are limited to 48 hours per week for men and 40 hours for women,[30] and union leaders benefit from special protection against dismissal.

It is possible to put in place a fixed-term employment contract, but the following conditions must be met:

- It must clearly state the performance of which specific work or service it applies to
- It must be in writing and approved by the competent officer at the *Ministerio de Trabajo*
- It can be used only in exceptional circumstances: temporary replacement of a current employee, increasing number of employees to cover a specific increase in demand or workload or for completion of projects with a pre-established delivery date
- It has a maximum term of one year that can be renewed only once for one year

Depending on the nature of a possible dispute between an employee and employer, the dispute is referred either to the *Ministerio de Trabajo*, in the case of administrative proceedings, or to a labour court.

At the beginning of 2021, the Bolivian Government passed the *DS 4218 (2021)*, recognising and regulating the 'work from home' concept, applicable to all sectors (public and private), as long as the nature of the activity allowed. This decree facilitates this concept being incorporated in a typical labour contract and imposes an availability obligation during work hours.

4.2.5 Safety culture

In Bolivia, occupational safety and health at work are governed by extensive provisions of the *Ley General de Higiene, Seguridad Ocupacional y Bienestar 1979*[31] as well as other complementary regulations, resolutions and decrees. But at the same time, the construction sector in the country is one of the most accident- and death-prone industrial sectors – on average 70% of the overall reported industrial accidents are in the construction sector.[32] Even though this percentage seems to be high, the basis for its calculation is questionable as the real number of accidents and deaths is not known. This can be explained by the culture of 'pacts of silence': financial arrangements between an owner of construction sites

30 *Ley General del Trabajo 1942* Art 46.

31 *Decreto Ley 16998*.

32 www.presidencia.gob.bo/index.php/prensa/noticias/1560-gobierno-lanza-el-seguro-obligatorio-de-accidentes-para-las-y-los-trabajadores-de-la-construccion-constructor-seguro (accessed 5 August 2021).

or a contractor and victims or their families so that the latter do not report the accident or fatality to the *Ministerio de Trabajo*, as they should.[33] The local construction companies consider reporting accidents and fatalities prejudicial, irrespective of such reporting being mandated by law. Another contributing factor to accidents and deaths, even when the employers provide safety gear and personal protection equipment, the employees at the construction site chose not to use them because they are considered uncomfortable, which demonstrates the absence of safety culture and education.

The Bolivian Government recognised the standing issue of the safety culture in construction and has ratified the *Safety and Health in Construction Convention, 1988 (No. 167)* in 2014,[34] the application of which is regulated by *DS 2936*[35] for all construction companies or companies linked to the construction industry.

The *Ministerio de Trabajo* took safety concerns one step further in 2017 by publishing, through a *Ministerial Resolution*, eight technical norms covering safety requirements in the construction sector for illumination, noise, work at heights, manipulation of ladders, scaffolding, demolition works, excavation works and works in confined spaces.[36]

4.2.6 Modular construction using factory-fabricated components

Most construction in Bolivia is site-based, with access to sites outside the major cities severely impacted by the poor quality of the roads, structural stability and weight capacity of the bridges, as well as weather impacts such as heavy rain and flooding during the rainy season (often resulting in bridge collapse[37] or a landslide[38]). Access to some sites also requires lengthy negotiations with local indigenous communities. Modular construction is yet to be deployed for construction in the major cities, but is widely used for resource projects in remote locations – the size of modules is restricted by the site connecting roads and bridges. The building construction is a mix between concrete panels and brick.

4.2.7 Technology/innovation/BIM

The latest construction technology and innovations are yet to find their way into the construction industry in Bolivia. Nonetheless, the two most innovative projects that Bolivia has seen to date are the building of the Centre for Nuclear Technology Research and Development (CNTRD)[39] and the cable-car public transportation system.[40] Building Information Management (**BIM**) has not yet been widely adopted as it was only officially

33 www.paginasiete.bo/especial01/2019/2/14/accidentes-laborales-entre-negligencia-omision-de-normas-pactos-de-silencio-209030.html (accessed 5 August 2021).

34 *Ley 545 (2014).*

35 *Reglamento de la Ley 545, 2016.*

36 *RM 387/17 (Ministerio de Trabajo) Aprobación de la normas técnicos de seguridad en la construcción, 2017.*

37 https://eldeber.com.bo/santa-cruz/colapsa-un-puente-en-el-norte-cruceno-la-crecida-del-rio-san-miguelito-se-llevo-parte-de-la-estructu_217632 (accessed 5 August 2021).

38 www.efe.com/efe/america/sociedad/sube-a-14-el-numero-de-fallecidos-en-dos-derrumbes-una-carretera-bolivia/20000013-3887759 (accessed 5 August 2021).

39 www.neimagazine.com/news/newsbolivias-nuclear-centre-will-see-first-two-phases-launched-this-year-8635279 (accessed 5 August 2021).

40 www.telegraph.co.uk/travel/destinations/south-america/bolivia/articles/la-paz-cable-cars/ (accessed 5 August 2021).

introduced in Bolivia in 2017 through the creation of *Comité BIM Bolivia*[41] and the launch of BIM Forum Bolivia[42] in 2020. There is no specific norm enacted governing the implementation of BIM for projects in Bolivia.[43]

4.2.8 Government/private sector procurement

In Bolivia, the strategic sectors of the economy such as oil and gas,[44] mining,[45] telecommunications[46] and electricity[47] are principally reserved for the State-owned entities; a foreign entity can invest in any of these industries through participation in close connection with a State-owned entity, either through a service type agreement, a joint venture arrangement or a public–private partnership (**PPP**).[48] PPPs are essentially defined as strategic alliances and *DS 3469* allows entering into strategic alliance contracts for joint investment between:

- Distinct Bolivian State-owned entities
- Bolivian State-owned entities and Bolivian private companies
- Bolivian State-owned entitles and foreign State companies that comply with legal requirements for commercial activities
- Bolivian State-owned entitles and foreign private companies that comply with legal requirements for commercial activities

There are four types of State-owned companies:[49]

- State Companies: 100% State capital
- Mixed State Companies: between 70% and 100% State capital
- Mixed Companies: between 51% and 70% State capital
- Intergovernmental companies: between 51% and 100% State capital; the rest of the capital is from Autonomous Territory Entities

State-owned entities have the right to enter into both administrative and commercial contracts.

The administrative contracts are signed between State and private entities or individuals and aimed at the execution of a construction contract or public service; their validity is subject to compliance with specific formalities.

All administrative contracts are subjected to Coercive Tax Jurisdiction as a method of dispute resolution with the exception of public entities that have external financing for

41 https://comitebimbolivia.com/acerca-de/ (accessed 5 August 2021).

42 www.e-zigurat.com/news/es/lanzamiento-bim-forum-bolivia/ (accessed 5 August 2021).

43 https://comitebimbolivia.com/2020/04/17/si-aun-no-hay-normas-bim-en-bolivia-de-que-nos-guiamos/ (accessed 5 August 2021).

44 *Ley de Hidrocarburos 2005 (Ley 3058).*

45 *Ley de Minería y Metalurgia 2014 (Ley 535).*

46 *Ley General de Telecomunicaciones, Tecnologías de Información y Comunicación 2011 (Ley 164).*

47 *Ley de Electricidad 1994 (Ley 1604).*

48 *Los preceptos y el contenido mínimo de los Contratos de Alianzas Estratégicas de Inversión Conjunta 2018 (DS 3469).*

49 *Ley de la Empresa Pública 2013 (Ley 466)* Art 6.

their projects[50] and companies listed as private entities that were part of the process of '*nacionalización*'; the latter can define their preferred dispute resolution method.[51]

In terms of the difference between administrative and commercial contracts, *AS 190/2013*[52] states that the contracts of the Public Administration are governed predominantly by public law and in some parts are also governed by private law. Predominately governed by private law are assignment contracts, swap contracts, donation, purchase and sale agreements, mandate contracts, deposits, bond contracts, contracts of carriage and contingent contracts. On the other hand, contracts of public function, borrowing contracts, concession of public services, concession of public works, public works and supply contracts are predominately governed by administrative law.

The *AS 281/2012* and *AS 286/2012*[53] define the difference between administrative contracts and commercial contracts: in commercial contracts parties are on equal footing in accordance with Art 454 of the *Código Civil*, but in administrative contracts such principle is restricted by public interest and special rules, thus there is inequality between the parties due to the supremacy of the State. The award of contracts with State or State-owned entities is regulated by *DS 181*[54] and complemented by *DS 4453*[55] in relation to electronic auctions and the State-owned online marketplace for procurement that now form an integral part of the State procurement website *Sistema De Contrataciones Estatales* (SICOES). It is imperative to note that *DS 181* provides for preferential margins and adjustment factors in bids including a certain percentage of Bolivian component content or labour.[56] *DS 2030 (2014)* allows State or State-owned entities in the strategic sectors to award public contracts to foreign companies when such awards are justified through legal and technical reports, and as long as such goods and services are not available in the domestic market. The State or State-owned entities in the strategic sectors have their sector-specific procurement regulations and processes, which generally follow the principles prescribed by *DS 181*; in the case of PPPs, specific conditions of *DS 3469* apply.

Amendment of the concluded contracts is allowed under *DS 181*, subject to specific conditions; in the case of construction contracts, the modifications can be carried out by means of change orders.[57]

4.2.9 Insurance requirements

In Bolivia, all workers who render their services within the construction sector are obliged to purchase annually the compulsory insurance *Seguro Obligatorio de Accidentes de la Trabajadora y el Trabajador en el Ámbito de la Construcción*.[58] This insurance covers medical expenses and provides compensation in case of death or permanent disability.[59]

50 *Ley 708*, (2015) *Art 5 no. 3.*

51 *Ley 708*, (2015) Transitory Article 4.

52 *Tribunal Supremo de Justicia Sala Civil*, April 2013.

53 *Tribunal Supremo de Justicia Sala Civil*, August 2012.

54 *Norma Básica del Sistema de Administración de Bienes y Servicios, 2009.*

55 *Subasta Electrónica y Mercado Virtual Estatal, 2021.*

56 *DS 181 (2009)* Art 30.

57 *DS 181 (2009)* Art 89.

58 *Ley de Seguro Obligatorio de Accidentes de la Trabajadora y el Trabajador en el Ámbito de la Construcción 2019 (Ley 1155).*

59 *DS 4058 (2019).*

Under the provisions of *Ley 1155*, public and private health establishments throughout the Bolivian territory are under an obligation to attend to the victims of work-related accidents. Therefore, all entities that hire and/or subcontract workers in the construction industry must require workers to present the current certificate of insurance coverage.

All other insurance requirements are governed by the provisions of *Ley de Seguros de la República de Bolivia 1998*[60] as modified and regulated by modification laws and regulating decrees.

4.2.10 Common forms of contract

Procurement by a State or State-owned entity is usually centred on the use of specific contracts based on the FIDIC rainbow suite and construed in favour of the State or State-owned entity; lump sum contracts are permitted under certain circumstances.[61] The State procurement framework agreement is called *Documento Base de Contratación* (DBC) and is prepared by the procuring entity for each procurement process, based on the Model DBC issued by the governing body, and contains the technical specifications or terms of reference, evaluation methodology, procedures and conditions for the procurement process.[62] The minimum required content of the contract package is defined in Art 86 and Art 87 of *DS 181* in the case of contracting with State and State-owned entities, and for PPPs, these are set out in *DS 3469*.

Private sector contracts are either modified standard forms of contract or tailored industry contracts. State or State-owned entities usually do not accept any modifications to the agreement presented as part of invitation to tender package. Engineering, procurement and construction (**EPC**) contracts are widely used.

4.2.11 Dispute resolution

Litigation in Bolivia is governed by the new *Código Procesal Civil 2013*;[63] however, arbitration is frequently chosen as the preferred form of dispute resolution by international entities doing business in Bolivia. In addition, most litigation proceedings in Bolivia take years to resolve due to the old-fashioned, paper-based, physical infrastructure of the courts and judges not known to be impartial.[64] If there is an arbitration clause or arbitration agreement in the contract, then the parties cannot initiate a judicial process in relation to a dispute already submitted to an arbitration proceeding. The judicial authority that becomes aware of a controversy in relation to an arbitration clause or arbitration agreement must refrain from hearing the case.[65]

As such, arbitration is also commonly chosen as a dispute resolution mechanism in contracts with the State and State-owned entities. The nationalisation spree by the government of Evo Morales between 2006 and 2019 resulted in a significant number of arbitration

---

60 *Ley 1883*.

61 *DS 181 (2009)* Art 76.

62 *DS 181 (2009)* Art 46.

63 *Ley 439*.

64 www.hrw.org/news/2020/11/25/will-luis-arce-rebuild-bolivias-broken-judiciary (accessed 18 August 2021).

65 *Ley 708* Art 45.

claims filed against the Bolivian State, which prompted Bolivia to withdraw from the *International Centre for Settlement Investment Disputes Convention* (***ICSID Convention***) in 2007.[66] In 2009, the new *CPE* provided for the State's new policies, especially concerning Bolivian sovereignty and authority over investment arbitration.[67] There are no valid bilateral investment treaties (**BIT**); these were abrogated in 2013.[68] Then in 2015, a new *Ley de Conciliación y Arbitraje 2015*[69] created a further step back in relation to arbitration with the State and State-owned entities.

Pursuant to *Ley 708*, any controversies of a contractual or non-contractual nature that involve the State or State-owned entities and arise from or are related to an investment made under *Ley de Promoción de Inversiones 2014*[70] shall be bound by the following rules:

- Investment controversies shall be subject to Bolivian jurisdiction, laws and authorities
- The parties must submit the controversy to conciliation before arbitration
- Conciliation or arbitration will be local
- Conciliation or arbitration will have the territory of Bolivia as its seat; hearings, evidence production and other procedures could be conducted outside of Bolivian territory
- The existence of an arbitration clause or the willingness to conciliate does not limit or restrict the attributions and competencies of control and supervision from the corresponding regulatory entities and competent authorities

Notwithstanding the foregoing, *Ley 708* allows for the parties to freely determine the applicable arbitration rules; if no consensus is reached, the applicable arbitration rules shall be those of a centre for the solution of investment controversies of an organisation of which Bolivia is a member. Administrative contracts are a subject matter excluded from conciliation and arbitration.[71]

The challenge of an arbitral award must be addressed to the court of the seat of the arbitration: Bolivia. Thus, the award can only be challenged by means of a nullity recourse, providing the following grounds for challenge: arbitrability, public policy, invalidity of the agreement to arbitrate, arbitral tribunal's excess of powers and procedural irregularities.

The use of Dispute Boards in Bolivia has not yet occurred. Most administrative contracts must follow the contract model of the *DS 181*; in that model of contract, there is no definition of Dispute Boards. Some private companies in the oil and gas industry consider including the option of Dispute Boards in their model contracts, but these contracts are yet to be signed in Bolivia.

In 2018, the State Company called ENDE signed with the VESTAS MEDITERRANEAN Company (external financing), a contract for the design, procurement, assembly,

66 https://scholar.smu.edu/cgi/viewcontent.cgi?article=1464&context=lbra (accessed 18 August 2021).

67 *Art 320*, CPE.

68 http://justinvestment.org/wp-content/uploads/2014/07/Bolivia-denounces-its-Bilateral-Investment-Treaties-and-attempts-to-put-an-end-to-the-Power-of-Corporations-to-sue-the-country-in-International-Tribunals1.pdf (accessed 18 August 2021).

69 *Ley 708*.

70 *Ley 516*.

71 *Ley 708* Art 4.

installation and commissioning of wind turbines for the Santa Cruz wind project,[72] under a modified FIDIC Yellow Book. However, the clause referring to Dispute Boards was deleted.

The contracts financed by German KfW Development Bank in Bolivia usually use FIDIC standard forms, but there is no evidence they have kept the provision regarding Dispute Boards. The contract 'Construction of the Itangua-Cuevo irrigation project' signed between the *Gobierno Autónomo Departamental de Chuquisaca* and the *Asociación Accidental FRAMA y ECCSA*[73] has a 'Commission for the Resolution of Disputes' but it consists of one member.

4.2.12 Current challenges

In the General State Budget (*Presupuesto General del Estado*)[74] for 2021, approved in December 2020, the Bolivian Government allocated approximately USD 4 billion towards public investments, of which only USD 1.452 billion was allocated for infrastructure projects.

4.2.13 Unique features of the construction industry in Bolivia

The uniqueness of the construction industry in Bolivia is the bureaucracy concerning the time required to obtain all the required contraction permits – on average 265 days in comparison with the average of 191 for Latin America and the Caribbean.[75]

4.3 The impact of COVID-19 in Bolivia

4.3.1 The impact of COVID-19 on the execution of construction projects in Bolivia

Almost all commercial activities, including the construction sector, were impacted by the initial 13-day-long lockdown in 2020 (*DS 4199 [2020]*[76]). The lockdown was further extended to 30 April 2020 (*DS 4200 [2020]* and *DS 4214 [2020]*) with much more stringent sanitary measures in place. Then the lockdown was relaxed during May 2020, but with some controls still in place (*DS 4229 [2020]*). *DS4229* allowed each Municipality to define the level of risk due to COVID-19 and to define accordingly which commercial activities were permitted. The decree provided that regardless of the level of risk, the activities in the construction sector starting 10 May 2020 were allowed subject to regulation by the *Ministerio de Obras Públicas*, the *Ministerio de Trabajo, Empleo y Seguridad Social* and the *Ministerio de Salud* through the *Resolución Multiministerial.*

72 www.infosicoes.com/licitacion/empresa-nacional-de-electricidad-ende/diseno-provision-montaje-instalacion-y-puesta-en-marcha-de-aerogeneradores-para-el-proyecto-eolico-santa-cruz-parques-eolicos-de-warnes-san-julian-y-el-dorado-en-bolivia-/nacional/345253/form-400.html (accessed 28 September 2021).

73 www.infosicoes.com/licitacion/gobierno-autonomo-departamental-de-chuquisaca/construccion-del-proyecto-de-riego-itangua-cuevo/nacional/378034/form-120.html (accessed 28 September 2021).

74 *Ley del Presupuesto General del Estado 2020 (Ley 1356).*

75 www.doingbusiness.org/content/dam/doingBusiness/country/b/bolivia/BOL.pdf (accessed 8 August 2021).

76 *DS 4199 (2020)* – this decree provided some exceptions in relation to essential commercial activity, but the construction sector was not included in the exception.

The *Reglamento para el Desarrollo de Actividades Económicas del Sector de Construcción*[77] was also passed in May 2020, requiring the construction companies to provide safe working conditions to all workers involved in construction and establishing the following precautionary and safety measures:

- Social distance of at least 1.5 metres
- Compulsory use of face masks
- Regular hand washing and disinfection
- Cleaning and disinfection of the footwear
- Cleaning and disinfection of the workplace and personal objects
- Strict control of the persons who enter the worksite
- Temperature measurement of site workers and declaration of the existence of any symptom related to COVID-19

The Bolivian Government also restricted travel and closed borders (partially or fully) during the waves of the pandemic – *DS 4430 (2021)* was extended by *DS 4443 (2021)* and *DS4464 (2021)* (the entrance of European residents was restricted, with some exceptions, until 31 May 2021).

4.3.2 The impact of COVID-19 on the operation of construction contracts in Bolivia

COVID-19 significantly impacted the construction industry as the lockdowns prevented parties from complying with their contractual obligations. Luckily, the Bolivian Government didn't pass any laws or decrees governing contractual compliance in this period, thus leaving parties to negotiate the new terms or conditions freely in the context of COVID-19.

The pandemic reached Bolivia when the country was socially and politically fragile as a result of a crisis generated by the failed 2019 general election, which led the incumbent president, Evo Morales, to resign, and the macroeconomic context that had had a slowdown in economic growth since 2015.[78]

The construction sector has one of the highest percentages of informal workers in urban areas (10.8%) that were hit by the crisis generated by the pandemic. It was one of the most affected activities up to July 2020, resulting in 23% of workers being dismissed/unemployed, followed by trade and food.[79]

Even though the lockdowns prevented parties from complying with their contractual obligations, the Bolivian Government did not pass any laws or decrees governing

77 *Resolución Multiministerial 001/20 (Ministerio de Obras Públicas, Servicios y Vivienda; Ministerio de Salud; Ministerio de Trabajo) 2020.*

78 UNDP Bolivia Office, COVID-19 in Bolivia: On the path to recovering development (2020) LAC C19 PDS No 22, page 7. file:///Users/claulmont/Downloads/undp-rblac-CD19-PDS-Number22-Bolivia-EN-1.pdf (accessed 29 August 2021).

79 UNDP Bolivia Office, COVID-19 in Bolivia: On the path to recovering development (2020) LAC C19 PDS No 22, page 15. file:///Users/claulmont/Downloads/undp-rblac-CD19-PDS-Number22-Bolivia-EN-1.pdf (accessed 29 August 2021).

contractual compliance in this period, thus leaving parties to negotiate the new terms or conditions freely in the COVID-19 context.

To compensate for the income loss of households due to the lockdown, the government provided three bonuses targeting the vulnerable population, estimated to be about USD 500 million, proven to be insufficient to cover even the basic needs of the vulnerable population.[80]

The Bolivian Government made an effort to temporarily relax economic constraints and burdens, extending the terms to repay loans. Through *DS 4206*,[81] regulating *Ley 1294*,[82] there was an automatic extension of loan payments on capital and interests for the full term of the COVID-19 emergency. The benefits prescribed by this legislation were further extended through passing *DS 4248 (2020)* and *DS 4409 (2020)* focusing on allowing the credit of two years to be re-scheduled over a five-year period. As a result, in 2020, the banking system deferred USD 3,543 million in repayments. This amount represents 1.4 times the banking system's equity. In addition, the non-performing loan portfolio as of February 2021 amounted to USD 501 million, a decrease of 5% compared to 2020.[83]

During this period also a financial relief program was adopted of up to USD 216 million for loans to micro, small and middle-sized companies, for up to five years, with a grace period from six months to a year and an interest rate regulated by the *Ministerio de Economía y Finanzas*.[84, 85]

Additionally, through *DS 4198*[86] the payment of the corporate profit tax (*Impuesto a las Utilidades de las Empresas IUE*) was postponed until 31 May 2020, in addition to the option to pay it in up to three monthly instalments without interest and maintaining the debt levels. Furthermore, through *DS 4298* (2020), among other measures, the declaration and payment of the value-added tax complementary regime (*Régimen Complementario al Valor Agregado RC-IVA*) transaction tax (*Impuesto a las Transacciones IT*) were postponed as follows: (i) July and August 2020 fiscal periods, to be paid in September 2020, (ii) October and November 2020 fiscal periods to be paid in December 2020. Moreover, the *DS 4298* allowed companies to access accelerated depreciation for their fixed assets acquired between 1 April and 31 December 2020, thus the uncollectible provisions from the fiscal year 2019 were deductible from the *IUE* in the fiscal year 2020.

Finally, through *DS 4216*, in order to support labour stability, an emergency plan was enacted offering resources to companies with a valid payroll of employees to pay for their workers for a term of up to 18 months and with a six-month grace period, for an amount

80 UNDP Bolivia Office, COVID-19 in Bolivia: On the path to recovering development (2020) LAC C19 PDS No 22, page 27. file:///Users/claulmont/Downloads/undp-rblac-CD19-PDS-Number22-Bolivia-EN-1.pdf (accessed 29 August 2021).

81 *Reglamento de Diferimiento de Pagos de Créditos y Reducción Temporal del Pago de Servicios Básicos, 2020 (DS 4206).*

82 *Ley excepcional de diferimiento de pagos de créditos y reducción temporal del pago de servicios básicos 2020 (Ley 1294).*

83 www.lostiempos.com/actualidad/economia/20210426/creditos-reprogramados-suben-64-afectan-flujos-banca (accessed 8 August 2021).

84 *Programa Especial de Apoyo a la Micro, Pequeña y Mediana Empresa, y el Plan de Emergencia de Apoyo al Empleo y Estabilidad Laboral a las empresas legalmente constituidas 2020 (DS 4216).*

85 UNDP Bolivia Office, COVID-19 in Bolivia: On the path to recovering development (2020) LAC C19 PDS No 22, page 27. file:///Users/claulmont/Downloads/undp-rblac-CD19-PDS-Number22-Bolivia-EN-1.pdf (accessed 29 August 2021).

86 *Diferimiento y facilidades de pago del impuesto sobre las utilidades de las empresas 2020 (DS 4198).*

equal to two national minimum salaries per worker per month up to a maximum of two months.

The judicial system was among those hit the hardest by COVID-19. During March and April 2020, all courts in the country were closed. In May 2020, the Judicial Council passed a resolution establishing restrictions for court operations based on the COVID-19 risk in each district.[87]

Vis-à-vis legal proceedings in the area of corporate and commercial law, the *Ministerio de Desarrollo Productivo* passed *Ministerial Resolutions*[88, 89] that suspended administrative, penalty and other procedures concerning commercial entities. Further, the *Ministerio de Desarrollo Productivo* passed a *Ministerial Resolution*[90] allowing a time extension for the payment of commercial obligations in order to ease the financial burden for commercial entities.

4.4 Bolivian governing law of the contract

4.4.1 Constraints on the governing law of a construction contract

In Bolivia, under Art 454 of the *Código Civil 1975*, parties can freely define the content and type of the contracts they enter, with the only exception being an interest worthy of legal protection (there is no legal definition or case law for kind of interest).

The specific provisions regarding construction contracts are established in Chapter V, Articles 732 to 749:

- The Contractor may not subcontract the performance of the work if it has not been authorised by the contracting party (the Employer)[91]
- If the exercise of an activity requires a professional title, and the service was provided without fulfilling that requirement, it is not possible to demand any remuneration[92]
- The Contractor cannot change the scope of a project if the Employer has not authorised it in writing and has not agreed to modify the remuneration. The Employer may arrange for Variations, provided the amount does not exceed one-fifth of the total agreed payment. In this case, the Contractor is entitled to a proportional increase in the payment[93]
- The Employer has the right to control the work, at its own expense, or to carry out the work. When the Employer verifies that work was not executed in accordance with the agreement or the rules of the construction, it can demand the Contractor

87 *Circular PRES-06/2020. Órgano Judicial de Bolivia, Consejo de la Magistratura, 2020.*

88 *Resolución Ministerial MDPyEP/DESPACHO/N°060-2020 (2020) – Ministerio de Desarrollo Productivo.*

89 *Resolución Ministerial MDPyEP/DESPACHO/N°244.2020 (2020) – Ministerio de Desarrollo Productivo.*

90 *Resolución Ministerial MDyEP/DESPACHO/N°0173.2020 (2020) – Ministerio de Desarrollo Productivo.*

91 *Código Civil 1975* Art 733.

92 *Código Civil 1975* Art 735.

93 *Código Civil 1975* Art 737.

to rectify the work, and if this is not done, the Employer can request the resolution of the contract and claim damages[94]

- If the increases or decreases in the value of materials or workforce are greater than one-tenth of the total agreed contract price and derive from unforeseen circumstances, then the agreed contract price can be adjusted for difference exceeding one-tenth[95]
- When a project suffers from defects or does not meet the required quality standards, the Contractor must, at its own expense, rectify defects and compensate for the damages.[96] Latent defects are subject to a time limit of six months for identification and notification to the Contractor
- Those who have provided materials for the execution of the work or have contributed their activity as dependents of the Contractor may take direct action against the Employer to recover owed amounts[97]
- If, for reasons not attributable to either party, the work perishes or deteriorates, then the loss is borne by the party that provided the material[98]

4.4.2 Formal requirements for a construction contract

When the contract is signed between private entities there are no formal requirements, the contract is the law between the parties as long as it does not go against Bolivian laws or public order.[99] In the case that the parties wish to enhance the legal enforceability of the contractual obligations, the contract can be authenticated by the Notaries Public.

In the case of a contract with the State or State-owned entities, the formal requirements for signature and protocols are defined in *DS 181*.[100] Electronic contracts, electronic signatures and digital signatures are recognised and regulated by the *Ley General de Telecomunicaciones, Tecnologías de Información y Comunicación*, 2011. Additionally, *DS 3946 (2019)* establishes the implementation of acceptance of digital signatures in the Notaries Public.

4.5 What Special Provisions in the Particular Conditions are necessary for consistency with applicable laws in Bolivia?

4.5.1 FIDIC General Conditions are incompatible or inconsistent with Bolivian governing law of the contract

The following are potential issues which may require Special Provisions for consistency with Bolivian governing law of the contract.

94 *Código Civil 1975* Art 738.
95 *Código Civil 1975* Art 740.
96 *Código Civil 1975* Art 741 and 742.
97 *Código Civil 1975* Art 748.
98 *Código Civil 1975* Art 745.
99 *Código Civil 1975* Art 454.
100 *DS 181 (2009)* Art 88.

4.5.1.1 Illegality/unenforceability of certain contractual terms

A contract shall be deemed to be ineffective if the contract exonerates or limits the non-performing party in their duty to compensate for the damage due to deceit or gross fault or an act that violates obligations established by rules of public order.[101]

4.5.1.2 Allocation of ground risk

Latent defects are subject to a time limit of six months for identification and notification to the Contractor.

If the defects are known or recognisable and the Employer receives the work, the Contractor is not responsible for such defects; however, the Contractor is liable for latent defects.[102]

If the execution of the work has been made impossible for a cause not attributable to either party, the Employer must pay the Contractor for the part of the work carried out in proportion to the total agreed contract price and within the limits in which the work is useful to the Employer.[103]

4.5.1.3 Burdensome obligations on the Contractor in the EPC Silver Book

When the Contractor does not comply with the obligations assumed in the contract, the Contractor must compensate for the damages.[104]

As noted in section 4.4.1, if for reasons not attributable to either party, the work perishes or deteriorates, then the loss is borne by the party that provided the material.[105]

4.5.1.4 Principles relating to a lump sum contract

Provisions relating to contracts with State or State-owned entities are discussed in section 4.2.10. Other provisions relevant to lump sum contracts are discussed in the third, fourth and fifth bullet points in section 4.4.1.

4.5.1.5 Proving entitlements to extension of time

In the case of temporary impossibility, the Contractor is not liable for the delay in contractual performance[106] as long as the pending obligations that are possible to fulfil are completed.[107]

4.5.1.6 Payment for Variations

The Contractor cannot change the scope of a project if the Employer has not authorised it in writing and has not agreed to modify the remuneration. The Employer may arrange for Variations, provided the amount does not exceed one-fifth of the total agreed payment. In this case, the Contractor is entitled to a proportional increase in the payment.[108]

---

101 *Código Civil 1975* Art 350.
102 *Código Civil 1975* Art 742.
103 *Código Civil 1975* Art 744.
104 *Código Civil 1975* Art 399.
105 *Código Civil 1975* Art 745.
106 *Código Civil 1975* Art 380.
107 *Código Civil 1975* Art 382.
108 *Código Civil 1975* Art 737.

4.5.1.7 Termination

If one party to the contract voluntarily fails to comply with its contractual obligations, the other party that has complied with its contractual obligations may judicially request compliance or termination of the contract plus compensation for damage.[109]

When a contract includes an arbitration clause, the appointed arbitrators can apply Art 568 *Código Civil* to replace a judge. Arbitration as a method of legal dispute resolution enables the arbitrator to dictate the remedy (Art 40 of *Ley 708*).

The Constitutional Court has considered this point in some cases, specifically whether when the text of the article indicates 'judicially' it means that only a judge can make an order; however, it was in relation to the declaration of nullity of the contract.[110] There is no precedent that refers to the impossibility for the arbitrator to decide on the fulfilment or termination of the contract, therefore, the arbitrators in Bolivia usually resolve cases through the application of Art 40 of *Ley 708*.

The parties may expressly agree that the contract will be terminated if a certain obligation is not fulfilled.[111]

4.5.1.8 Force majeure

In the *Código Civil 1975*, there are no specific provisions in relation to *force majeure*; however, there is the doctrine of unforeseeability of events.

If a party to a contract is released from the performance of its obligations due to supervening impossibility, it cannot claim compensation from the other party.[112]

The same also applies when the performance of the contract becomes partially impossible unless the party in compliance gives consent for partial compliance; in such case the parties can agree to a proportional reduction in the contract price.[113]

4.5.2 FIDIC General Conditions are incompatible or inconsistent with the law of the Site/Country

The following sub-clauses refer to Laws in the FIDIC 2017 Yellow Book that may require additional explanation in the context of contracts with a State or State-owned entity.

4.5.2.1 Health and safety (sub-clause 4.8)

If the contract is with a State or State-owned entity, this clause might be modified as the State entity might require that the health and safety manual be provided within a shorter period from the commencement date. The reporting and recording of accidents shall be in accordance with applicable laws and health and safety regulations.

109 *Código Civil 1975* Art 568.

110 *Sentencia Constitucional* 17/2001 of 19 March, which established that an arbitrator can declare nullity of a contract and the subsequent *Sentencia Constitucional Plurinacional* 2471/2012 of 22 November, settled that an arbitrator cannot declare nullity of a contract on grounds of public order.

111 *Código Civil 1975* Art 569.

112 *Código Civil 1975* Art 577.

113 *Código Civil 1975* Art 578.

4.5.2.2 Environment (sub-clauses 4.18, 5.4)
The Contractor shall comply with the specific regulations applicable to the management of dangerous substances and obtain all corresponding licenses and permits.

4.5.2.3 Subcontractors (sub-clause 4.4)
In contracts with the State or State-owned entities, the sub-contracting could be limited to a certain percentage of the total value of the contract.

4.5.2.4 Design (sub-clauses 5.1, 5.2, 5.3)
State or State-owned entities might require that the qualification documentation for engineers and other professionals be provided with legalised translation if they are qualified in a non-Spanish speaking jurisdiction.

4.5.2.5 Ownership of Plant and Materials (sub-clause 7.7)
State or State-owned entities might modify this clause to extend their ownership and control.

4.5.2.6 Employer's sale of Contractor's Equipment, surplus material, wreckage and Temporary Works (sub-clause 11.11)
Depending on the location of the Site, very stringent conditions might be imposed concerning reinstating all parts of the Site not occupied by the Permanent Works to the original state.

4.5.2.7 Bankruptcy, insolvency, liquidation (sub-clauses 15.2, 16.2)
In relation to termination, particular care should be exercised when entering into a contractual relationship with a State or State-owned entity. The general position in Bolivia based on the provisions of the *Ley de Administración y Control Gubernamentales, 1990*[114] is that in the case of a person or legal entity causing monetary damage to the State, this act of damage will be referred by the affected entity to the corresponding legal entity which in turn will directly seek a judgment in respect to the damage. In relation to certain types of Notices, State or State-owned entities might require that these notices be notarised – with recognised notarisation being one in Bolivia only.

4.5.2.8 Insurance (sub-clause 19.2)
The insurance shall be in the name of the Contractor only. Refer also to section 4.2.9.

4.5.3 FIDIC General Conditions are incompatible or inconsistent with the relevant laws on dispute determination in Bolivia

4.5.3.1 Mandating the way in which a court or tribunal is to settle disputes or determine contractual rights
Art 4 of the *Ley de Conciliación y Arbitraje*[115] excludes administrative contracts from conciliation and arbitration, except as provided by law and discussed in section 4.2.8.

114 *Ley 1178* Art 47.
115 *Ley 708*.

Administrative construction contracts that have external financing and contracts with companies with a majority State share may incorporate clauses in relation to dispute resolution through conciliation or arbitration, subject to the following conditions: (1) dispute resolution must take place in Bolivia, (2) dispute resolution must be subject to Bolivian regulations and (3) the arbitration will be according to law. This dispute resolution exception applies only to contracts signed with types of companies that will migrate to the legal regime of *Law No. 466* of 26 December 2013[116] (refer to section 4.2.8).

4.5.3.2 Disputes relating to non-contractual claims may not be arbitrable
In the case of a malicious or negligent act the redress of the damage shall be by means of courts and is not subject to arbitration.

Jurisprudence in Bolivia establishes civil liability as the obligation to compensate and repair, as far as possible, the damage caused.[117]

4.6 What Special Provisions in the Particular Conditions are desirable for consistency with applicable laws in Bolivia?

4.6.1 Outsourcing

Although it is covered by sub-clauses 6.2 and 6.4 of the FIDIC GCs, it is important to highlight that any company that requires to contract another in activities that are not its own or part of the permanent work establishment must necessarily include in the contract a clause that establishes that the contracted company will comply with the socio-labour obligations regarding its workers.[118]

4.6.2 Archeological discovery

The Contractor shall comply with the specific regulations and notification procedures applicable in the case of an archaeological discovery at the construction site. They must carry out studies of Archaeological Diagnosis, Archaeological Rescue, Archaeological Monitoring and Preventive Conservation, in all stages of the project, having to hire specialists in archaeology to carry out such activities.[119]

4.6.3 Penalty clause

When the parties include a penalty clause in the contract which has been breached during the performance of the contract, the total penalty cannot exceed the total contract price.[120]

116 *Artículo Transitorio 4.*

117 *Auto Supremo: AS 472/2017 09 May 2017. Tribunal Supremo de Justicia.* https://tsj.bo/wp-content/uploads/2019/11/revista-de-jurisprudencia-nro-8-2017.pdf (accessed 23 August 2021).

118 *DS 521 (2010)* Art 3.

119 *Reglamento de Autorizaciones para Actividades Arqueológicas, Resolución Ministerial N° 349/2012 (2012)* Art 4.

120 *Código de Comercio de Bolivia 1977* Art 801.

4.6.4 Applicable law

Contracts signed outside of Bolivia and to be executed in Bolivia are governed by Bolivian law.[121]

This rule applies in the case that the parties have not exercised their right of autonomy and defined the governing law.

4.6.5 Good faith

The Contract must be executed in good faith and parties are subject not only to the contract conditions but also to all the effects that are derived in accordance with the nature of the contract, applicable laws or customs and equity principles.[122]

4.6.6 Implying terms in all contracts of a particular type

When a contractual clause is susceptible to different meanings, the interpretation must be the one that can produce a tangible effect.[123]

The contract has force of law between the parties and cannot be dissolved except by mutual consent or for causes authorised by law.[124]

The clauses of the contract provided by one of the contracting parties are interpreted, in case of doubt, in favour of the other party[125] (*contra proferentum*).

The signature on a contract implies that the parties do it for themselves unless otherwise agreed in the contract or prescribed by the nature of the contract.[126]

4.6.7 Delay damages/penalties

If a penalty clause has been stipulated for the case of non-compliance or delay in the execution of a contract, the contractual penalty replaces the judicial compensation for damage that would have been awarded for the delay or the non-compliance.[127]

It is not possible to demand at the same time the fulfilment of the contractual obligations and the contractual penalty.[128]

4.6.8 Limitation period for liability

The limitation period for contractual liability is five years unless applicable law provides differently.[129]

Non-contractual liability is three years unless it concerns a criminal offence.[130]

---

121 *Código de Comercio de Bolivia 1977* Art 804.
122 *Código Civil 1975* Art 520.
123 *Código Civil 1975* Art 511.
124 *Código Civil 1975* Art 519.
125 *Código Civil 1975* Art 518.
126 *Código Civil 1975* Art 524.
127 *Código Civil 1975* Art 532.
128 *Código Civil 1975* Art 533.
129 *Código Civil 1975* Art 1507.
130 *Código Civil 1975* Art 1508.

4.7 Summary of applicable legislation for Bolivia governing law of the contract

4.7.1 Entry into a construction contract

Contracts generally	*Código Civil 1975* Art 450 and Art 451
Construction contracts	*Código Civil 1975* Art 732 to Art 749

4.7.2 Operation of a construction contract

Force majeure	*Código Civil 1975* Arts 380, 382, 577, 578
Hardship	*Código de Comercio 1977* Art 802 *Código Civil 1975* Art 581
Guarantees under forms of Security (Tender Security, Demand Guarantee, Surety Bond, Advance Payment Guarantee, Retention Money Guarantee, Payment Guarantee by Employer)	*Código de Comercio 1977* Arts 806, 810, 1447 *Norma Básica del Sistema de Administración de Bienes y Servicios 2009 (DS 181)* Art 20

4.7.3 Termination of a construction contract

Frustration	*Código Civil 1975* Arts 380, 382, 577, 578
Bankruptcy, insolvency, liquidation	*Código de Comercio 1977* Arts 1509, 1513, 1593

4.7.4 Dispute resolution

Limitation periods	*Código Procesal Civil 2013* *Código Civil 1975*
Liability	*Código Procesal Civil 2013* *Código Civil 1975*
Adjudication	*Código Procesal Civil 2013* *Código Civil 1975*
Arbitration	*Ley de Conciliación y Arbitraje 2015* (as modified by *Ley 936 [2017]*)

4.8 Summary of applicable legislation if the Site/Country is in Bolivia

4.8.1 Operation of a construction contract

Registration and administration of professionals – Engineers, Architects, HSE professionals	*Ley del Ejercicio Profesional de la Ingeniería 1993* *Ley del Ejercicio Profesional del Arquitecto 1992* *RM 595/16 (Ministerio de Trabajo) Aprobación del Reglamento de Registro Nacional de Profesionales y Técnicos en Higiene, Seguridad Ocupacional y Medicina del Trabajo*

Registration/licencing of Contractors and subcontractors	*Código de Comercio 1977* *Código Tributario 1992* *Reglamento para actividades con sustancias peligrosas 1995 (DS 24176)* *Ley del Medio Ambiente 1992* *Tramitación de la licencia ambiental 2011 (DS 902)* *RM 105/18 (Ministerio de Trabajo) Registro Obligatorio de Empleadores – ROE*
Use of liens/Assignment of debts	*Código Civil 1975* Art 391 *Código de Comercio 1977* Arts 818, 820
Labour	*Ley General del Trabajo 1942* *Reglamento de la Ley General del Trabajo (DS 224) 1943* *Código Civil 1975* Art 992
Design/Moral rights	*Reglamento para diseño, construcción, operación y abandono de ductos en Bolivia 1997 (DS24721)* *Reglamento para la Construcción y Operación de Refinerías, Plantas, Petroquímicas y Unidades de Proceso 1999 (DS 25502)*
Copyright	*Ley de Derecho de Autor 1992* *Reglamento de la Ley de Derecho de Autor 1994 (DS 23907)*
The product being produced from the Works	*Código Civil 1975*
First Nation people's land rights	*DS 29033 (2007)* *DS 29124 (2007)* *DS 2195 (2014)* *DS 2298 (2015)*
Planning	*Ley del Sistema de Planificación Integral del Estado de Bolivia 2016*
Work affecting adjacent property to the Site	*Código Civil 1975* Art 998
Heritage	*Código de Comercio 1977* Art 1585
Environment	*Ley del Medio Ambiente 1992* *Ley Forestal 1996* *Ley de gestión integral de residuos 2015* *Reglamento del saneamiento del medio ambiente 1982 (DS 18886)* *Reglamento general de gestión Ambiental 1995 (DS 24176)* *Protección de Fauna Silvestre 2021 (DS 4489)*
Public procurement	*Los preceptos y el contenido mínimo de los Contratos de Alianzas Estratégicas de Inversión Conjunta 2018 (DS 3469)* *Norma Básica del Sistema de Administración de Bienes y Servicios 2009 (DS 181)* *Subasta Electrónica y Mercado Virtual Estatal 2021 (DS 4453)*

(*Continued*)

(Continued)

Building and construction permits, execution of construction work, standard of construction work	*Código Civil 1975* *RM 186/14 (Ministerio de Obras Publicas) Guía Boliviana de Construcción de Edificaciones*
Health and safety	*Ley General de Higiene, Seguridad Ocupacional y Bienestar 1979* *Código de Salud 1978* *Convenio sobre seguridad y salud en la construcción 2014* *Reglamento de higiene, seguridad y medicina del trabajo 1982 (DS18886)* *RM 388/17 (Ministerio de Medioambiente) Aprobación de las normas técnicas de seguridad en la construcción*
Ownership of Plant and Materials	*Código Civil 1975*
Employer's sale of Contractor's Equipment, surplus material, wreckage and Temporary Works	*Código Civil 1975* *Código de Comercio 1977*
Insurance	*Código de Comercio 1977* *Ley de Seguros 1998* (as modified by *Ley 2064 [2000], Ley 65 [2010], Ley 365 [2013], Ley 455 [2013], Ley 737 [2015]* and *Ley 856 [2016]*) *Ley de Seguro Obligatorio de Accidentes de la Trabajadora y el Trabajador en el Ámbito de la Construcción 2019*
Statutory rights that coexist with contractual rights	*Código de Comercio 1977*
Liability for defective work	*Código Civil 1975*
Liability for nuisance	*Código Civil 1975*

4.8.2 Termination of a construction contract

Bankruptcy, insolvency, liquidation	*Código de Comercio 1977*
Decennial liability and liability generally for the total or partial collapse of structures	*Código Civil 1975*

4.8.3 Dispute resolution

Dispute before a local board/Adjudication	*Código Procesal Civil 2013*
Limitation periods	*Código Civil 1975*

4.9 Summary of applicable legislation if the 'seat' of the dispute determination is Bolivia

Dispute resolution	*Código Procesal Civil 2013* *Código Civil 1975*
Limitation periods	*Código Procesal Civil 2013* *Código Civil 1975*
Adjudication	*Código Procesal Civil 2013* *Código Civil 1975*
Arbitration	*Ley de Conciliación y Arbitraje 2015* (modified by *Ley 936 [2017]*)

4.10 Additional references for Bolivia

4.10.1 Books

Carlos Morales Guillen, *Código Civil Concordado y Anotado* (4th edn, CMG, last printed version 2004) *Tomo II, Parte II De las Fuentes de las Obligaciones, De los Contratos en General*

Carlos Morales Guillen, *Código de Comercio Concordado y Anotado* (1st edn, CMG, 1999) *Libro Tercero, De los Contratos y Obligaciones Comerciales*

4.10.2 Internet

4.10.2.1 Online publications

La cláusula de Fuerza Mayor y su aplicación en el contexto de la pandemia de Covid-19 [The *force majeure* clause and its application in the context of the COVID-19 pandemic] www.lostiempos.com/actualidad/opinion/20200416/columna/clausula-fuerza-mayor-su-aplicacion-contexto-pandemia-covid-19

4.10.2.2 Legislation

National Laws and Decrees www.gacetaoficialdebolivia.gob.bo

4.10.2.3 Court decisions

Jurisprudence https://jurisprudencia.tsj.bo/jurisprudencia

Constitutional jurisprudence https://jurisprudenciaconstitucional.com

AS 180/2012. July 2016. Tribunal Supremo de Justicia [Arbitration clause does not apply to those who are not part of the Contract] blob:https://jurisprudencia.tsj.bo/bf2f83a0-ffce-cf4d-b17f-645e6ec7c66f

AS 0287/2013. June 2013. Tribunal Supremo de Justicia I [Arbitration exception] blob:https://jurisprudencia.tsj.bo/400baafb-2ae1-d742-9040-74a7877eef20

AS505/2014. September 2014. Tribunal Supremo de Justicia [Ambiguous clauses interpretation] blob:https://jurisprudencia.tsj.bo/af1303eb-a45b-3548-b7c2-33620D204358

Circular N° 01/2019 Sala Plena – TSJ/OJ Uniformización de criterios procedimentales para la tramitación de procesos contenciosos y contenciosos administrativos. Tribunal Supremo de Justicia [Standardization of procedural criteria for the processing of contentious and contentious administrative processes. Supreme justice court] https://tsj.bo/wp-content/uploads/2019/CIRCULAR-001-2019.pdf

4.10.3 Websites for the Ministries and other government entities

Ministerio de Obras Públicas, Servicios y Vivienda www.oopp.gob.bo
La Dirección General de Sustancias Controladas www.dgsc.gob.bo/
Ministerio de Medio Ambiente y Agua www.mmaya.gob.bo
Ministerio de Hidrocarburos y Energías www.mhe.gob.bo/
Ministerio de Trabajo, Empleo y Previsión Social www.mintrabajo.gob.bo
Directorio de la Administradora Boliviana de Carreteras www.abc.gob.bo
Ministerio de Desarrollo Rural y Tierras www.ruralytierras.gob.bo/
Ministerio de Desarrollo Productivo y Economía Plural https://produccion.gob.bo

CHAPTER 5

Applying FIDIC Contracts in Brazil

Thiago Fernandes Moreira and Caio Gabra

CONTENTS

5.1	Outline of Brazil's legal environment	107
	5.1.1 Constitutional structure of Brazil	107
	5.1.2 The legal system in Brazil	107
	5.1.3 The court system in Brazil	107
5.2	The construction industry in Brazil	108
	5.2.1 Overview	108
	5.2.2 Structure	108
	5.2.3 Licensing/registration	109
	5.2.4 Labour relations	110
	5.2.5 Safety culture	110
	5.2.6 Modular construction using factory-fabricated components	111
	5.2.7 Technology/innovation/BIM	112
	5.2.8 Government procurement	112
	5.2.10 Common forms of contract	114
	5.2.11 Dispute resolution	114
	5.2.12 Current challenges	115
	5.2.13 Unique features of the construction industry in Brazil	115
	5.2.13.1 Language barriers	115
	5.2.13.2 Infrastructure	116
5.3	The impact of COVID-19 in Brazil	116
	5.3.1 The impact of COVID-19 on the execution of construction projects in Brazil	116
	5.3.2 The impact of COVID-19 on the operation of construction contracts in Brazil	117
	5.3.2.1 Force majeure and exemption of liability	117
	5.3.2.2 Cost impacts	117
	5.3.2.3 Change of law	118
	5.3.2.4 Contracts executed after the beginning of the COVID-19 pandemic	118
	5.3.2.5 Statutes of limitation and prescription periods	119
	5.3.2.6 Corporate governance	119

DOI: 10.4324/9781003201250-5

5.4 Brazilian governing law of the contract 119
5.4.1 Constraints on the governing law of a construction contract 119
5.4.2 Formal requirements for a construction contract 120
5.5 What Special Provisions in the Particular Conditions are necessary for consistency with applicable laws in Brazil? 120
5.5.1 FIDIC General Conditions are incompatible or inconsistent with Brazilian governing law of the contract 120
5.5.1.1 Indirect damages 120
5.5.1.2 Notice of Claim 120
5.5.2 FIDIC General Conditions are incompatible or inconsistent with the law of the Site/Country 121
5.5.2.1 Defect Notice Period 121
5.5.3 FIDIC General Conditions are incompatible or inconsistent with the laws on dispute determination in Brazil 121
5.5.3.1 The Engineer 121
5.5.3.2 Dispute Adjudication Boards 122
5.6 What Special Provisions in the Particular Conditions are desirable for consistency with applicable laws in Brazil? 122
5.6.1 Gross negligence 122
5.6.2 Loss of profits 123
5.6.3 Compliance with laws – Brazilian Association of Technical Regulation 123
5.7 Summary of applicable legislation for Brazilian governing law of the contract 123
5.7.1 Entry into a construction contract 123
5.7.2 Termination of a construction contract 124
5.7.3 Dispute resolution 124
5.8 Summary of applicable legislation if the Site/Country is in Brazil 124
5.8.1 Operation of a construction contract 124
5.8.2 Termination of a construction contract 125
5.8.3 Dispute resolution 126
5.9 Summary of applicable legislation if the 'seat' of the dispute determination is in Brazil 126
5.10 Issues that a court or arbitrator may construe differently from that expected from the words of the Contract because of local law or custom 126
5.10.1 Deemed acceptance of Variations 126
5.10.2 Termination for reorganisation 127
5.10.3 Hardship 127
5.11 Additional references for Brazil 128
5.11.1 Books 128
5.11.2 Legislation 128
5.11.3 Case law 128

5.1 Outline of Brazil's legal environment

5.1.1 Constitutional structure of Brazil

The country is organised as a federative republic formed by the indissoluble union of the States and municipalities and of the Federal District. Under the principles established in the *Federal Constitution*, Brazil's 26 Federative States have powers to adopt their own organic constitutions and laws.

Municipalities also enjoy restricted autonomy as their legislation must follow the dictates of the *State Constitutions* where they are located and, consequently, those of the *Federal Constitution* itself. As for the Federal District, it blends functions of Federative States and of municipalities, and its equivalent to a constitution, named *Organic Law*, must obey the terms of the *Federal Constitution*.

The Brazilian *Constitution* provides for a structure of checks and balances between the three branches of government: executive, legislative and judicial.

The head of the executive branch is the President of the Republic, who is both the chief of state and the head of government and is directly elected by the citizens.

The legislative branch, embedded in the form of the National Congress, consists of two houses or chambers: the Chamber of Congressmen and the Federal Senate; the members of both chambers are representatives directly elected by the citizens.

5.1.2 The legal system in Brazil

Brazil adopts a civil law system, based on the Roman-Germanic tradition. Although customs and case law are part of the legal framework, statutes remain the primary source of law and prevail over secondary sources. In that sense, Article 4 of *Federal law No. 4,657/1942* (*Decree of Introduction to Brazilian Law*) determines that a judge may only resort to analogy, customs and general principles of law where the letter of the law itself is silent on a respective matter.[1]

With regard to legal principles, the principle of good faith has gained significant strength since the enactment of Brazil's latest *Constitution* in 1988. As discussed later, the principle of good faith is often used to adapt the law, the Contract and the will of the parties to the circumstances of the case, being of ultimate relevance to the outcome of construction disputes in Brazil.

5.1.3 The court system in Brazil

The judicial system structure comprises the Federal Supreme Court; the Superior Court of Justice; the regional Federal and State Courts; and federal and state judges. There are also specialised courts to deal with electoral, labour and military disputes.

There are five constitutional divisions of competence for the Brazilian Judiciary:

- i Federal jurisdiction, competent to adjudicate civil and criminal matters directly or indirectly related to the Federal Government
- ii Labour jurisdiction, competent to adjudicate disputes concerning labour relations

1 *Federal law No. 4,657/1942*, Article 4. When the law is silent, the judge shall decide the case on the basis of analogy, customs and general principles of law.

iii Electoral jurisdiction, competent to adjudicate electoral litigation
iv Military jurisdiction, competent to adjudicate federal military crimes, and
v State jurisdiction, competent to adjudicate all other civil and criminal disputes

Generally, each case is decided by a single judge – there is a jury only in cases concerning crimes against human life – and, as a rule, it is possible to appeal to a State or District Court against this kind of decision. Moreover, every branch of competence – ordinary (meaning both federal and state jurisdictions), labour, electoral and military branches – has a superior court responsible for harmonising the interpretation of the law (Superior Court of Justice, Superior Labour Court, Superior Electoral Court and Superior Military Court).

Each State territory is divided into judicial districts named *comarcas*, which are composed of one or more Municipalities. The 27 courts of justice have their headquarters in the capital of each State and have jurisdiction only over their respective State territories.

There are two national Superior Courts, which rule on both civil and criminal cases: the Superior Court of Justice, also known as STJ, which rules on offences to non-constitutional legal provisions, and the Supreme Federal Court, known as STF, the highest Brazilian court, which is, as a rule, in charge of deciding issues concerning offences to the Brazilian *Constitution*.

5.2 The construction industry in Brazil

5.2.1 Overview

Brazil and its construction market have been facing a very turbulent political and economic situation since the beginning of 2015. This is mainly due to the *operação lava-jato* (car wash investigation), in which political leaders and businesses have been investigated for tax evasion, bribery and misuse of public funds. Brazil's major construction companies have been at the centre of these investigations and have suffered from a lack of credit and opportunities.

Due to the decrease in public financing for infrastructure projects, the government created the *Programa de Parcerias de Investimentos* (Programme of Investment Partnerships) (**PPI**) to increase the contribution of private capital to infrastructure projects in Brazil. The purpose of the PPI is to expand and strengthen the relationship between the State and the private sector through partnership contracts (including concessions, public–private partnerships, permissions or leasing of public assets and other public–private arrangements with similar legal structures).

Due to the deterioration of major construction companies involved in the car wash investigation, there has been an increase in the activity of medium-sized construction companies and foreign players in the construction market, especially in the concession of highways, airports and transmission lines throughout the country.

5.2.2 Structure

As discussed in section 5.2.1, the split of market share, size and structure of contractors has changed widely over the last decade. In the past, large national contractors also acted as concessionaires for infrastructure projects. They would then contract the scope of construction of the assets within the corporate group.

After the car wash investigation, many of these companies have been unable to secure stable financing for large projects and/or were unsuitable to contract with public entities due to anti-corruption sanctions. Because of that, international contractors have gained space both as concessionaires of public services and as main contractors of large and mid-sized projects.

In turn, international contractors and technology providers subcontract or work together with mid-sized Brazilian contractors.

In terms of the extent of subcontracting, it is worth mentioning that Brazil is a country of continental dimensions and, as such, multi-layered subcontracting structures are usually necessary for projects in less central areas in order to enable the supply of materials and manpower.

5.2.3 Licensing/registration

Professional licensing of engineering and construction works and services is mainly regulated by *Law No. 5,194 of 24 December 1966*, which regulates the professions related to engineering, architecture and agronomy, and provides for the requirement of registration with the *Conselho Regional de Engenharia, Arquitetura e Agronomia* (Regional Council of Engineering, Architecture and Agronomy) (**CREA**) for professionals who handle the performance of activities such as (i) management of natural resources; (ii) construction works, installations and access routes; and (iii) industrial or rural developments.

Resolution No. 1,121 of 19 December 2019 of CREA further details the procedure and requirements for the registration and clearance of individuals and legal entities for developing construction and engineering activities.

Resolution No. 1,025 of 30 October 2009 issued by CREA requires that any engineering, architecture or agronomy activity is signed by a responsible professional through a Technical Responsibility Annotation (**ART**). The ART records the authorship of the works and assigns liability to the responsible professional(s).

Law No. 12,378 of 31 December 2010 segregated the oversight of architecture and created the Regional Councils for Architecture and Urbanism (**CAU**). CAU has a similar structure and regulation to CREA but is related to architects and architecture services instead of engineering, including registration requirements for companies and professionals and ART requirements.

Registration and ARTs for design, supervision and testing activities in relation to construction works are subject to the same rules and standards as construction works.

The request registration of companies will be assessed by CREA based on the academic or educational qualifications of its professionals and their capacity to handle the fields of knowledge that are deemed necessary for the company's activities.[2]

Without the applicable registrations, professionals may suffer sanctions, both of a civil and criminal nature. Furthermore, without the applicable registration of the responsible

2 *Regional Councils of Engineering and Agronomy/Architecture's Resolution No. 1,125 of 19 December 2019*, Article 11. The competent specialised chamber will only grant the registration to the legal entity in the fullness of its social objectives when it has in its technical staff professionals with capabilities consistent with those objectives.

engineers, it is not possible to obtain or maintain the necessary construction and environmental permits required for the development of the project. This may cause delays and impacts on the schedule and budget.[3]

Engineering Councils do not authorise or grant permits to specific projects, but merely register and authorise an individual or legal entity to perform a certain scope of activities based on their technical capacity and the general description of the activities intended, and do not examine the technical feasibility of the project itself. The authorisations and permits required for the development of specific projects must be granted by the applicable Municipality, environmental authorities and other regulatory authorities, depending on the type of project.

Foreign entities may apply for registration if they are certified in Brazil and have a Brazilian-qualified responsible engineer. Foreign engineers may apply for registration by CREA and therefore become Brazilian-qualified if they have their diplomas validated in Brazil.

5.2.4 Labour relations

Brazilian labour relations are relatively complex. As explained in section 5.1.3, Brazil relies on specific courts to rule on labour relations. That is because labour law relies on several layers of rules.

First, several key labour rights are already set forth in Article 7 of the *Brazilian Constitution*, such as the right to go on strike, maximum working hours per day and per week, duration of maternity leaves, paid vacations and many others.

Below the *Federal Constitution*, labour relationships are mostly subject to *Decree 5,452*, issued on 1 May 1943 (*Consolidated Labor Laws*). However, union agreements and collective agreements have a major weight in the governing of labour relationships and often overrule the *Consolidated Labor Laws*. In that regard, construction and industrial labour unions are known to be particularly strong and politically influential, especially in certain regions of the country.

5.2.5 Safety culture

In Brazil, health and safety are among the main concerns in a construction contract and are extensively regulated by labour laws and executive regulations, which include the following:

- The *Federal Constitution*, which establishes employees' rights and includes, among others, the reduction of risks inherent to works through compliance with health, hygiene and safety rules
- The *Consolidação das Leis Trabalhistas* (*Consolidation of Labour Laws*) (*Labour Code*)

3 *Law No. 5,194 of 24 December 1966*, Article 6. Article 6 defines someone who illegally exercises the profession of engineer, architect or agronomist: 'a) the individual or legal entity that performs acts or provides public or private services reserved to the professionals referred to in this law and who does not have registration with the Regional Councils'.

- Administrative rulings (e.g. *Portaria No. 3,214, de 8 de Junho de 1978* (*Ordinance No. 3,214 of 8 June 1978* of the Ministry of Labour and Employment)
- Rules and standards issued by the Brazilian Standards Association, and
- International Labour Organization conventions

Furthermore, according to Normative Resolution No. 7 from the Ministry of Labor and Employment at each company, at least one staff member for each group of employees must be trained in providing first aid in case of emergencies.

The Ministry of Labour and Employment enacted the Normative Resolutions through *Ordinance No. 3,214 of 8 June 1978* regarding health and safety norms, which established rules that must be complied with by employers and employees. The key provisions are as follows:

- Prior Inspection (*Inspeção Prévia*): A company must request an inspection by the Ministry of Labour and Employment before starting its activities[4]
- Specialised Work Safety and Medicine Services (*Serviços Especializados em Engenharia de Segurança e em Medicina do Trabalho*) (**SESMET**): Companies hiring more than 50 employees must have SESMET, aiming to promote the protection of health and safety in the workplace. The size of SESMET will vary in accordance with the risk of a company's business (established by law) and the number of employees[5]
- Accident Prevention Commission (*Comissão Interna de Prevenção de Acidentes*) (**CIPA**): Companies hiring more than 20 employees must have a CIPA, aiming to prevent occupational accidents or diseases. The size of a CIPA will vary in accordance with the number of employees[6]
- *Personal Protective Equipment* (*Equipamentos de Proteção Individual*) (**EPI**): The employer must provide its employees with EPI, aiming to neutralise or reduce their exposure to chemical, physical, and biological agents[7]

5.2.6 Modular construction using factory-fabricated components

Modular construction is most common in real estate and standard civil construction projects, but not usually in more sophisticated infrastructure projects. Hence, Brazilian law and market practices do not have any specific approach to modular construction.

4 *Norma Regulamentadora No. 2 – Inspeção Prévia* (Normative Resolution No. 2 – Prior Inspection).

5 *Norma Regulamentadora No. 4 – Serviços Especializados em Engenharia de Segurança e em Medicina do Trabalho* (Normative Resolution No. 4 – SESMET).

6 *Norma Regulamentadora No. 5 – Comissão Interna de Prevenção de Acidentes* (Normative Resolution No. 5 – CIPA).

7 *Norma Regulamentadora No. 6 – Equipamentos de Proteção Individual* (Normative Resolution No. 6 – EPI).

5.2.7 Technology/innovation/BIM

The increase of international players in the Brazilian construction industry either as contractors, developers or consultants has also brought advances in the use of design and project management technologies.

The use of building information modelling (BIM) solutions has been introduced over the past few years into Brazilian projects. Even public concessions and public procured works have been relying on or even requiring BIM solutions to increase efficiency in both the development and operation of assets. In fact, *Federal Decree No. 10,306/2020* issued on 2 April 2020 requires public entities related to the Ministry of Defence and the Ministry of Infrastructure to implement BIM solutions in projects engaged by their related entities.

Hence, contractors and suppliers must be well-versed in operating these solutions in order to comply with increasingly more common bidding requirements.

5.2.8 Government procurement

Article 37, item XXI, of the *Federal Constitution*[8] provides for the requirement of public bidding procedures for the procurement of construction, engineering works, services, purchases and sales by the government. In April 2021 the Brazilian government enacted a new public procurement law to set the basic regulation for public procurement which can be found in *Law No. 14,133/2021* (*New Public Procurement Law*). Nonetheless, many active public contracts were entered prior to it and are still governed by *Law No. 8,666/1993* (*Public Procurement Law*).

Both the *Public Procurement Law* and the *New Public Procurement Law* regulate public procurement procedures and contracts entered into by Federal, State and Municipal Governments. In theory, the *Public Procurement Law* is meant to provide general rules, which would be complemented by State or Municipal legislation based on local circumstances. However, the *Public Procurement Law* is relatively detailed, leaving little margin for the States and Municipalities to further legislate on the matter.

State-owned companies, however, rely on a specific regime set forth by *Law No. 13,303 of 30 June 2016*. It establishes specific rules for the management, corporate governance and procurement procedures for State-owned companies, where the State has a direct or indirect controlling interest.

Additional rules on public procurement include:

- *Law No. 9,472 of 16 July 1997*, which provides for the National Communications Agency and authorises the agency to create its own public procurement rules
- *Law No. 9,478 of 6 August 1997*, which established the National Oil Agency and authorises the agency to create its own public procurement rules, whilst also

8 *Federal Constitution*, Art. 37, item XXI. Except in the cases specified in the legislation, the works, services, purchases and disposals will be contracted through a public bidding process that ensures equal conditions among bidders, with clauses that establish payment obligations, maintaining the effective conditions of the proposal, under the terms of the law, limiting technical and economic qualification requirements only to the extent necessary to guarantee the fulfilment of obligations.

allowing Petrobras (a state-owned oil company) to comply with a simplified tender procedure
- *Law No. 12,598 of 21 March 2012*, which provides special rules for the purchase and development of defence systems

The fundamental principles for tender procedures (publicity, transparency, objective evaluation criteria, equal treatment, competition, value-for-money pursuit, efficiency, morality and probity) are all stated in Article 37 of the *Federal Constitution*, Article 5 of the *New Public Procurement Law* and Article 3 of the *Public Procurement Law*.[9]

Article 22 of the *Public Procurement Law*[10] provides for the three main public procurement procedures that can be followed:

- Invitation to tender, which mandates the procuring entity to invite at least three companies to participate in the competition
- Price survey, a tender procedure that occurs with competitors that were previously registered with the procuring entity, and
- Public tender, which is open to whoever wants to participate, provided the tenderer can meet all qualifying criteria prior to the beginning of the bidding procedure

Article 28, item V of the *New Public Procurement Law* also added the procedure for competitive dialogue,[11] during which the procuring entity conducts dialogues with previously selected bidders according to objective criteria, with the aim of developing one or more alternatives capable of meeting their needs, with bidders submitting a final proposal after the dialogue has ended. As per Article 32 of the same law, this modality is particularly suited for the procurement of technological innovations or where the procuring entity is not able to draft appropriate technical specifications for bidding.[12]

In any case, at this date, Brazilian public authorities do not usually use FIDIC forms of contract nor other international forms of contract. In some instances, public entities and

9 *New Public Procurement Law*, Article 5. In the application of this Law, the principles of legality, impersonality, morality, publicity, efficiency, public interest, administrative probity, equality, planning, transparency, effectiveness, segregation of functions, motivation, binding to the notice, objective judgment, legal certainty, reasonableness, competitiveness, proportionality, speed, economy and sustainable national development, as well as the provisions of Decree-Law No. 4,657 of 4 September 1942 (Law of Introduction to the Rules of Brazilian Law), are considered.

10 *Public Procurement Law*, Article 22. The bidding modalities are: I – competition; II – pricing; III – invitation; IV – competition; V – auction.

11 *New Public Procurement Law*, Article 28, V. The bidding modalities are: I – trading floor; II – competition; III – contest; IV – auction; V – competitive dialogue.

12 *New Public Procurement Law*, Article 32. The competitive dialogue modality is restricted to contracts in which the Administration:

I – aims to contract an object that involves the following conditions:

a) technological or technical innovation;
b) impossibility for the entity to have its need satisfied without adapting solutions available on the market; and
c) impossibility of the technical specifications being defined with sufficient precision by the procuring entity.

state-owned companies will have their own standard form of contract, which they may open or not for discussion during biddings, on a case-by-case basis.

5.2.10 Common forms of contract

The increase in international contractors' market share as explained in section 5.2.2 has led to a slight increase in the use of international forms of contract, the main ones being the FIDIC Yellow and Silver Books.

The increase in international financing sources over the last decade, where sponsors and lenders often require the use of standard forms of contracts, has also contributed to the increase in their use in Brazil.

With that said, standard forms of contracts are still not the most common practice in Brazil, and companies, as well as public entities, tend to have their own standard forms based on their past experiences with bespoke contracts.

5.2.11 Dispute resolution

Contracting parties may contractually provide for the forum that will examine their disputes where they cannot be resolved amicably, including foreign courts, if the contract relies on an international element (e.g. foreign parties, object or applicable law).[13]

Either the court or an arbitration tribunal may act as the competent forum, based on the contractual agreement. In construction and infrastructure disputes, if no amicable settlement is reached, disputes are usually resolved by arbitration. However, Brazil does not have courts specialised in construction disputes. This, in addition to the pathologic sluggishness of state courts, has made arbitration the most popular dispute resolution method for construction disputes related to mid-sized and large projects.

Unlike in the UK, Brazilian law does not provide for statutory adjudication. However, the inclusion of Dispute Boards in construction contracts has become more common in the past few years, which in practice creates a contractual adjudication mechanism for certain projects.

In 2018, the Municipality of São Paulo through *Lei No. 16,873/2018* (*Law No. 16,873/2018*) passed the first law allowing and regulating the use of Dispute Review and Adjudication Boards in public procurement contracts executed by the Municipality.

Brazilian arbitration is regulated by the *Brazilian Arbitration Act* (which is based on the *UNCITRAL Model Law*) and the *New York Convention*. Therefore, some important principles and features are applied in arbitration proceedings, such as due process, the right to be heard, impartiality and independence of arbitrators, *kompetenz-kompetenz* (competence-competence) and separability of the arbitration agreement, among many others.

Any party that can enter into a contract is permitted to submit disputes to arbitration. However, the dispute must relate to rights and assets that can be freely transferred or disposed of by the parties (Article 1).

13 *Civil Procedure Code*, Article 25. It is not the responsibility of the Brazilian judicial authority to process and judge the claim when there is a clause for the selection of an exclusive foreign jurisdiction in an international contract, defended by the defendant in the defence.

Domestic awards – those rendered inside Brazilian territory – are considered final judgments and do not require any confirmation by courts for the purposes of enforcement. Foreign awards, on the other hand, are subject to recognition proceedings within the High Court of Justice, in accordance with the *New York Convention* and with the *Brazilian Arbitration Act* (Article 34).

Parties may choose the arbitral institution to administer the case, the language of the proceedings, the law applicable to the dispute and the number of arbitrators to constitute the tribunal, as well as other procedural aspects related to the arbitration.

5.2.12 Current challenges

As with many countries around the world, the Brazilian construction industry is trying to overcome the impacts of the COVID-19 pandemic. On one hand, those effects include problems related to the supply of materials, such as:

1. The restructuring of supply chains to be less dependent on imported products, which are more susceptible to further restrictions and shortages in case of a new wave of the pandemic
2. Shortage of materials such as steel, microchips and systems made thereof
3. High currency fluctuation and weakening of the national currency, increasing costs for importation of equipment and materials

On the other hand, the COVID-19 pandemic, allied with some measure of political instability and uncertainty about the results of the upcoming presidential elections of 2022, has made the market currently cautious in the investment in new projects.

5.2.13 Unique features of the construction industry in Brazil

Although not necessarily unique, the Brazilian construction industry does rely on its particular aspects which mostly derive from other social, economic and political aspects of the country.

5.2.13.1 Language barriers

As mentioned in section 5.2.2, Brazil is a country of continental dimensions, formed by very different cultures across its regions. Hence, when managing projects in Brazil, parties may need to account for regional habits, standards and available resources.

One key resource that comes to mind when managing projects outside of major urban centres in Brazil is the availability of an English-speaking workforce. Having Portuguese as its official language and an under-developed education system, it is normal that not all personnel involved in the Works will be fluent in English or other foreign languages, at least not at a technical level. Thus, foreign contractors, developers or consultants are often forced to hire or partner with Brazilian professionals that can help translate relevant communications.

Also, as a consequence of the shortage of foreign-language-speaking personnel, public entities do not normally accept documents in English and most documents required for public procurement and licensing proceedings need to be in Portuguese.

5.2.13.2 Infrastructure
As a massive developing country, Brazil has many remote areas with poor infrastructure, which may include difficult access routes, lack of means of transportation and difficulty accessing power or water supplies. Hence, infrastructure has to be carefully accounted for by any parties developing projects in Brazil.

5.3 The impact of COVID-19 in Brazil

5.3.1 The impact of COVID-19 on the execution of construction projects in Brazil

After the breakout of the COVID-19 pandemic in Brazil in March 2020, a vast amount of regulation was issued to tackle the disease and avoid the spread of the virus. To add complication to the situation, as a federal republic, the *Brazilian Constitution* grants States and Municipalities powers to legislate over matters of public health concurrently with the Federal Government (Article 24, XII).

Due to these concurrent powers and the different political views on how to best address the pandemic, there was often conflict between the laws and regulations issued at the three levels (Federal, State and Municipality).

In the State of Rio de Janeiro, for example, *Decree No. 46,973* issued on 16 March 2020 and *Decree No. 47,209* issued in August 2020 brought several restrictions to the performance of economic activities, including:

1. Restriction on the hours of functioning of industrial and commercial activities
2. Requirements for companies to comply with good practices recommended by the World Health Organization, including social distancing
3. Requirements for companies to perform asepsis routines for disinfecting taps, door handles, bathrooms and their premises, in addition to providing individual protection equipment and antiseptics based on alcohol for use by the general public

The Municipality of Buzios, also in the State of Rio de Janeiro, for example, went further and entered into lockdown and closed exits and entries to the city both from highways and waterways, by means of the *Municipality Decree 1,405* issued on 8 May 2020. This measure was replicated in other Municipalities throughout Brazil. Although these lockdowns did not directly shut down the functioning of construction sites, in practice, this restriction on going in and out of Municipalities posed a challenge to works in remote places where the workforce comes from or is lodged in a different Municipality than the Site.

On the other hand, the Federal Government, in a less restrictive approach issued, for example, emergency measures declaring several activities as public essential interests, including civil works (provided that the works obey health and safety regulations) and engineering works related to power generation and transmission.

In this sense, Brazilian contractors faced situations where they would be allowed to resume works on a project in accordance with Federal regulations but would be restricted or impeded to perform either directly or indirectly due to State or Municipality restrictions.

On the subject of the conflicts between regulations issued by Federal, State and Municipality Governments, the Brazilian Federal Supreme Court has ruled on multiple occasions and has upheld the constitutional provisions in the sense that State and

Municipality legislation are not necessarily overruled by Federal legislation since all three levels are competent to legislate on the subject of health and sanitary measures.

Hence, parties to the projects often need to comply with regulations from Federal, State and Municipality levels, as well as engage in dialogue with State and Municipality authorities to allow for the continuation of works.

5.3.2 The impact of COVID-19 on the operation of construction contracts in Brazil

5.3.2.1 Force majeure and exemption of liability

One of the most common effects of the COVID-19 pandemic on contracts in general, including construction contracts, was parties being unable to fulfil their obligations due to restrictions imposed by government entities aiming to stop the spread of the virus. Project owners were sometimes unable to obtain licences due to the disruptions and stopping of public authorities' activities and Contractors were often unable to deploy their full workforce to the Site.

In those situations, if the Contract lacks further specification, parties could often rely on Article 393 of the *Brazilian Civil Code*, which provides that a party is exempted from liability if such liability derives from an event of *force majeure*. Contractors can more specifically resort to Article 625, I, which provides that the Contractor is entitled to suspend the Works due to an event of *force majeure*.

The main consequence of the application of Articles 393 and 625 is that the Contractor would generally be entitled to an extension of time for the completion of its scope with consequent relief from Delay Damages. Costs, on the other hand, are not necessarily awarded unless the Contract provides otherwise since the Brazilian law approach to *force majeure* is that each party bears its own losses.

It is important, however, that the party suffering from the effect of *force majeure* demonstrates the actual impacts of the *force majeure* and that it is possible to identify whether and to what extent delays or disruptions were actually caused by the pandemic and were not the result of other concurring or even prior events. In addition, parties need to comply with other requirements provided for in the Contract for the enforcement of their right to claim *force majeure*.

5.3.2.2 Cost impacts

For impacts on cost caused by the COVID-19 pandemic (e.g. increased health and safety requirements, deviations in supply chains, longer mobilisation of workforce), in cases where the contract does not provide for a specific remedy, parties may benefit from Article 317 of the *Brazilian Civil Code* and request for the rebalancing of the relationship due to the occurrence of the unforeseeable and inevitable event. Nonetheless, Article 317 requires that the Contract becomes materially disproportionate for the aggrieved party to have the right to review.

In contracts for mid-sized and large projects, it is more common that the Contract itself provides rules for determining the possibility and the extension of the Contractor's cost relief for the impacts of unforeseeable circumstances.

Once again, the party claiming reimbursement of costs or increases in price should evidence the amount of the increase and the causality between the pandemic and the increase in its costs.

5.3.2.3 Change of law

As explained in section 5.3.1, several laws and regulations were issued to fight the spread of COVID-19. Some of those laws and regulations caused impacts on construction works either directly (e.g. restricting hours of work, number of workers on site) or indirectly (e.g. blocking of roads, disruption in supply chains).

In this scenario, a common debate arose in contracts where the remedies available for change of law were different than the ones available for *force majeure* on whether the effects of COVID-19 should be treated as *force majeure* or as effects of the changes in law arising of COVID-19. The main difference usually being that under change-in-law provisions, Contractors would be entitled to both extensions of time and reimbursement of costs arising out of impacts of the change, while, in case of *force majeure*, Contractors would only be entitled to extensions of time and not reimbursement of costs.

Formally speaking, some of these changes are indeed caused by the change in the law and not by the effects of the pandemic itself. Nonetheless, from a material perspective, these changes in law differ from normal changes in law as they are a mere reaction to the pandemic rather than the will of legislators to change the legal framework. This argument is supported by the text and official justification of most of these decrees, laws and regulations which specifically justify them based on the pandemic and describe them to be transitory and emergency measures related to the pandemic as well. For example, *Federal Law No. 14,010/2020* issued on 10 June 2020, also in response to the COVID-19 pandemic, specifically describes itself as providing 'for the Emergency and Transitional Legal Regime of private legal relationships during the coronavirus pandemic period (Covid-19)'.

Naturally, the final assessment of the impacts of COVID-19 on the Contract will rely on the particular words in the Contract. However, given the circumstances of the pandemic and the approach taken by Brazilian regulations on the subject, it seems reasonable that the impacts of the government restrictions in virtue of the pandemic will be treated as *force majeure* rather than proper changes in law.

In view of that, after the beginning of the pandemic, parties have been trying to more specifically regulate the effects of the pandemic and specify if its impacts are to be treated as *force majeure*, changes in law or shall be subject to its own specific regime.

5.3.2.4 Contracts executed after the beginning of the COVID-19 pandemic

For contracts executed after the beginning of the COVID-19 pandemic, it is still uncertain whether remedies related to *force majeure*, hardship or review of contract could apply, since the effects of the pandemic and new fluctuations may now, to a certain extent, not be completely unforeseeable or unavoidable and, therefore, may not fulfil the applicable requirements.

In view of that, parties have generally been more conscious of trying to address possible impacts of the COVID-19 pandemic by either: (i) clarifying who will bear the time and cost impacts arising therefrom or (ii) designing tailor-made solutions and splitting of liabilities to address stoppages to the Works or increase of costs caused by necessary changes to the Works, including additional health and safety requirements.

Another issue parties to construction and supply contracts have been trying to limit after the COVID-19 pandemic is the geographical limit for which they are willing to undertake risk. For example, although some owners may be willing to undertake some degree of risk for impacts of the pandemic in the country of the Site, they may not be willing to take risks for impacts caused by the COVID-19 pandemic in the Contractor's supply chain, especially if that supply chain involves supplies being sourced from places with a very different risk profile from a health perspective.

5.3.2.5 Statutes of limitation and prescription periods
Article 3 of *Federal Law No. 14,010/2020* issued on 10 June 2020 suspended statutes of limitation and prescription periods from the date of issuance of the law until 30 October 2020.

5.3.2.6 Corporate governance
Law No. 14,010/2020 issued on 10 June 2020, also in response to the COVID-19 pandemic, allowed legal entities to conduct their members' and shareholders' meetings by virtual means. The Company Registration Department and the Brazilian Stock and Exchange Commission also issued regulation in the same sense.[14]

5.4 Brazilian governing law of the contract

5.4.1 Constraints on the governing law of a construction contract

Brazilian civil law expressly allows and recognises the parties' freedom to contract and agree on the terms of the contract, subject to the limits of the law.[15] However, it is doubtful whether it recognises the parties' right to choose non-state rules of law, since, although it is a signatory to the *Hague Convention on Choice of Law*, it has not to this date taken the legislative measures necessary to effectively implement it internally.

Instead, the *Decree of Introduction to Brazilian Law* still provides the rules of conflict of laws applicable to contracts. Its Article 9 provides that obligations, or contracts, are governed by the law of the place where they are executed. Moreover, in the case of international contracts, it details that the place of execution is deemed to be the place of residence of the proponent.[16]

However, the situation is different when the parties submit their dispute to international arbitration. If the seat of the arbitration is in Brazil, *Federal Law No. 9,307/1996* (*Brazilian Arbitration Act*) shall apply to the proceedings.

The first paragraph of Article 2 of the *Brazilian Arbitration Act* expressly authorises parties to agree on the law applicable to the dispute, as long as they do not violate public policies. Additionally, the second paragraph of Article 2 also includes the possibility for parties to agree on the application of general principles of law, customs, business practices and international trade rules.

14 Normative Ruling No. 79 of the Company Registration Department, dated 14 April 2020, and Normative Ruling No. 622, dated 17 April 2020.

15 *Civil Code*, Article 425. Subject to the provisions of the Code, the parties are allowed to stipulate the terms of bespoke contracts.

16 Article 9: obligations are governed by the law of the place where they are constituted.

5.4.2 Formal requirements for a construction contract

Brazilian law provides no specific formal requirements for the formation of a construction contract. In fact, Brazilian case law has already acknowledged the possibility of the execution of verbal construction contracts.[17] Nevertheless, construction contracts shall comply with the general requirements for the validity and effectiveness of binding contracts according to Brazilian law, which are:

- i The contracting parties shall have full capacity and authority to contract
- ii The object of the contract shall be lawful, possible, determined or determinable
- iii The formalities required by law, if any, must be observed

5.5 What Special Provisions in the Particular Conditions are necessary for consistency with applicable laws in Brazil?

5.5.1 FIDIC General Conditions are incompatible or inconsistent with Brazilian governing law of the contract

5.5.1.1 Indirect damages

Sub-clause 1.15 of the General Condition of Contract of the Yellow and Red Books and sub-clause 1.14 of the Silver Book provide that the Parties shall not be liable for loss of profits, loss of contract or indirect damages, except in the cases listed thereunder. Article 403 of the *Brazilian Civil Code* only allows for parties to claim damages and losses of profits that arise directly from the breach committed by the other party.[18] Hence, as a rule, indirect damages are widely excluded from liability under Brazilian law.

Although there is no specific determination by law or by case law with regard to the possibility of parties agreeing on the inclusion of indirect damages, it is possible that a court or arbitral tribunal would reject a claim for damages which it understands to be indirect, even if they are claimed to fit under the exclusions provided by FIDIC General Conditions of Contract.

5.5.1.2 Notice of Claim

Sub-clause 20.2 of the General Conditions requires the Contractor to present a Notice of Claim 28 days after the Party has become aware or should have become aware of the events or circumstances giving cause to the claim. Although case law and the majority of scholars accept that it is feasible for Parties to agree on claim limitations, Article 209[19] of the *Brazilian Civil Code* does not allow Parties to reduce or waive statutory limitations.[20] In this scenario, statutory limitations may apply to claims between the Parties, making the time limitations provided for in sub-clause 20.2 not applicable to such claims.

Additionally, in relation to standard forms of contract, Article 424 of the *Brazilian Civil Code* establishes that provisions granting the Party who drafted or proposed the standard

17 Brazilian Superior Court of Justice, Interim Special Appeal No. 16121 SP 2018/0155547-5, Reporting Justice Marco Buzzi, 24 August 2018.

18 Article 403. Losses and damages only comprise actual direct damages and loss of profits, even if the non-performance arises out of willful misconduct of the debtor, without prejudice to procedural law provisions.

19 Article 209. Waivers of statutory limitations are void.

20 Tepedino, Barboza, & De Moraes, *Código Civil Interpretado, Vol. I* [2011] 425.

terms of the contract an anticipated waiver of rights are void.[21] Hence, in the case of a specific transaction where one of the Parties is considered to be subscribing to a standard form of contract, for example where there are no Particular Conditions of Contract, the contractual limitations imposed by sub-clause 20.2 of the FIDIC General Conditions of Contract may be considered void.

5.5.2 FIDIC General Conditions are incompatible or inconsistent with the law of the Site/Country

5.5.2.1 Defect Notice Period

Article 618 of the *Brazilian Civil Code* provides that the Contractor is liable for the defects relating to the soundness and safety of the Works for a period of five years. This warranty is considered to guard not only the interests of the Employer but of the whole community that may be exposed to structural defects of the project. For this reason, the five-year term may not be waived or reduced by contract.[22]

In view of that, the limitation brought by the Defect Notice Period as described in the General Conditions may not be applicable to defects relating to the soundness and safety of the Works.

5.5.3 FIDIC General Conditions are incompatible or inconsistent with the laws on dispute determination in Brazil

5.5.3.1 The Engineer

Sub-clause 3.7.5 of the General Conditions of the Red and Yellow Books provides that, in the case where no Notice of Dissatisfaction is issued by the defeated Party, the decision by the Engineer (or part thereof) shall become final and binding. Also, any non-compliance with such decision shall be treated in the same manner as non-compliance with a DAAB's decision.

Nevertheless, Brazilian law may impose several obstacles to the enforcement of an Engineer's decision as binding and final. Firstly, as a civil law jurisdiction, the Brazilian legal system is highly resistant to attributing final and binding force to decisions unless their nature derives from the provisions of law, such as with arbitral awards, which are expressly equivalent to a judicial award by virtue of Article 31 of the *Brazilian Arbitration Law*.[23]

Moreover, Brazilian courts and arbitrators may also challenge the final and binding effects of the Engineer's decision based on the partiality of the Engineer. Brazilian law requires both court judges and arbitrators to act impartially and independently, with no financial or political interest in the management or in the resolution of the dispute. Overall, despite its obligations to act fairly, the Engineer is described in the General Conditions as

21 Article 424. In forms of contract, clauses which stipulate anticipated waiver of rights inherent to the nature of the contract are void.

22 Court of Appeals of the State of Goiás, Appeal No. 0151633-54.2015.8.09.0051, Reporting Judge Fernando de Castro Mesquita, 19 July 2016.

23 Article 31. The arbitral award produces the same effects as an award issued by a state court to the parties and its successors and, being a condemnation, it constitutes a bond.

first and foremost considered to act on behalf of the Employer and is in no way considered to be fully impartial.[24]

Therefore, decisions rendered by the Engineer are less likely to be considered final and binding even if unchallenged, due to the lack of impartiality and independence of an Employer-appointed Engineer.

5.5.3.2 Dispute Adjudication Boards

Although Dispute Adjudication Boards have already been acknowledged by case law and also by state laws relating to public contracts, Brazilian courts have not yet directly faced the issue of whether decisions issued by Dispute Adjudication Boards may eventually become final if no Notice of Dissatisfaction is presented. The Superior Court of Justice has already expressed, however, that it considers an adjudicator to which the parties have granted the power to issue a final and binding decision to be acting as an arbitrator, regardless of the title given to such third party.[25]

Although this could mean in the future that a Dispute Adjudication Board could have powers comparable to those of an arbitrator, this could also mean that the court does not see a Dispute Adjudication Board itself as having powers to issue a final and binding decision. This last understanding seems to be corroborated by the position adopted by *Law No. 16,873/18* of the Municipality of São Paulo, governing Dispute Boards in contracts executed by the Government of São Paulo. Its Article 2, II, provides that the Dispute Adjudication Board shall issue 'contractually binding' decisions to the parties. At first sight, this expression seems to diminish the extension and binding effects of the decision in order to differentiate it from the final and binding award issued by an arbitral tribunal, consequently indicating that the Dispute Board decision must be ratified by an arbitral award or a court before it becomes final and binding.

5.6 What Special Provisions in the Particular Conditions are desirable for consistency with applicable laws in Brazil?

5.6.1 Gross negligence

Brazilian law presents no clear definition of gross negligence or reckless misconduct. As in English law, some scholars claim that gross negligence is conduct of such a reckless nature that it would constitute almost a deliberate action towards harm (willful misconduct) or at least the assumption of the possibility or risk of a harmful outcome.

However, there are also those who contest that gross negligence is not an objective or absolute concept but should rather be construed in the light of the circumstances of the case, such as the nature, size and objective of the transaction, as well as the qualification of the parties or of the agent.[26] According to this second line of thought, an expert Engineer could not be expected to act with the same degree of care, diligence and know-how as an

24 Baker, Mellors, Chalmers, & Lavers, *FIDIC Contracts: Law and Practice* (Informa Law: London 2009) 287.

25 Brazilian Superior Court of Justice. Special Appeal no. 1.569.422/RJ, Reporting Justice Marco Aurélio Belizze. 7 May 2016.

26 De Azevedo, 'Nulidade de cláusula limitativa de responsabilidade em caso de culpa grave. Caso de equiparação entre dolo e culpa grave. Configuração da culpa grave em caso de responsabilidade profissional', *Novos estudos e pareceres de direito privado* [2009] 436–437.

average person. The standards should be naturally much higher, given the extraordinary diligence expected from such an expert, which is, by definition, what makes him or her an expert in the first place.

Due to this difficulty of extracting an accurate or even predictable definition of the concept of gross negligence and its relevance to the General Conditions of Contract as exceptions to limitations of liability (e.g. Yellow Book sub-clauses 1.14, 8.8, 11.10 and 14.14), parties are recommended to include a definition for such term in the Special Conditions of Contract in order to provide more clarity and certainty to the exceptions at hand.

5.6.2 Loss of profits

Although the *Brazilian Civil Code* provides for the possibility of an aggrieved party to claim loss of profits along with actual damages (Article 403) and for the possibility of a Contractor to claim them in the case of unlawful termination by the Employer (Article 623), the Brazilian benchmark for mid-size and/or large construction and infrastructure projects is set by contractual provisions excluding the liability of the parties for loss of profits, loss of opportunity or investment. Hence, the provisions of the General Conditions of Contract are usually amended by Particular Conditions of Contract with regard to limitation of liability or to the payments upon termination in order to exclude the application of loss of profits and loss of contracts from the parties' liability.

5.6.3 Compliance with laws – Brazilian Association of Technical Regulation

The Brazilian Association of Technical Regulation (ABNT) issues several rules or recommended standards with regard to engineering, formatting, standardisation and quality assurance. Some of those rules and standards are made mandatory by virtue of laws and regulations of higher rank, but others, although not specifically mandatory, are considered to be a reasonable or minimum standard.

Considering the definition of Laws provided in the General Conditions of Contract, it could be assumed that the Contractor would not be bound by the non-mandatory rules issued by ABNT. For this reason, in cases where there are relevant rules from ABNT applicable to the Works or to the Site, it is important that the Special Conditions of Contract revise the definition of Laws and/or sub-clauses 1.12 of the Yellow and Red Books or 1.13 of the Silver Book (Compliance with Laws) in order to specify that ABNT rules should be followed or which rules specifically should be followed.

5.7 Summary of applicable legislation for Brazilian governing law of the contract

5.7.1 Entry into a construction contract

Contracts generally	*Brazilian Civil Code (Federal Law No. 10,406/2002)*
Construction contracts	*Brazilian Civil Code (Federal Law No. 10,406/2002)* *Public Procurement Law (Federal Law No. 8,666/1993)*

5.7.2 Termination of a construction contract

Frustration	*Brazilian Civil Code (Federal Law No. 10,406/2002)*
Bankruptcy, insolvency, liquidation	*Brazilian Civil Code (Federal Law No. 10,406/2002)* *Bankruptcy Law (Federal Law No. 11,101/2005)*
Guarantees under forms of Security (Tender Security, Demand Guarantee, Surety Bond, Advance Payment Guarantee, Retention Money Guarantee, Payment Guarantee by Employer)	*Brazilian Civil Code (Federal Law No. 10,406/2002)*

5.7.3 Dispute resolution

Limitation periods	*Brazilian Civil Code (Federal Law No. 10,406/2002)* *Several special laws may apply depending on the right or obligation under discussion*
Liability	*Brazilian Civil Code (Federal Law No. 10,406/2002)*
Adjudication	*No applicable Brazilian law*
Arbitration	*Brazilian Arbitration Law (Federal Law No. 9,307/1996)* *Brazilian Code of Civil Procedure (Federal Law No. 13,105/2015)*

5.8 Summary of applicable legislation if the Site/Country is in Brazil

5.8.1 Operation of a construction contract

Registration and administration of professionals – Engineers, Architects	*Brazilian Engineering Professional Law (Federal Law No. 5,194/1966)*
Registration/licencing of Contractors and subcontractors	No applicable Brazilian law
Subcontractors	No applicable Brazilian law
Use of liens/assignment of debts	*Brazilian Civil Code (Federal Law No. 10,406/2002)*
Labour	*Brazilian Consolidation of Labour Laws (Decree-Law No. 5,452/1943)*
Design/Moral Rights	*Brazilian Copyright Law (No. 9,610/1998)*
Copyright	*Brazilian Copyright Law (No. 9,610/1998)*
The product being produced from the Works	*Brazilian Civil Code (Federal Law No. 10,406/2002)*
First Nation people's land rights	*Brazilian Federal Constitution of 1988 Indian Statute (Federal Law No. 6,001/1973)*
Planning	No applicable Brazilian law
Work affecting adjacent property to the Site	*Brazilian Civil Code (Federal Law No. 10,406/2002)*

Heritage	*Brazilian Civil Code (Federal Law No. 10,406/2002)*
Environment	Brazilian environmental law is scattered among several laws, such as, but not limited to: *Brazilian Federal Constitution of 1988 Forest Law (No. 12,651/2012)* *Nuclear Activities Act (No. 6,453/1977)* *Mineral Exploration Act (No. 7,805/1989)* *Water Resources Act (No. 7,805/1989)* *Brazilian Environmental Policy (No. 6,938/1981)* *Pesticides Law (No. 7,802/1989)* *Environmental Crimes Law (No. 9,605/1998)*
Local procurement	*Public Procurement Law (Federal Law No. 8,666/1993)*; *New Public Procurement Law (Federal Law No. 14,133/2021)*
Building and construction permits, execution of construction work, standard of construction work	Building and construction permits are usually regulated by Municipal or State laws which differ among the 26 Brazilian States and over 5,000 Municipalities
Health and safety	Health and safety regulations are scattered in regulations issued by governmental entities and agencies
Calibration of testing apparatus, equipment and instruments	No applicable Brazilian law
Ownership of Plant and Materials	*Brazilian Civil Code (Federal Law No. 10,406/2002)*
Employer's sale of Contractor's Equipment, surplus material, wreckage and Temporary Works	No applicable Brazilian law
Insurance	*Private Insurance Law (Federal Decree No. 73/1966)*
Statutory rights that coexist with contractual rights	No applicable Brazilian law
Liability for defective work	*Brazilian Civil Code (Federal Law No. 10,406/2002)*
Liability for nuisance	*Brazilian Civil Code (Federal Law No. 10,406/2002)* Nuisance is often regulated by State or Municipality laws

5.8.2 Termination of a construction contract

Bankruptcy, insolvency, liquidation	*Bankruptcy Law (Federal Law No. 11,101/2005)*
Decennial liability and liability generally for the total or partial collapse of structures	*Brazilian Civil Code (Federal Law No. 10,406/2002)*

5.8.3 Dispute resolution

Dispute before a local board/adjudication	No applicable Brazilian law
Limitation periods	*Brazilian Civil Code (Federal Law No. 10,406/2002)*

5.9 Summary of applicable legislation if the 'seat' of the dispute determination is in Brazil

Dispute resolution	*Brazilian Mediation Law (Federal Law No. 13,140/2015)* *Brazilian Arbitration Law (Federal Law No. 9,307/1996)* *Brazilian Code of Civil Procedure (Federal Law No. 13,105/2015)*
Limitation periods	*Brazilian Civil Code (Federal Law No. 10,406/2002)*
Adjudication	No applicable Brazilian law
Arbitration	*Brazilian Arbitration Law (Federal Law No. 9,307/1996)* *Brazilian Code of Civil Procedure (Federal Law No. 13,105/2015)*

5.10 Issues that a court or arbitrator may construe differently from that expected from the words of the Contract because of local law or custom

5.10.1 Deemed acceptance of Variations

The sole paragraph of Article 619 of the *Brazilian Civil Code* provides that, even where no express written authorisation or instruction has been given by the Employer, the Contractor will be entitled to a Variation in a case where the project is modified, and the Employer, due to its constant visits, inspections or presence at the Site, could not have been unaware of such modifications but never objected to them.

According to Brazilian scholars and case law, this deemed acceptance by the Employer as provided by Article 619's sole paragraph is a direct consequence of the principle of good faith and a necessary tool to avoid unlawful enrichment by the Employer.[27] Since both the principles of good faith and unjust enrichment are considered to be public policy matters, it would not be possible for an Employer to avoid such responsibility by virtue of provisions in the Contract to the contrary.

Hence, provisions of the General Conditions of Contract requiring (i) express consent of the Employer, (ii) agreement of the Parties or (iii) a specific procedure for the submission and approval of Claims may be overruled in view of the specifics of the case, where the Employer could not deny its knowledge or awareness of the alterations to the original project by being constantly engaged in or micromanaging the Works or by comparable events of acknowledgement.

Naturally, the requirements for the assessment of this deemed acknowledgement by the Employer must take into consideration the specificities of the case, including the expertise

27 Superior Court of Justice, Interim Special Appeal No. 979663/MG, Reporting Justice Vasco Della Giustina, 22 October 2010.

of the Employer and the complexity of the project or of the specific alterations being implemented to the project or Works.

5.10.2 Termination for reorganisation

The FIDIC General Conditions of Contract provide for either Party's right to terminate the Contract if the other Party becomes insolvent, bankrupt or goes into liquidation, reorganisation or other situations where the company becomes extinct or loses access to its assets. Brazilian *Federal Law No. 11,101/05* provides for the procedure of *recuperação judicial*, similar to reorganisation, where the company is put under the administration of a manager appointed by the court, with the goal of restructuring its debts and allowing for the resumption of its activities.

In those cases, there is case law in Brazil establishing that clauses providing for the right of termination of the Contract exclusively due to one of the parties entering into reorganisation are void in relation to those contracts which are essential to the maintenance of the business activity of the party under reorganisation.[28] In other words, Brazilian courts consider that such provisions, if applied widely, would disable and stultify the functionality of the reorganisation.[29]

Thus, although termination clauses including the possibility of reorganisation by the parties are common in the Brazilian market, they may, on occasion, be set aside by courts in cases where they present an imminent threat to the continuity of the business under reorganisation.

5.10.3 Hardship

As can be observed in some common-law jurisdictions, the degree of risk assumed by a Contractor may be extremely high in regard to unanticipated adverse ground conditions. English courts tend to relieve the Contractor's burden only when the hardship renders the obligation impossible to perform or when it is unforeseeable.

On the other hand, under Brazilian law, it is possible to shift the risk to the Employer on an exceptional basis, i.e. in the case of an extraordinary supervening event which places an excessively onerous obligation on one of the Parties, even if the Contract has originally provided otherwise. Articles 478 to 480[30] of the *Brazilian Civil Code* provide a general rule regarding Contract termination and revision due to excessively onerous obligations. In sum, if supervening, extraordinary and unpredictable conditions arise which make the Contract more onerous to one of the Parties and extremely advantageous to the other, the

28 Court of Appeals of the State of Paraná, Appeal No. 1.292.381-0, Reporting Judge Luis Sergio Swiech, 22 July 2015.

29 Court of Appeals of the State of São Paulo, Appeal No. 21099854520158260000, Reporting Judge Carlos Alberto Garbi, 31 August 2015.

30 Article 478: in contracts for continuous or deferred execution, if the performance of one of the parties becomes excessively burdensome, with great advantage to the other, due to extraordinary and unforeseeable events, the debtor may request the termination of the contract. The effects of the decision to be decreed retroactively at the date of the citation. Article 479: the resolution can be avoided, offering the defendant to modify the conditions of the contract equitably. Article 480: if in the contract the obligations fall on only one of the parties, it may claim the reduction of its burden or the alteration of the performance in order to avoid excessive burden.

aggrieved Party may request the termination of the Contract. Such termination may be avoided if the benefited party agrees to review the terms of the Contract.

In this regard, the Brazilian Federal Supreme Court has already decided that these general rules apply to construction contracts, which may be revised and supplemented in a case of extraordinary modifications of the objective conditions in which the Contract was executed.

Furthermore, it is important to point out that there are also specific rules which can be applied to add to the general rules of hardship. Article 625, item II of the *Brazilian Civil Code*[31] provides for the right of the Contractor to suspend the Works in a case of unforeseeable geological or hydraulic conditions (or other similar conditions) which make the Works excessively onerous, in case the Employer refuses to revise the Contract Price.

The purpose of this provision is to make an objective application of the principle of good faith, which is of ultimate relevance in Brazilian law. This prevents the unjust enrichment of the beneficiary of the Works, the Employer, due to unforeseeable Site conditions.

Due to its direct connection with the principle of good faith, it is therefore possible that, on occasion, Brazilian courts will allow for the review of the terms of the Contract based on Articles 478 and 625, straying from the exact words of the Contract.

5.11 Additional references for Brazil

5.11.1 Books

Antônio Junqueira de Azevedo, *Nulidade de cláusula limitativa de responsabilidade em caso de culpa grave. Caso de equiparação entre dolo e culpa grave. Configuração da culpa grave em caso de responsabilidade profissional. Novos estudos e pareceres de direito privado* (Saraiva, 2009).

Gustavo Tepedino, Heloisa Helena Barboza, & Maria Celina Bodin De Moraes, *Código Civil Interpretado*, Vol. I (Renovar, 2014).

5.11.2 Legislation

www4.planalto.gov.br/legislacao/ (in Portuguese)

5.11.3 Case law

Court of Appeal of the State of Goiás: www.tjgo.jus.br
Court of Appeals of the State of Paraná: www.tjpr.jus.br
Court of Appeals of the State of São Paulo: www.tjsp.jus.br
Federal Supreme Court of Justice: www.stf.jus.br
Superior Court of Justice: www.stj.jus.br/sites/STJ

31 Article 625, section II. The contractor may suspend the work 'when, during the course of the services, unforeseeable difficulties arise due to geological or water causes or similar, so that the work is excessively burdensome and the employer opposes the adjustment of the price'.

CHAPTER 6

Applying FIDIC Contracts in Canada

Sharon C Vogel[1]

CONTENTS

6.1	Outline of Canada's legal environment	131
	6.1.1 The constitutional structure of Canada	131
	6.1.2 The legal system in Canada	132
	6.1.3 Indigenous Peoples	132
	6.1.4 Distinction between private law and public law	133
	6.1.5 Construction lien legislation	133
	6.1.6 The court system in Canada	135
6.2	The construction industry in Canada	137
	6.2.1 Overview	137
	6.2.1.1 Investing in Canada's construction industry	138
	6.2.1.2 Public Infrastructure Projects	139
	6.2.2 Licencing/registration of professionals and skilled trades	140
	6.2.2.1 Municipal licencing	142
	6.2.3 Labour relations	142
	6.2.4 Safety culture	143
	6.2.5 Technology and innovation	144
	6.2.6 Procurement	145
	6.2.7 Anti-corruption measures	146
	6.2.8 Insurance requirements	147
	6.2.9 Common forms of contract	147
	6.2.10 Dispute resolution	148
6.3	The impact of COVID-19 in Canada	149
	6.3.1 The impact of COVID-19 on the execution of construction projects in Canada	149
	6.3.2 The impact of COVID-19 on the operation of construction contracts in Canada	150

1 The author wishes to thank Alegria Indio, an articling student with Singleton Urquhart Reynolds Vogel LLP, for her extensive assistance in the preparation of this chapter.

DOI: 10.4324/9781003201250-6

6.4 Canadian governing law of the contract 152
6.4.1 Constraints on the governing law of a construction contract 152
6.4.2 Formal requirements for a construction contract 152
6.5 What Special Provisions in the Particular Conditions are necessary for consistency with applicable laws? 153
6.5.1 FIDIC General Conditions are incompatible or inconsistent with the governing law of the contract 153
6.5.2 FIDIC General Conditions are incompatible or inconsistent with the law of the Site/Country 153
6.5.3 FIDIC General Conditions are incompatible or inconsistent with the laws of the seat of the arbitration or relevant laws on dispute determination 155
6.6 What Special Provisions in the Particular Conditions are desirable for consistency with applicable laws? 156
6.7 Summary of applicable legislation if the governing law is that of Canada 156
6.7.1 Entry into a construction contract 157
6.7.2 Termination of a construction contract 157
6.7.3 Dispute resolution 157
6.8 Summary of applicable legislation if the Site/Country is in Canada 157
6.8.1 Operation of a construction contract 157
6.8.2 Termination of a construction contract 158
6.8.3 Dispute resolution 158
6.9 Summary of applicable legislation if the 'seat' of the dispute determination is Canada 158
6.10 Issues that a court or arbitrator may construe differently than expected from the words of the Contract because of local law or custom 159
6.11 Additional references for Canada 159
6.11.1 Books 159
6.11.2 Journals/guides/encyclopaedias 160
6.11.3 Federal legislation 160
6.11.4 Provincial and territorial legislation 160
6.11.5 Case law 161

6.1 Outline of Canada's legal environment

6.1.1 The constitutional structure of Canada

Canada is a federal state.[2] The *Constitution Act, 1867* is the basis of Canada's constitutional documents. This document establishes Canada's three institutions of government – the legislature, judiciary and executive branches. In addition, the *Constitution Act, 1867* divides legislative jurisdiction between the Federal and Provincial Governments based on subject matter.

For example, section 92(13) of the *Constitution Act, 1867* grants Provincial and Territorial legislatures the exclusive jurisdiction to develop and implement laws relating to property and civil rights. This jurisdiction gives the Provinces and Territories jurisdiction over most areas related to the construction industry which is why most of the relevant legislation is Provincial or Territorial. Provincial and Territorial legislation varies, so for the purpose of this chapter, Ontario is frequently cited as an example of relevant legislation given that it is the most populous Province.

The *Constitution Act, 1982* is the constitutional document which incorporates the *Canadian Charter of Rights and Freedoms* and explicitly designates the *Constitution* as the supreme law of Canada. The *Constitution Act, 1982* also provides a schedule of constitutional documents and a procedure for amending the *Constitution.*

Canada is a constitutional monarchy such that the Crown (the Sovereign) is the formal head of state represented in Canada by the Governor General of Canada. The Governor General is appointed by the British monarch on the recommendation of the Prime Minister. The *Constitution* reserves certain formal powers to the Crown including giving royal recommendation to bills that propose to spend government revenues, giving royal assent to bills passed by the House of Commons and the Senate and dissolving parliament, opening and closing parliamentary sessions, etc.

Canada's parliamentary system is based on the British or Westminster tradition. There are two chambers – the House of Commons and the Senate. The representatives of the House of Commons are elected, and representatives of the Senate are appointed. Most bills are introduced in the House of Commons and each bill is subject to review, debate, examination and amendment through both Houses before receiving final approval.

Other sources of Canadian constitutional law include non-entrenched quasi-constitutional statutes, constitutional conventions and unwritten principles like the rule of law, separation of powers and democracy.

In Canada, laws which are inconsistent with the *Constitution* are, to the extent of the inconsistency, of no force or effect.

2 Parliament of Canada, 'The Canadian Parliamentary System'. www.ourcommons.ca/about/OurProcedure/ParliamentaryFramework/c_g_parliamentaryframework-e.htm#:~:text=Canada%20is%20a%20constitutional%20monarchy,or%20%E2%80%9CWestminster%E2%80%9D%2C%20tradition (accessed 21 April 2022). See also Peter W. Hogg & Wade Wright, *Constitutional Law of Canada*, (5th edn, The Carswell Company Ltd Subscriptions, 2021).

6.1.2 The legal system in Canada

The two primary sources of law in Canada are legislation and common law. Canada is composed of ten Provincial Governments, three Territorial Governments and a Federal Government. The Provincial and Territorial legislatures along with the Parliament of Canada have the power to enact legislation within their constitutional jurisdiction. The judiciary is responsible for resolving disputes in accordance with the law and, in doing so, administering justice.[3]

Overall, Canada is a multi-juridical country rooted in common law and civil law. Canada is primarily a common law jurisdiction with the exception of the Province of Quebec which is a civil law jurisdiction based on the *Civil Code of Quebec* (the ***Civil Code***). Both the common law and civil law systems were brought to Canada by colonists in the 17th and 18th centuries. The common law is rooted in the English legal system and is based on judicial precedent rather than a code or body of legislation.[4] On the other hand, the *Civil Code* is a comprehensive statement of private law rules based on the French *Napoleonic Code*.[5]

As noted earlier, each common law Province in Canada has its own court system through which the law is developed, and the Supreme Court of Canada's jurisprudence is binding on all jurisdictions.

6.1.3 Indigenous Peoples

In respect to land rights, the *Constitution Act, 1867* allocates legislative jurisdiction over '[l]ands reserved for the Indians' to the Federal Government.[6] The Federal Government has jurisdiction over reserve lands, lands which are subject to aboriginal title and unceded lands. Reserve lands are those lands which the Crown has set aside for the communal use and benefit of an Indigenous band. Title to reserve lands remains with either the Federal or Provincial Crown pursuant to the *Indian Act*.[7] Pursuant to the *First Nations Land Management Act*,[8] there are a number of First Nation bands[9] who can opt out of the *Indian Act's* land management regime and develop their own land codes.

In addition, section 35 of the *Constitution Act, 1982* recognises and affirms '[t]he existing aboriginal and treaty rights of the aboriginal peoples of Canada'.[10] Indigenous rights are those rights which arise from the historic occupation and use of traditional lands. For instance, aboriginal title is a type of Indigenous right which acknowledges the historic occupation of Indigenous peoples on traditional land and establishes a continued right to

3 Government of Canada, 'How Does Canada's Court System Work?' www.justice.gc.ca/eng/csj-sjc/ccs-ajc/01.html (accessed 22 April 2022).

4 Government of Canada, 'Where Our Legal System Comes From'. www.justice.gc.ca/eng/csj-sjc/just/03.html (accessed 21 April 2022).

5 *Ibid.*

6 *Constitutional Act, 1867* s 91(24).

7 R.S.C., 1985, c. I-5 [*Indian Act*].

8 *First Nations Land Management Act*, S.C. 1999, c. 24.

9 *Ibid.* The *First Nations Land Management Act* defines a First Nation as 'a band named in Schedule 1'. Schedule 1 of the *First Nations Land Management Act* provides a list of bands to which the *Act* applies.

10 Margaret Buist, *Halsbury's Laws of Canada – Aboriginal* (LexisNexis Canada, 2020 Reissue) at HAB-19 [HLC].

occupation.[11] Further, historically, certain treaties were entered into which are agreements entered into by the Crown and Indigenous peoples in Canada. These treaties have historically delineated the rights and relationships of certain Indigenous groups across Canada. In addition, in more recent times, the Federal and Provincial Governments have entered into land claim agreements with Indigenous groups who assert title to traditional lands not subject to historical treaties.[12]

6.1.4 Distinction between private law and public law

Canadian law can be categorised into public and private law. Public law governs the legal relationships between individuals and society. Constitutional law, administrative law and criminal law are subsets of public law.

On the other hand, private law governs the relationships between individuals. For example, contract law is considered a private law matter. In addition, the laws pertaining to construction contracts are generally governed by the common law of contracts, albeit in Quebec, the *Civil Code* codifies the law of contracts. Therefore, in the common law Provinces and Territories, construction law is based on rules which evolve from case law. Judges will consider themselves bound by higher court decisions within the same jurisdiction on similar issues in the area of construction law. In the Province of Quebec, judges will adjudicate construction law disputes based on the rules set out in the *Civil Code*. For clarity, judges in the Province of Quebec are not bound by precedent but they may consider prior court decisions when deciding construction issues.

6.1.5 Construction lien legislation

Further, most Provinces and Territories have enacted construction lien legislation which modifies the common law of construction contracts in their respective jurisdiction. Statutory liens give a person who provides labour or material to an improved premise an extra-contractual right to place a charge on that property.[13] In Ontario, lien legislation dates back to the 1870s. In particular, amendments made in 1874 to the *Mechanics Lien Act of 1873*[14] gave subcontractors the right to lien an owner's property. Lien legislation in Ontario has since evolved. The *Construction Act*,[15] formerly known as the *Construction Lien Act*, R.S.O. 1990, c. C. 30, is Ontario's current lien legislation.

Apart from the common law jurisdictions, the *Civil Code of Quebec* also contains provisions for liens against land which are referred to as 'construction hypothecs'.[16]A construction hypothec is a form of security against real property in favour of certain entities who provide materials or services for the construction or renovation of real property. The *Civil Code* indicates that architects, engineers, suppliers of material, workmen, contractors and subcontractors are entities who may exercise a construction hypothec against an

11 *Ibid.*

12 *Ibid* at HAB-256 and 257.

13 LexisNexis Canada, *Halsbury's Laws of Canada – Construction* (2021 Reissue) at HCU-120.

14 Maria Ruberto and Kyle Kuczynski, 'The "Holdback": The Ontario Experience – From the *Mechanics Lien Act* to the *Construction Act*' (2021) *Journal of the Canadian College of Construction Lawyers*.

15 R.S.O. 1990, c. C. 30 [*Construction Act*].

16 Justice Leonard Ricchetti and Timothy J Murphy, *Construction Law in Canada* (LexisNexis Canada Inc, 2010), Chapter 4.I.

owner. The construction hypothec provides the construction participant with a secured right to the increased value of the property arising from the material or services contributed by them.[17]

By way of example, Ontario's current lien legislation, the *Construction Act*, contains a number of provisions relating to construction liens including holdback provisions. It also contains trust provisions which establish statutory trusts. Construction contracts in Ontario are deemed to be amended in accordance with the *Construction Act*.[18] Parties to such contracts cannot limit the application of the *Construction Act* through contractual drafting given that section 4 of the *Construction Act* indicates that '[a]n agreement by any person who supplies services or materials to an improvement that this Act does not apply to the person or that the remedies provided by it are not available for the benefit of the person is **void**'.[19] The *Construction Act* contains prompt payment and adjudication provisions which came into force on 1 October 2019 and apply to both Ontario's public and private sectors.

In addition to the legislative changes in Ontario, the Province of Saskatchewan now has implemented prompt payment and adjudication legislation. The *Builders' Lien (Prompt Payment) Amendment Act, 2019*[20] came into force on 1 March 2022. This *Act* amended the *Builders' Lien Act*[21] to include prompt payment timelines and interim adjudication provisions. *The Builders' Lien Amendment Regulations, 2020* elaborate on these provisions. The Province of Alberta has also introduced prompt payment and adjudication legislation through its Bill 37 titled the *Builders' Lien (Prompt Payment) Amendment Act, 2020*.[22] This *Act* received royal assent on 9 December 2020 and will come into force on 29 August 2022,[23] along with accompanying regulations.[24] Likewise, the Province of Nova Scotia has introduced prompt payment and adjudication legislation through its Bill 119[25] which received royal assent on 12 April 2019. Once in force, Bill 119 will amend the *Builders' Lien Act*.[26] However, the Province of Nova Scotia has not announced the date on which this *Act* will come into force.

Some other Canadian Provinces are currently in the process of considering the development of prompt payment and adjudication legislation. For instance, on 24 January 2022, the Province of British Columbia established a working group to provide guidance on the development of prompt payment legislation to the Ministry of the Attorney General.[27] In the Province of New Brunswick, the Legislative Services Branch of the Office of the

17 *Ibid.*, Chapter 13.

18 *Construction Act*, *supra* n15, s 5(1).

19 *Ibid.* at s 4 (emphasis added).

20 SS 2019, c. 2.

21 SS 1984-85-86, c. B-7.1

22 Legislative Assembly of Alberta, Bill 37: Builders' Lien (Prompt Payment) Amendment Act, 2020. www.assembly.ab.ca/assembly-business/bills/bill?billinfoid=11872&from=bills (accessed 21 April 2022).

23 Government of Alberta, *Introducing Prompt Payment for Construction Industry*. www.alberta.ca/introducing-prompt-payment-for-construction-industry.aspx (accessed 21 April 2022).

24 See for example, Prompt Payment and Adjudication Regulation, Alta Reg 23/2022.

25 Bill 119, *Builders' Lien Act (Amended)*. https://nslegislature.ca/legc/bills/63rd_2nd/3rd_read/b119.htm (accessed 21 April 2022).

26 RSNS 1989, c. 277.

27 British Columbia Construction Association, 'BC Government Takes Action Toward Prompt Payment Legislation, Establishes Industry Working Group as Next Step'. https://bccassn.com/bc-government-takes-action-toward-prompt-payment-legislation-establishes-industry-working-group-as-next-step/ (accessed 21 April 2022).

Attorney General has indicated that it is monitoring prompt payment and adjudication regimes in other jurisdictions.[28]

The Province of Quebec is currently engaged in a pilot project testing various measures to facilitate prompt payment to businesses that are engaged in certain public contracts and subcontracts. Bill 108,[29] which received royal assent on 1 December 2017, amended the *Act respecting contracting by public bodies*.[30] Both prompt payment timelines and an adjudication regime are being tested and the Chair of the Conseil du trésor is responsible for implementing this pilot project.[31] Further, the *Act respecting the acceleration of certain infrastructure projects*[32] extended the pilot project to include those projects listed in Schedule I.

In addition, the Province of Manitoba has unsuccessfully attempted to enact prompt payment legislation on two occasions.[33] Recently, the Government of Manitoba introduced Bill 28 titled the *Prompt Payment for Construction Act*[34] which is currently in its first reading before the Legislative Assembly of Manitoba.[35]

In the federal sphere, the Canadian Government is in the process of enacting the *Federal Prompt Payment for Construction Work Act*.[36] The purpose of this *Act* is to address the non-payment of contractors and subcontractors who perform work on federal real property and federal immovable property as well as to encourage the timely carrying out and completion of these projects.[37] Once in force, this federal legislation will generally apply to projects involving federal real property and federal immovable property.

6.1.6 The court system in Canada

The Canadian court system contains various levels of Provincial, Territorial and Federal courts as well as certain specialised courts. Most Provinces and Territories have three levels of court, a lower court as well as a superior court with a trial level and an appellate level. However, the territory of Nunavut has a single-level trial court.

---

28 New Brunswick's *Construction Remedies Act* received royal assent on 18 December 2020 and the majority of its provisions came into force on 1 November 2021. This Act replaced the old *Mechanics' Lien Act*. The *Construction Remedies Act* does not currently include prompt payment and adjudication mechanisms. However, the Legislative Services Branch of the Office of the Attorney General has indicated that it is monitoring other prompt payment and adjudication regimes. See, for example, New Brunswick, Law Reform Notes of July 2019 (www2.gnb.ca/content/dam/gnb/Departments/ag-pg/PDF/en/LawReform/Notes42.pdf); New Brunswick, Law Reform Notes of April 2020 (www2.gnb.ca/content/dam/gnb/Departments/ag-pg/PDF/en/LawReform/Notes43.pdf); New Brunswick, Law Reform Notes of February 2021 (www2.gnb.ca/content/dam/gnb/Departments/ag-pg/PDF/en/LawReform/notes-44.pdf).

29 Bill 108, *An Act to facilitate oversight of public bodies' contract and to establish the Autorité des marchés publics* (www2.publicationsduquebec.gouv.qc.ca/dynamicSearch/telecharge.php?type=5&file=2017C27A.PDF).

30 Chapter C-65.1.

31 *Ibid.* at 24.3.

32 Chapter A-2.001.

33 See for example, Bill 218, *The Prompt Payment in the Construction Industry Act* https://web2.gov.mb.ca/bills/41-3/b218ei.php (accessed 21 April 2022) and Bill 245, *The Prompt Payment in the Construction Industry Act* https://web2.gov.mb.ca/bills/41-4/b245ei.php (accessed 21 April 2022).

34 Bill 28, *The Prompt Payment for Construction Act*, 4th Session, 42nd Legislature. https://web2.gov.mb.ca/bills/42-4/b028e.php (accessed 21 April 2022).

35 Legislative Assembly of Manitoba, Status of Bills Fourth Session, Forty-Second Legislature, 2021–2022. www.gov.mb.ca/legislature/business/billstatus.pdf (accessed 21 April 2022).

36 S.C. 2019, c. 29, s 387 (not in force).

37 *Ibid.* at s 4.

Trial-level superior courts can review the decisions of lower Provincial and Territorial courts and the appeal-level superior court can hear appeals from the trial-level superior court. Within the Provincial and Territorial courts, the superior courts tend to hear serious criminal and private law cases.

Generally, the trial-level superior court will be the court of first instance for a construction law dispute. Thereafter, the decision may be appealed to the appellate court level. In Ontario, disputes involving monetary claims of less than 35,000 Canadian dollars (US$28,000), may be heard at the Small Claims court which is a branch of the superior court.[38] Also, if the dispute at issue involves a monetary value or property value of 200,000 Canadian dollars (US$160,000) or less, parties in Ontario may use the Simplified Procedure process of the superior court.[39]

Some Federal and Provincial/Territorial statutes establish quasi-judicial administrative boards and tribunals. These boards and tribunals adjudicate disputes relating to the interpretation and application of particular laws and regulations. Administrative boards and tribunals are not part of the court system. However, board and tribunal decisions may be reviewed in court through an appeal or judicial review process, in certain circumstances.[40] In Ontario, for example, the Divisional Court hears statutory appeals from administrative tribunals in Ontario and applications for judicial review of administrative decisions.[41]

Canada also has a Federal Court with both a trial and an appellate level. The Federal Court has jurisdiction in relation to federal matters such as construction law issues relating to Federal Government procurement. The Federal Court also has jurisdiction to hear most judicial review applications with respect to federal boards and tribunals.[42] The Federal Court of Appeal only has jurisdiction to hear applications for judicial review arising from certain federal boards and tribunals listed in section 28(1) of the *Federal Courts Act*.[43]

The Supreme Court of Canada is the highest court in the country. The Supreme Court of Canada hears appeals from the Provincial and Territorial appellate courts, the Federal Court of Appeal, as well as the military court and the Court Martial Appeal Court. In civil cases, to appeal a decision to the Supreme Court of Canada, an applicant must first apply for leave to appeal by filing a written application. For the Supreme Court of Canada to grant leave to appeal, the case in dispute must raise issues of public importance, raise an important issue of law or mixed fact and law or otherwise be an issue of 'such a nature or significance as to warrant [a] decision by [the Supreme Court]'.[44] The Supreme Court of Canada has discretion to grant or deny leave and will not usually provide reasons for its

38 Superior Court of Justice, 'About the Small Claims Court'. www.ontariocourts.ca/scj/small-claims-court/ (accessed 21 April 2022).

39 Government of Ontario, 'Civil Claims: Simplified Procedure'. www.ontario.ca/page/civil-claims-simplified-procedure (accessed 21 April 2022).

40 Government of Canada, 'The Judicial Structure'. www.justice.gc.ca/eng/csj-sjc/just/07.html (accessed 21 April 2022).

41 Superior Court of Justice, 'Divisional Court'. www.ontariocourts.ca/scj/divisional-court/ (accessed 21 April 2022).

42 Federal Court, 'Administrative Law'. www.fct-cf.gc.ca/en/pages/about-the-court/jurisdiction/administrative-law#cont (accessed 21 April 2022).

43 R.S.C., 1985, c. F-7 at s 28(1). The Federal Court of Appeal has the jurisdiction to hear judicial review applications arising from the boards and tribunals listed in section 28(1) of the *Federal Courts Act*.

44 *Supreme Court Act*, R.S.C., 1985, c. S-26 at s 40(1).

decision.[45] If an application for leave to appeal is dismissed, the appeal will not be heard and this decision is final. However, if an application for leave to appeal is granted, parties will have an opportunity to argue their appeal and the Supreme Court of Canada will then render a judgement. Overall, hundreds of applications for leave to appeal are filed each year but the Supreme Court of Canada only hears about 80 appeals per year.[46]

The Federal Government appoints judges to the Supreme Court of Canada as well as the Federal Courts and the Provincial and Territorial Superior Courts. However, the Provincial and Territorial Governments appoint all other Provincial and Territorial judges.

Common law courts in Canada apply the principle of *stare decisis et non quieta movere*. In other words, judges in Canada consider themselves bound by higher court decisions within the same jurisdiction. For example, a construction law decision of the Ontario Court of Appeal would bind the Ontario Superior court. However, this decision would not bind the Manitoba Court of Queen's Bench because decisions of appellate courts in one Province do not bind trial-level courts in another Province but can be relied upon for their persuasive value. Decisions of the Supreme Court of Canada bind all Provincial and Territorial appellate-level courts.

6.2 The construction industry in Canada

6.2.1 Overview

The construction industry is a critical part of the Canadian economy. In 2021, there were over 1.432 million people in the Canadian labour force.[47] Further, the construction industry contributes billions of dollars to Canada's Gross Domestic Product (GDP) each month. For example, in 2021, the construction industry contributed between 145.72 and 155.50 billion Canadian dollars (US$115.7b to US$123.5b) to the GDP each month.[48]

The Canadian construction industry is composed of many construction firms engaged in the construction, development, repair, renovation and engineering of structures. For example, in 2020, there were approximately 376,987 construction businesses across Canada.[49] This number is exclusive of businesses which primarily manufacture and/or install building equipment as well as businesses that provide administrative and support services to the industry. Therefore, there is a multitude of construction-related businesses in Canada.

Most construction establishments in Canada are small businesses with one to 99 employees. In fact, in 2020 less than 1% of construction businesses employed between

45 Supreme Court of Canada, 'Role of the Court'. www.scc-csc.ca/court-cour/role-eng.aspx#:~:text=First%2C%20in%20most%20cases%2C%20a,to%20appeal%20is%20not%20required (accessed 21 April 2022).

46 See Supreme Court of Canada, 'Guide'. www.scc-csc.ca/unrep-nonrep/app-dem/guide-eng.aspx (accessed 21 April 2022).

47 Statistics Canada, 'Labour Force Characteristics by Industry'. www150.statcan.gc.ca/t1/tbl1/en/tv.action?pid=1410002301 (accessed 22 April 2022).

48 Statistics Canada, 'Gross Domestic Product (GDP) at Basic Prices, by Industry, Monthly (× 1,000,000)'. www150.statcan.gc.ca/t1/tbl1/en/tv.action?pid=3610043401&pickMembers%5B0%5D=2.1&pickMembers%5B1%5D=3.1&cubeTimeFrame.startMonth=01&cubeTimeFrame.startYear=2021&cubeTimeFrame.endMonth=12&cubeTimeFrame.endYear=2021&referencePeriods=20210101%2C20211201 (accessed 22 April 2022).

49 Government of Canada, 'Summary – Canadian Industry Statistics (Construction)'. www.ic.gc.ca/app/scr/app/cis/summary-sommaire/23 (accessed 22 April 2022).

100 and 499 employees.[50] The average revenue of a small and medium-sized enterprise (SME) was 499,700 Canadian dollars (US$396,800).[51] In 2020, less than 0.1% of construction businesses in Canada were considered large businesses, employing over 500 people.[52] However, large construction companies in Canada play a critical role in the industry and in stimulating the Canadian economy. For instance, in 2020, the top ten largest contractors in Canada produced a total collective revenue of over US$ 30 billion.

6.2.1.1 Investing in Canada's construction industry

The Federal and Provincial/Territorial Governments are investing in the Canadian construction industry. For instance, in 2016, the Government of Canada committed 180 billion Canadian dollars (US$143b) over 12 years to infrastructure investment through the Investing in Canada Plan (the **Plan**). The Plan aims, in part, to build new urban transit networks and extensions to existing networks. The Plan has the following five investment streams:

- Public transit infrastructure stream (28.7 billion Canadian dollars [US$22.8b])
- Green infrastructure stream (26.9 billion Canadian dollars [US$21.3b])
- Social infrastructure stream (25.3 billion Canadian dollars [US$18.6b])
- Trade and transportation infrastructure stream (10.1 billion Canadian dollars [US$8b]), and
- Rural and northern communities infrastructure stream (2 billion Canadian dollars [US$1.6b])

With respect to the public transit infrastructure stream, the Government of Canada has invested over 13 billion Canadian dollars (US$10.3b) in over 1,300 public transit projects across the country. This funding has contributed to the development of over 240 kilometres of public transit subways and light rail transit lines in Canada.[53]

Further, the Investing in Canada Infrastructure Program (the **Program**) delivers funding to Provinces and Territories through bilateral agreements. Through the Program, the Canadian Government will contribute 33.5 billion Canadian dollars (US$26.6b) to public infrastructure projects across the country over the next 11 years.[54] The Canada Community-Building Fund (the **Fund**) is another example of federal funding used to support infrastructure development in Canada. Each year, the Fund provides 2 billion Canadian dollars (US$1.6b) to communities across the country. Once received, communities can direct the

50 Government of Canada, 'Canadian Industry Statistics'. www.ic.gc.ca/app/scr/app/cis/businesses-entreprises/23 (accessed 22 April 2022).

51 'Summary – Canadian Industry Statistics', *supra* n49.

52 'Canadian Industry Statistics', *supra* n50.

53 Government of Canada, 'Investing in Canada Plan – Building a Better Canada'. www.infrastructure.gc.ca/plan/about-invest-apropos-eng.html (accessed 22 April 2022). See also, Government of Canada, 'Investing in Canada Plan Funding Steam – Public Transit Infrastructure'. www.infrastructure.gc.ca/plan/pti-itc-eng.html (accessed 22 April 2022).

54 Government of Canada, 'Investing in Canada Infrastructure Program'. www.infrastructure.gc.ca/plan/icp-pic-INFC-eng.html (accessed 22 April 2022); see also, 2022 Budget, 'A Plan to Grow Our Economy and Make Life More Affordable'. https://budget.gc.ca/2022/pdf/budget-2022-en.pdf (accessed 22 April 2022).

funds into any of the permitted project categories which include public transit, wastewater infrastructure, highways and local and regional airport development.[55]

Canada's Budget for 2022, which was released on 7 April 2022, indicates that the Government of Canada will also contribute 150 million Canadian dollars (US$119m) to the Territorial Governments in an effort to support affordable housing initiatives and infrastructure development over the next two years.[56] The Government of Canada also plans to contribute 396.8 million Canadian dollars (US$314.9m) to support Transport Canada and Infrastructure Canada in their development of a high-frequency rail system between the City of Toronto in Ontario and Quebec City in the Province of Quebec.[57]

The Canada Infrastructure Bank (the **CIB**) is a Crown corporation created in 2017 which operates at arm's length from the Government of Canada. The CIB will also invest 35 billion Canadian dollars (US$27.8b) in infrastructure development.[58]

Provincial and Territorial Governments across Canada are also investing in infrastructure. For example, the Government of Ontario indicated in its March 2021 Budget that the Provincial Government would invest approximately 145.5 billion Canadian dollars (US$115.5b) in infrastructure projects over the next decade. Namely, the Government of Ontario plans to invest in the development and improvement of transit lines, highways, education and healthcare facilities, as well as broadband in order to stimulate economic growth and ease post-pandemic economic recovery.[59]

Lastly, investment in residential and non-residential construction has also increased in recent times. For example, in January 2022, investment in residential construction rose by 4.1% to 14.1 billion Canadian dollars (US$11.2b) and investment in non-residential construction increased by 1.5% to 5 billion Canadian dollars (US$4b).[60] Therefore, individuals and governments continue to invest in Canadian construction projects.

6.2.1.2 Public Infrastructure Projects

Public–Private Partnerships (**P3s**) are often used on large public infrastructure projects. P3s can take a number of different forms. In Canada, the Design Build Finance and Maintain model (**DBFM**) is common.[61] Generally, a government authority (commonly referred to as **Contracting Authority**) will contract with a special-purpose entity (commonly referred to as **Project Co**). Project Co is often composed of joint ventures, depending on the size of the project. Project Co contracts with a design-builder for the design and construction phase of a project who will then subcontract the work to trade contractors and suppliers. Project Co will provide all or part of the financing for the project's design and construction.

55 Government of Canada, 'The Canada Community-Building Fund'. www.infrastructure.gc.ca/plan/gtf-fte-eng.html (accessed 22 April 2022).

56 2022 Budget, *supra* n54, 61.

57 *Ibid.*, 101.

58 Government of Canada, 'Canada Infrastructure Bank'. www.infrastructure.gc.ca/CIB-BIC/index-eng.html (accessed 22 April 2022).

59 2021 Ontario Budget, 'Ontario's Action Plan – Protecting People's Health and Our Economy'. https://budget.ontario.ca/2021/pdf/2021-ontario-budget-en.pdf (accessed 22 April 2022).

60 Statistics Canada, 'Investment in Building Construction', January 2022. www150.statcan.gc.ca/n1/daily-quotidien/220314/dq220314a-eng.htm?indid=19277-1&indgeo=0 (accessed 22 April 2022).

61 Thomson Reuters Practical Law, 'Construction and Projects in Canada: Overview'. https://uk.practicallaw.thomsonreuters.com/9-502-1837?transitionType=Default&contextData=(sc.Default)&firstPage=true#co_anchor_a868360 (accessed 22 April 2022).

The design-builder may also be responsible for the project's operation and maintenance after completion for a period of time specified in the parties' Project Agreement. This period of time often spans 30 years in the Canadian context.[62]

There are currently 291 active P3s in Canada with a total market value of approximately 139.48 billion Canadian dollars (US$110.8b).[63]

6.2.2 Licencing/registration of professionals and skilled trades

In Canada, professions are generally a matter of Provincial and Territorial jurisdiction. Therefore, the Provinces and Territories generally enact laws respecting the professions. In Ontario, the *Architects Act*,[64] the *Professional Engineers Act*[65] and the *Surveyors Act*[66] set out laws pertaining to the architecture, engineering and surveying professions, respectively.

Further, the aforementioned *Acts* also sanction governing bodies to regulate the respective profession. For example, the *Architects Act* authorises the Ontario Association of Architects to regulate the practice of architecture and to govern members of the profession. Likewise, the *Professional Engineers Act* authorises the Association of Professional Engineers of Ontario to regulate the engineering profession and the *Surveyors Act* authorises the Association of Ontario Land Surveyors to regulate the surveying profession.

The bodies responsible for governing professions protect the public interest by ensuring that only properly qualified individuals practice a given profession. Therefore, governing bodies generally ensure that members adhere to standards of practice and ethics and ensure that prospective licencees meet certain professional standards and competencies. For example, persons wishing to practice legal boundary surveying in Ontario must complete an approved baccalaureate-level programme in professional surveying (Geomatics), followed by the completion of an articling period and professional examinations. Thereafter, a licencee must continue to adhere to codes of ethics and standards of professional practice.

Further, certification requirements for skilled trades are also a matter of Provincial and Territorial jurisdiction in Canada. For example, Ontario's *Building Opportunities in the Skilled Trades Act, 2021* authorises the Minister to, for example, prescribe the scope of practice for a given trade[67] and classify trades as compulsory trades.[68]

A compulsory trade is one which requires a tradesperson to obtain a Certificate of Qualification or a Provisional Certificate of Qualification issued by Skilled Trades Ontario to work in the trade.[69] Alternatively, a compulsory trade may require a tradesperson to reg-

62 Infrastructure Canada, 'Project Agreement: New Bridge for St. Lawrence Project'. www.infrastructure.gc.ca/nbsl-npsl/agreement-entente-eng.html (accessed 22 April 2022).

63 Spectrum, 'Public–Private Partnership Statistics in Canada'. www.p3spectrum.ca/project/ (accessed 22 April 2022).

64 R.S.O. 1990, c. A.26.

65 R.S.O. 1990, c. P.28.

66 R.S.O. 1990, c. S.29.

67 *Building Opportunities in the Skilled Trades Act, 2021*, S.O. 2021, c. 28 at s 2(c).

68 *Ibid.* at s 2(b).

69 Skilled Trades Ontario, 'Compulsory Trades'. www.skilledtradesontario.ca/about-trades/compulsory-trades/ (accessed 22 April 2022). See also, Saskatchewan Apprenticeship and Trade Certification Commission. https://saskapprenticeship.ca/ (accessed 22 April 2022).; Government of Alberta, 'Apprenticeship and Industry

ister as an apprentice with the Ministry of Labour, Training and Skills Development and to hold a Registered Training Agreement to legally work in the trade.[70] In either case, the information of a tradesperson working in a compulsory trade must appear in the Skilled Trades Ontario Public Register.

On the other hand, a tradesperson working in a non-compulsory trade is not required to obtain a Certificate of Qualification, a Provisional Certificate of Qualification or a Registered Training Agreement. The information of a tradesperson working in a non-compulsory trade will not appear in the Skilled Trades Ontario Public Register. However, a tradesperson working in a non-compulsory trade can choose to pursue an apprenticeship programme and, in some instances, write a certifying examination and obtain a Certificate of Qualification.[71]

For example, plumbing is a compulsory trade which requires the completion of an apprenticeship programme and a certifying exam. Once a Certificate of Apprenticeship is obtained and a certifying exam is passed, Skilled Trades Ontario will issue a Certificate of Qualification in plumbing. Thereafter, the tradesperson's name will appear in the Skilled Trades Ontario Public Register and the Certificate of Qualification in plumbing must be renewed periodically.

On the other hand, the general contractor trade is not a compulsory trade in Ontario. A general contractor may choose to obtain a Certificate of Qualification but a renewal of this certificate is not necessary and the tradespersons' information will not appear in the Skilled Trades Ontario Public Register. However, general contractors and developers are required to be licenced in the Province of British Columbia.

A number of trades are regulated in the Province of Quebec. Tradespersons in Quebec seeking to practice a regulated trade must obtain either a competency certificate from the Commission de la construction du Québec (**CCQ**) or a certificate of qualification from Emploi-Québec (**EQ**). For example, to become an electrician or plumber in the Province of Quebec, a tradesperson must obtain a certificate of qualification from EQ.[72] Subject to particular exemptions, anyone who carries out construction work or who has construction work carried out in Quebec requires a licence issued by the Régie du bâtiment du Québec (the **RB**).[73]

Like in the Province of British Columbia, general contractors in Quebec typically require a licence.[74] A licence granted by the RB is required for general contractors who organise, coordinate or carry out certain construction works. With a licence, a general contractor can bid on and carry out construction work covered by their licence and have certain construction work carried out on their behalf.[75]

Training'. https://tradesecrets.alberta.ca/ (accessed 22 April 2022); Province of British Columbia, 'Work BC'. www.workbc.ca/Training-Education/Trades-Training.aspx (accessed 22 April 2022).

70 Skilled Trades Ontario, 'Mandate'. www.skilledtradesontario.ca/about-us/mandate/ (accessed 22 April 2022).

71 Skilled Trades Ontario, 'Non-Compulsory Trades'. www.skilledtradesontario.ca/about-trades/non-compulsory-trades/ (accessed 22 April 2022).

72 Province of Quebec, 'Regulated Professions and Trades'. www.quebec.ca/en/employment/trades-occupations/regulated-professions-trades/regulated-construction-trades (accessed 22 April 2022).

73 Quebec, 'All the Steps for Obtaining a Licence'. www.rbq.gouv.qc.ca/en/licence/obtaining-your-licence/all-the-steps-for-obtaining-a-licence.html (accessed 22 April 2022).

74 Province of Quebec, 'General Contractor Subclasses'. www.rbq.gouv.qc.ca/en/licence/determining-your-licence-subclasses/general-contractor-subclasses.html (accessed 22 April 2022).

75 *Ibid.*

Across Canada, both the plumbing and general contractor trades are part of the Interprovincial Red Seal Program. Upon passing an exam and obtaining a Red Seal endorsement, a tradesperson will be seen as having the requisite knowledge and skill needed to practise the trade anywhere in Canada.[76]

6.2.2.1 Municipal licencing

The Provinces and Territories of Canada along with the Municipalities within them generally have laws dealing with the use, development and redevelopment of land. Also, Municipalities generally require Municipal licencing prior to the commencement of a construction project. For example, the City of Toronto in Ontario requires constructors to obtain a building permit prior to the construction, demolition, addition or renovation of a building. Once construction plans are submitted to the City of Toronto, the plans will be reviewed for compliance with the *Ontario Building Code*, municipal zoning by-laws and various laws such as the *Planning Act*[77] and the *Environmental Protection Act*.[78] Once the City of Toronto issues a building permit, the *Ontario Building Code* requires mandatory inspections at various stages throughout the construction process as well as the issuance of an Occupancy Permit towards the end of construction.[79] Various Municipalities across the country have comparable laws and processes with respect to construction projects.

Projects within the jurisdiction of the Federal Government may require the issuance of federal permits or licences prior to the commencement of construction work.

6.2.3 Labour relations

In Canada, both the Federal Government and the Provincial/Territorial Governments have enacted laws relating to labour and employment in the country. The common law and the *Civil Code* in Quebec also govern the law relating to labour and employment. In Ontario, the *Labour Relations Act*[80] sets out laws governing the relationship between employers, employees and trade unions. For example, the *Labour Relations Act, 1995* outlines laws pertaining to collective agreements as well as bargaining rights and includes sections focused specifically on labour relations in the construction industry.[81]

Further, Ontario's *Employment Standards Act*[82] sets out the minimum standards that employers must meet in areas such as payment of wages, vacation with pay, overtime pay and the minimum wage. There are various *Regulations* made under the *Employment Standards Act* such as *O. Reg. 288/01*[83] which provides greater detail with respect to the lawful termination and severance of an employee.

---

76 Red Seal, 'The Red Seal Program'. www.red-seal.ca/eng/w.2lc.4m.2.shtml (accessed 22 April 2022).

77 R.S.O. 1990, c. P.13.

78 R.S.O. 1990, c. E. 19.

79 City of Toronto, 'Legislated Mandatory Inspections'. www.toronto.ca/services-payments/building-construction/building-inspections/about-building-inspections/ (accessed 22 April 2022).

80 S.O. 1995, c. 1, Sched. A.

81 *Ibid.* at s 126-150.6.

82 S.O. 2000, c. 41.

83 O. Reg. 288/01: Termination and Severance of Employment.

There are various tribunals across Canada which review applications involving labour and employment laws. For example, the Ontario Labour Relations Board[84] has jurisdiction over the *Labour Relations Act* and the *Employment Standards Act*. The tribunal reviews applications for certification of a trade union in a workplace and applications concerning unfair labour practices, amongst other things.

Provincial and Territorial *Codes* also affect labour and employment laws across the country. In Ontario, the *Human Rights Code*[85] provides that all employees have a right to equal treatment without discrimination[86] and that employees have a right to freedom from harassment in the workplace.[87] The Human Rights Tribunal of Ontario has jurisdiction to hear applications relating to discrimination and harassment in the workplace.[88]

Overall, there are many laws across the country governing labour relations and the employment of workers, including those workers engaged in the construction industry.

6.2.4 Safety culture

Federal and Provincial labour and employment laws, as well as Provincial health and safety laws generally impose significant health and safety requirements on construction projects across Canada. For example, the *Occupational Health and Safety Act*[89] governs health and safety laws in Ontario and provides specific duties on the part of constructors and project owners.[90] There are various *Regulations* passed under the *Occupational Health and Safety Act*.[91] This particular *Regulation* imposes requirements with respect to a wide range of topics such as protective clothing to be worn on site, proper use of ladders and scaffolds, as well as safety standards applicable to work in tunnels, shafts, caissons and cofferdams.[92]

Further, under the *Occupational Health and Safety Act*, employers and constructors are required to report workplace incidents and occupational illness to the Ministry of Labour, Training and Skills Development and to provide a written report. Employers are also responsible for reporting to their joint health and safety committee or representative as well as to the employee's union, if applicable.

In addition, inspectors under the *Occupational Health and Safety Act* have broad powers to enter workplaces without obtaining a warrant as well as to inspect equipment and/ or physical agents in or around the workplace, amongst other things.[93] Those who fail to comply with the *Occupational Health and Safety Act* may face significant consequences. For instance, a person who fails to comply with a provision of the *Act* or its regulations may

84 Ontario Labour Relations Board, 'Does Your Concern Fall under the Board?' www.olrb.gov.on.ca/Jurisdiction-EN.asp (accessed 22 April 2022).

85 R.S.O. 1990, c. H. 19.

86 *Ibid.* at s 5(1).

87 *Ibid.* at s 5(2).

88 Tribunals Ontario, 'Human Rights Tribunal of Ontario'. https://tribunalsontario.ca/hrto/ (accessed 22 April 2022).

89 R.S.O. 1990, c. O.1 [*Occupational Health and Safety Act*].

90 *Ibid.* at s 23, 30.

91 O. Reg. 213/91: Construction Projects.

92 *Ibid.*

93 *Occupational Health and Safety Act*, *supra* n89, s 54.

be guilty of an offence and charged a fine of up to 100,000 Canadian dollars (US$79,400) and/or a term of imprisonment of not more than 12 months.[94]

Further, construction industry employers are often responsible for obtaining workers' compensation coverage through Provincial plans and reporting accidents to compensation boards. The Workplace Safety and Insurance Board (the **WSIB**) in Ontario provides workplace insurance to employees in exchange for employer-paid premiums,[95] and employers are responsible for reporting accidents to the WSIB. The *Workplace Safety and Insurance Act, 1997*[96] governs the WSIB in Ontario.

Overall, the health and safety of construction workers in Canada is of crucial importance. Canadian Provinces have developed robust health and safety legislation and enforcement mechanisms. Parties to a construction project need to ensure that they are aware of and meet all applicable health and safety laws and obtain appropriate coverage under Provincial compensation plans for their workers.

6.2.5 Technology and innovation

The Canadian construction industry is adopting technologies that will aid in increasing productivity and efficiency throughout the industry. In November 2020, the Canadian Construction Association and KPMG Canada joined forces to conduct a survey to determine how Canadian construction businesses are adapting to technological innovation.[97] The survey asked companies to rate their digital capabilities in a number of areas. The most commonly adopted technologies in the industry appear to be those relating to cyber security and cloud technologies. However, some Canadian construction companies are planning to implement technologies such as intelligent automation, bid data and augmented decision support. Some Canadian construction companies are also planning to integrate more internet-connected devices on construction sites. These devices include but are not limited to drones, machine control systems and site access and time tracking devices.[98]

Many countries around the world have developed national Building Information Management (**BIM**) mandates which require the use of BIM technologies on public and/or private projects. Although Canada does not currently have a national mandate outlining standards of practice and/or use requirements pertaining to BIM, it is becoming widely used throughout the country.[99] BIM is expected to significantly impact the future of project information and design practices in fields such as construction management, engineering and architecture.[100]

---

94 *Ibid.* at s 66.

95 WSIB Ontario, 'Register with Us'. www.wsib.ca/en/businesses/registration-and-coverage/register-us (accessed 22 April 2022).

96 S.O. 1997, c. 16, Sched. A.

97 KPMG Canada and the Canadian Construction Association, 'Construction in a Digital World'. https://assets.kpmg/content/dam/kpmg/ca/pdf/2021/05/construction-in-the-digital-age-report-en.pdf (accessed 22 April 2022).

98 See Daniel S Brennan, 'The Internet of Things in Construction: Opportunity, Risk and Insurance Considerations' (2019) Volume 13, Issue 2 *Journal of the American College of Construction Lawyers* 1.

99 AECO Innovation Lab, *3rd Annual BIM Report* (2020). https://static1.squarespace.com/static/5eff5bdef5beea28d155a50f/t/5fa09661054854317d528b46/1604359784353/AEC111_BIMReport_02b.pdf (accessed 22 April 2022).

100 *Ibid.*

Overall, Canadian businesses and the overall construction industry will benefit greatly from the use and implementation of various construction technologies.

6.2.6 Procurement

In Canada, owners, particularly public sector owners (collectively, Project Owners) frequently engage in competitive procurement processes to procure goods and services in accordance with their own policies and procedures and relevant trade treaties. Procurement processes often commence with either the Project Owner's issuance of a call for tenders or a request for proposals (**RFP**).

With respect to tendering, there is a set of principles established through the common law governing the tender process as it relates to construction contracts. The overarching proposition is that a Project Owner will receive the best value for contracted service through competition, not negotiation. To further this proposition, courts have developed the following principles:

- The tendering system must be safeguarded and maintained
- An owner must treat all tenders fairly, and
- One tender should not gain an unfair advantage over another[101]

Therefore, these principles are aimed at ensuring that Project Owners obtain competitive prices through the tender or RFP process and that bidders are treated equally.

During the tender process, a tenderer will submit a bid to provide labour or materials for a project. If the bid is compliant, a binding contract will be formed between the Project Owner and tenderer. This contract is known as Contract A. Generally, the Project Owner must then award the construction contract to the bidder with the lowest bid price. This contract is known as Contract B. The tenderer must agree to enter into Contract B and perform the work as set out in the bid documents.[102] A Project Owner who fails to follow the tender process may face claims for lost profits from unsuccessful tenderers.

In an RFP process, the Project Owner may initially issue a request for qualifications (**RFQ**). The RFQ is usually issued together with background information describing the project scope, the necessary proponent qualifications and prospective proponent evaluation criteria.[103] In response to the RFQ, prospective proponents will provide the Project Owner with requested information such as information regarding its design, construction and maintenance teams, as well as information demonstrating the prospective proponent's ability to obtain financing for the project. The Project Owner will then issue an RFP to certain proponents who satisfy the RFQ requirements. The RFP will provide detailed information to proponents such as information regarding the project scope, the selection process and the evaluation criteria for the proposal. In response to the RFP, proponents will submit a non-binding proposal to the Project Owner. In preparation for the submission, proponents will submit requests for information and engage in meetings with the Project Owner to collect relevant information about the project and to determine how best

101 *Construction Law in Canada, supra* n16, Chapter 4.I.
102 *The Queen (Ont.) v Ron Engineering*, [1981] 1 SCR 111.
103 *Construction Law in Canada, supra* n16, Chapter 4.

to formulate their proposals. The proponents will develop construction designs, schedules and maintenance plans for the project. Once the shortlist of proponents has submitted their proposals, the Project Owner will evaluate the proposals and select a preferred proponent to complete the project, and the contract will be finalised.[104]

In determining whether tendering law applies to an RFP process, the specific language of the RFP must be considered.[105] If tendering law does not apply to an RFP process, an RFP will be considered an invitation to treat. However, a hybrid procurement process is possible whereby tendering law applies in part to an RFP process. For example, there have been instances where a Project Owner initiates a two-part RFP process whereby proponents submit two proposal packages, involving a technical submission and a financial submission and the financial submission in particular may be found to constitute Contract A.[106]

Whether a Project Owner chooses to pursue a tender or RFP procurement method will be dependent on the specific project under consideration.

6.2.7 Anti-corruption measures

On or around 17 December 1997, Canada became a signatory to the Organization for Economic Co-operation and Development **(OECD)** *Convention on Combating Bribery in International Business Transactions*.[107] The *OECD Convention* aims to criminalise and deter the bribery of foreign public officials engaged in international transactions.[108]

Since then, Canada has strengthened its anti-corruption regime through the enactment or enhancement of various statutes. For example, the *Corruption of Foreign Public Officials Act*[109] (***CFPO Act***) has since been enacted. The *CFPO Act* makes it an offence to bribe a foreign official in an attempt to influence the award of a construction contract. In addition, section 121 of Canada's *Criminal Code*[110] makes it an offence to directly or indirectly give, offer or agree to offer a benefit to a government official in exchange for assistance in government-related business transactions such as government procurements.[111] Further, the federal *Competition Act*[112] contains provisions which criminalise bid rigging. For example, section 47 indicates that individuals who engage in bid-rigging are guilty of an indictable offence. Upon conviction, individuals can be liable to a fine and/or a term of imprisonment of up to 14 years.[113]

---

104 Thomson Reuters Practical Law, 'Construction and Projects in Canada: Overview'. https://uk.practicallaw.thomsonreuters.com/9-502-1837?transitionType=Default&contextData=(sc.Default)&firstPage=true#co_anchor_a868360 (accessed 22 April 2022).

105 *Buttcon Ltd v Toronto Electric Commissioners*, 2003 CanLII 9258 (ON SC).

106 Glaholt Bowles, Paul Sandori & William M. Pigott, *Bidding and Tendering – What Is the Law?* (6th edn, LexisNexis Canada, 2020).

107 Government of Canada (Global Affairs Canada), 'Bribery and Corruption'. www.international.gc.ca/trade-agreements-accords-commerciaux/topics-domaines/other-autre/corruption.aspx?lang=eng#:~:text=On%20December%2017%2C%201997%2C%20Canada,and%20Development%20(OECD%20Convention (accessed 22 April 2022).

108 OECD, 'OECD Convention on Combating Bribery of Foreign Public Officials in International Business Transactions' (www.oecd.org/corruption/oecdantibriberyconvention.htm (accessed 22 April 2022).

109 S.C. 1998, c. 34.

110 R.S.C., 1985, c. C-46.

111 *Ibid.* at 121(1)(a).

112 R.S.C., 1985, c. C-34.

113 *Ibid.* at s 47(2).

Lastly, the Government of Canada introduced an 'Integrity Regime' in 2015 which attempts to ensure that Canada only engages in business transactions with ethical suppliers.[114] Therefore, suppliers who have been convicted of offences such as accounting offences under the *CFPO Act*, bribery of officials under the *Criminal Code* or offences related to bid rigging under the *Competition Act* will be ineligible to transact with the Government of Canada.[115] Individuals or entities with these or similar convictions are disqualified from the award of government construction contracts.

6.2.8 Insurance requirements

There are many types of insurance policies available for construction projects in Canada. Insurance is necessary to effectively manage risk on a project. In Canada, the Insurance Bureau of Canada provides benchmark insurance policies which are used by underwriters throughout the country. The most important policies on a construction project are generally the builder's risk policy, the wrap-up liability policy and the professional liability policy.

Builder's risk insurance generally covers physical loss or damage to property on the construction site arising from an insured event. Whereas a wrap-up liability policy generally provides blanket liability coverage to all stakeholders participating in the construction project. In addition, professional liability policies are available for designers, consultants and engineers.

In addition, the following types of insurance policies are commonly used on Canadian construction projects:

- Commercial general liability policies
- Boiler and machinery and contractor's equipment insurance
- Delayed completion/*force majeure*/liquidated damages insurance
- Project-specific and owner-controlled insurance
- Default insurance, and
- Pollution insurance/insurance for environmental hazards

The types of insurance required on a construction project may vary depending on the language of the parties' contract.

As mentioned previously, construction industry employers are also generally responsible for obtaining workers' compensation coverage for their employees through provincial plans.

6.2.9 Common forms of contract

Standard-form contracts are often used on construction projects in Canada. Construction stakeholders in the public and private sectors often use the CCDC suite of contracts. For example, project owners and contractors often use the CCDC 2 Stipulated Price Contract

114 Government of Canada, 'Guide to the *Ineligibility and Suspension Policy*'. www.tpsgc-pwgsc.gc.ca/ci-if/guide-eng.html (accessed 22 April 2022).

115 *Ibid.*

to arrange their affairs. However, contracting parties often amend or supplement standard form provisions through the drafting of supplementary General Conditions.

The Canadian Construction Association (the **CCA**) publishes standard form subcontracts that are commonly used in the industry. For instance, Contractors and Subcontractors will often arrange their affairs through the use of the CCA 1 – 2008 Stipulated Price Subcontract.

Further, when retaining a prime consultant, the Royal Architectural Institute Contract Form[116] is commonly used to retain an architect and the Association of Consulting Engineers of Canada forms are commonly used to retain an engineer.[117]

Currently, the FIDIC suite contracts are not commonly used domestically in Canada.

6.2.10 Dispute resolution

Construction disputes in Canada are generally dealt with in either a public or private forum. In regard to the public forum, construction litigation often falls within the jurisdiction of the Provincial and Territorial Superior Courts. For instance, a party to a construction dispute in Ontario may commence a civil action in the Superior Court of Justice. In addition, in the City of Toronto, there are specialised associate judges who resolve disputes relating to construction lien matters arising from the *Construction Act*.

Further, in Ontario, contracting parties have the right to refer the following disputes to adjudication based on the *Construction Act*:

1. The valuation of services or materials provided under the contract.
2. Payment under the contract, including in respect of a change order, whether approved or not, or a proposed change order.
3. Disputes that are the subject of a notice of non-payment …
4. Amounts retained under section 12 (set-off by trustee) or under subsection 17 (3) (lien set-off).
5. Payment of a holdback under section 26.1 or 26.2.
6. Non-payment of holdback under section 27.1.
7. Any other matter that the parties to the adjudication agree to, or that may be prescribed.[118]

The Ontario Dispute Adjudication for Construction Contracts (**ODACC**) is the Authorized Nominating Authority responsible for administering adjudications under the *Construction Act*.[119]

More commonly, parties to construction disputes in Canada engage in alternative dispute resolution (**ADR**), often as a result of the construction contract containing a mandatory dispute resolution process. ADR includes amicable negotiation and neutral, non-binding mediation which is a commonly used form of ADR. Mediation is sometimes

116 Royal Architectural Institute of Canada, 'Canadian Standard Form of Contract for Architectural Services'. https://raic.org/raic/canadian-standard-form-contract-architectural-services-document-six-2018-edition (accessed 22 April 2022).

117 Association of Consulting Engineering Companies Canada, 'Products'. www.acec.ca/products.html/shopping/index/view-category/id/5 (accessed 22 April 2022).

118 *Construction Act*, *supra* n15, s 13.5(1).

119 *Ibid.* at s 13.2.

mandated through contract. Otherwise, in some jurisdictions such as Ontario, it is mandatory to engage in mediation prior to trial.[120]

Arbitration is another form of ADR used in Canada to resolve construction disputes. Provincial and Territorial Governments have enacted legislation governing arbitration. For example, the *Arbitration Act, 1991*[121] governs arbitration proceedings in Ontario. Further, parties who agree to partake in arbitration proceedings often follow the ADR Institute of Canada's Arbitration Rules.[122]

Dispute Boards are not commonly used in Canada yet. However, the use of Dispute Boards may become more prominent in Canada over time.

6.3 The impact of COVID-19 in Canada

6.3.1 The impact of COVID-19 on the execution of construction projects in Canada

At the outset of the global COVID-19 pandemic, Provincial Governments implemented measures to halt segments of the construction industry. For example, in March 2020, the Government of Ontario enacted a regulation under the *Emergency Management and Civil Protection Act* which mandated the closure of businesses other than those that were deemed to be essential.[123] Construction projects relating to critical provincial infrastructure including transit and transportation were permitted to remain open. On the other hand, certain construction projects which were not included on the essential workplaces list, such as certain residential construction projects, were paused for a period of time. All construction projects in Ontario have since been permitted to resume operation.

Further, industry stakeholders modified their health and safety practices to align with new standards. Parties adapted to physical distancing measures, sanitisation requirements and the use of personal protective equipment, amongst other things.[124] These precautions continue to constitute best practices on construction sites.

In addition, the COVID-19 pandemic has caused widespread changes in the Canadian construction industry. For instance, the industry continues to experience labour shortages. For example, in the fourth quarter of 2021, employers in the construction industry were actively seeking to fill 69,000 vacant positions as compared to 32,900 vacancies in the fourth quarter of 2019.[125] Many labourers have declined to return to work due to COVID-19-related health concerns. Canada has also offered financial assistance to those Canadians whose employment was affected by the COVID-19 pandemic.[126] Overall, the demand for construction labour has been high while the supply of labour has diminished.

120 *Courts of Justice Act*, R.R.O. 1990, c. C. 43 – Reg. 194: Rules of Civil Procedure at R 24.1.

121 S.O. 1991, c. 17.

122 ADR Institute of Canada, 'ADRIC Arbitration Rules'. https://adric.ca/wp-content/uploads/2017/08/2016_ARBITRATION_RULES_Booklet_2016_Aug2017.pdf (accessed 22 April 2022).

123 *Order Under Subsection 7.0.2(4) – Closure of Places of Non-Essential Businesses*, O. Reg. 82/20.

124 Government of Ontario, 'Construction Site Health and Safety during COVID-19'. www.ontario.ca/page/construction-site-health-and-safety-during-covid-19) (accessed 22 April 2022).

125 Statistics Canada, 'Job Vacancies, Fourth Quarter 2021'. www150.statcan.gc.ca/n1/daily-quotidien/220322/dq220322a-eng.htm (accessed 22 April 2022).

126 Government of Canada, 'Canada Emergency Response Benefit (CERB)'. www.canada.ca/en/services/benefits/ei/cerb-application.html (accessed 22 April 2022). CERB has since ended.

Until recently, interest rates in Canada have been low since the pandemic began. This has led, in part, to demand for new home construction.[127] However, labour has become increasingly more expensive as a result of widespread skilled labour shortages. For instance, from the fourth quarter of 2019 to the fourth quarter of 2021, the average offered hourly wages for small businesses in the construction industry increased by 11.1% to an average of 25.55 Canadian dollars (US$20.20) per hour.[128]

At the same time, Canada has experienced a shortage of construction materials due to supply chain issues. In the fourth quarter of 2021, Statistics Canada reported that increased prices of wood, plastics and composites were the largest contributors to increased residential building construction costs. On the other hand, increased prices of metal fabrication products and concrete elements were the largest contributors to increased non-residential building construction costs.[129] Overall, the COVID-19 pandemic has led to increased labour and material prices which has caused record yearly price increases for both residential and non-residential construction costs.[130] Material shortages are expected to continue as a result of both the pandemic and the recent Russian invasion of Ukraine.

Recently, interest rates in Canada have risen.[131] It remains to be seen how rising interest rates will indirectly affect demand for skilled labour and impact the overall construction industry in Canada.

6.3.2 The impact of COVID-19 on the operation of construction contracts in Canada

Contractors on construction projects have alleged certain COVID-19-related impacts and have relied on certain contractual provisions, including the following provisions:

- *Force majeure*
- Relief event
- Change in law, and
- Emergency provisions

The foregoing contractual provisions have been applied to give some relief in certain circumstances, depending on the wording of the contractual provision at issue. The determination of whether there is entitlement to relief is very fact-specific, depending on the wording of the contract at issue. A number of claims have been successfully negotiated in relation to requests for extensions of time. In respect of entitlement to compensation, certain categories of claim have been easier to address including direct

127 See Statistics Canada, 'Building Permits, by Type of Structure and Type of Work (× 1000)' (www150.statcan.gc.ca/t1/tbl1/en/tv.action?pid=3410006601). The number of building permits in Canada and the value of those permits increased for both residential and non-residential construction in 2021 as compared to the previous year.

128 'Job vacancies', *supra* n125.

129 Statistics Canada, 'Building Construction Price Indexes, Fourth Quarter 2021'. www150.statcan.gc.ca/n1/daily-quotidien/220204/dq220204c-eng.htm.

130 *Ibid.*

131 Bank of Canada, 'Bank of Canada Increases Policy Interest Rate'. www.bankofcanada.ca/2022/03/fad-press-release-2022-03-02/ (accessed 22 April 2022).

costs such as those associated with personal protective equipment, cleaning and sanitation. Other categories of claims have been much more difficult to address including those claims related to loss of productivity, disruption and delay. Much of the Canadian construction industry was not subject to work stoppages of any length over the course of the pandemic, though there were some stoppages in certain sectors, including the residential construction sector, and in these sectors some extensions of time have been granted, again depending on the wording of the contractual provisions at issue. In respect of some claims, Contractors have had difficulty establishing entitlement to certain costs such as supply chain impacts or material price escalation, absent specific contractual mechanisms for recovery.

To date, there is a dearth of case law in Canada regarding the enforcement of the referenced provisions. The case of *Crosslinx v Ontario Infrastructure*[132] involved an attempt by Crosslinx, the ProjectCo on the Eglinton Crosstown Light Rail Transit Project, to apply the emergency provisions of the Project Agreement. Crosslinx was successful before an applications judge who determined that the provision applied given that COVID was an emergency. But, on appeal, the Ontario Court of Appeal determined that no notice was actually given by the owner of a requirement to comply with any additional or overriding procedures such that there was a palpable and overriding error made by the trial judge such that the matter was sent back for re-hearing.

In the Province of Quebec, the *Civil Code* contains provisions pertaining to *force majeure* events. The *Civil Code* uses the term 'superior force' to refer to these events. Superior force provisions in the *Civil Code* provide that a contracting party can be relieved from contractual liability in instances where a superior force event occurs.[133] The *Civil Code* defines a superior force as 'an unforeseeable and irresistible event, including external causes with the same characteristics'.[134] A superior force event under the *Civil Code* is one which a reasonable contracting party could not have predicted at the time the contract was formed and one which the party could not control. To obtain relief under these provisions, the superior force must render impossible the performance of the contractual obligation at issue.[135]

Whether the COVID-19 pandemic can constitute a *force majeure* or superior force event is dependent on the wording of the contract at issue. In the case of *Hengyun International Investment Commerce Inc v 9368-7614 Quebec Inc*,[136] the Superior Court of Quebec held that the COVID-19 pandemic was a *force majeure* or superior force event which prevented a commercial landlord from fulfilling its obligation to provide its tenant with peaceful enjoyment of a rental unit. The commercial tenant, who leased the premise for the purpose of operating a fitness facility, was ultimately relieved of its obligation to pay rent for a period of time during which the Province of Quebec was under a Provincial-wide COVID-19 lockdown and during which fitness facilities remain closed. However, the question of

132 2022 ONCA 187.

133 See *Civil Code of Quebec*, chapter CCQ-1991, ss 1470, 1693, 1694 and 2100.

134 *Ibid.* at 1470.

135 Gowling WLG, 'COVID-19: Force Majeure and Construction – A Quebec Law Perspective'. https://gowlingwlg.com/en/insights-resources/articles/2020/covid-19-force-majeure-and-construction/#_ftn3 (accessed 4 May 2022).

136 2020 QCCS 2251.

whether COVID-19 can constitute a *force majeure* or superior force event in the context of a construction dispute has not yet been considered by the Quebec Courts.

6.4 Canadian governing law of the contract

6.4.1 Constraints on the governing law of a construction contract

In Canada, the freedom of contract principle is well recognised and subject to limited restrictions.[137] Canadian courts are reluctant to imply terms into a construction contract.

There have been recent developments in the law of good faith. For instance, the Supreme Court of Canada has held that all contracts are subject to the organising principle of good faith. In other words, parties to a construction contract must generally perform their contractual duties honestly and reasonably as opposed to capriciously or arbitrarily.[138] This duty is not an implied contractual term but rather a general doctrine that imposes a minimum standard of honest contractual performance which means that parties must not lie or knowingly mislead one another regarding matters directly linked to contractual performance.[139] Further, the duty of good faith performance encompasses a duty to exercise contractual discretion in good faith.[140] Discretionary powers under a contract must be exercised reasonably, in accordance with the purpose of the underlying discretion.

As well and as noted earlier, in some jurisdictions parties are not permitted to contract out of lien legislation.

Parties to a construction project are free to include foreign law provisions and jurisdiction clauses within their contract. In other words, parties to a construction contract are free to specify the substantive law that will govern their contractual relationship as well as the court system that will hear disputes that arise. These provisions are generally upheld and enforced under Canadian contract law.

6.4.2 Formal requirements for a construction contract

In Canada, the law of construction contracts is generally the common law of contracts, subject to Provincial and Territorial statutory lien laws.

In Canada, consideration is also required to establish a legally binding contract. However, courts are generally not concerned with the adequacy of consideration so long as the consideration is of some value.[141] A contract that is executed as a deed does not require consideration. The need for consideration is circumvented by the existence of a seal on the contract and evidence of the parties' intention to execute a deed.[142]

137 See *Uber Technologies Inc v Heller*, 2020 SCC 16, [107]. Here, the Supreme Court of Canada indicated that 'a hallmark of a free society is the freedom of individuals to arrange their affairs without fear of overreaching interference by the state, including the courts'.

138 *Bhasin v Hrynew*, 2014 SCC 71, [63].

139 *C.M. Callow Inc. v Zollinger*, 2020 SCC 45.

140 *Wastech Services Ltd v Greater Vancouver Sewerage and Drainage District*, 2021 SCC 17.

141 Thomas G Heintzman, Bryan G West and Immanuel Goldsmith, *Heintzman, West and Goldsmith on Canadian Building Contracts*, (5th edn, Carswell, 2022), $1:45–$1:47.

142 Angela Swan, Jakub Adamski & Annie Y Na, *Canadian Contract Law* (3rd edn, LexisNexis Canada, 2018), $2.283–$2.310.

Lastly, parties to a construction contract in Canada must have the legal capacity to enter into a contract and they must intend to create a binding contractual relationship. In Canada, construction contracts are often in writing which serves as evidence of a party's objective intention to enter into the contract at issue.[143] Nonetheless, a construction contract entered into under either duress or coercion is not a valid contract.[144]

6.5 What Special Provisions in the Particular Conditions are necessary for consistency with applicable laws?

6.5.1 FIDIC General Conditions are incompatible or inconsistent with the governing law of the contract

The FIDIC suite of contracts is not commonly used in Canada. However, no Special Provisions are needed for the FIDIC General Conditions to be consistent with the general law of contracts in Canada. As mentioned earlier, freedom of contract is an important principle in the Canadian legal system. Parties to a construction contract are generally free to contract with whom they choose and to draft contractual provisions as they see fit. However, as noted earlier, mandatory Provincial and Territorial construction lien laws may modify the common law of construction contracts in a particular jurisdiction. Therefore, it may be prudent to consider the relevant construction lien legislation, if any, and to include Special Provisions to accord with those laws. Nevertheless, in provinces such as Ontario, Manitoba and Saskatchewan, a construction contract is deemed to be amended in accordance with the relevant statute.

There are various relevant regulatory requirements that parties must comply with. For instance, in Ontario, parties to a construction contract must be aware of and comply with the provisions of and regulations under various statutes including the *Occupational Health and Safety Act*,[145] the *Building Code Act*,[146] the *Planning Act*[147] and the *Environmental Protection Act*.[148] The FIDIC Red Book does contain provisions which state that a Contractor must comply with all applicable health and safety laws and regulations[149] and obtain permits, licences and/or approvals as required by law.[150] However, Special Provisions in the FIDIC contract may be appropriate to ensure that all environmental requirements must be complied with.[151]

6.5.2 FIDIC General Conditions are incompatible or inconsistent with the law of the Site/Country

Prior to entering into a FIDIC contract in Canada, parties to a construction project should consider how best to align FIDIC General Conditions with applicable statutory lien

143 *Canadian Building Contracts, supra* n141, $1:28.
144 *Ibid.*, $1:30.
145 *Occupational Health and Safety Act, supra* n89.
146 *Building Code Act*, 1992, S.O. 1992, c. 23.
147 R.S.O. 1990, c. P. 13.
148 R.S.O. 1990, c. E. 19.
149 2017 Red Book sub-clause 4.8.
150 *Ibid.*, sub-clause 1.13.
151 *Ibid.*, sub-clause 4.18.

legislation, if any. The following discussion will focus solely on adapting FIDIC contracts for use in Ontario.

In Ontario, prompt payment and construction dispute interim adjudication provisions have been legislated through the *Construction Act.* These provisions aim to curb lengthy payment periods, thereby ensuring that stakeholders within the construction pyramid are paid promptly. The adjudication regime aims to coincide with the prompt payment provisions and assist parties in resolving payment disputes.[152]

Generally in Ontario, an Employer must pay a Contractor the amount payable under a proper invoice within 28 days after receipt of a proper invoice.[153] Thereafter, a Contractor who has received full payment of a proper invoice must pay each Subcontractor who supplied services or materials included in the proper invoice, the amount payable to them within seven calendar days.[154] The Subcontractor is then required to pay its sub-subcontractor within seven calendar days[155] and this prompt payment regime continues through the construction pyramid.

However, the FIDIC Red Book provides for a rather elongated payment process which would not align well with the *Construction Act.* For instance, the FIDIC Red Book proposes that when requesting payment, a Contractor provide an application for payment to the project Engineer. The Engineer must issue an Interim Payment Certificate (**IPC**) to the Employer within 28 days. The IPC will outline the amount which the Engineer fairly considers to be due and owing to the Contractor.[156] Thereafter, the Employer must pay the Contractor the amount certified in the IPC within the period stated in the Contract Data. If the Contract Data is silent, the Employer must pay the Contractor within 56 days.[157]

Therefore, the timeframe for payment between the Employer and Contractor under the FIDIC Red Book is potentially longer than the maximum legislated 28-day timeframe in Ontario. Parties seeking to use the FIDIC Red Book in Ontario may draft Special Provisions to amend this payment timeframe to ensure that Contractors are paid within 28 days of receipt of an application for payment. Also, to align with Ontario's legislation, a Contractor's application for payment should meet the definition of a proper invoice as written in provision 6.1 of the *Construction Act.*

Further, under the *Construction Act*, an Employer who disputes a proper invoice can refuse to pay all or a portion of the amount payable under the proper invoice. To do so, an Employer must provide a notice of non-payment to the Contractor within 14 days of receipt of the proper invoice.[158] The notice of non-payment must detail the amount in dispute and the reasons for non-payment.

Similarly, FIDIC contracts provide that an Engineer has the ability to review the Contractor's Statement and determine the amount that is fairly due and owing. If the Engineer wishes to dispute the Statement or a portion thereof, the Interim Payment

152 Singleton Urquhart Reynolds Vogel LLP, 'A Guide to Prompt Payment and Adjudication in Ontario'. www.singleton.com/2019/10/a-guide-to-prompt-payment-and-adjudication-in-ontario/ (accessed 22 April 2022).

153 *Construction Act*, *supra* n15, s 6.4(1).

154 *Ibid.* at s 6.5.

155 *Ibid.* at s 6.6.

156 Red Book, *supra* n149 at s 14.6.1.

157 *Ibid.* at s 14.7.

158 *Construction Act*, *supra* n15, s 6.4(2).

Certificate must include supporting particulars and must be provided to the Employer within 28 days of receipt of the Statement.

Although these non-payment mechanisms have similarities, the FIDIC contract should be modified for use in Ontario. Namely, an IPC which disputes payment should be delivered within the statutory 14-day notice of non-payment period. Also, it is prudent for contracting parties to ensure that the notice of non-payment requirements is satisfied by the delivery of an IPC to an Employer and Contractor.

It is also worth noting that the FIDIC Red Book appears to be silent on the timeframe for payment of Subcontractors. As mentioned earlier, the *Construction Act* indicates that a Contractor who has received full payment of a proper invoice must pay each Subcontractor who supplied services or materials included in the proper invoice the amount payable to them within seven calendar days.[159] Therefore, parties to a FIDIC contract in Ontario may choose to draft a Special Provision calling for the payment of subcontractors in accordance with the *Construction Act*.

As mentioned earlier, the CCDC 2 is frequently used on construction projects in Canada. Interestingly, the latest 2020 version of this standard form contract was amended to reflect the prompt payment provisions of the *Construction Act*. For example, General Condition 5.3.1.2 now states that an '*Owner* shall make payment to the *Contractor* ... on or before **28 calendar days** after the receipt by the *Owner* and the *Consultant* of the application for payment, and in any event, in compliance with ***Payment Legislation***'.[160] Therefore, the CCDC 2 is now in general conformance with the *Construction Act* and can be easily altered for use in other Canadian jurisdictions. Parties who wish to contract using the FIDIC Red Book should include similar modifications to reflect the *Construction Act*.

6.5.3 FIDIC General Conditions are incompatible or inconsistent with the laws of the seat of the arbitration or relevant laws on dispute determination

Parties to a construction project seeking to use a FIDIC contract in Canada should consider how best to incorporate provisions related to statutory construction adjudication legislation within the FIDIC contract. The following discussion will focus solely on modifying FIDIC contracts for use in Ontario.

In Ontario, contracting parties have the right to refer payment-related disputes to adjudication regardless of whether the same matter is the subject of a court action or of an arbitration under the *Arbitration Act*.[161] Further, once an adjudicator has received all required documentation, a decision must be rendered within 30 days.[162] The adjudicator's determination is binding until otherwise determined by a court, arbitrator under the *Arbitrations Act* or written agreement between the parties.[163]

As written, the FIDIC Red Book states that a Dispute Avoidance/Adjudication Board (**DAAB**) is to resolve disputes that arise between the parties.[164] Determinations are to

159 *Ibid.* at s 6.5.

160 Canadian Construction Documents Committee, CCDC 2 Stipulated Price Contract (2020), s 11 [CCDC 2] (emphasis added).

161 *Construction Act, supra* n15, s 13.5(5).

162 *Ibid.*, s 13.13.

163 *Ibid.*, s 13.5.

164 Red Book, sub-clause 21.1.

be made within 84 days of receiving a reference. Otherwise, the DAAB can propose a different period of time within which to render a determination.[165] Therefore, the FIDIC Red Book provides for the use of a Dispute Board but is silent with respect to adjudication.

If construction operations are carried out under a FIDIC contract in Ontario, the interim adjudication provisions of the *Construction Act* will be implied into the contract. Accordingly, it is open to parties using a FIDIC contract to specifically modify the standard contract by way of Special Provisions to make reference to the adjudication provisions within the *Construction Act* or any other relevant provincial statute. For example, the CCDC 2 includes a provision which states that '[n]othing in this *Contract* shall be deemed to affect the rights of the parties to resolve any dispute by adjudication as may be prescribed by applicable legislation'.[166] The incorporation of a similar provision may be prudent when using a FIDIC contract in Canada.

6.6 What Special Provisions in the Particular Conditions are desirable for consistency with applicable laws?

As mentioned earlier, parties to a construction project seeking to use a FIDIC contract in Canada should consider incorporating provisions pertaining to applicable statutory prompt payment and adjudication laws in their contract. Aside from this, parties may consider adding a provision relating to workers' compensation insurance.

In Canada, construction industry employers are responsible for obtaining workers' compensation insurance. Therefore, it may be prudent to include a provision within the FIDIC contract which ensures that stakeholders obtain coverage. By way of example, the CCDC 2 includes a provision which states that '[p]rior to commencing the *Work*, and again with the *Contractor*'s applications for payment, **the *Contractor* shall provide evidence of compliance with workers' compensation legislation at the *Place of Work***'.[167] A similar clause may be incorporated within a FIDIC contract by way of Special Provision.

6.7 Summary of applicable legislation if the governing law is that of Canada

The following table reflects the law in Ontario with reference to federal legislation where applicable. As noted earlier, the *Constitution Act, 1867* divides legislative jurisdiction between the Federal and Provincial Governments based on subject matter. Therefore, each Province and Territory has developed its own body of legislation with respect to matters of Provincial/Territorial jurisdiction. The law of Ontario is used as an example in the following to illustrate relevant Provincial laws. Federal statutes pertaining to matters of federal jurisdiction are also outlined.

165 *Ibid.*, sub-clause 21.4.3.
166 CCDC 2, *supra* n160, s 8.2.1.
167 *Ibid.* at s 10.4.1 (emphasis added).

6.7.1 Entry into a construction contract

Contracts generally	*Sale of Goods Act*, R.S.O. 1990, c. s 1. *Consumer Protection Act, 2002*, S.O. 2002, c. 30, Sched. A. *Frustrated Contracts Act*, R.S.O. 1990, c. F. 34.
Construction contracts	*Construction Act*, R.S.O. 1990, c. C. 30.

6.7.2 Termination of a construction contract

Frustration	*Frustrated Contracts Act*, R.S.O. 1990, c. F. 34.
Bankruptcy, insolvency, liquidation	*Bankruptcy and Insolvency Act*, R.S.C., 1985, c. B-3.
Guarantees under forms of Security (Tender Security, Demand Guarantee, Surety Bond, Advance Payment Guarantee, Retention Money Guarantee, Payment Guarantee by Employer)	*Personal Property Security Act*, R.S.O. 1990, c. P. 10.

6.7.3 Dispute resolution

Limitation periods	*Limitations Act, 2002*, S.O. 2002, c. 24, Sched. B.
Liability	*Negligence Act*, R.S.O. 1990, c. N.1.
Adjudication	*Construction Act*, R.S.O. 1990, c. C. 30.
Arbitration	*Arbitration Act, 1991*, S.O. 1991, c. 17. *International Commercial Arbitration Act, 2017*, S.O. 2017, c. 2, Sched. 5. *Commercial Arbitration Act*, R.S.C., 1985, c. 17 (2nd Supp.)

6.8 Summary of applicable legislation if the Site/Country is in Canada

The following table reflects the law in Ontario with reference to federal legislation where applicable.

6.8.1 Operation of a construction contract

Registration and administration of professionals – Engineers, Architects, Surveyors	*Professional Engineers Act*, R.S.O. 1990, c. P.28. *Architects Act*, R.S.O. 1990, c. A.26. *Surveyors Act*, R.S.O. 1990, c. S.29.
Registration/licencing of Contractors and subcontractors	*Building Opportunities in the Skilled Trades Act, 2021*, S.O. 2021, c. 28.
Subcontractors	*Construction Act*, R.S.O. 1990, c. C. 30.
Use of liens/assignment of debts	*Construction Act*, R.S.O. 1990, c. C. 30. *Assignment and Preferences Act*, R.S.O. 1990, c. A. 33.

(*Continued*)

(Continued)

Labour	*Employment Standards Act, 2000*, S.O. 2000, c. 41. *Human Rights Code*, R.S.O. 1990, c. H. 19. *Labour Relations Act, 1995*, S.O. 1995, c. 1, Sched. A. *Canada Labour Code*, R.S.C., 1985, c. L-2.
Design/moral rights	*Copyright Act*, R.S.C., 1985, c. C-42.
Copyright	*Copyright Act*, R.S.C., 1985, c. C-42.
First Nation people's land rights	*First Nations Land Management Act*, S.C. 1999, c. 24
Planning	*Planning Act*, R.S.O. 1990, c. P. 13.
Heritage	*Ontario Heritage Act*, R.S.O. 1990, c. O. 18
Environment	*Environmental Protection Act*, R.S.O. 1990, c. E. 19.
Local procurement	*Fairness in Procurement Act, 2018*, S.O. 2018, c. 4.
Building and construction permits, execution of construction work, standard of construction work	*Building Code Act, 1992*, S.O. 1992, c. 23 *Ontario New Home Warranties Plan Act*, R.S.O. 1990, c. O. 31.
Health and safety	*Occupational Health and Safety Act*, R.S.O. 1990, c. O.1
Insurance	*Insurance Act*, R.S.O. 1990, c. I. 8. *Workplace Safety and Insurance Act, 1997*, S.O. 1997, c. 16, Sched. A.
Statutory rights that coexist with contractual rights	*Courts of Justice Act*, R.S.O. 1990, c. C. 43 – R.R.O. 1990, Reg. 194: Rules of Civil Procedure.
Liability for defective work	*Negligence Act*, R.S.O. 1990, c. N.1.
Other issues	*Evidence Act*, R.S.O. 1990, c. E.23. *Canada Evidence Act*, R.S.C. 1985, c. C. 5.

6.8.2 Termination of a construction contract

Bankruptcy, insolvency, liquidation	*Bankruptcy and Insolvency Act*, RSC, 1985, c. B-3. *Companies' Creditors Arrangement Act*, RSC, 1985, c. C-36
Decennial liability and liability generally for the total or partial collapse of structures	*Negligence Act*, R.S.O. 1990, c. N.1. *Insurance Act*, R.S.O. 1990, c. I. 8.

6.8.3 Dispute resolution

Dispute before a local board/ Adjudication	*Construction Act*, R.S.O. 1990, c. C. 30.
Limitation periods	*Limitations Act, 2002*, S.O. 2002, c. 24, Sched. B.

6.9 Summary of applicable legislation if the 'seat' of the dispute determination is Canada

The following table reflects the law in Ontario with reference to federal legislation where applicable.

Dispute resolution	*Commercial Mediation Act*, 2010, S.O. 2010, c. 16, Sched. 3.
Limitation periods	*Limitations Act, 2002*, S.O. 2002, c. 24, Sched. B.
Adjudication	*Construction Act*, R.S.O. 1990, c. C. 30.
Arbitration	*Arbitration Act, 1991*, S.O. 1991, c. 17.
	International Commercial Arbitration Act, 2017, S.O. 2017, c. 2, Sched. 5.
	Commercial Arbitration Act, R.S.C., 1985, c. 17 (2nd Supp.).

6.10 Issues that a court or arbitrator may construe differently than expected from the words of the Contract because of local law or custom

Parties to a construction dispute in Canada can expect judges and arbitrators to carefully consider the language of the contract at issue and to read the contract as a whole with regard for all provisions.[168] Judges and arbitrators will also consider the surrounding circumstances or factual matrix of the contract. Evidence of the factual matrix is always admissible regardless of ambiguity in the contract and is generally broad in scope.[169] However, the words of the contract will prevail in cases of conflict between the words and the factual matrix.[170] Therefore, parties to a FIDIC contract in Canada should be aware of these principles and should draft any Special Provisions with care. Lastly, parties to a contract should be aware that subjective intent is inadmissible and will not form part of the factual matrix in court or alike.[171]

6.11 Additional references for Canada

6.11.1 Books

Allan S Cutler, *A Practical Guide to Public Procurement* (LexisNexis Canada, 2018)

Angela Swan, Jakub Adamski & Annie Y Na *Canadian Contract Law* (4th edn, LexisNexis Canada, 2018)

Dianne Dyck, *Occupational Health and Safety: Theory, Strategy and Industry Practice* (4th edn, LexisNexis Canada, 2020)

Elliot A Smith, *The Canadian Construction Contracts Guidebook* (Thomson Reuters, 2019)

Glaholt Bowles, Paul Sandori & William M Pigott, *Bidding and Tendering – What is the Law?* (6th edn, LexisNexis Canada, 2020)

Guy Regimbald, *Canadian Administrative Law* (3rd edn, LexisNexis Canada, 2021).

Harvey Kirsh & Matthew R Alter, *A Guide to Construction Liens in Ontario* (3rd edn, LexisNexis Canada, 2011)

Harvey Kirsh & Paul A Ivanoff, *Canadian Construction Law Dictionary* (LexisNexis Canada, 2006)

J Kenneth McEwan & Ludmila B Herbst, *Commercial Arbitration in Canada: A Guide to Domestic and International Arbitrations* (Carswell, 2022)

John Borrows, *Canada's Indigenous Constitution* (University of Toronto Press, 2010)

168 Geoff R Hall, *Canadian Contractual Interpretation Law* (4th edn, LexisNexis Canada, 2020), 10.

169 *Ibid.*, 11–12, 31–32.

170 *Ibid.*, 35.

171 See *Sattva Capital Corp v Creston Moly Corp*, 2014 SCC 53, the seminal Supreme Court of Canada decision on contractual interpretation.

Jules B Bloch et al., *Canadian Construction Labour and Employment Law* (LexisNexis Canada, 2022)
Michael Silver & Gary Furlong, *Construction Dispute Resolution Handbook* (LexisNexis Canada, 2004)
Patrick Macklem et al., *Canadian Constitutional Law* (5th edn, Emond Publishing, 2016)
Patrick J Monahan, Byron Shaw & Padraic Ryan, *Constitutional Law* (5th edn, Irwin Law, 2017)
R Bruce Reynolds & Sharon C Vogel, *A Guide to Canadian Construction Insurance Law* (1st edn, Carswell, 2013)
Timothy Murphy, *Public–Private Partnerships in Canada: Law, Policy and Value for Money* (LexisNexis Canada, 2019)

6.11.2 Journals/guides/encyclopaedias

Canadian Employment Safety and Health Guide (LexisNexis Canada)
Canadian Encyclopedic Digest (Thomson Reuters)
Construction Law Reports (Thomson Reuters)
Halsbury's Laws of Canada (LexisNexis Canada)
Journal of the Canadian College of Construction Lawyers (Thomson Reuters)

6.11.3 Federal legislation

Federal legislation can be accessed through the Government of Canada's Justice Laws webpage (https://laws-lois.justice.gc.ca/eng/acts/)

The *Canada Gazette* is the official newspaper of the Government of Canada. Part II of the *Canada Gazette* contains enacted regulations and statutory instruments and Part III includes Acts of Parliament published after they receive royal assent. The *Canada Gazette* can be accessed through the Government of Canada webpage (www.gazette.gc.ca/rp-pr/publications-eng.html)

The Parliament of Canada publishes the current status of federal legislation (**Bills**) as they proceed through the parliamentary review process. Information regarding federal Bills can be accessed through the Parliament of Canada's LEGISInfo webpage (www.parl.ca/legisinfo/en/overview)

Both federal and provincial/territorial legislation can be accessed through the Canadian Legal Information Institute (CanLII) (www.canlii.org/en/)

6.11.4 Provincial and territorial legislation

Alberta's legislation can be accessed through the Government of Alberta's webpage (www.qp.alberta.ca/Laws_Online.cfm)

British Columbia's legislation can be accessed through the Government of British Columbia webpage (www.bclaws.gov.bc.ca/)

Manitoba's legislation can be accessed through the Government of Manitoba webpage (https://web2.gov.mb.ca/laws/index.php)

New Brunswick's legislation can be accessed through the Government of New Brunswick webpage (www2.gnb.ca/content/gnb/en/departments/public-safety/attorney-general/content/acts_regulations.html)

Newfoundland and Labrador's legislation can be accessed through the House of Assembly Newfoundland and Labrador webpage (www.assembly.nl.ca/default.aspx)

Nova Scotia's legislation can be accessed through the Nova Scotia Legislature webpage (https://nslegislature.ca/legislative-business/bills-statutes)

Ontario's legislation can be accessed through the Government of Ontario's e-Laws webpage (www.ontario.ca/laws)

Prince Edward Island's legislation can be accessed through the Government of Prince Edward Island webpage (www.princeedwardisland.ca/en/legislation/all/all/a)

The Civil Code of Quebec as well as Quebec statutes and regulations can be accessed through the Publications Quebec webpage (www.legisquebec.gouv.qc.ca/en/document/cs/CCQ-1991)

Saskatchewan's legislation can be accessed through the Government of Saskatchewan webpage (https://publications.saskatchewan.ca/#/freelaw)

Legislation of the Northwest Territories can be accessed through the Government of Northwest Territories webpage (www.justice.gov.nt.ca/en/legislation/)

Nunavut's legislation can be accessed through the Government of Nunavut webpage (www.nunavutlegislation.ca/en)

Yukon's legislation can be accessed through the Government of Yukon webpage (https://laws.yukon.ca/cms/)

6.11.5 Case law

Many court decisions can be accessed through the Canadian Legal Information Institute (CanLII) (www.canlii.org/en/)

Case law can also be accessed through Lexis Advanced Quicklaw (LexisNexis Canada) (www.lexisnexis.ca/en-ca/products/lexis-advance-quicklaw-overview.page) as well as Westlaw Canada (Thomson Reuters) (www.westlawcanada.com/)

CHAPTER 7

Applying FIDIC Contracts in Chile

Dr Elina Mereminskaya, Alex Wagemann and Fernando Landeros

CONTENTS

7.1 Outline of the Chilean legal environment 164
7.1.1 The constitutional structure of Chile 164
7.1.2 The legal system in Chile 164
7.1.3 The court system in Chile 164
7.2 The construction industry in Chile 165
7.2.1 Overview 165
7.2.2 Structure 165
7.2.3 Licencing/registration 166
7.2.4 Labour relations 167
7.2.5 Safety culture 167
7.2.6 Modular construction using factory fabricated components 168
7.2.7 BIM 168
7.2.8 Government procurement 168
7.2.9 Insurance requirements 169
7.2.10 Common forms of contract 170
7.2.11 Dispute resolution 170
7.2.12 Current challenges 171
7.2.13 Unique features of the construction industry in Chile 171
7.3 The impact of COVID-19 in Chile 172
7.3.1 The impact of COVID-19 on the execution of construction projects in Chile 172
7.3.2 The impact of COVID-19 on the operation of construction contracts in Chile 173
7.4 Chilean law as the governing law of the contract 175
7.4.1 Constraints on the governing law of a construction contract 175
7.4.2 Formal requirements for a construction contract 175
7.5 What Special Provisions in the Particular Conditions are necessary for consistency with applicable law in Chile? 176
7.5.1 Good faith 176
7.5.2 Delay damages/penalties 177

 DOI: 10.4324/9781003201250-7

7.5.3 Employer's Taking Over 178
7.5.4 Termination 179
7.5.5 Time period for the submission of the Notice of Claim 180
7.6 What Special Provisions in the Particular Conditions are desirable for consistency with applicable laws in Chile? 181
7.7 Applicable legislation for Chilean governing law of the contract 181
7.8 Summary of applicable legislation for Chilean governing law of the contract 181
7.8.1 Entry into a construction contract 181
7.8.2 Operation of a construction contract 182
7.8.3 Termination of a construction contract 182
7.8.4 Dispute resolution 182
7.9 Applicable legislation if the Site is in Chile 182
7.10 Summary of applicable legislation if the Site is in Chile 183
7.10.1 Operation of a construction contract 183
7.10.2 Termination of a construction contract 183
7.10.3 Dispute resolution 183
7.11 Applicable legislation if the 'seat' of the dispute determination is Chile 184
7.12 Summary of applicable legislation if the 'seat' of the dispute determination is Chile 184
7.13 Issues that a court or arbitrator may construe differently than expected from the words of the Contract because of local law or custom 184
7.14 Additional references for Chile 185
7.14.1 Books 185
7.14.2 Journals 185
7.14.3 Internet 185

7.1 Outline of the Chilean legal environment

7.1.1 The constitutional structure of Chile

The current *Constitution* of Chile dates to 1980 and thus to the time of the Augusto Pinochet government. After the country's return to democracy, the original text was considered to have lacked democratic legitimacy and has been subject to various modifications. However, the reforms have been deemed vastly insufficient to safeguard certain political, social and economic rights.

In 2015, the President of the Republic, Michelle Bachellet, initiated a national participatory and institutional constitutional process to enact a new *Constitution*. In October 2019, social riots took place as a testimony of broad social discontent. As a consequence, in 2021 the Constitutional Convention was set up to write a new *Constitution* that should be then submitted to a plebiscite. The current *Constitution* has been amended to allow for this constitutional process to be carried out. It is expected that the drafting process will culminate by the end of 2022.

7.1.2 The legal system in Chile

The Chilean legal system belongs to the civil law family, which means that it relies on written statutes and codification of the law.

Chile is a unitary state as opposed to a federal state. Thus, the same legislation applies in all its territory.

The *Chilean Civil Code* was prepared single-handedly by Chilean-Venezuelan scholar Andrés Bello, who based his work on the *Napoleonic Civil Code* from 1804 and the *Louisiana Civil Code*, enacted in 1808. The *Chilean Civil Code* (***CC***) entered into force in 1857. Its Chapter VI 'About the obligations in general and the contracts' has not been substantially amended since that date.

As set forth in Article 1545 of the *CC*, the sanctity, pre-eminence and intangibility of the contract (*pacta sunt servanda* principle) is one of the most fundamental principles of Chilean private law. This provision states: 'Every legally concluded contract is a law for the contracting parties, and cannot be invalidated except by their mutual consent or for legal causes'.

Therefore, as a rule, the parties' bargain will be binding upon them and will be enforced by the courts. The *CC* establishes some specific legal causes that invalidate parties' contractual agreements. Pursuant to Article 1462 of the *CC*, 'there is an illicit object in everything that contravenes Chilean public law'. In turn, pursuant to Article 1682 of the *CC*, a contractual relationship that aims at an illicit object is voidable and null.

7.1.3 The court system in Chile

The judiciary in Chile is an autonomous and independent branch of government not subject to any other. The Chilean judicial system is divided into three levels: the Supreme Court, Courts of Appeals and tribunals of the first instance.

In addition, various specialist tribunals exist that are not formally included in the judicial system, e.g. Constitutional Tribunal and the Tribunal for the Defence of Free Competition, as well as customs and revenue tribunals, which – despite their names – fulfil administrative functions.

At the top of the judiciary courts, there is a Supreme Court, with 21 judges appointed by the President of the Republic pending approval of the Senate, who are selected from a list of five judges made by current Supreme Court members. The Supreme Court has the administrative and regulatory control of all judges.

There are 17 Courts of Appeals. The first-instance tribunals are divided into civil, criminal, family and labour tribunals.

As is common in many civil law jurisdictions, the law assigns judges a rather relegated position, that is, they do not create rules of law and, following Montesquieu's approach, act as *la bouche de la loi*.[1] There are no precedents or *stare decisis* rule, which makes it difficult to predict the outcome of court proceedings.

Access to the ordinary courts is free and not subject to payment of any kind of administrative fees. However, the system is overloaded with a huge volume of cases, which renders it less efficient. Before the COVID-19 pandemic, the average time period for a construction case to be completed (including the cassation recourse to the Supreme Court) was five to seven years.

7.2 The construction industry in Chile

7.2.1 Overview

According to Central Bank figures, the GDP of the construction sector has a relatively important share of Chilean GDP, close to 7%, and is more or less stable over time.[2] Private investments in the construction sector account for 64% while public sector investments comprise 36%.[3]

The productivity of the construction sector in Chile is lower than the OECD average and the rest of the Chilean economy. First, the construction productivity gap between Chile and the OECD benchmark average increased by 20% during the 2009–2018 period, from 43 percentage points (pp) to 52 pp, concluding that the benchmark productivity is more than double the Chilean one. Second, construction productivity in Chile is lower than that of most other sectors, being equivalent to 80% of the average of the rest of the economy.[4]

7.2.2 Structure

In Chile, there is no formal record of the number of existing construction companies, which, if possible, would be a relative measurement anyway, since most construction companies are small and medium-sized and tend to form consortia among themselves to bid for projects.

1 The mouth of the law.

2 Andrea Alvarado Duffau and Sebastian Spolmann Pasten, 'Análisis de competencia del sector de la construcción chileno y sus procesos de licitaciones públicas de contratos de obras: Estructura, Agentes y Prácticas', (2009) 13, www.fne.gob.cl/wp-content/uploads/2011/03/estu_0001_2009.pdf (accessed 22 March 2022); Comisión Nacional de Productividad, 'Productividad en el Sector de la Construcción', (2020) 25, www.comisiondeproductividad.cl/estudios/hallazgos-recomendaciones/construccion/ (accessed 22 March 2022).

3 https://media.elmostrador.cl/2017/12/mach-47-05-diciembre-2017-ok.compressed.pdf (accessed 22 March 2022).

4 Comisión Nacional de Productividad, 'Productividad en el Sector de la Construcción', note 2, 27.

The only existing description in this regard is an approximation of the type and composition of existing construction companies according to the registry of members of the Chilean Chamber of Construction (**CChC**). This trade association has almost 1,500 members throughout the country.[5]

There are at least four prominent construction companies (or rather economic groups) of national origin, that is, SalfaCorp, Besalco, Sidgo Koppers and Claro, Vicuña y Valenzuela.[6]

Spanish construction companies arrived in Chile more than two decades ago, starting with Sacyr when in 1996 it was awarded the first contract to build and operate the Los Vilos-La Serena highway, at the beginning of the country's implementation of the concession system.[7]

The concession sector (public–private partnership or **PPP**) in Chile was for years mainly controlled by large Spanish construction companies such as Abertis, Sacyr, OHL, Acciona and FCC, managing the country's main roads, working with both the public and private sectors. Between 1994 and 1998, Spanish investors were present in 11 concession projects, out of a total of 14 awarded between those years. Spanish companies continue to have a prominent presence in Chile, Spain being the second most important foreign investor after the USA, even despite the COVID-19 pandemic. However, Chinese interest in these assets has translated into strong competition for traditional firms with a presence in the country.[8]

Nowadays, the Chilean construction industry – including national and foreign contractors – can be described as highly mature and competitive, which in turn creates pressure on contractors in order for them to remain competitive and profitable.

7.2.3 Licencing/registration

The construction sector is one with high barriers to entry for foreign companies, so there is no disciplining pressure on established construction companies from this potential competition. This market entry condition for foreign companies is defined on the basis of the fixed costs of various types that a foreign company must incur when carrying out a project in national territory. However, when it comes to large projects, such as public works concessions, in practice it is possible to observe greater competition from foreign construction companies.[9]

The General Directorate of Public Works of the Ministry of Public Works is responsible for the administration of the Contractor's Register, which is comprised of the Register of Major Works and the Register of Minor Works. These registers include natural persons and construction companies that are authorised to serve as contractors in projects administered by the Ministry of Public Works (**MOP**).

5 Andrea Alvarado Duffau and Sebastian Spolmann Pasten, note 2, 24.

6 www.mch.cl/2011/09/26/los-negocios-que-se-disputan-las-grandes-constructoras/# (accessed 23 March 2022).

7 www.sacyrinfraestructuras.com/chile (accessed 23 March 2022).

8 www.latercera.com/pulso/noticia/el-rearme-de-las-inversiones-espanolas-en-chile/XLXFMYSV7BCQPOAJETDLW53E6M/ (accessed 23 March 2022).

9 Andrea Alvarado Duffau and Sebastian Spolmann Pasten, note 2, 19–22.

For the purpose of classifying contractors, the Register of Major Works is divided into Specialities of Civil Works and Assembly, which in turn are divided into registers according to the type of work and whose experience requires accreditation. Contractors may request registration in one or more of the categories and specialities of the Contractor's Register. Each record will, in turn, be categorised according to experience, economic ability, professional quality and professional plant staff.

To be admitted to any of the registers, a contractor must gain accreditation for the speciality required and prove a minimum level of experience, which is measured by the amount of work it has carried out.

The literature has described the Contractor's Register as an entry barrier as it imposes some technical requirements that are excessive and obsolete, such as the parameters for certifying the accumulation of experience in certain specialities; the requirement of a minimum permanent staff, when what is relevant is the field staff of temporary contracts for works; and the requirement of minimum capital to be permanently accredited to be part of a category, which is established as a percentage of the value of the works that is not related to economic efficiency requirements.[10]

7.2.4 Labour relations

Labour relations are subject to the *Labour Code* from 1931, updated through numerous reforms. One of its most relevant features is the high level of protection for the workers of contractors and subcontractors. Article 183-A of the *Labour Code* treats the workers of a contractor as 'subcontractors' of the owner or client. Pursuant to Article 183-B, the latter is jointly liable for the compliance of the 'subcontractors'' rights. The same rule applies to contractors regarding their subcontractors' personnel.

7.2.5 Safety culture

The first *Organic Law No 3170 of 1916* on matters of health and safety, covered occupational accidents only. In 1922, it was modified by *Law No 4055* to provide regulation of occupational diseases, but always from a compensatory point of view, covering medical care, subsidy payments and compensation for permanent disability and death.

Law No 16.744 that 'Establishes Rules on Occupational Accidents and Occupational Diseases' from 1968, which is still in force today, created compulsory social insurance for work accidents and occupational diseases. It provides for the protection of workers in both medical and economic aspects and requires the employer and the worker to carry out activities for the prevention of accidents and occupational diseases.

Because of those developments, Chile continues to lower its accident rates. The current accident rate fluctuates around 5%, which is a substantial improvement, considering that ten years ago it was almost twice as high. Unfortunately, among the characteristics of the industry are the low level of training of its workers, the high turnover and low specialisation, the intensive use of labour, a large number of activities of varying complexity and the significant use of subcontracts at all stages, factors that push the rates higher.[11]

10 Andrea Alvarado Duffau and Sebastian Spolmann Pasten, note 2, 108–109.

11 www.emb.cl/construccion/articulo.mvc?xid=2835 (accessed 23 March 2022).

7.2.6 Modular construction using factory fabricated components

This type of construction method is used for the erection of small private houses. Its use in big infrastructure projects is still rare or not being reported.[12]

7.2.7 BIM

Although BIM programs have existed for more than 15 years, starting from 2009 they have been used more actively through the geometric coordination of projects, which several companies are implementing based on BIM models.[13]

Currently, there is an ongoing government plan called Planbim, which is a ten-year initiative, aimed at promoting the use of BIM methodology for the development and operation of building and public infrastructure projects. Its objective is to increase the productivity and sustainability – social, economic and environmental – of the construction industry.[14]

7.2.8 Government procurement

The MOP plays a preponderant role in public infrastructure investment. The MOP plans, projects, builds and maintains the public infrastructure, which is entrusted by other Ministries that by law have the power to build works, institutions or companies of the State, Regional Governments and Municipalities. The MOP determines project conditions, modalities and financing, as well as conserving and administering them. It is also responsible for the administration of all water in the country.

The total investment in infrastructure of the MOP includes the investment made through sectoral funds, private financing via concessions, by mandate of other public institutions such as Ministries, Regional Governments, etc. and the investment in infrastructure that is decided by the Regional Governments.[15]

The most important laws regulating Government procurement and administrative actions in general are *Law No 19.880* called 'Establishes the Basis for the Administrative Procedures Governing the Acts of the Agencies of the State Administration' and *Law No 19.886* called 'Basic Law about Administrative Procurement Contracts and Provision of Services'.

Each public entity such as Ministries or Municipalities tends to regulate its own construction activity. In some cases, it may mandate the MOP to act as its agent to oversee construction.

The MOP uses *Supreme Decree No 75* of the MOP of 2004 that approves the 'Regulation for the construction of public works'. This document regulates a classical construction contract in which the design is provided by the MOP.

The MOP also has carried out various projects such as public hospitals or prisons under the *Supreme Decree No 108 of 2009*, which uses the design and build delivery method and reimburses the Contractor once it reaches contractually agreed milestones.

12 www.df.cl/noticias/site/artic/20200601/asocfile/20200601175753/20200602suple.pdf (accessed 23 March 2022).

13 www.emb.cl/construccion/articulo.mvc?xid=2739 (accessed 23 March 2022).

14 https://construye2025.cl/plan-bim-6/ (accessed 23 March 2022).

15 Andrea Alvarado Duffau and Sebastian Spolmann Pasten, note 2, 34.

Another relevant regulation is the *Supreme Decree No 236* of the Ministry of Housing and Urban Development, called 'Approves General Regulatory Bases for the Contracting of Works for Housing and Urbanisation Services'.

The Ministry of Health, through its Undersecretariat of Health Care Networks, applies *Resolution No 160 of 2015* for the construction of public hospitals, which also follows the design and build approach.

The Government's plan aimed at economic recovery after the pandemic comprises 2,550 projects to be carried out between 2020 and 2022 for US$ 14 billion, involving public and private investment.[16] The MOP will be investing over US$ 3 billion, its highest investment ever, while the total public investment will involve US$ 9.8 billion.[17]

Traditionally, despite its highly developed legal framework, among the OECD countries Chile has been highlighted as the one that takes the longest to award a public contract, identifying extremes of around 15 months in road works. In turn, that same procedure takes five months in South Korea.[18] For approval of a mining project, the companies must submit more than 1,500 requests for approval and the entire procedure takes an average of 3.5 years.[19]

7.2.9 Insurance requirements

The most common insurance required by owners or Employers is a construction all-risks insurance policy (**CAR**), subject to general provisions on insurance entailed in the *Commercial Code.* However, because there are no legal provisions that define construction risks, the specific scope of this insurance may vary.

In general terms, this kind of insurance covers material damage affecting the Works suffered by the beneficiaries. The insurance includes the machinery, man hours, fixed expenses of the work and all direct and some indirect costs that are associated with the work, such as materials or equipment if they are part of the contract or if they are not excluded from the policy. By its nature, it covers from machinery and process failures to fires and contingencies caused by nature. In addition, this insurance may cover the Contractor's general liability to third parties.

The second most common insurance form is the so-called 'Civil Liability Insurance'. This insurance protects the Employer or Contractor against claims from third parties who may suffer property damage or personal injury as a result of the construction site; for example, neighbours adjacent to the project, passers-by or the construction site workers themselves. Both the legal expenses and the corresponding indemnities are covered by this type of policy.

16 planeamiento.mop.gob.cl/noticias/Paginas/DetalledeNoticias.aspx?item=212 (accessed 23 March 2022).

17 concepcionconstruye.cl/mop-confirmo-que-ejecutara-entre-2020-y-2022-el-presupuesto-mas-alto-de-su-historia/ (accessed 23 March 2022).

18 Comisión Nacional de Productividad, 'Productividad en el Sector de la Construcción', note 2, 25.

19 www.bnamericas.com/es/noticias/proyectos-mineros-chilenos-por-us22000mn-a-la-espera-de-permisos (accessed 28 March 2022).

7.2.10 Common forms of contract

The most common delivery methods are the traditional construction contract achieved by the design-bid-build strategy, as well as EPC. As mentioned earlier, the design and build modality is applied rather exceptionally within the public sector.

Other forms of delivery such are partnering, alliancing or other forms of collaboration are very rare and are encountered within the private sector only.

The prevailing pricing modality is the lump sum, which is often used for EPC or turnkey contracts as well as for common construction contracts. The second most common modality comprises unitary prices for direct costs and lump sum agreements for overhead and fees.

The modality of delegated administration conducted on an open book plus fees basis is rather exceptional and is limited to fast-track contracts.

The PPP regulations follow the **BOT** (build, operate and transfer) model.

7.2.11 Dispute resolution

There are no specialised courts in the field of construction law. In matters of public works, disputes are resolved through the ordinary courts of justice.

In the case of PPPs, the *Public Works Concessions Law* was amended in 2010 to establish a so-called Concessions Technical Panel. The Concessions Technical Panel is composed of two lawyers, two engineers and one professional specialised in economic or financial sciences, with a professional or academic career in technical, economic or legal matters related to the infrastructure concessions sector.

Pursuant to Article 36 of the *Public Works Concessions Law*, the Technical Panel hears matters related to technical or economic discrepancies during the execution of the concession contract. As of November 2017, with the publication of *Law No 21.044*, the Panel may receive requests for opinion from the MOP and concession companies, jointly or separately. The Technical Panel issues 'recommendations' within the scope of its competence, which are not binding on the parties. The parties may choose to reach an agreement on the basis of the recommendation or resort to arbitration.

Recourse to the Technical Panel is a condition precedent for subsequent arbitration. Article 36bis of the *Public Works Concessions Law* provides for *ad hoc* arbitration before the so-called Arbitration Commission. At the beginning of each concession contract, the parties appoint members of the Arbitration Commission from two pre-approved lists of candidates. The first list includes 20 lawyers and is drawn up by the Chilean Supreme Court. The other list gathers ten non-lawyers such as economists or engineers and is drawn up by the Court for the Defence of Free Competition. At least two of the members of the Arbitration Commission must be lawyers.

Within the private sector, parties to more complex and sophisticated contracts tend to agree on institutional arbitration. The main local arbitral institution is the Arbitration and Mediation Center (**CAM Santiago**) established in 1992. Nowadays, approximately 21% of all cases relate to the construction sector.

In international contracts with foreign parties, the most preferred institution seems to be the International Court for Arbitration of the International Chamber of Commerce (**ICC**).

Disputes arising from smaller private contracts with no arbitration agreement fall within the jurisdiction of the general courts. The main disadvantage of these is the excessive length of the proceedings which fluctuates between five and seven years.

7.2.12 Current challenges

A key challenge is to substantially improve the content of *Supreme Decree No 75* from 2004 applicable to the construction of public works, in several aspects, especially those related to risk distribution, eliminating entrance barriers and the incorporation of forms of alternative dispute resolution, in particular, Dispute Boards.

While this *Supreme Decree* is applied to projects undertaken by the MOP only, it is the main public entity in charge of public sector infrastructure, which makes a modification of its rules a necessity and a priority.

7.2.13 Unique features of the construction industry in Chile

The unique feature of the construction industry in Chile is the wide usage of concessions for public works or PPP. Chile introduced a system of concessions for public works during the last decade of the 20th century. Its legal framework begins with the *Decree with the Power of Law No 164* from 1991 (*Public Works Concessions Law*), which has been updated on various occasions, the *Law No 20.410* of 2010 being one of its most relevant modifications.

The Concessions Directorate is a department within the MOP, which designs and plans public infrastructure works within the framework of PPP. In more specific terms, the Concessions Directorate is in charge of:

- The programming of bidding procedures for the contracting of studies, projects and execution of fiscal public works through the concession system
- The establishment of the administrative and economic conditions to which the bidding processes for the granting of concessions will be subject
- Bidding processes for the awarding of public works concessions, and the rules for the supervision of the concession contracts
- The elaboration of the modifications that may be necessary to incorporate into the concession contracts under construction or operation, and the concession contracts under construction or operation

The Concessions Directorate has reported that between 1993 and 2020, the concession system allowed works worth US$ 18.378 billion to be implemented.[20]

20 https://concesiones.mop.gob.cl/quienes_somos/Paginas/default.aspx (accessed 28 March 2022).

7.3 The impact of COVID-19 in Chile

7.3.1 The impact of COVID-19 on the execution of construction projects in Chile

Due to the spread of COVID-19, on 18 March 2020, Chile declared the so-called Catastrophic Situation, which lasted until 30 September 2021.

On 22 March 2020, a nationwide curfew was imposed from 10 p.m. to 5 a.m. in order to reduce social contact and facilitate verification of compliance with mandatory quarantine. Starting on 26 March 2020, the Chilean government began quarantining areas most affected by the disease spread.

However, lockdown of construction sites, even if imposed, was lifted shortly after, and the works resumed under new health and safety constraints. The most relevant constraints were the usage of face masks; physical distancing; cleaning and disinfection; record keeping; compulsory quarantine on arrival from abroad; and long distance work for certain categories of workers, among others.

At the onset of the pandemic, various administrative bodies issued instructions and regulations to recommend adequate management during the pandemic.

The Comptroller General of the Republic, the body overseeing the legality of the public administration, described the situation as follows:

> The COVID-19 outbreak constitutes a *force majeure* and unforeseeable event, and, given the serious consequences that its spread among the population may cause, allows the adoption of internal emergency measures by the public authorities and the services of the public administration.

This exceptional situation allows the authorities 'to take special measures, to exempt from liability, to exempt from compliance with certain obligations or deadlines, or to establish special conditions of performance, among other consequences that are not allowed by the legal system in normal situations'.[21]

In turn, the MOP issued two contradictory instructions. In the first instruction, the MOP recognised that construction personnel could be absent from work due to preventive sick leave, which could slow down the progress of Works. The Ministry urged public entities acting as clients to treat this situation with the appropriate flexibility: cases of breach of contracts usually involve fines, which, however, in view of the Catastrophic Situation declared due to the epidemiological emergency in the country, must be treated these days according to special criteria.[22]

A week later, the MOP issued a second instruction, calling for the avoidance of work stoppage and indicating that those Contractors who choose to stop the Works relying on the *force majeure* provisions will not receive any compensation.[23]

On 6 April 2020, *Employment Protection Law No 21.227* was approved, which allowed employees to receive unemployment benefits while maintaining their jobs and banned employers from firing them due to *force majeure*.[24] Following this law, many companies decided to stop their construction projects. For example, CODELCO, an independent

21 Recommendation of the Office of the Comptroller General of the Republic 'On management actions that can be taken by public administration agencies in connection with the COVID-19 outbreak' dated 17 March 2020.

22 General Directorate of Public Works, Ministry of Public Works, ORD. No 222 of 18 March 2020.

23 General Directorate of Public Works, Ministry of Public Works, ORD. No 239 of 27 March 2020.

24 www.leychile.cl/Consulta/m/norma_plana?idNorma=1144080&org=ulp (accessed 23 March 2022).

state-owned enterprise and the country's main copper producer, suspended a third of its projects, advising Contractors to take advantage of the rights granted by *Law No 21.227*.[25]

At the time of writing (March 2022), the virus containment measures continue impacting projects located in Chile. The uncertainty caused by the pandemic has prompted delays in the investment schedules for building and infrastructure works. The supply of construction materials has been interrupted on national and international levels. Workers have deserted the labour market causing an acute shortage of personnel. In addition, credit access conditions are not entirely favourable for the construction sector with short and long-term interest rates on the rise.[26]

Currently, while the Government is looking to reactivate the economy affected by COVID-19, the procedures of the public tenders are being streamlined through administrative measures and controls carried out by the MOP. Among the initiatives to speed up the implementation of projects is the reduction of the number of days between the opening and awarding of projects from 84 days in 2020 to 56 at present.[27]

7.3.2 The impact of COVID-19 on the operation of construction contracts in Chile

In view of the current pandemic, the primacy of the contractually agreed terms has been putting a lot of pressure on the parties, as there are no contractual or legal mechanisms to adapt their obligations to the new reality.

The only way to be – partially – liberated from the weight of contractual obligations is by invoking the *force majeure* clause or legal provision. *Force majeure* is regulated in Article 45 of the Chilean CC, in the following terms:

> the unforeseen [event] impossible to resist, such as a shipwreck, an earthquake, the capture by enemies, acts of authority exercised by a public officer, etc.

Force majeure operates as a disclaimer or exculpation possibility that justifies a party's non-compliance with contractual obligations. However, while a party can be discharged from liability, it should bear its own costs. For construction projects, it means that the Contractor will receive an extension of time but won't receive compensation for costs incurred during the *force majeure* event.

For *force majeure* provisions to apply, the inability to comply with the contractual obligations needs to be absolute. Conversely, if the unforeseen circumstances make compliance more onerous for one of the parties, the situation cannot be deemed a *force majeure* event.

In some cases, and for a short period of time, construction sites were closed by local authorities and the population was in lockdown, making it absolutely impossible for personnel to circulate or reach the Site. In these cases, Contractors seemed to be better equipped to rely on *force majeure* if they wanted to. But in other cases, the impact has been caused by new social distancing rules, which required the provision of additional

25 www.poderyliderazgo.cl/codelco-suspende-relacion-con-empresas-contratistas-y-llamo-a-acogerse-a-ley-de-proteccion-del-empleo/ (accessed 23 March 2022).

26 Informe MACh 57 Macroeconomía y Construcción, Gerencia de Estudios Cámara Chilena de la Construcción, June 2021, 5, https://cchc.cl/uploads/archivos/archivos/mach-57.pdf (accessed 23 March 2022).

27 https://concepcionconstruye.cl/mop-confirmo-que-ejecutara-entre-2020-y-2022-el-presupuesto-mas-alto-de-su-historia/ (accessed 23 March 2022).

transportation; new accommodation and catering facilities for the workers; and creating remote working opportunities, among other measures. In several contracts, the parties disputed how these types of measures should be contractually and legally treated.

Within the realm of concessions of public works, the Technical Panel dealt with a concessionaire request for time-related costs and cost overruns because of the pandemic. A dispute arose between *Sociedad Concesionaria Nuevo Pudahuel* (SCNP) in charge of the amplification of the Santiago airport, and the MOP (No D05-2021-16). SCNP avoided qualifying the pandemic as *force majeure*. However, the MOP did so and accepted the 57-day extension of the deadline for the provisional commissioning.

Article 22 of the Public Works Concessions Law assigns the risk and losses arising in the course of the execution of the works, to the concession company or its contractor:

> The legal regime of the concession, during the construction phase of the works, shall be as follows: …
>
> 2. The works will be carried out at the concessionaire's entire risk, and it will be incumbent upon the concessionaire to meet any disbursements that may be necessary until its total completion, whether due to unforeseen circumstances, *force majeure*, or any other cause. The State will not be responsible for the consequences derived from the contracts entered into by the concessionaire with the contractors or suppliers. However, the State will contribute to the payment of damages caused by acts of God or *force majeure*, if so established in the bidding conditions.

Regarding the costs associated with the effects of the pandemic, the Technical Panel argued that, according to Article 22 of the *Public Works Concessions Law*, the SCNP assumed all the risk of the construction stage and must make all the necessary disbursements 'regardless of the origin or cause of such disbursements, whether or not they were foreseen in its valuation presented in the bidding process'.[28]

It indicated that 'all contractors should have considered in their bid or not – the decision is theirs –, a variable for construction risks, being clear that the construction costs are their responsibility'. The Panel added that the provision's wording is 'so broad that it does not rule out any hypothesis, except those that the regulation itself contemplates', but no exception was provided for.

It is safe to assume that the Panel exceeded the limits of its mandate when it based its decision on deliberations of a legal nature. In addition, it is hard to share its view on risk assignment as it seems to argue that the concessionaire is liable for all remote or unthinkable risks unknown at the time of the contract formation.

Curiously, in a previous dispute between those same parties, regarding the economic rebalancing of that same concession contract, the Technical Panel recognised that the 'pandemic is a supervening event of nature, an extraordinary and unforeseen situation, totally beyond the will of the parties' and 'escapes the natural, rational and foreseeable risk of the business to which SCNP's responsibility extends' (No D02-2021-16). As explained earlier, the Panel's decisions are non-binding recommendations to the parties, who will certainly want to have them reviewed in binding arbitration.

28 Concessions Technical Panel, No D05-2021-16, www.panelconcesiones.cl/OpenNews/Default.aspx?argInstanciaId=1&argnoticiaid=196 (accessed 23 March 2022).

7.4 Chilean law as the governing law of the contract

Chile follows the so-called territorial approach to the determination of the law applicable within its national territory. Article 14 of the *Chilean Civil Code* provides: 'The law is mandatory for all inhabitants of the Republic, even the foreigners'. This has been construed as a mandate to apply the substantive Chilean law over foreign laws potentially applicable. In other words, with some minor exceptions allowed by specific provisions contained in the conflict of laws rules, Chilean substantive law would apply within the national territory.

Thus, Chilean law would apply to contracts executed by Chilean nationals or companies incorporated in Chile which are deemed Chilean. In addition, if a contract involves a foreign party but there is no stipulation regarding the applicable law, Chilean law will apply as well. The same goes for a contract executed between two or more foreign parties regarding a project located in Chile.

7.4.1 Constraints on the governing law of a construction contract

There is no legal requirement to submit construction contracts to Chilean law and there is no express prohibition of foreign choice-of-law clauses. However, there are some rather antique court decisions that misapplied Article 16 of the Chilean *CC*. This legal provision states: 'All assets situated within Chile subject to Chilean law'.

Based on the foregoing, the courts have argued that the national law applies to all contracts that refer to assets located in Chile. Thus, choice-of-law clauses in favour of foreign law could be challenged in courts.

This position has been correctly criticised by national doctrine arguing that Article 16 of the *CC* does not apply to the contractual relationships between the parties, but only establishes the law applicable to the so-called 'real status' of the assets.[29]

If the contract has foreign elements (e.g. foreign nationality of one of the parties), the safer option would be to submit the disputes arising from that contract to international arbitration. In that case, the foreign choice-of-law clause would be enforceable under Article 28 of *Law No 19.971 on International Commercial Arbitration.*

Despite the foregoing, it is customary that in large-scale projects in the areas of private mining and energy, the contracts are drafted at the Employer's headquarters, many of them in accordance with common law rules and concepts. Pursuant to the *pacta sunt servanda* principle, those contractual provisions will prevail over the non-mandatory legal provisions of the local law. Thus, the parties can draft their contractual provisions in alignment with provisions of a foreign law.

7.4.2 Formal requirements for a construction contract

There are no legal requirements regarding formalities applicable to private construction contracts. For the sake of greater legal certainty, the contracts are usually formalised in writing. In the public sector, pursuant to Article 89 of the *Supreme Decree No 75* from 2004, the contract requires a specific approval or decree by the public entity.

29 Mario Ramirez Necochea, *Análisis crítico del derecho internacional privado chileno* (LexisNexis Matthew Bender, 2007) 44–51.

7.5 What Special Provisions in the Particular Conditions are necessary for consistency with applicable law in Chile?

The Chilean private law (but not its public or administrative law) is based on the principle of autonomy of will. According to Article 1545 of the *Civil Code*, the contract entered into by the parties is deemed binding upon them as if it were law. Following this basic principle, there seem to be no obstacles for the parties to agree on the application of the FIDIC contract models when the applicable substantive law is Chilean law.

FIDIC clauses would override the *Civil Code* provisions which will apply in a supplementary manner only. Not all of the FIDIC contract types are expressly recognised in Chilean Law as only limited provisions on construction contracts exist, while there is no general regulation of design and build or EPC contracts.

FIDIC contracts under Chilean law will be described as 'unnamed', that is, not identified within the *Civil Code*, since they do not strictly respond to the modalities of construction contracts as specified by the *Chilean Civil Code*. Nonetheless, this does not endanger its validity or enforceability.[30]

There is virtually no practical experience with FIDIC contracts in Chile. Thus, there is no case law or overarching academic studies that address their possible consistency with Chilean law. As explained earlier, the general understanding is that the FIDIC contracts are compatible with Chilean law and should prevail over the legal provisions by virtue of the Parties' autonomy of will.

However, because FIDIC contracts are based on common law, some provisions might be construed differently or require an additional explanation. On the other hand, some domestic law provisions might influence the way FIDIC provisions could be construed. The following addresses some of the issues that might bring to light differences between FIDIC forms and Chilean law.

7.5.1 Good faith

Good faith obligations do not play a relevant role in FIDIC contracts. It is only mentioned in sub-clause 6.3 of the General Conditions of Dispute Avoidance/Adjudication Agreement that establishes the Parties' general obligation to cooperate with the DAAB, and in the Notes on the Preparation of Special Provisions example on mediation rules under sub-clause 21.5 that establishes the Parties' obligation to engage with the Mediator and with each other in co-operation, in a timely manner and in good faith.

Article 1546 of the *CC* enshrines the general duty of good faith in contractual matters, also known as objective good faith. There is consensus in the doctrine and national jurisprudence that the principle of objective good faith underlines all Chilean law.[31]

The duty to act in good faith translates into the following requirements:

> It is an extension of the duty of performance, in accordance with the commands of contractual good faith, linking the contracting parties in a conduct of mutual collaboration in the fulfillment of their obligations, oriented to everything that derives from the nature of the obligation that each one must abide by. Regarding contractual good faith, it has been said that it is 'an

30 Juan Eduardo Figueroa Valdés, *Construcción y arbitraje* (DER Ediciones, 2019) 101.

31 Hernán Corral, 'La aplicación jurisprudencial de la buena fe objetiva en el ordenamiento civil chileno' (2007) No 3 *Cuadernos de Análisis Jurídico*, 187, 189.

> attitude of cooperation that binds the obligor to put its own energies at the service of the interests of others, in view of a performance that responds with all its assets.[32]

The Supreme Court has been emphatic in deriving from the principle of good faith a requirement of an attitude of collaboration and loyalty:

> Both the doctrine and the jurisprudence of this Supreme Court have considered good faith, in its objective aspect, as the conduct that can be expected from a correct person, since it is a standard of conduct which is employed as a synonym of probity, loyalty, trust, confidence, security, honourability, of non-contradiction of the observed behaviour and fair play, considering, as the case may be, the economic function of contract, which imposes cooperation, collaboration, advice and information between the parties, behaving in an active manner, since he has the obligation to safeguard the interest of the other party.[33]

This overarching meaning of the good faith obligation could lead courts and arbitral tribunals to construe contractual provisions in a more liberal way, highlighting Parties' loyalty and cooperation duties.

This is also in line with the rules of interpretation under Chilean law. The supreme rule in Chilean legislation is Article 1560 of the *CC*, which reads: 'The intention of the contracting parties being clearly known, it must be followed rather than the literal meaning of the words'. It exhorts the judge to look for what has been the intention of the parties. Other rules of contract implementation prompt courts and tribunals to search for the authentic and intrinsic parties' understanding of their contractual relationship.

In addition to the Article 1546 of the *CC*, Article 1564 provides for a subsidiary but nonetheless relevant rule on contract interpretation:

> The clauses of a contract shall be interpreted one by the other, each one being given each one the meaning that better suits the contract as a whole. They may also be interpreted by clauses of another contract between the same parties and on the same subject matter. Or by the practical application made of them by both parties, or by one of the parties with the approval of the other.

For example, if the Parties did not follow the notification procedure during the contract performance, none of them should be allowed to rely on the contractual provisions that make timely notices and claim submissions a condition precedent in material and procedural matters.

7.5.2 Delay damages/penalties

Sub-clause 8.7 sets out the Employer's right to 'Delay Damages' and is derived from Clause 47 of the fourth edition Red Book. It was previously called 'Liquidated Damages for Delay', and the discussion of this provision often focuses on that last concept.[34] It is our understanding that liquidated damages must be a genuine pre-estimate of loss. Thus, they have a compensatory function for damages suffered by the Employer and cannot be aimed at penalising the Contractor.

---

32 Supreme Court, Case No 2073-2013, 29 May 2014.

33 Supreme Court, Case No 3965-2011, 2 May 2012.

34 Corbett & Co, 'Clause 8 Commencement Delays and Suspension', www.corbett.co.uk/wp-content/uploads/Clause-8-Commencement-Delays-and-Suspension-.pdf (accessed 24 March 2022).

In Chile, construction contracts usually include provisions on penalties (***multas***) payable by the Contractor in the event of delay. While *multa* is translated as penalty, it can also be equated to the anticipated estimation of damages. The relevant provision here is Article 1542 of the *CC* which states:

> The penalty may be demanded in all cases in which it has been stipulated, without the debtor being able to allege that the non-performance of the agreed performance has not caused any damage to the creditor or has produced a benefit for him.

The distinction between the punitive or compensatory nature of the specific clause will have to be assessed within a specific contractual context.[35] Independent from the characterisation of the clause, as a rule, it will be upheld by the court or arbitral tribunal.

As argued in academic writings:

> The creditor has the right to collect the penalty, even if there were really no damages; he does not need to prove them, nor can the debtor exempt himself from paying them, alleging that there were none. This is provided for in Article 1542, so that in the end it may well happen that the debtor is obliged to pay the penalty, even if the creditor has not suffered any damage, or, on the contrary, has been benefited.[36]

Not only is the creditor exempted from proving damages, but also the debtor cannot argue or show that there were no damages.

Article 1543 of the *CC* highlights the difference between penalty and compensation of damages: 'The penalty and the compensation of damages cannot be demanded at the same time, unless it has been expressly stipulated; but it will always be at the creditor's discretion to claim the compensation or the penalty'. In other words, Chilean law treats *multas* as penalties, which could create a dissonance with the common law resistance towards penalties. Nonetheless, if a contract is subject to Chilean law, Delay Damages, *multas* or liquidated damages should be deemed valid and enforceable.

Exceptionally, according to Article 1544 of the *CC*, the court or arbitral tribunal may reduce the penalty, but only when it exceeds the value of the main obligation twice (so-called 'huge penalty' or ***pena enorme***).

Therefore, courts' or arbitral tribunals' approaches to the interpretation of sub-clause 8.7 may vary. If the common law concept of liquidated damages is followed, a review of the agreement on Delay Damages could be exceptionally admissible. In turn, if the Chilean law approach is preferred, sub-clause 8.7 will be applied with no room for review unless the Delay Damages are deemed *pena enorme*.

7.5.3 Employer's Taking Over

Under sub-clause 10, Taking Over refers to a physical completion of the Works that transfers the responsibility for the care of the Works to the Employer.

In Chilean practice, two kinds of reception or acceptance of the Works can be distinguished. The first one is the so-called provisional acceptance (***recepción provisoria***), which usually means that all works and tests have been completed by the Contractor and,

35 This seems to be the contemporary position of the English courts. See: *Eco World – Ballymore Embassy Gardens Company Limited v Dobler UK Limited* [2021] EWHC 2207 (TCC) [54].

36 René Abeliuk Manasevich, *Las Obligaciones*, Volume II, 5th edn (ThomsonReuters, 2009) 180.

beyond the punch list of minor corrections, no activities are pending. At that moment, the Contractor would usually submit a final invoice and replace its performance security with a security covering its liability for potential defects and clear the Site. Starting from that point, the contractual warranty period begins. As a matter of custom, it lasts between one and two years. Once that period has passed or once the Contractor has cured the defects, the final reception (***recepción definitiva***) or acceptance by the Employer takes place and all the contractual obligations will be deemed extinguished.

In turn, pursuant to sub-clause 11.9 of the FIDIC Red Book, performance of the Contractor's obligations is certified through the Performance Certificate. According to sub-clause 11.10, the Contractor cannot be made liable for Defects or damage occurring more than two years after expiry of the Defects Notification Period for the Plant.

It must be noted that the *General Law of Urbanism and Constructions* approved by the *Decree with the Power Law No 458* in 1975, establishes the Contractor's liability during the ten-year period starting from the final reception or acceptance of the works (Article 18). The question is when this liability period starts running, whether from the issuance of the Taking Over Certificate or from the issuance of the Performance Certificate.

In order to align FIDIC concepts with the local practice and *Decree No 458*, the Parties could clarify in the Particular Conditions that Taking Over should be assimilated to the provisional acceptance and that the Performance Certificate should be assimilated to the final acceptance. It should be made clear that the legal liability period would be calculated starting from the Performance Certificate.

If the legal liability period was calculated from Taking Over onwards, it would reduce the Contractor's liability (by one or two years), which can be deemed contrary to the mandatory provisions of *Law No 458*.

7.5.4 Termination

National law does not contemplate the possibility of unilateral termination of the Contract. On that topic, Article 1489 of the *CC* provides:

> In bilateral contracts the resolutory condition is included if one of the contracting parties does not comply with its obligations. But in such case the other contracting party may request at its discretion either the termination or the specific performance of the contract, with compensation of damages.

This provision authorises the diligent party to file for certain actions before a court or arbitral tribunal. *A contrario sensu*,[37] the diligent party is not authorised to take justice into its own hands, for example, by walking out of an uncommercial bargain, the competent court being the one who must declare the termination of the contract or order its compulsory performance.

It is accepted and in common practice in Chile to include in construction contracts clauses on contract termination in case of contractual breaches or defaults committed by one of the parties. Therefore, the corresponding FIDIC provisions should be deemed valid and enforceable under Chilean law. Nonetheless, as a matter of experience, the Parties

37 In a contrary sense (Latin).

tend to take their disputes to courts or tribunals arguing that the termination of the contract lacked contractual or legal bases.

In addition, it is doubtful whether the Employer's right under sub-clause 15.5 on termination for convenience can be enforced. The sanctity of a contract (*pacta sunt servanda*) is a highly ranked principle under Chilean law, and at the same time, Article 1478 of the *CC* declares void 'obligations contracted under an optional condition that consists of the sheer will of the person who is bound' (*condición potestativa*).

At least in one known case, the arbitral tribunal declared unlawful termination at will, which was confirmed by the Supreme Court. In that case, both Parties had the right to terminate the long-term contract upon prior notice. The Employer made use of that right alleging loss of trust previously deposited in the Contractor. A month before that termination at will, the Parties were trying to renegotiate the contract. The Supreme Court relied extensively on the good faith principle to establish that the termination was unlawful. There was no reasonable ground for such termination; it was termination at whim rather than at will. According to the Court, good faith requires the Party to pursue not only its own commercial interests but those of the other Party as well. This included the Employer's obligation to refrain from conduct that would prevent the Contractor from obtaining the advantages it was expecting to achieve. Those advantages were specifically the profit the Contractor had expected to obtain. An unreasonable termination by the Employer deprived the Contractor of its expected profit, which it was entitled to receive.[38]

7.5.5 Time period for the submission of the Notice of Claim

Pursuant to sub-clause 20.2.1, if Notice of a Claim is not filed within 28 days of the occurrence of the event or knowledge of its effects, the claiming Party will not be entitled to any of the remedies and the other Party will be discharged from any liability in connection with the events that gave rise to the Claim.

However, it remains to be seen whether this provision will be given effect under Chilean law. As it precludes a Party from performing actions in defence of its rights, it can be equated to a statutory limitation provision. It might not be deemed acceptable to reduce four or five years of the statutory limitation period to 28 days. Such a limitation may be deemed contrary to Chilean public policy, as it would dramatically reduce and shorten access to justice.

Therefore, the omission to submit the Notice of Claim within the limitation period under sub-clause 20.2.1 will most probably be construed as extinguishing the right to file a Claim under the Contract. Nonetheless, it will not extinguish the right to file a claim against the counterparty before an arbitral tribunal. In this case, the arbitral tribunal will be faced with a challenge to accommodate such a claim to the notion of a Dispute, which has a very specific definition under FIDIC 2017 (sub-clause 1.1.29).

However, the notion of Dispute seemingly includes matters that are different from a Claim or different from a matter to be determined by the Engineer. As provided under

38 Supreme Court, 22 May 2019, Case No 38.506-2017.

sub-clause 1.1.29: 'Dispute' means any situation where: (a) one Party makes a claim against the other Party (which may be a Claim, as defined in these Conditions, or a matter to be determined by the Engineer under these Conditions, or otherwise).

While it is not suggested that an arbitral tribunal acting under Chilean law will automatically disregard the limitation period under sub-clause 20.2.1, it is plausible that, based on public policy concerns, they would do so.

7.6 What Special Provisions in the Particular Conditions are desirable for consistency with applicable laws in Chile?

As explained earlier, there is no practical experience with FIDIC contracts under Chilean law. From the sensitive issues identified earlier, some might be addressed by way of specific provisions in order to achieve a desirable consistency with Chilean law or in order to ensure that the FIDIC General Conditions prevail.

7.7 Applicable legislation for Chilean governing law of the contract

A construction contract in Chile is regulated in Articles 1996 and following of the *Civil Code*, as a type of service lease, following the Roman tradition. Pursuant to Article 1996 of the *Chilean Civil Code*, a construction contract is classified according to which Party supplies the materials for the Works. Thus, the construction contract is a 'sale' contract when it is the Contractor who supplies the materials, while the contract will be a 'service lease' contract when the materials are supplied to the Contractor by the Employer who ordered the construction of the Works.

The importance of the distinction in the construction contract between 'sale' and 'lease of services' lies in the assumption of the risks of loss of the materials (Article 2000 of the *CC*). Thus, if the thing/Works perish, the Contractor loses not only the materials but also the price of its work, unlike what happens if the contract is classified as a lease, in which the loss of the materials will fall on the Employer who ordered the work, unless the thing perishes due to the fault of the Contractor or its dependents, as indicated in paragraph 2 of the same Article 2000 of the *Chilean Civil Code*.[39]

7.8 Summary of applicable legislation for Chilean governing law of the contract

7.8.1 Entry into a construction contract

Contracts generally	*Código Civil*, Libro 4, Títulos 1 to 2; *Código de Comercio*, Art 96 to Art 106
Construction contracts	*Código Civil*, Art 1996 to Art 2005

39 Juan Eduardo Figueroa Valdés, note 29, 99–100.

7.8.2 Operation of a construction contract

Force majeure	*Código Civil*, Art 45
Hardship	Not recognised under Chilean law
Guarantees under forms of Security (Tender Security, Demand Guarantee, Surety Bond, Advance Payment Guarantee, Retention Money Guarantee, Payment Guarantee by Employer)	Not expressly regulated by law with the only exception of Art 69 No 13 of the *General Banking Law* that authorises the banks to issue guarantees as forms of security

7.8.3 Termination of a construction contract

Frustration	Not recognised under Chilean law
Bankruptcy, insolvency, liquidation	*Ley No 20.720 de 'Reorganización y Liquidación de Empresas y Personas, y Perfecciona el Rol de la Superintendencia del Ramo'*

7.8.4 Dispute resolution

Limitation periods	*Código Civil*, Art 2014 to 2015
Liability	*Decreto con Fuerza de Ley No 458 'Ley General de Urbanismo y Construcción'*, Art 18
Arbitration	*Ley de Arbitraje Comercial Internacional No 19.971*, 2004 *Código Orgánico de Tribunales*, Art 222 to Art 243 *Código de Procedimiento Civil*, Art 628 to Art 644

7.9 Applicable legislation if the Site is in Chile

As explained earlier, Chile follows the so-called territoriality principle for the determination of the law applicable to international transactions. In other words, unless the parties have stipulated a different choice-of-law provision, Chilean law will apply to a project carried out in Chile. The practical experience shows that the parties to international construction contracts tend to agree on the application of Chilean law as far as the project is situated within the national territory.

In addition, if the parties have submitted their contractual relationship to a foreign law, certain local provisions will apply anyway. These kinds of provisions are the so-called laws of police (*lois de police*), that is, they are mandatory provisions applicable notwithstanding the substantive applicable law (labour law, health and safety, environmental law, tax, custom, etc.).

7.10 Summary of applicable legislation if the Site is in Chile

7.10.1 Operation of a construction contract

Registration and administration of professionals	Non-existent
Registration/licencing of Contractors and subcontractors	Non-existent with the sole exception of registration before the Ministry of Public Works per *Decreto Ley No 75 'Reglamento de Construcción de Obras Públicas'*, Art 5
Use of liens/assignment of debts	*Código Civil*, Art 1991 to Art 1908
Labour	*Código de Trabajo*
Design/moral rights	*Ley No 17.336 'Propiedad Intelectual'*
Copyright	*Ley No 17.336 'Propiedad Intelectual'*
Work affecting adjacent property to the Site	*Código Civil*, Art 2003
Heritage	*Código Civil*, Art 624 to Art 626
Environment	*Ley No 19.300 sobre Bases Generales del Medio Ambiente*
Public procurement	*Ley No 19.886 de 'Compras Públicas'*
Building and construction permits, execution of construction work, standard of construction work	*Decreto con Fuerza de Ley No 458 'Ley General de Urbanismo y Construcción'*
Health and safety	*Ley No 16.744 'Establece normas sobre accidentes del trabajo y enfermedades profesionales', 1968*
Calibration of testing apparatus, equipment and instruments	Not expressly regulated by law
Ownership of Plant and Materials	*Código Civil*, Art 1996
Employer's sale of Contractor's Equipment, surplus material, wreckage and Temporary Works	Not expressly regulated by law
Insurance	*Ley 20.667 'Regula el contrato de seguro', Código de Comercio*, Art 512 to Art 601
Liability for defective work	*Decreto con Fuerza de Ley No 485 'Ley General de Urbanismo y Construcción'*, Art 18
Liability for nuisance	*Código Civil*, Art 2314 to Art 2334

7.10.2 Termination of a construction contract

Bankruptcy, insolvency, liquidation	*Ley No 20.720 de 'Reorganización y Liquidación de Empresas y Personas, y Perfecciona el Rol de la Superintendencia del Ramo'*
Decennial liability and liability generally for the total or partial collapse of structures	*Decreto con Fuerza de Ley No 485 'Ley General de Urbanismo y Construcción'*, Art 18

7.10.3 Dispute resolution

Limitation periods	*Código Civil*, Art 2014 to 2015

7.11 Applicable legislation if the 'seat' of the dispute determination is Chile

If parties have submitted their disputes to Chilean ordinary courts, *Civil Procedure Code* as well as *Organic Tribunal Codes* will apply.

If the Parties have opted for arbitration, a distinction needs to be made. If all the Parties to the contract and to the arbitration agreement have their place of business in Chile, then the arbitration will be deemed domestic and subject to the *Civil Procedure Code* as well as *Organic Tribunal Codes*. One of the unique features of the Chilean legal system is that, in domestic cases, the arbitrators are deemed judges of the Republic and entrusted with certain jurisdictional functions unknown within the realm of domestic arbitration in other jurisdictions. By way of an example, the arbitrators in domestic proceedings are authorised to issue interim measures that must be complied with by third parties such as banks or public registers.

International commercial arbitration is subject to a different legal regime based upon *Law No 19.971 on International Commercial Arbitration*, which is almost identical to the *UNCITRAL Model Law on International Commercial Arbitration.*

Therefore, one of the most important challenges when dealing with arbitration clauses and arbitration in general in Chile is to determine which of the two legal regimes is applicable: the domestic arbitration regime or the international commercial arbitration regime.

7.12 Summary of applicable legislation if the 'seat' of the dispute determination is Chile

Dispute resolution	*Ley de Arbitraje Comercial Internacional No 19.971, 2004* *Código Orgánico de Tribunales* *Código de Procedimiento Civil*
Limitation periods	*Código Civil*, Art 2014 to 2015
Arbitration	*Ley de Arbitraje Comercial Internacional No 19.971, 2004* *Código Orgánico de Tribunales*, Art 222 to Art 243 *Código de Procedimiento Civil*, Art 628 to Art 644

7.13 Issues that a court or arbitrator may construe differently than expected from the words of the Contract because of local law or custom

Theoretically, a court or arbitrator might be faced with difficulties reconciling some of the concepts described in section 7.5.1. However, in Chilean law, the sanctity of the contract is one of the most highly regarded legal principles. Based on the binding force of the contractual agreement stipulated in Article 1545 of the *Civil Code*, the first working assumption should be that the contract will be construed as expected by the parties, in accordance with its wording.

7.14 Additional references for Chile

7.14.1 Books

Carlos Molina Zaldívar & Víctor Ríos Salas, *Derecho de la Construcción* (O'Print Impresores, 2016).

Juan Eduardo Figueroa (ed), *Derecho de Construcción: Análisis Dogmático y Práctico* (Der Ediciones Limitada, 2017).

Jaime Arancibia & Alejandro Romero (eds), *La concesión de obra pública: Aspectos jurídicos y económicos* (Universidad de los Andes, 2018).

7.14.2 Journals

Álvaro Araya Ibáñez, 'El Contrato de Construcción en Chile. Análisis Económico y Jurisprudencial', (2018) No 31 *Revista Chilena de Derecho Privado* 221–276 (The Construction Contract in Chile. Economic and Jurisprudential Analysis).

Arturo Prado Puga, 'El contrato general de construcción, y en especial la modalidad EPC y sus principales características', (2014) Vol. 41 No 2 *Revista Chilena de Derecho* 765–783 (The general construction contract, and especially the EPC modality and its main characteristics).

7.14.3 Internet

National Laws and Decrees: www.bcn.cl (Spanish)
Court Decisions: www.pjud.cl (Spanish)

CHAPTER 8

Applying FIDIC Contracts in Ecuador

Dr Mario Alejandro Flor, Juan Carlos Herrera-Quenguan and Alejandro Pérez

CONTENTS

8.1 Outline of Ecuador's legal environment 188
8.1.1 The constitutional structure of Ecuador 188
8.1.2 The legal system in Ecuador 188
8.1.3 The court system in Ecuador 189
8.2 The construction industry in Ecuador 189
8.2.1 Overview 189
8.2.2 Structure 190
8.2.3 Licensing/registration 191
8.2.4 Labour relations 191
8.2.5 Employment 192
8.2.5.1 Salary 192
8.2.5.2 Work shifts 192
8.2.5.3 Vacations and holidays 193
8.2.5.4 Disabled persons 193
8.2.5.5 Termination of labour contracts 193
8.2.5.6 Compensation for termination 193
8.2.5.7 Social Security 194
8.2.6 Safety culture 194
8.2.7 Modular construction using factory-fabricated components 195
8.2.8 Innovation 195
8.2.9 Government/private sector procurement 195
8.2.10 Insurance requirements 196
8.2.11 Common forms of contract 196
8.2.12 Dispute resolution 197
8.2.13 Current challenges 198
8.2.14 Unique features of the construction industry in Ecuador 198
8.3 The impact of COVID-19 in Ecuador 198
8.3.1 The impact of COVID-19 on the execution of construction projects in Ecuador 198
8.3.2 The impact of COVID-19 on the operation of construction contracts in Ecuador 199
8.3.2.1 Labour matters 199
8.3.2.2 Bankruptcy special rules 200

 DOI: 10.4324/9781003201250-8

8.4 Ecuadorian governing law of the contract 200
8.4.1 Constraints on the governing law of a construction contract 200
8.4.2 Formal requirements for a construction contract 200
8.5 What Special Provisions in the Particular Conditions are necessary for consistency with applicable laws in Ecuador? 201
8.5.1 FIDIC General Conditions are incompatible or inconsistent with Ecuadorian governing law of the contract 201
8.5.2 FIDIC General Conditions are incompatible or inconsistent with the law of the Site/Country 201
8.5.3 FIDIC General Conditions are incompatible or inconsistent with the relevant laws on dispute determination in Ecuador 201
8.6 What Special Provisions in the Particular Conditions are desirable for consistency with applicable laws in Ecuador? 201
8.7 Applicable legislation for Ecuadorian governing law of the contract 201
8.7.1 Freedom of contract 201
8.7.2 Applicable laws 202
8.7.3 The plurality of regulation sources 202
8.7.4 Outdated rules 203
8.7.5 Mandatory rules – public policy 203
8.8 Summary of applicable legislation for Ecuador governing law of the contract 203
8.8.1 Entry into a construction contract 203
8.8.2 Operation of a construction contract 203
8.8.3 Termination of a construction contract 203
8.8.4 Dispute resolution 204
8.9 Summary of applicable legislation if the Site/Country is in Ecuador 204
8.9.1 Operation of a construction contract 204
8.9.2 Termination of a construction contract 205
8.10 Summary of applicable legislation if the 'seat' of the dispute determination is Ecuador 206
8.11 Issues that a court or arbitrator may construe differently from that expected from the words of the Contract because of local law or custom 206
8.12 Additional references for Ecuador 206
8.12.1 Books 206
8.12.2 Journals 206
8.12.3 Legislation 206

8.1 Outline of Ecuador's legal environment

8.1.1 The constitutional structure of Ecuador

Pursuant to Article 1 of the *Ecuadorian Constitution* of 2008, Ecuador is:

> a constitutional **state of rights and justice**, social, democratic, sovereign, independent, unitary, intercultural, plurinational and secular.
>
> It is organised in the form of a **republic** and is **governed in a decentralised** manner. **Sovereignty is vested in the people**, whose will is the basis of authority, and is exercised through the organs of public power and the forms of direct participation provided for in the Constitution.[1]

Consequently, Ecuador is a republic with a strong emphasis on citizen participation and a decentralised structure that recognises the local governments' autonomy to rule on matters relevant to their corresponding jurisdiction.[2]

Furthermore, apart from the traditional republican structure of the State,[3] Ecuador adopted a more complex branch structure. It created the Transparency and Social Control Branch in charge of the coordination and organisation of citizens' participation in state affairs[4] and elevated the election authorities, the National Electoral Council and the Contentious Electoral Tribunal, to the Electoral Branch.[5]

8.1.2 The legal system in Ecuador

The legal system in Ecuador is an amalgamation of influences derived from the *French Civil Code of 21 March 1804* – the *Napoleonic Code* – which influenced the *Chilean Civil Code* and the *Spanish Civil Code*. The *Chilean Civil Code* or the *Bello Code*[6] was adopted in Ecuador on 21 November 1857.[7] Consequently, the Ecuadorian legal tradition is civil law and it is based largely on law statutes, with its general regulations and written norms enacted by governmental agencies.[8] Notwithstanding the aforementioned, judicial rulings from the highest tribunals, the National Court of Justice and the Constitutional Court, may become binding law – precedent – in certain situations.

1 *Constitution of Ecuador* 2008, Article 1, emphasis added. Excerpt translated from Spanish: '*El Ecuador es un Estado constitucional de derechos y justicia, social, democrático, soberano, independiente, unitario, intercultural, plurinacional y laico. Se organiza en forma de república y se gobierna de manera descentralizada. La soberanía radica en el pueblo, cuya voluntad es el fundamento de la autoridad, y se ejerce a través de los órganos del poder público y de las formas de participación directa previstas en la Constitución*'.

2 The Ecuadorian *Constitution* and the *Organic Code of Territorial Organisation* establish the differentiated regime of competencies (powers) that the central and local government exercises.

3 EB Abdrasulov, SR Shalabaev and AI Mugauova, *The Concept of the Triad of Branches of State Power and Issues of its Modernisation* (2015) Vol. XVIII *European Research Studies Journal*, 75.

4 *Constitution of Ecuador* Article 204.

5 *Ibid.*, Article 217.

6 In reference to the Venezuelan-Chilean Jurist and Diplomat Andrés de Jesús María y José Bello, also known as Andrés Bello.

7 J Reig Satorres and J Larrea Holguin, *Manual de Historia del Derecho en el Ecuador* (2nd edn, Corporación de Estudios y Publicaciones 2000) 310.

8 It is important to note that not only the Legislative Branch (National Assembly) has the power to enact binding rules. Pursuant to Articles 137 *et seq.* of the *Constitution of Ecuador*, the President has a key role in the creation of laws and, similarly, pursuant to Article 147 (13), the President is entitled to issue the *General Regulations* that develop the provisions of a given law statute.

8.1.3 The court system in Ecuador

Ecuador's judiciary is regulated by the *Organic Code of the Judiciary*[9] and its top-down organic structure is as follows:

(a) The National Court of Justice (highest court)
(b) Provincial Courts
(c) Judicial Units (courts)/Contentious Administrative and Tax Tribunals

Pursuant to Article 429 of the *Constitution*, the Constitutional Court is 'the highest organ of control, constitutional interpretation and administration of justice in this area' and it is differentiated from the aforementioned structure of ordinary justice. In some cases established in the law, matters that were adjudicated in ordinary justice may be directed to the constitutional system of justice (constitutionality control) via an Extraordinary Protection Action (*Acción Extraordinaria de Protección*).[10]

Furthermore, in the constitutional system of justice, judicial units and Provincial Courts do participate via Protection Actions (*Acción de Protección*)[11] that rule on the constitutionality of non-judicial measures (e.g. administrative acts).

Arbitration and mediation are other forms of dispute resolution that are enshrined in the *Constitution*.[12] Notwithstanding that neither arbitral tribunals nor mediators are considered courts, their awards and mediation agreements, respectively, have the value or binding effect as if they were rulings from the highest court: the National Court. Furthermore, their binding and final character render them as enforcement instruments (*títulos de ejecución*)[13] with limited grounds to be challenged, for instance, an annulment action.[14]

8.2 The construction industry in Ecuador

8.2.1 Overview

There are two very different construction segments in Ecuador; the first is related to construction for commercial sectors, such as factories, warehouses and offices, and the second is related to the infrastructure sector.

Although the commercial sector maintained a high level of activity for several years, it has now slowed down mainly due to a less dynamic real estate market, which has resulted in many units available, ultimately leading to depreciation.

Additionally, during 2019 and 2020 there was a contraction in the placement of credit by local financial institutions, which prevented existing units from being acquired due to financing restrictions. This resulted in a significant increase in available units, in addition to those vacated during the pandemic. As a result, the level of new construction stagnated, affecting the commercial sector.

As for the infrastructure sector, it has been affected since 2017 due to the cutback of public resources for the financing and execution of public projects. This situation remains

9 *Organic Code of the Judiciary*, Article 170 *et seq.*
10 *Constitution of Ecuador*, Article 94.
11 *Ibid.*, Article 88.
12 *Ibid.*, Article 190.
13 *General Organic Code of Procedures*, Article 363, (2) and (3).
14 *Arbitration and Mediation Act*, Article 31.

as there is a considerable deficit in public resources. However, there is a high need to carry out new projects, as well as to provide maintenance to the existing ones.

Currently, new alternatives are being explored for the design, operation and financing of infrastructure projects, such as concessions and public–private partnerships, which will allow projects to be executed with private resources in exchange for a concession or delegation for a specific period.

8.2.2 Structure

It is necessary to differentiate the regulatory framework that applies to the private sector from that applying to the public sector. Many of the provisions of the regulatory framework apply to both sectors; however, specific provisions must also be considered.

Among the existing law statutes and regulations, the following are relevant to construction:

- The *Law of the National Registry of Machinery and Equipment* (*Ley del Registro Nacional de Maquinaria y Equipo*), published in the Official Gazette 93 of 3 July 1972. Its purpose is to create the registry of equipment and machinery used in the construction of civil engineering works, which the Ministry of Public Works is in charge of
- The *Law on the Professional Practice of Architecture* (*Ley del Ejercicio Profesional de la Arquitectura*), published in the Official Gazette 708 of 24 December 1974. Its purpose is to create exclusive competencies for architecture professionals, establishing specific conditions for the exercise of the profession of architecture
- The *Law of the Professional Practice of Civil Engineering* (*Ley del Ejercicio Profesional de la Ingeniería Civil*), published in the Official Gazette 590 of 30 September 1983. It establishes exclusive competencies for civil engineers, such as the performance of preliminary studies, projects, designs, appraisals, construction, planning, supervision, oversight, supervision and consulting
- The *Law of the Professional Practice of Engineering* (*Ley del Ejercicio Profesional de la Ingeniería*), published in the Official Gazette 709 of 26 December 1974. It provides that only professionals with engineering degrees in any of its branches may sign technical documents (which have been prepared by them or by personnel under their technical direction) such as plans, calculations, technical specifications, drawings, reports, memoranda, expert reports, appraisals and appraisals. They also require that national or foreign companies, to carry out engineering work in Ecuador, must have the services of an Ecuadorian engineer in the legal exercise of his profession, as a technical representative related to the nature of the work being performed
- The *Ecuadorian Construction Standard* (*Norma Ecuatoriana de la Construcción*), published in the Official Gazette Supplement 413 of 10 January 2015, contains the technical standards that construction projects must comply with to be approved by the various public entities, according to the scope of their competencies

8.2.3 Licensing/registration

There are certain limitations to the number of foreign professionals that can be hired for the execution of projects, which are summarised below:

(a) The *Law on the Professional Practice of Architecture* provides that for the execution of architectural works, it is mandatory to have, for the execution of such works, a staff of national architects not less than 96% of the total number of architects employed on the project. If there are no national architects in the country specialised in the required work, the companies are obliged to employ national architects for their training in that field of speciality.

It also establishes that foreign professionals, to practice their profession in Ecuador, must comply with the following requirements: (i) revalidate their degree in any of the Faculties or Schools of Architecture of the Institutes of Higher Education of Ecuador, recognised by the applicable Law; and (ii) obtain the corresponding visa (temporary or permanent) in accordance with the applicable law.

(b) The *Law of the Professional Practice of Civil Engineering* establishes a minimum percentage of Ecuadorian civil engineers, which may not be less than 90% of the total number of civil engineers employed on the project. If there are no civil engineers in the country specialised in the work performed by such companies, they may hire foreigners, but they are obliged to employ and carry out technical training programmes for nationals in that field of speciality.

(c) The *Law of the Professional Practice of Engineering* establishes a minimum percentage of Ecuadorian engineers, which cannot be less than 90% of the total number of engineers employed in the project. If there are no national professionals in the country specialised in the work performed by the companies or consortiums, they are obliged to employ them for their training in that field of expertise.

It also establishes that foreign professionals, to practice their profession in Ecuador, must meet the following requirements: (i) revalidate their degree at any of the country's Institutes of Higher Education, recognised by the applicable law; and (ii) obtain the corresponding visa (temporary or permanent) in accordance with the applicable law.

It is important to mention that for projects under the public procurement regime, the contractors and subcontractors must be registered with the National Public Procurement Service. For further details please refer to section 8.2.9.

8.2.4 Labour relations

Ecuadorian labour legislation recognises the existence and validity of labour unions. Their use has not been widespread and there are currently few unions in the construction sector.

Unlike other countries, in Ecuador, one of the conditions for joining a union is that the person must be a current worker. As the types of employment contracts used in the construction sector are temporary (usually tied to the duration of the project), this makes it difficult for people to join unions or for unions to have a large number of members.

8.2.5 Employment

In Ecuador, two legal frameworks apply depending on the sector in which the professional works. For the private sector, the *Labour Code* applies, while for the public sector, the *Organic Law of Public Service* applies.

It should be mentioned that there are provisions that are common to both sectors, such as the labour benefits to which employees are entitled, among which the following stand out.

8.2.5.1 Salary

An employee is entitled to receive the 13th and the 14th salary. The 13th salary is equivalent to the 12 portions of all remunerations that the employee had received in the period December–November of each year. The payment must be made by 24 December.

The 14th salary is equivalent to the Minimum Legal Wage applicable for the last year (for the year 2021, US$ 400.00). This applies for the period March–February of each year. The payment must be made by 15 March for the Coast and Galapagos Regions, and by 15 August for the Highlands and Amazon Regions.

The Reserve Fund payment is equivalent to a monthly gross salary for each year of work and is mandatory from the first year of the employment contract. The employee is entitled to request to receive directly or to be deposited at the Social Security Institute. In addition, he/she could decide if the payment was to be paid monthly or in a single payment.

8.2.5.2 Work shifts

The ordinary daily work hours are eight and the weekly work hours are 40. Overtime cannot exceed the limit of four hours in a day or 12 hours in a week. Two types of overtime are paid. Overtime pay is calculated for the salary received by the employee and depending on the time. If overtime work is performed before 24h00 (midnight), payment will be equal to time and a half; if overtime work is performed between 24h00 and 06h00, payment will equal double time.

Regarding special rosters, if special shifts are required for a longer or shorter duration for the specific needs of the business, the Ministry of Labour must approve those shifts. The law also considers shorter shifts for specific cases, such as minors, working mothers and underground work. Any work shift that is different from the ordinary regime must obtain the express authorisation of the Ministry of Labour. This applies to the following special work shifts:

- More than five consecutive days, or those that have more than two consecutive rest days
- Less than five consecutive days, or those that have less than two consecutive rest days
- Shifts that have rotational shifts between day and night time

It is possible to have more than one special work shift depending on the needs of the company.

The special work shifts can be also considered in the company's Internal Regulations that must be approved by the Ministry of Labour. Overtime and surcharge are also applicable to these special work shifts, depending on each specific case. In the case of work shifts, overtime pay will apply to night shifts even if the limit of 40 hours per week is not reached, so people working the night shift always earn an overtime rate. Overtime is calculated over the regular working hour during the day.

8.2.5.3 Vacations and holidays

All workers are entitled to a vacation each year for an uninterrupted period of 15 days, including non-working days. This right cannot be replaced with payment for vacation days.

Extra vacation days because of seniority cannot exceed an additional 15 days including non-working days (for a total of 30 days), unless more vacation days are granted pursuant to an individual or collective contract.

8.2.5.4 Disabled persons

If a company reaches the threshold of 25 employees or more, it is obliged to hire at least one disabled person. However, the company must hire at least 4% of disabled persons, based on the total payroll of permanent employees. The disabled worker is protected by law and cannot be dismissed. If he or she is dismissed, an additional compensation equivalent to 18 times the best-earned salary must be paid, plus the pro-rata legal benefits.[15]

8.2.5.5 Termination of labour contracts

An employee can terminate a labour contract by: (i) eviction or (ii) '*Visto bueno*' or unilateral termination if one of the following causes is fulfilled by the employer: (a) insults or injuries against the employee and his/her direct family; (b) reduced or lack of payment or delay in the payment of the salary; (c) request of the employer to perform other types of activities from those established and agreed in the labour contract; or (d) if the employee is a victim of employment and sexual harassment by the employer.

The employer can terminate a labour contract by (i) dismissal or (ii) '*Visto bueno*' or unilateral termination if one of the following causes is fulfilled by the employee: (a) repetitive and unjustified unpunctuality for more than three consecutive days in the same month; (b) indiscipline or disobeying the company's internal regulations; (c) lack of probity or immoral conduct; (d) insults or injuries against the employer and its direct family; (e) manifest negligence; (f) an unjustified claim before the Social Security Institute against the employer, regarding its labour obligations; (g) lack of compliance with the safety measures, health and safety regulations, contained in the law or promulgated by a competent authority, or for non-compliance of the recommendations issued by a physician; and (h) committing employment and sexual harassment.

8.2.5.6 Compensation for termination

In evictions, the employer must generally either pay a bonus or compensate the worker when the worker's services are terminated. The decision to terminate an employment contract is called '*Desahucio*' and the employer must pay the worker a bonus equal to 25% of the worker's last monthly salary times the number of years of service. Only very few employment contracts may be terminated without having to pay any compensation.

15 *Disabilities Organic Act* (*Ley Orgánica de Discapacidades*) published in Official Gazette Supplement 796 of 25 September 2012

Dismissal without a fair cause exists when the employer terminates an employment contract and fires a worker without a cause, or if there is a fair cause, fails to follow the procedure established by the law. Compensation for dismissal without cause is:

(a) Compensation concerning the employee's time of service:
- Up to three years of service: three times the monthly salary
- Over three years of service: one month's salary for each year of service, without exceeding in any case 25 times the monthly salary

(b) Eviction bonus, equal to 25% of the last monthly salary for each year of service. Any fraction of a year will be regarded as a complete year and the salary to be considered is that which the worker was earning when dismissed

In the case of piecework employees, salary is calculated based on the average salary earned by the worker during the year preceding the dismissal.

8.2.5.7 Social Security

Every employee must be affiliated with the Social Security Institute (IESS). The monthly contributions are: 9.45% of the base salary must be contributed by the employee and 11.15% of the base salary must be contributed by the company.

It should also be noted that it is possible to hire a professional (e.g. architect, civil engineer, etc.) under the civil and not the labour regime. That is to say, they are not workers under a dependency relationship, but only contractors.

8.2.6 Safety culture

Pursuant to Article 434 of the *Labour Code*, every company that has more than ten employees or workers must have a Health and Security Regulation. In this instrument are established all the specific procedures that the employees and workers must consider, concerning the activities that must be performed. This Regulation must be renewed every two years.

However, specific requirements in the Health and Security Regulation are mandated depending on the number of employees hired by the company.

From one to nine employees:

- Risk analysis
- Health and safety policy
- Minimum Prevention Plan
- First aid kit
- Health and safety delegate
- Responsibilities for risk prevention

From ten to 49 employees:

- The same requirements as for up to nine employees
- Internal Health and Safety Regulation
- Prevention program

- Training program
- Emergency plan
- Parity Health and Safety Committee (15 employees or more)
- A permanent nurse or medical service (25 employees or more)

For 100 or more employees:

- The same requirements as for up to 49 employees
- Health and Safety Unit
- Health and Safety Manager

In respect of medical examinations, every person who will perform any labour activity must obtain a medical certificate granted by a physician of the Social Security Institute, which must certify the person's health condition. This medical examination must be performed at least once a year.

8.2.7 Modular construction using factory-fabricated components

Current legislation does not regulate any aspect regarding the use of prefabricated components for modular construction. However, this may be regulated at the sectional level by municipal ordinances and be applicable only at this level of jurisdiction.

To the best of our knowledge, there are currently no projects that have been constructed using factory-fabricated modules.

8.2.8 Innovation

The Government has presented a bill that seeks to reactivate the construction sector by simplifying procedures, as well as allowing private and public banking institutions to carry out mortgage portfolio securitisation processes, in order to develop financial products such as residential mortgage-backed securities (**RMBS**) in local and international markets.

The bill must be analysed and debated by the National Assembly and could be subject to modifications.

8.2.9 Government/private sector procurement

Freedom of contracting is recognised and guaranteed for the private sector, as long as it is aligned with the legal framework in force and complies with the minimum percentages of local contracting. In the case of the public sector, the contracting of works is regulated by the *Public Procurement Law* (*Ley Orgánica del Sistema Nacional de Contratación Pública*), published in the Official Gazette Supplement 395 of 4 August 2008. This law requires the Contractor to be registered in the Single Registry of Suppliers (RUP), administered by the National Public Procurement Service, the competent entity in matters of public procurement.

In addition, it is important to mention that according to Article 6 of the *Company Law* in force, any company that (i) executes public works (ii) provides public services, or (iii) exploits natural resources, must establish itself in the country.

It should be added that in the case of the private sector, there is no legal limitation on the percentage of subcontracting that may be contracted in a specific project, while in the case of public sector projects under the public procurement regime, no more than 30% of the contract amount may be subcontracted.

Likewise, if it is necessary to expand, modify or complement a work under the public contracting regime, due to unforeseen or technical causes that are duly justified, the State or the contracting entity may enter into complementary contracts with the same Contractor, without bidding or competition, to cover the aforementioned modifications. The proviso is that the prices of the items of the original contract are maintained and adjusted to the date of execution of the respective complementary contract. These complementary contracts may not exceed 15% of the value of the main contract.

8.2.10 Insurance requirements

Article 1937, paragraph 2 of the *Civil Code* establishes a ten-year warranty period from the delivery of the property, concerning possible construction defects or soil defects that the builder should have known about and foreseen because of its trade.

In public procurement scope, the law requires the issuance of the following guarantees:

- Proper use of advance payment: the policy must cover 100% of the amount paid by the contracting entity as advance payment
- Performance guarantee: guarantees the execution of the contract in the terms foreseen. The bond is equivalent to 5% of the amount of the contract granted by means of a refundable bank guarantee
- Technical guarantee: the term is usually established between one and three years from the delivery of the work. This is the guarantee that the constructor grants in favour of the contracting entity. This guarantee must be granted without prejudice to the provisions contained in Article 1937 of the *Civil Code* (ten-year warranty period from the delivery of the property)

In addition, in private projects, it is also possible to take out several additional insurance policies, such as:

- Good quality of materials: guarantees the proper execution of the work and the good quality of the materials that have been used in the execution of the contract
- Personal accidents: covers bodily injury caused by any type of accident. This is in addition to the workers' compensation to be paid by the Social Security Institute
- Contractual liability: this covers the repair of damage due to a breach of an obligation arising from a contract
- Non-contractual civil liability: this covers repairing damage due to negligence or fault to a third party with whom there is no prior contractual relationship

8.2.11 Common forms of contract

There is a diversity of contracts that can be used depending on the type of project, as well as the regime to which it is subject. Although there is no express legal recognition of the FIDIC contract forms, it is possible to condition their use in public projects that are financed with resources from financial or multilateral entities. For example, the *Public Procurement Law* refers to the conditions provided for in such financing and may even establish procedures and conditions additional to those provided for in local legislation, as well as the obligation to use certain standardised contract models or forms, such as FIDIC.

For projects related to concessions or delegations under public–private partnerships, there is freedom to establish between the delegating entity and the concessionaire or private operator, the standards and forms that best suit the needs of the project.

As for private projects, there is freedom to establish the standards and formats that the parties voluntarily agree upon, the most common formats being BOT, EPC and DBOT contracts.

8.2.12 Dispute resolution

Article 190 of the *Constitution of Ecuador* recognises arbitration, mediation and other alternative dispute resolution procedures. It also provides that these procedures shall be applied subject to the law, in matters which by their nature can be compromised. It also establishes that in matters of public contracting, arbitration in law shall be applicable. As a consequence of the enactment of the *General Regulation to the Arbitration and Mediation Act*, the State Attorney General's Office (*Procurador General del Estado*) has the authority to review, prima facie, the legality of an arbitration agreement and the law applicable at the seat of the arbitration.[16]

The *Arbitration and Mediation Law* provides that in the case of public sector entities that may submit to arbitration, they must meet the following additional requirements:

(a) To enter into an arbitration agreement before the controversy arises; if the agreement is to be signed after the controversy has arisen, the State Attorney General must be consulted
(b) The legal relationship to which the agreement refers must be contractual
(c) The arbitration agreement shall include the manner of selection of the arbitrators
(d) The arbitration agreement in which the public sector institution waives the ordinary jurisdiction, must be signed by the person authorised to contract on behalf of said institution

It is further stipulated that failure to comply with the aforementioned requirements will result in the nullity of the arbitration agreement.

It is important to mention that in matters of public procurement related to large infrastructure projects, international arbitration has been foreseen, mainly based in Santiago de Chile. Therefore, it is common to find arbitration clauses in construction contracts with public entities that refer to such a seat of arbitration. However, other seats may be provided such as in New York, Paris or London.

Concerning PPP projects, the *Organic Law on Incentives for Public–Private Partnerships* (*Ley Orgánica de Incentivos para Asociaciones Público Privadas*) published in the Official Gazette Supplement 652, 18 December 2015, provides that if contractual disputes are submitted to international arbitration, such arbitration shall be carried

16 *Presidential Decree No. 165* published in the Official Gazette 254 of 26 August 2021.

out before a Latin American regional arbitration body. Additionally, the following rules must be followed:

(i) When the party that considers itself affected informs the other party of the subject matter of the dispute, the parties may settle the dispute through direct dialogue or mediation
(ii) If the parties do not reach an agreement to settle the dispute through direct dialogue or mediation and after exhausting administrative channels, the dispute may be settled by national or international regional arbitration, as a last resort, following the provisions of the PPP contract

A limitation is also established since tax matters will not be submitted to arbitration, as well as any other act derived directly from the legislative and regulatory power of the Ecuadorian State.

Dispute Boards have recently been used in some public works projects, although their use is still marginal. However, the experience so far has been favourable, since it has avoided in most cases the activation of the arbitration clause, in technical aspects that could have been resolved promptly by this mechanism.

Finally, if arbitration, whether national or international, has not been provided as a dispute resolution mechanism, in the case of public contracts, the administrative courts have jurisdiction, while in the case of private projects, civil courts have jurisdiction.

8.2.13 Current challenges

Among the challenges faced by the construction sector is the lack of access to credit for both construction companies and individuals who wish to acquire units. As for public projects, the lack of public resources makes it necessary to consider contracting alternatives that ensure financing by the Contractor. In addition, the use of PPP mechanisms to carry out infrastructure projects with private resources is currently being explored.

8.2.14 Unique features of the construction industry in Ecuador

In greenfield projects, there is currently a significant infrastructure gap that needs to be closed through projects that improve people's quality of life. Likewise, with respect to brownfield projects, there is a lot of infrastructure that needs to be rebuilt and maintained, so asset recycling could be an important business opportunity.

It should be noted that Ecuadorian construction companies have become regional references due to the type of projects they have developed. This has allowed them to expand into other jurisdictions such as Colombia, Peru and Panama.

8.3 The impact of COVID-19 in Ecuador

8.3.1 The impact of COVID-19 on the execution of construction projects in Ecuador

In March 2020 the Government ordered the first national lockdown that was extended up to June 2020. Then it allowed some essential activities to be carried out. However, the construction sector was not included in such 'essential activities'.

Only in August 2020 did the first pilot projects begin, which allowed the sector to be gradually reactivated. At that time, it was ordered that field workers could not leave the construction site, forcing the companies to maintain a permanent camp.

As in other sectors, the main challenge was generated by problems in the supply chain, as many ports and logistic companies were still closed. This situation caused many projects to be suspended due to the lack of materials and raw materials for their execution.

The biosafety measures that were still in force as of September 2021 were the compulsory use of face masks, social distancing and prohibition of public events, and private events with limited seating. For people that travel from abroad to Ecuador, it was mandatory to submit at least one of the following requirements: (i) vaccination passport/certificate or (ii) a negative PCR test performed at least 48 hours before the flight.

Compulsory quarantine on arrival varied from time to time and depended on the situation in other countries, such as India and Brazil. All the land borders were still closed in September 2021; only ports and airports were open.

8.3.2 The impact of COVID-19 on the operation of construction contracts in Ecuador

As a measure to mitigate the effects of the pandemic, the government enacted the *Humanitarian Support Act* (*Ley Orgánica de Apoyo Humanitario*), published in Official Gazette Supplement No. 229, 22 June 2020. This law established some limitations such as the following.

8.3.2.1 Labour matters

- Agreements for the preservation of sources of employment by which workers and employers could, by mutual agreement, modify the economic conditions of the labour relationship to preserve the sources of employment and guarantee stability to the workers. The agreements could not affect the basic salary or sectorial salaries
- Special emerging contract, by which the employer was able to hire for a fixed term (up to one year, renewable for a single occasion), for the sustainability of production and sources of income in emerging situations or new investments or lines of business, products or services, expansions or extensions of the business, modification of the line of business or increase in the supply of goods and services
- Emergency reduction of working hours, for duly justified events of *force majeure* or fortuitous cause, the employer may reduce the working day, up to a maximum of 50%. The employee's salary or wage will correspond, in proportion, to the hours worked, and will not be less than 55% of that fixed before the reduction; the social security contribution will be paid based on the reduced working day. This reduction may be applied for up to one year, renewable for the same period, only once
- From the implementation of the reduced working day and during the time it lasts, the companies that have implemented the reduction of the working day may not reduce the capital stock of the company nor distribute dividends obtained in the fiscal years in which this working day is in force
- Vacations/holidays: until the year 2022, employers may unilaterally notify the employee of the vacation schedule or, in turn, establish the compensation of those days of absence from work as vacation days already accrued

8.3.2.2 Bankruptcy special rules

- The legislation established an exceptional bankruptcy regime from 2020 and up to 2023 by which the debtor and its creditors can sign pre-bankruptcy agreements. If it is not possible to reach such agreements, the debtor is entitled to request a judge for a bankruptcy proceeding. In normal situations, there is a Reorganisation Proceeding (*Concurso Preventivo de Acreedores*), by which a company that is under financial stress can request the Corporate Superintendence to initiate a Reorganisation Proceeding to avoid the company's bankruptcy. There are no bankruptcy courts for companies, only for individuals. The reorganisation proceeding is administrative, not judicial
- Eviction moratorium, during the lockdown and for 60 days after, landlords will not be able to evict tenants; except in cases of danger of destruction or ruin of the building in the part comprising the leased premises and making repairs necessary, as well as the use of the property for illegal activities

The *Humanitarian Support Act* contains an interpretation of Article 169, paragraph 6 of the *Labour Code*, which limits the termination of employment contracts for *force majeure* only when there is:

> the impossibility of performing the work due to an act of God or force majeure will be linked to the total and definitive cessation of the economic activity of the employer, whether a natural or legal person. This means that there will be an impossibility when the work cannot be carried out by the usual physical means or by alternative means that allow its execution, not even by telematic means.

8.4 Ecuadorian governing law of the contract

8.4.1 Constraints on the governing law of a construction contract

Under the principle of freedom of contract (see section 8.7.1) the parties to a private construction project in Ecuador are entitled to choose the governing law of the contract, as long as it is not contrary to Article 1477 of the *Ecuadorian Civil Code* nor contravenes Ecuadorian public policy.

The governing law for any public procurement is Ecuadorian law, pursuant to the provisions of the *Public Procurement Act*.

8.4.2 Formal requirements for a construction contract

As per the *Ecuadorian Civil Code*,[17] generally, a contract shall have the following elements for its validity: (i) legal capacity of the parties, (ii) consent, (iii) a lawful purpose and (iv) a lawful cause.[18]

There are no other specific requirements for a construction contract, which does not have to be in writing (although they usually are). Many construction projects do not

17 Articles 1453 *et seq.*
18 *Ibid.*, Article 1461.

have written contracts governing the project. This mainly occurs in small-scale projects. Although verbal contracts are valid, they are difficult to enforce or adjudicate.

8.5 What Special Provisions in the Particular Conditions are necessary for consistency with applicable laws in Ecuador?

8.5.1 FIDIC General Conditions are incompatible or inconsistent with Ecuadorian governing law of the contract

FIDIC General Conditions are not incompatible nor inconsistent with the Ecuadorian governing law of the contract. In case of conflict, Ecuadorian legislation would prevail to the extent that contractual obligations are against public order (see section 8.7).

8.5.2 FIDIC General Conditions are incompatible or inconsistent with the law of the Site/Country

FIDIC General Conditions are not incompatible nor inconsistent with applicable laws in Ecuador. In case of conflict, Ecuadorian legislation would prevail to the extent that contractual obligations are against public order (see section 8.7).

8.5.3 FIDIC General Conditions are incompatible or inconsistent with the relevant laws on dispute determination in Ecuador

FIDIC General Conditions are not incompatible nor inconsistent with Ecuadorian laws on dispute determination (resolution).

Similar to section 8.5.1 and section 8.5.2, the limits to any adjudicating exercise are in the law, namely, the authority (by law or agreement) to administer the dispute (e.g. judges, arbitrators, mediators) and the due process in the adjudication/determination process. In cases of arbitration, if that is the dispute resolution method chosen by the parties, it will also depend on whether it is international or domestic, where, in the former, there is an interplay of different applicable laws: substantive law, *lex arbitri*, arbitration rules, etc.

8.6 What Special Provisions in the Particular Conditions are desirable for consistency with applicable laws in Ecuador?

No Special Provisions in the Particular Conditions are desirable for consistency with applicable laws in Ecuador.

8.7 Applicable legislation for Ecuadorian governing law of the contract

8.7.1 Freedom of contract

In accordance with Ecuadorian law and the principle of party autonomy, the parties to a contract can freely agree on the terms and conditions to be performed according to the contract. However, this freedom (party autonomy) is not absolute but limited. Article 1477 of the *Ecuadorian Civil Code* provides that:

> If the object [contract's purpose] is a fact, it must be physically and morally possible. It is physically impossible if it is contrary to nature, and morally impossible if it is forbidden by law, or contrary to morality or public order.[19]

Consequently, the parties' contracting freedom is limited by the law and public order. As aforementioned, public order considerations will entail, for instance, a contractual provision changing the Ecuadorian labour regime, e.g. minimum wage of the workers involved in the project.[20] Any contractual provision that alters, modifies or changes rights and obligations that are not at the disposition of the parties will be deemed null and void.

8.7.2 Applicable laws

Depending on the nature of the project, different types of laws may be involved in a project. For instance, in public procurement infrastructure projects, administrative laws such as the *Organic Law on Incentives for Public–Private Partnerships* and the *Public Procurement Law* will be the governing law on the project, while on private real estate projects, the *Ecuadorian Civil Code* will be the governing law.

Considering the aforementioned categories, it is also important to bear in mind that irrespective of the public or private nature of the project, there are secondary legal rules that will still be applicable – for instance, the specific regulations issued by local Governments (Municipalities, Prefects, Parishes, etc.) for the use of land, the payment of taxes, etc. These legal rules will establish the limitations and regulations for urban planning, the conditions for urbanisation, the division and subdivision of land and the required green zones and communal areas.[21]

The concurrence of all these applicable rules makes it a complex task for developers to establish with certainty all the regulatory regimes that will govern the project.

8.7.3 The plurality of regulation sources

As aforementioned, Ecuador is a republic that is organised in a decentralised fashion which to some extent gives independence and autonomy to local governments to adopt their own rules and regulations within their legal prerogatives.[22] In projects that take place in more than one jurisdiction, a conflict of regulations may arise.

19 *Ecuadorian Civil Code*, Article 1477, translated from Spanish: 'Art. 1477 – No sólo las cosas que existen pueden ser objeto de una declaración de voluntad, sino las que se espera que existan; pero es menester que las unas y las otras sean comerciables, y que estén determinadas, a lo menos en cuanto a su género. La cantidad puede ser incierta con tal que el acto o contrato fije reglas o contenga datos que sirvan para determinarla. Si el objeto es un hecho, es necesario que sea física y moralmente posible. Es físicamente imposible el contrario a la naturaleza, y moralmente imposible el prohibido por las leyes, o contrario a las buenas costumbres o al orden público'.

20 Pursuant to Article 336 of the *Constitution*, '[l]abour rights are inalienable and intangible'.

21 *Organic Code of Territorial Organisation*, Article 54.

22 *Ibid.*, Article 32.

8.7.4 Outdated rules

One of the main problems with Ecuadorian law is its lack of modernity. The *Ecuadorian Civil Code* has not been comprehensively amended since 2005 and has only had minor revisions normally related to the amendment of other law statutes.[23]

8.7.5 Mandatory rules – public policy

Irrespective of the terms and conditions agreed by the parties of a contract, there are legal limits that cannot be disposed of by the parties. For instance, those related to labour, taxes and health cannot be subject to self-regulation. Any contractual provision contrary to these mandatory rules may be deemed null and void.

8.8 Summary of applicable legislation for Ecuador governing law of the contract

8.8.1 Entry into a construction contract

Contracts generally	*Civil Code*
Construction contracts	*Civil Code* *Public Procurement Act* (*Ley Orgánica del Sistema Nacional de Contratación Pública*), for public (government) projects

8.8.2 Operation of a construction contract

Force majeure	*Civil Code*
Hardship	*Civil Code*
Guarantees under forms of Security (Tender Security, Demand Guarantee, Surety Bond, Advance Payment Guarantee, Retention Money Guarantee, Payment Guarantee by Employer)	*Insurance Act* *Civil Code* *Public Procurement Act* (*Ley Orgánica del Sistema Nacional de Contratación Pública*), for public (governmental) projects

8.8.3 Termination of a construction contract

Frustration	*Civil Code*
Bankruptcy, insolvency, liquidation	*General Procedures Code*, for individuals *Reorganisation Proceeding Law*, for companies

23 The last revision of certain provisions of the *Civil Code* took place on 14 May 2021 in the Official Gazette Supplement 452 and was related to the public servant in the electric public service.

8.8.4 Dispute resolution

Limitation periods	*Civil Code*
Liability	*Civil Code*
Adjudication	*Civil Code* *Public Procurement Act* (*Ley Orgánica del Sistema Nacional de Contratación Pública*), for public (governmental) projects
Arbitration	*Arbitration and Mediation Act*

8.9 Summary of applicable legislation if the Site/Country is in Ecuador

8.9.1 Operation of a construction contract

Registration and administration of professionals – Engineers, Architects	*Law on the Professional Practice of Architecture* (*Ley del Ejercicio Profesional de la Arquitectura*) *Law of the Professional Practice of Civil Engineering* (*Ley del Ejercicio Profesional de la Ingeniería Civil*) *Law of the Professional Practice of Engineering* (*Ley del Ejercicio Profesional de la Ingeniería*)
Registration/licencing of Contractors and subcontractors	*Public Procurement Act* (*Ley Orgánica del Sistema Nacional de Contratación Pública*) (A contractor is required to be registered in the Single Registry of Suppliers (RUP) for public sector work) *Company Law* (Any company that [i] executes public works, [ii] provides public services or [iii] exploits natural resources must establish itself in the country)
Subcontractors	Same requirements as for the Contractor
Use of liens/assignment of debts	*Civil Code*
Labour	*Labour Code* (private sector) *Organic Law of Public Service* (public sector)
Design/moral rights	*Civil Code*
Copyright	*IP Law* (*Código Orgánico de la Economía Social de los Conocimientos, Creatividad e Innovación*)
The product being produced from the Works	*Labor Code* *IP Law* (*Código Orgánico de la Economía Social de los Conocimientos, Creatividad e Innovación*)
First Nation people's land rights	*Organic Code of Territorial Organisation, Autonomy and Decentralisation* (*Código Orgánico de Organización Territorial, Autonomía y Descentralización*)
Planning	*Organic Code of Territorial Organisation, Autonomy and Decentralisation* (*Código Orgánico de Organización Territorial, Autonomía y Descentralización*)

Work affecting adjacent property to the Site	*Civil Code*
Heritage	*Civil Code*
Environment	*Environmental Code*
Local procurement	*Law on the Professional Practice of Architecture* (*Ley del Ejercicio Profesional de la Arquitectura*) *Law of the Professional Practice of Civil Engineering* (*Ley del Ejercicio Profesional de la Ingeniería Civil*) *Law of the Professional Practice of Engineering* (*Ley del Ejercicio Profesional de la Ingeniería*)
Public procurement	*Public Procurement Law* (*Ley Orgánica del Sistema Nacional de Contratación Pública*) *Organic Law on Incentives for Public–Private Partnerships* (*Ley Orgánica de Incentivos para Asociaciones Público Privadas*)
Building and construction permits, execution of construction work, standard of construction work	*Ecuadorian Construction Standard* (*Norma Ecuatoriana de la Construcción*)
Health and safety	*Labour Code* *Safety Regulations for Construction and Public Works* (*Reglamento de Seguridad para la Construcción y Obras Públicas*)
Ownership of Plant and Materials	*Law of the National Registry of Machinery and Equipment* (*Ley del Registro Nacional de Maquinaria y Equipo*)
Employer's sale of Contractor's Equipment, surplus material, wreckage and Temporary Works	*Law of the National Registry of Machinery and Equipment* (*Ley del Registro Nacional de Maquinaria y Equipo*)
Insurance	*Insurance Act*
Liability for defective work	*Civil Code*
Liability for nuisance	*Civil Code*
Registry of equipment and machinery used in the construction of civil engineering works	*Law of the National Registry of Machinery and Equipment* (*Ley del Registro Nacional de Maquinaria y Equipo*)

8.9.2 Termination of a construction contract

Bankruptcy, insolvency, liquidation	*General Procedures Code*, for individuals *Reorganisation Proceeding Law*, for companies
Decennial liability and liability generally for the total or partial collapse of structures	*Civil Code* Article 1937, paragraph 2

8.10 Summary of applicable legislation if the 'seat' of the dispute determination is Ecuador

Dispute resolution	*Arbitration and Mediation Act* *Organic General Code of Procedures*
Limitation periods	*Arbitration and Mediation Act* *Organic General Code of procedures*
Mediation	*Arbitration and Mediation Act*
Arbitration	*Arbitration and Mediation Act*

8.11 Issues that a court or arbitrator may construe differently from that expected from the words of the Contract because of local law or custom

As aforementioned, issues that are related to constitutional rights that have been breached and issues that were regulated by the parties in a way that is in breach of the law or public order may be deemed null and void by the adjudicator.

8.12 Additional references for Ecuador

8.12.1 Books

J Reig Satorres & J Larrea Holguin, *Manual de Historia del Derecho en el Ecuador* (2nd edn, Corporación de Estudios y Publicaciones, 2000).

8.12.2 Journals

EB Abdrasulov, SR Shalabaev & AI Mugauova, 'The Concept of the Triad of Branches of State Power and Issues of its Modernisation' (2015) Vol. XVIII ERS 75.

8.12.3 Legislation

www.worldlii.org/catalog/50471.html

CHAPTER 9

Applying FIDIC Contracts in Mexico

Roberto Hernández García and Juan Pablo Sandoval García

CONTENTS

9.1	Outline of Mexico's legal environment	210
	9.1.1 The constitutional structure of Mexico	210
	9.1.2 The legal system in Mexico	210
	9.1.3 The court system in Mexico	210
9.2	The construction industry in Mexico	211
	9.2.1 Overview	211
	9.2.2 Structure	212
	9.2.3 Licencing/registration	212
	9.2.4 Labour relations	213
	9.2.5 Safety culture	213
	9.2.6 Modular construction using factory fabricated components	213
	9.2.7 Technology/innovation/BIM	214
	9.2.8 Government/private sector procurement	214
	9.2.9 Insurance requirements	215
	9.2.10 Common forms of contract	215
	9.2.11 Dispute resolution	216
	9.2.12 Current challenges	218
9.3	The impact of COVID-19 in Mexico	218
	9.3.1 The impact of COVID-19 on the execution of construction projects in Mexico	218
	9.3.2 The impact of COVID-19 on the operation of construction contracts in Mexico	219
9.4	Mexico governing law of the contract	220
	9.4.1 Constraints on the governing law of a construction contract	220
	9.4.2 Formal requirements for a construction contract	220
9.5	What Special Provisions in the Particular Conditions are necessary for consistency with applicable laws in Mexico?	221
	9.5.1 FIDIC General Conditions are incompatible or inconsistent with Mexican governing law of the contract	221
	9.5.2 FIDIC General Conditions are incompatible or inconsistent with the law of the Site/Country	221
	9.5.3 FIDIC General Conditions are incompatible or inconsistent with the relevant laws on dispute determination in Mexico	221

DOI: 10.4324/9781003201250-9

9.6 What Special Provisions in the Particular Conditions are desirable for consistency with applicable laws in Mexico? 222
9.7 Applicable law for Mexican governing law of the contract 222
9.7.1 Entry into a construction contract 222
9.7.2 Operation of a construction contract 223
9.7.2.1 Force majeure 223
9.7.2.2 Hardship 223
9.7.2.3 Guarantees under forms of Security 223
9.7.3 Termination of a construction contract 223
9.7.3.1 Frustration 223
9.7.3.2 Bankruptcy, insolvency, liquidation 224
9.7.3.3 Limitation periods 224
9.7.3.4 Liability 224
9.7.3.5 Arbitration 224
9.8 Summary of applicable legislation for Mexican governing law of the contract 225
9.8.1 Entry into a construction contract 225
9.8.2 Operation of a construction contract 225
9.8.3 Termination of a construction contract 225
9.8.4 Dispute resolution 225
9.9 Applicable law if the Site/Country is in Mexico 225
9.9.1 Operation of a construction contract 225
9.9.1.1 Registration of professionals 225
9.9.1.2 Registration/licencing of contractors and subcontractors 225
9.9.1.3 Use of liens/assignment of debts 226
9.9.1.4 Design/moral rights 226
9.9.1.5 First Nation people's land rights 226
9.9.1.6 Heritage 226
9.9.1.7 Environment 226
9.9.1.8 Health and safety 226
9.9.1.9 Employer's sale of Contractor's Equipment 226
9.9.1.10 Statutory rights that coexist with contractual rights 226
9.9.1.11 Liability for nuisance 227
9.9.1.12 Other issues 227
9.9.2 Termination of a construction contract 227
9.9.2.1 Bankruptcy, insolvency, liquidation 227
9.9.2.2 Decennial liability and liability generally for the total or partial collapse of structures 227
9.9.2.3 Dispute resolution 227
9.9.2.4 Limitation periods 227
9.10 Summary of applicable legislation if the Site/Country is in Mexico 228
9.10.1 Operation of a construction contract 228
9.10.2 Termination of a construction contract 228

9.11 Applicable law if the 'seat' of the dispute determination is Mexico 229
9.11.1 Dispute resolution 229
9.11.2 Limitation periods 229
9.11.3 Arbitration 229
9.12 Summary of applicable legislation if the 'seat' of the dispute determination is Mexico 229
9.13 Issues that a court or arbitrator may construe differently than expected from the words of the Contract because of local law or custom 229
9.14 Additional references for Mexico 230
9.14.1 Books 230

9.1 Outline of Mexico's legal environment

9.1.1 The constitutional structure of Mexico

Mexico is a Federation consisting of 32 Federal Entities (States) with autonomy and sovereignty. Thus, there are three levels of government: the Federal Government, the State Governments and local governments.

Both the Federal Government and the State Governments are divided into three powers: an executive power, a legislative power and a judicial power.

The federal executive power is held by a President who is elected for a six-year period and cannot be re-elected.

The federal legislative power is constituted by a Congress divided into (i) the Chamber of Representatives and (ii) the Chamber of Senators (comprising 500 federal representatives of the 32 States, and 128 senators, respectively).

The federal judicial power is presided over by the Supreme Court which is constituted of two Chambers: (i) the First Chamber is empowered to decide on civil and criminal matters; and (ii) the Second Chamber can resolve administrative and labour cases in relation to constitutional matters. Electoral matters are excluded since there is the Constitutional Tribunal for Electoral Matters. Below the Supreme Court, there are courts and tribunals with competence over federal matters.

Each State has an equivalent structure to the one described here.

9.1.2 The legal system in Mexico

Mexico belongs to the civil law system. The *Constitution* is the founding rule from which the rest of the legislation derives. It is worth mentioning that according to Article 133 of the *Constitution*, the international treaties related to human rights will be at the same level as the *Constitution*.

Pursuant to the foregoing, is important to mention that derived from the transcendent case *Rosendo Radilla Pacheco v Mexico*,[1] the Mexican legal system enacted a relevant amendment in connection with human rights and the obligation of the entire judicial authorities to act to protect human rights.

Below the *Federal Constitution* and the international treaties of human rights are the federal laws, and finally, the local laws.

9.1.3 The court system in Mexico

As mentioned earlier, the judicial system in Mexico is presided over by the Supreme Court, which is the head of the judicial system, managed by a Federal Judiciary Board and also presided over by the President of the Supreme Court. Below the Supreme Court are the Collegiate Tribunals which are formed by three Magistrates. The jurisdiction of both the Supreme Court and the Collegiate Tribunals is reserved for constitutional cases (judicial review).

After the Collegiate Tribunals are the Tribunals of Appeal which are also collegiate tribunals comprising three Magistrates, but their jurisdiction is not reserved for constitutional

1 Varios 912/2010.

matters. As their name establishes, they can also act as tribunals of appeal (or Tribunals of Second Instance). Before 2021, these tribunals were known as Unitary Tribunals which were formed by one Magistrate only, but they transformed from unitary to collegiate as a result of a judicial amendment enacted in March 2021.

Below the Collegiate Tribunals of Appeal, there are the District Judges; these are also Federal Courts, but their jurisdiction can be in *Amparo* (constitutional) and also in civil or commercial matters. The foregoing will depend on the distribution that each State gives to such Courts. It is also common to see different kinds of specialisation of the District Judges. For example, there are District Judges with specialised competence in bankruptcy or oral process, among others.

Additionally, there is the Federal Court in Administrative and Tax Matters which, as its name indicates, resolves administrative cases. The particularity is that its jurisdiction covers tax cases and intellectual property, among others. It is also important to emphasise the importance of this tribunal in the context of construction disputes since this tribunal is in charge of resolving any dispute derived from 'administrative relationships'. According to Mexican law, contractual relations with the Ministries and some public organisations are considered 'administrative', so the relationship between the contracting party (the State) and the Contractor is not understood as a traditional private (civil) relationship. On the contrary, the contracts to which the State is party are considered 'administrative contracts' and follow the 'exorbitant principle' of civil law, which means that the administrative contracts go further in the civil environment.

As administrative contracts cannot be treated as civil (private) contracts, any related dispute shall be resolved by the Federal Court in Administrative Matters, unless the parties agree on arbitration. It is also important to note that, even if the parties in an administrative contract agree on arbitration, if the contract is cancelled by the public entity, the nullity of the cancellation resolution is a subject matter strictly reserved for the jurisdiction of this tribunal. Additionally, there are some State-owned companies that have their own regulations, and in some cases, these establish that the contracts executed with them are civil (commercial) in nature (for example Pemex and CFE).

Finally, each State has their local courts, which are also divided by subject (commercial, civil, family, etc).

9.2 The construction industry in Mexico

9.2.1 Overview

According to public numbers, Mexico in 2021 had approximately 27,300 construction companies[2] and an approximate value of 281 billion Mexican pesos (US$ 14 billion).[3] Being the second largest economy in Latin America,[4] Mexico has an incredible construction market of public and private projects. However, the construction market tends to be like a heavy elephant that does require a lot of time to move and improve.

2 https://es.statista.com/estadisticas/596201/empresas-del-sector-de-la-construccion-por-entidad/ (accessed 19 October 2022).

3 https://es.statista.com/estadisticas/592624/produccion-valor-de-la-construccion-mexico/#:~:text=En%202021%2C%20el%20valor%20de,281.000%20millones%20de%20pesos%20mexicanos (accessed 19 October 2022).

4 www.bancomundial.org/es/country/mexico/overview#1 (accessed 19 October 2022).

Construction companies and chambers have had for many years a way of doing things that is 'conservative', not to say 'old' and 'flawed'.

In the book *Construction Law in Mexico: Perspectives and Challenges*[5] the first author of this chapter explained that the construction sector in Mexico still needs to develop areas such as:

A) Fight against corruption
B) Adequate use of technology
C) Effective prevention and resolution of disputes, and
D) Standard forms of contract

Of course, this chapter focuses on the latter, which we think is a very important area for the development of a well-balanced and developed construction market in the country, but will explain why the fight against corruption, the use of technology and effective dispute prevention and resolution are concepts and issues directly related to the use of FIDIC contracts.

9.2.2 Structure

The industry in Mexico is very diverse, and it is common to see many contractors of many sizes and many jurisdictions working on the same project. In fact, it is common to see big and global construction companies working along with small-sized local companies jointly (it is common to see joint ventures) in order to perform specific projects.

In general, in most public projects the bidding process is international, i.e., open to foreign companies to apply for the project, and, depending on the complexity of the project, can be reserved for companies from a country where Mexico has a bilateral or multilateral trade agreement or for any company notwithstanding its nationality. However, it is common that in public projects, the contracting entity requires a certain percentage of local manpower. Also, Mexico has signed several bilateral, trilateral or multilateral commercial treaties in order to regulate the national content of materials, component of materials and/or percentage of local manpower. A good example of this is the **USMCA**, the United States–Mexico–Canada Agreement that regulates trade in North America.[6]

9.2.3 Licencing/registration

First, in Mexico, obtaining membership of a bar or chamber is not mandatory in order to exercise a profession or an activity. Thus, construction companies do not have to register anywhere in order to work on a project.

In order to provide design and engineering services legally, the professionals need to have a professional licence that allows them to exercise such activities.

5 Roberto Hernandez Garcia, *Derecho de la Construcción en México: perspectivas y retos* [*Construction Law in Mexico: perspectives and challenges*] (Editorial Bosch, 2020).

6 https://usmca.com (accessed 19 October 2022).

9.2.4 Labour relations

The labour field is governed by the *Federal Labour Law* (*Ley Federal del Trabajo*) which regulates the relationship between the employer and the employee, both parties' rights and obligations and most of the procedures. One of the main characteristics of this law is that it protects the employee from the employer. Thus, in procedural matters, the employer has the burden of proof.

However, the *Federal Labour Law* is just one piece of the Mexican construction industry puzzle, which makes labour a complex topic in Mexico since it considers several obligations that need to be complied with.

Some of the most important issues are:

1. 'Individual Contract'. According to the *Federal Labour Law*, the employees have to have a contract with the minimum requirements including: (i) place of work; (ii) time; (iii) salary; (iv) work schedule; (v) resting days.
2. 'Collective Contract', this is, the contract executed with the union.
3. Registry of the project. Each company working on a project shall register its contract with the *Instituto Mexicano del Seguro Social* (**IMSS**) (Mexican Institute of Social Security).
4. Payment of the employer fees.
5. Obtaining the **REPSE** (*Registro de Prestadoras de Servicios Especializados y Obras Especializadas* [Special Services Provider or Specialised Works Registry]) depending on the type of works to be contracted. It is worth mentioning that this requirement came with a recent amendment regarding outsourcing.

9.2.5 Safety culture

Construction companies shall comply with the *Obligatory Rules of Social Security for the Construction Workers by Work or Time* (*Reglamento del Seguro Social Obligatorio para los Trabajadores de la Construcción por Obra o Tiempo Determinado*) as well as the Mexican Official Regulation called *NOM-031-STPS-2011, Construcción – Condiciones de seguridad y salud en el trabajo.*

Regarding safety as a 'culture', it can be mentioned that indeed, in general terms, the construction sector in Mexico normally complies with the safety requirements; however, it is a reality that on small projects, it is common to see contractors and workers not complying with such requirements.

It is also important to mention that there are authorities empowered to perform random visits and/or due diligence in order to review if the construction companies on the projects comply with such rules. Such authorities will perform specific reviews depending on each one's scope. Reviews can be related to tax, compliance with social security obligations and security compliance on site, among other issues.

9.2.6 Modular construction using factory fabricated components

Modular construction in Mexico is still a work in progress. There are some efforts in the country to develop this means of construction.

9.2.7 Technology/innovation/BIM

Construction is one of the sectors that worldwide is using more technology: robotics, IA, cloud tools, digital twins and BIM represent only some of the major advances in the sector.

The 2019 editions of the FIDIC model contracts include Advisory Notes to Users of FIDIC Contracts Where the Project is to Include Building Information Modelling Systems.

These Advisory Notes clearly establish that

> BIM is one of the digital data technologies used in all aspects of project planning, investigation, design, construction and operation. Digital data technologies include systems for: data acquisition; document management; design and process management; estimating, planning, and scheduling; contract management; performance management; and building information modelling.
>
> BIM has varying degrees of complexity ranging from rather isolated use of computer aided design tools to full sharing of models and information by the entire project team. Currently, BIM is more often used and better understood in developed countries, many of which are encouraging or even mandating its use to improve quality, accuracy and delivery times for projects as well as to provide cost savings. BIM has the potential to dramatically improve productivity in the construction industry and reduce operational costs of facilities as well.
>
> BIM is not a set of contract conditions; it is a mechanism to provide an environment where all parties have access to information relevant to their role in the design and construction of a project. Wherever possible, a combined (sometimes called federated or collaborative) model is developed for all parties to share, even if, as is often the case, various designers have used different computer aided design programs to develop their respective designs. Drawings and specifications are held in a common database accessible to everyone. These can be used for clash detection, coordination of designs, communication of changes, and construction sequencing.

In Mexico's complex projects, it is relatively common to see 'BIM clauses'; however, on many occasions, parties do not really understand the essence and use of BIM. This represents a major burden and challenge since BIM may be considered a mere formality instead of a team approach.

As the Advisory Note says:

> FIDIC contracts are designed to be fair to all parties and are considered suitable for use with projects featuring the use of BIM – providing that the parties recognise the difference in approach and use the contract appropriately.

Therefore, using FIDIC contracts is a good way to promote the use of this technology in order to avoid situations that BIM can clearly resolve timeously.

9.2.8 Government/private sector procurement

Public procurement and private procurement in Mexico are quite different. Private procurement can follow the principle of *pacta sunt servanda*; whatever is agreed is enforceable for the parties, the only limitation being the public order and general interest. In this regard, in private procurement, a contracting party is free to implement as many requirements as it considers necessary.

On the other hand, public procurement is more complicated since it has to follow strict rules.

It is worth mentioning at the start that the public projects shall respond to the public necessities and, thus, shall strictly comply with the public order and social interest.

Consequently, the procurement procedure shall be transparent. Such procedure is established in the *Public Works and Related Services Law* (*Ley de Obras Públicas Servicios Relacionados con las Mismas*).

According to this law, there are three procedures to award public contracts:

1. The public tender. This procedure shall be followed as a general rule and consists of the publication of the project on the public official platform (CompraNet) in order to enable every interested person to review the bidding basis. This basis generally contains the timeframes of submission for proposals, dates for the clarification meetings, and dates for the issuance of the decision
2. Restricted call for bidders. This process shall be exceptionally used when there are not too many bidders in the market. The call is performed through letters notified personally to the bidders in order for them to submit an 'intention letter' to demonstrate their interest in participating in the process
3. Finally, the direct award. This option shall be the last one. It is common to see direct awards to extend contracts in order to maintain the same price and conditions

9.2.9 Insurance requirements

In practice, the warranty sector in Mexican practice is divided into two: bonds and insurance. Bonds are regulated by the *Federal Act for Bond and Insurances Institutions*, while insurance is governed by the *Law of the Insurance Contract*.

It is common to have insurance as a requirement and some other warranties for the Contractor (such as the down payment, performance and hidden defects). Also, it is common to use insurance for damages caused by reasons not attributable to the parties (such as *force majeure* and/or Acts of God). There are also 'Civil Responsibility Insurances' that can cover any damage caused by any work to an adjacent property.

In public procurement the issuance of bonds is mandatory.

9.2.10 Common forms of contract

As previously noted, there is little to discuss about standard forms of contract in Mexico: they are absolutely absent.

Ironically, the lack of discussion goes further: there are no organisations, associations or even serious academic discussions looking for them, or making an argument about whether they are a good or not good option for the country or for specific sectors or institutions; the conversation has never started in a formal way.

As explained in the book of the first author of this chapter:

> In general terms, we consider that the lack of model contracts in Mexico, leads to several practical matters such as the following:
>
> 1. There are no objective texts that more than protect one of the contracting parties, privilege the project and its execution.
> 2. The time that parties take to draft a contract, comment it, modify it and sign them, leads to a situation of delay in its formalization, that on many occasions generate that the parties, complete the project, without a signed contract and that its 'signing' is more a formality, rather than a guide for its performance.

3. As no common drafts exist, there are no general interpretations that allow the improvement or evolution of the contracts, attending reality and practice. In this context, model contracts are sometimes interpreted by judges, arbitrators, and even academics, in such a way as to allow the prompt resolution of disputes, and a 'bank of interpretations' that allow the parties to use such, and not in accordance with 'self-made' interpretations that are far from reality.[7]

In this order of ideas when thinking of such an important country, with so many challenges and needs for public and private construction, it is clear that there should be important efforts to promote and foster the use of model contracts, such as FIDIC, as stated in the first author's work, which explains:

> In this context, and considering the above benefits, our proposal would be as follows:
>
> 1. That construction chambers, professional associations, and other interested groups in Mexico, seriously consider the possibility of using international model contracts, such as FIDIC, or take the initiative to create local contract models, based on national efforts, in order to improve the industry from the contractual and legal point of view.
> 2. That serious efforts be made to determine the desirability of adapting public procurement laws for works to Model contracts.
> 3. That working groups be established to monitor model contracts in public works to see their continuous evolution and improvement.[8]

9.2.11 Dispute resolution

Maybe one of the most important and needed tools in today's construction sector in Mexico is an accessible means of dispute prevention and resolution.

FIDIC is, without doubt, *the* standard of dispute resolution in construction worldwide. FIDIC has included in its 2017 standard suite of contracts a series of multi-tier dispute prevention and resolution mechanisms that are illustrated in Figure 9.1.

The stages in this multi-tier process are explained as follows:

- **Engineer**: Has to invite the Parties to reach amicable settlements. If the Parties cannot agree, the Engineer has to decide Claims fairly
- **DAAB**: Has the power to prevent Disputes as well as to resolve Disputes in a decision that is binding but not final if either Party issues a Notice of Dissatisfaction. This process allows the Parties to resolve their Disputes in a timely manner
- **Negotiation (cool-down period)**: Intended to allow the Parties an opportunity to resolve their differences in respect of a DAAB decision before going to arbitration
- **Arbitration**: The ultimate final and binding method of resolving Disputes that have not been resolved previously by the other mechanisms

7 Roberto Hernandez Garcia, footnote 5.
8 *Ibid.*

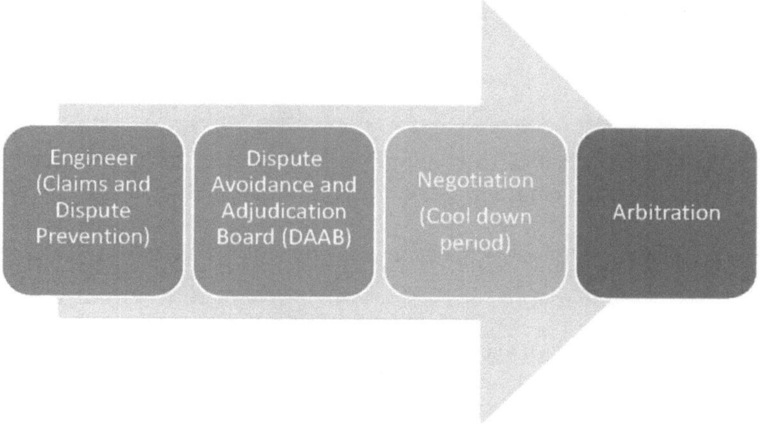

Figure 9.1 The multi-tier dispute prevention and resolution mechanisms in the 2017 FIDIC rainbow suite.

In Mexico, the current system (in public and private construction contracts) has the following features:

a) It does not include an Engineer that has to decide fairly
b) There are no DABs, DAABs or the like
c) Arbitration may be absent for public contracts and will be present in private contracts only in certain cases

The strongest effort to introduce Dispute Boards in the construction sector was on 18 March 2020, when the College of Civil Engineers of Mexico presented the 'Legislative Initiative Project of the Public Works Law'. This document was the product of the great force that this professional association has tried to give to best practices in the field of construction of public works, contemplated in the following proposal for Article 122:

> Article 122. Dispute Resolution Committees. Major works contracts entered into by the parties may incorporate in the contract or by separate agreement, subject to compliance with the requirements established in the contract, a permanent dispute resolution committee in charge of resolving differences of an economic or technical nature that arise, which will follow the guidelines of the institutional regulations derived from international best practices.

Unfortunately, this proposal has not seen the light of day and it is not expected to be approved or accepted in the coming years.

The very urgent importance of having a mechanism such as a Dispute Board is reflected in the FIDIC Golden Principle 5, which states:

> Unless there is a conflict with the governing law of the Contract, all formal disputes must be referred to a Dispute Avoidance/Adjudication Board (or a Dispute Adjudication Board, if applicable) for a provisionally binding decision as a condition precedent to arbitration.[9]

9 https://fidic.org/sites/default/files/_golden_principles_1_12.pdf (accessed 19 October 2022).

This shows the importance of having effective and timely dispute resolution in construction projects.

9.2.12 Current challenges

The use of FIDIC model contracts brings to a country a high respect for construction contracts and projects. Usually, these contracts are used by multilateral banks because of their balanced elements.[10]

FIDIC chief executive Dr Nelson Ogunshakin outlined the benefits of the World Banks's adoption of the 2017 editions:

> the World Bank has agreed to adopt our 2017 editions of the Rainbow suite of contracts and use them as a key part of their standard bidding documents. This will create more certainty in the market as by adopting the FIDIC contacts on major projects the World Bank is saying that they endorse … the fair and balanced approach that these documents offer to parties on major construction contracts. The familiarity that the FIDIC contracts bring make it easier to get projects underway as many of the typical commercial risks are clearly addressed in the contracts and all the parties understand their obligations and responsibilities.[11]

Clear obligations and responsibilities allow parties to reduce their intention to abuse the other party, by contractual or other malicious means.

But beyond the balance of the contracts, we can find specific anticorruption provisions in the 2017 FIDIC contracts, such as in the following: sub-clause 6.9 (Contractor's personnel) paragraph (e); sub-clause 15.2 (Termination for Contractor's default) paragraph (h); sub-clause 16.2 (Termination by Contractor) paragraph (j); and Guidance sub-clause 3.2.

Mexico is ranked in the Transparency International Index (2021), in position 124 out of 180 countries, from one being the least corrupt, to 180 being the most corrupt.[12] Considering that 'The engineering & construction sector is the industry most affected by bribery and corruption. Nearly half of respondents experiencing economic crime say it included bribery and corruption, far more than the next closest sector',[13] this mortal cocktail should be enough for Mexico to understand that we need international model contracts that foster integrity, meaning FIDIC.

Also, it is clear that FIDIC has a whole anticorruption and integrity group that promotes best practice conduct of construction players.

9.3 The impact of COVID-19 in Mexico

9.3.1 The impact of COVID-19 on the execution of construction projects in Mexico

As in the rest of the world, Mexico was not prepared for the impact of a global pandemic that would change the conditions of every industry.

10 https://fidic.org/node/26488 (accessed 25 November 2022).

11 https://fidic.org/world-bank-signs-five-year-agreement-use-fidic-standard-contracts (accessed 19 October 2022).

12 www.tm.org.mx/ipc2021/ (accessed 19 October 2022).

13 www.pwc.com/gx/en/economic-crime-survey/assets/economic-crime-survey-2014-construction.pdf (accessed 19 October 2022).

In Mexico, the pandemic (sanitary emergency) was declared by the Federal Government on 30 March 2020.[14] On the next day (31 March 2020) the correspondent authorities issued a new edict with extraordinary measures to be taken.[15] Some of the most relevant were:

1. Suspension of non-essential activities
2. Construction itself was not considered an essential activity unless it was related to sectors such as the energy sector, potable water, projects of communications (airports, ports and rail projects) or the health industry. In fact, those declared as 'essential projects' were those of special interest to the current administration
3. Regarding essential activities, several measures were mandatory such as:
    a. Not exceeding 50 people per meeting
    b. Frequent hand washing
    c. Coughing and sneezing according to the protocol
    d. In general, putting in practice social distancing rules

Some other measures were taken such as the separation of arriving, leaving and lunch times, not sharing materials, tools and PPE, etc.

Also, many protocols were implemented such as the mandatory testing of temperature and random COVID tests. When there was a positive case, the contagious person was required to go back home and rest until another test was negative.

Administrative work was mainly performed remotely.

9.3.2 The impact of COVID-19 on the operation of construction contracts in Mexico

There were of course impacts on the practice and operation of construction contracts in Mexico.

An immediate reaction was for every Contractor to invoke the *force majeure* clause, in order to try to suffer as little damage as possible. Consequently, non-essential projects were suspended. Despite the foregoing, it can be said that there was an environment of solidarity from the parties, and the animus was, in general, to try to reach agreements in order for the parties to minimise the impacts.

Notwithstanding, step by step, construction companies started to suffer an escalation of prices (for example the price of steel), an increase in transportation prices and a shortage of materials. These consequences were step by step transmitted to and absorbed by Contractors.

On the judicial side, Federal and Local Courts closed their doors until August 2020. Even though the courts are open in 2022, Federal Courts at least continue working with an appointment system. This significantly complicates attendance at court. However, it is also important to note that electronic files were implemented.

14 https://dof.gob.mx/nota_detalle.php?codigo=5590745&fecha=30/03/2020#gsc.tab=0 (accessed 19 October 2022).

15 https://dof.gob.mx/nota_detalle.php?codigo=5590914&fecha=31/03/2020#gsc.tab=0 (accessed 19 October 2022).

In respect of arbitration procedures, there was some suspension of procedures until the parties found very useful tools to continue with arbitration/mediation processes remotely. Institutions such as the ICC acted rapidly and enacted amendments to their rules.

However, no specific legislation was issued, nor were amendments implemented.

9.4 Mexico governing law of the contract

9.4.1 Constraints on the governing law of a construction contract

As mentioned earlier, construction contracts in Mexico follow the principle of *pacta sun servanda*, i.e., the contracts are the law that rules the relationship of the parties. In this regard, it is worth mentioning that the parties are free to agree on the contractual provisions they consider appropriate, even legislation from another jurisdiction. Even though the foregoing is possible, this is not recommended since it can complicate any judicial interpretation. The only constraint or limitation is the public order and the social interest. Thus, if any contract contains clauses against the public order or the social interest, such a clause can be declared a nullity by the correspondent judge.

On the other hand, for public contracts, the foregoing is not possible since the public entity is bound by national laws.

9.4.2 Formal requirements for a construction contract

Construction contracts follow the general rules for contracts. There are no special requirements for construction contracts. According to Article 1794 of the *Federal Civil Code*, there are only two requirements for a contract to be considered legally in existence and valid. For the existence of a contract, article 1794 of the *Federal Civil Code* requires that the Contract shall have the consent of the parties and an object.

For the validity of a contract, there are additional legal requirements:

1. The consent (Articles 1795 and 1796 of the *Federal Civil Code*):
   a. Shall be expressed according to the formalities of the law
   b. Shall be free of any flaw
2. The contracting parties shall be competent and able to be the subjects of rights and obligations. In the case of companies ('moral powers' as known in Mexican law), the representatives shall have sufficient powers to formalise the contract
3. The object (Article 1795 of the *Federal Civil Code*):
   a. Shall be a legal object
   b. Shall be in commerce
   c. Shall be determined or to be determined

Regarding public contracts, it is worth mentioning that in general, they follow the same rules as private contracts. However, in addition, a public contract shall contain the precise conditions of the *Public Works and Related Services Law*. Any disposition contrary to such law would be declared invalid by the Administrative Courts.

9.5 What Special Provisions in the Particular Conditions are necessary for consistency with applicable laws in Mexico?

9.5.1 FIDIC General Conditions are incompatible or inconsistent with Mexican governing law of the contract

As has been mentioned before, for private contracts in Mexico, the parties are free to agree on the terms and conditions of the contracts as they consider appropriate. Article 1796 of the *Federal Civil Code* contains the *pacta sunt servanda* principle as follows:

> Contracts are perfected by mere consent, except those that must have a form established by law. Since they are perfected, they oblige the contracting parties, not only to comply with what was expressly agreed, but also to the consequences that, according to their nature, are in accordance with good faith, use or the law.[16]

Thus, private parties are completely free to agree and/or formalise a FIDIC contract, and if the consent of both parties was granted legally, such contract will be perfectly valid under Mexican law. Accordingly, there are no Special Provisions required for consistency with applicable laws in Mexico for private contracts.

However, in public procurement, contracts shall follow the rules of the law. It is important to note that administrative law is governed by the principle of legality, which requires that the authorities shall act as is strictly established by the law.

In this regard, there are difficulties in using FIDIC contracts in public contracts in Mexico, since the possibility for the government to be forced by a model of contract is not specifically established in the law. This has been barely explored so there is no unified criterion in this regard. In any case, if an administrative entity agrees to use a FIDIC contract, the conditions of contract should follow what is established in the *Public Works and Related Services Law*, accordingly the General Conditions would need to be changed by Special Provisions.

The risk in this regard would be that the resulting amended contract would not comply with the FIDIC Golden Principles and the contract would lose its character as a 'FIDIC contract'.

9.5.2 FIDIC General Conditions are incompatible or inconsistent with the law of the Site/Country

The same considerations discussed in section 9.5.1 apply to this issue.

9.5.3 FIDIC General Conditions are incompatible or inconsistent with the relevant laws on dispute determination in Mexico

As mentioned earlier, the Dispute Boards in FIDIC contracts are a very useful tool for complex projects and can guarantee the continuance of the projects. Also, it has been mentioned that individuals can agree on whatever they consider appropriate as long as they

16 Translated from the original Spanish using Google translate: 'Artículo 1796. – Los contratos se perfeccionan por el mero consentimiento, excepto aquellos que deben revestir una forma establecida por la ley. Desde que se perfeccionan obligan a los contratantes, no sólo al cumplimiento de lo expresamente pactado, sino también a las consecuencias que, según su naturaleza, son conforme a la buena fe, al uso o a la ley'.

do not contravene the public order and the general interest. So, for private contracts, there is no incompatibility with the dispute resolution tools established in FIDIC contracts, as long as the procedure is perfectly defined.

On the other hand, applying the principle of legality to public contracts, the authority could only agree on provisions strictly established in the law. In this regard, neither the Engineer nor Dispute Boards are considered in Mexican law. In consequence, in the event of executing a FIDIC contract on a public project, it would be possible that the dispute resolution method is excluded, which can be contrary to FIDIC's Golden Principles, specifically Golden Principle No 5.

Thus, even though such concepts are not 'incompatible' with Mexican public law, as they are not specifically established in the law, it would be expected that the contracting entity would request not to agree on such elements. This would jeopardise the nature of the FIDIC contract as has happened in practice.

9.6 What Special Provisions in the Particular Conditions are desirable for consistency with applicable laws in Mexico?

In the case of private contracts, there are no limitations, with the exception of certain principles that apply according to the *Commercial Code* and/or the *Civil Code*.

9.7 Applicable law for Mexican governing law of the contract

For public procurement, there is the *Public Works and Related Services Law*, and for private contracts, there is the *Commercial Code* and the *Civil Code* (whether federal or local *Code*, depending on the place of the project and the jurisdiction agreed in each contract).

Notwithstanding the foregoing, it is important to mention that there are special laws that apply to construction in certain State entities. State Companies such as PEMEX (*Petróleos Mexicanos* [Mexican Petroleum]) and CFE (*Comisión Federal de Electricidad* [Federal Commission of Electricity]) have their own laws. These cases are special since the contracts executed by them are considered private.

9.7.1 Entry into a construction contract

Contracts in general are governed by the *Civil Code* (whether federal or local). *Civil Codes* contemplate general requirements of a contract such as the consent of the parties and the ways for the consent to be expressed. This includes but is not limited to representation (in the case of companies), as well as the requirement of the object of the contract and its rules to be determined and/or possible to determine, to be in commerce and to be legal. Also, *Civil Codes* contain general rules of interpretation and the consequences of breaches.

First of all, the *Commercial Code* establishes that any act performed by a commercial entity would be understood as a commerce act, and it will be then governed by the *Commercial Code*. Also, such legislation establishes that construction is considered a commercial act. Consequently, any contract related to construction will be understood as an act of commerce and will be governed by the principles of the *Commercial Code*.

Notwithstanding the foregoing, common legislation does not consider or regulate a construction contract in particular as a 'Construction Contract'. However, it does consider a lump sum contract and establishes the general rules of such a contract.

For public projects, the *Public Works and Related Services Law* specifically regulates lump sum contracts, construction contracts on a unitary prices basis and mixed contracts.

9.7.2 Operation of a construction contract

9.7.2.1 Force majeure

The general rule under the law is that nobody can be forced to perform in the case of *force majeure* (article 2111 of the *Federal Civil Code*). In this regard, the parties are free to agree on the consequences and remedies if an event of *force majeure* occurs.

In general, the parties agree on suspensions of the works in case of events of *force majeure*; the corresponding costs to be recognised (as standby costs); and the possibility of an anticipated termination of the contract if the *force majeure* event goes further than a specific period of time.

9.7.2.2 Hardship

According to the law, specifically the *Commercial Code*, it can be said that 'hardship' only exists in theory. Even though the *Civil Code* for Mexico City (i.e., a local *Code*) considers the possibility that a party to a contract affected by a 'national extraordinary and unforeseeable event'[17] can intend to recover the equilibrium of the contract, the truth is that in practice, hardship does not apply to Contractors.

The foregoing has been solved in a mandatory judicial precedent where the Constitutional Tribunal concluded that despite the fact that Article 1796 of the *Local Civil Code* applicable in Mexico City contains the *rebus sic stantibus* clause, the truth is that the applicable principle is the *pact sunt servanda* clause; thus, the contract shall be strictly fulfilled in the terms agreed.[18]

9.7.2.3 Guarantees under forms of Security

The most common practice for guarantees is to require a down payment bond, performance bond, hidden defects bond, bond for contractual penalties and a 'contingencies bond'.

Down payment, performance, hidden defects and contractual penalties are self-explanatory. With regard to the 'contingencies bond', it is commonly used to guarantee labour/social contingencies (labour demands and/or sanctions from the social security authorities). Depending on the scope specifically expressed in the bond policy, it can even guarantee civil actions.

9.7.3 Termination of a construction contract

9.7.3.1 Frustration

Construction projects can be frustrated for several reasons: due to administrative decisions, lack of investors, loss of resources or even by decision of the owner. Mexico has

17 Articles 1796 and 1796 Bis of the *Local Civil Code* applicable in Mexico City.

18 Mandatory precedent titled '*Contratos. Los legalmente celebrados deben ser fielmente cumplidos, no obstante que sobrevengan acontecimientos futuros imprevisibles que pudieran alterar el cumplimiento de la obligación, de acuerdo a las condiciones que privaban al concertarse aquélla*' (Contracts legally entered into must be faithfully fulfilled, notwithstanding the event of unforeseen future events that could alter the fulfillment of the obligation, according to the conditions that applied when it was agreed on). https://sjf2.scjn.gob.mx/detalle/tesis/186972 (accessed 21 March 2023).

suffered some examples of frustration of projects due to administrative decisions, such as the New Airport of Mexico City (the NAIM) and a beer factory in Mexicali City (the last one was relocated). In the case of the NAIM, while it was a public project, the Federal Government paid the Contractor a fee for termination of the Contract.

Regarding private contracts, the parties can agree on termination for convenience (anticipated termination), and the parties can agree on the costs of termination.

9.7.3.2 Bankruptcy, insolvency, liquidation

It is common practice that many contracts provide for termination if any of the parties is declared to be bankrupt. However, according to the *Bankruptcy Law* (*Ley de Concursos Mercantiles*), this kind of clause cannot be considered valid.[19]

9.7.3.3 Limitation periods

The parties can agree on a limitation of the periods for dispute resolutions. Indeed, it is common to see clauses stating that if the parties do not reach an agreement in the negotiation procedure within 30 days, the controversy will be referred to mediation or arbitration.

Such clauses are completely valid. However, the parties cannot withdraw any period for any procedure act/phase. Any agreement in that regard will be invalid and can even jeopardise the validity of the procedure.

9.7.3.4 Liability

If the parties agree on an ADR clause, they are bound to this procedure. In case any party tries to avoid this clause by applying to the court, the affected party can invoke a defence of lack of competence and request the judge to redirect the dispute to arbitration.

9.7.3.5 Arbitration

Depending on the requirements of the parties and the characteristics of the contract, the parties can agree on different types of arbitral procedures (whether expedited, *ad hoc*, institutional, etc.). The parties can agree to apply the principles of equity and have the arbitration decided ***ex aequo et bono***.[20]

Also, the parties can agree on the place and language of the arbitration, the number of arbitrators and speciality.

---

19 Article 87 of the *Bankruptcy Law*: '*Se tendrá por no puesta, salvo las excepciones expresamente establecidas en esta Ley, cualquier estipulación contractual que con motivo de la presentaciónde una solicitud o demanda de concurso mercantil, o de su declaración, establezca modificaciones que agraven para el Comerciante los términos de los contratos*' (Except for the exceptions expressly established in this Law, any contractual stipulation that, due to the presentation of an application or demand for commercial bankruptcy, or its declaration, establishes modifications that aggravate the terms of the contracts for the Merchant, shall be deemed not included).

20 Latin for 'according to the right and good' or 'from equity and conscience'. An arbitrator authorised to act *ex aqueo et bono* has the power to dispense with strict consideration of the law and consider solely what they consider to be fair and equitable in the circumstances.

9.8 Summary of applicable legislation for Mexican governing law of the contract

9.8.1 Entry into a construction contract

Contracts generally Construction contracts	*Civil Code* *Commercial Code* *Public Works and Related Services Law* (public contracts)

9.8.2 Operation of a construction contract

Force majeure	*Federal Civil Code* Article 2111
Guarantees under forms of Security (Tender Security, Demand Guarantee, Surety Bond, Advance Payment Guarantee, Retention Money Guarantee, Payment Guarantee by Employer)	*Federal Act for Bond and Insurances Institutions*

9.8.3 Termination of a construction contract

Bankruptcy, insolvency, liquidation	*Bankruptcy Law* (*Ley de Concursos Mercantiles*)

9.8.4 Dispute resolution

Arbitration	*Commercial Code*

9.9 Applicable law if the Site/Country is in Mexico

9.9.1 Operation of a construction contract

9.9.1.1 Registration of professionals

In Mexico, there is no special legislation for design, administration or engineering contracts. These kinds of contracts can be governed by the provisions of a 'Services Contract', where the special requirements needed by the parties can be agreed upon.

If the services will be provided by an individual, this shall be authorised through a 'Professional Licence' which is the evidence that such an individual possesses the professional training and has the knowledge to perform the technical speciality of the contract.

9.9.1.2 Registration/licencing of contractors and subcontractors

Due to a recent amendment of outsourcing (amendment to the *Labour Law*), specialised contractors and subcontractors are required to obtain the REPSE (*Registro de Prestadoras de Servicios Especializados u Obras Especializadas* [Registry for Special Services or Works Provider]).

9.9.1.3 Use of liens/assignment of debts

In construction contracts, it is not common to use liens unless they are ordered by a judge. Other cases where liens are common are while acquiring finance for a project, where the site and the project itself can be the guarantee.

Assignment of debts is not usually permitted unless it is expressly agreed upon by the parties.

9.9.1.4 Design/moral rights

Intellectual property can be agreed upon by the parties. Usually, the rights are retained by the designer, who provides a licence to the Employer to use the design.

9.9.1.5 First Nation people's land rights

In Mexico, it is very common to deal with native owners and/or '*ejidal*' regimes. It is possible to develop a project in lands subject to an *ejidal* regime, but the acquisition process is commonly much longer than with conventional private property. The process will vary from State to State.

For public projects, if the specific project is needed by the Federal State, the land where the project is going to be developed will be expropriated by the relevant authorities.

9.9.1.6 Heritage

There are administrative institutes or authorities that perform visits to the sites in order to review if there are heritage issues at the Site of the Works. In a case where historic objects are found, such authorities can suspend the Works in order to protect the heritage and even cancel the project.

9.9.1.7 Environment

The environment is one of the most important topics in a construction project. Before starting a project, the Employer is required to obtain an Environment Impact Statement according to the *General Law for the Equilibrium and Protection of the Environment*.

There is some other legislation for the treatment of water and hazardous waste that the construction companies shall comply with, otherwise, projects can be even cancelled.

9.9.1.8 Health and safety

There are specific regulations for safety in construction projects. In general, such rules consider PPE, regulations regarding fire detection and general rules for construction workers. Health and safety of workers is a federal matter.

9.9.1.9 Employer's sale of Contractor's Equipment

The Employer cannot dispose of any Contractor's property, and vice versa. The contravention of the foregoing can even constitute a crime.

9.9.1.10 Statutory rights that coexist with contractual rights

A good example of statutory rights coexisting with contractual rights is the power of cancelling a contract for breach. While the parties can agree on that possibility, the *Federal Civil Code* Article 1949 establishes that in the case that a Contractor breaches its obligations, the facility to resolve the obligations is implicit.

9.9.1.11 Liability for nuisance

In the case that the nuisance causes expenses, the affected party can claim its reimbursement and even damages.

9.9.1.12 Other issues

The *Civil Code* considers the 'damages and losses' concept that can be claimed by the affected party. The *sine qua non* requirement for damages and losses is that they are directly related to the original contract. As a general rule, damages and losses cannot be claimed jointly with the execution of the contractual penalty.

9.9.2 Termination of a construction contract

9.9.2.1 Bankruptcy, insolvency, liquidation

It is common in practice that many contracts provide for termination if any of the parties is declared to be bankrupt. However, according to the *Bankruptcy Law* (*Ley de Concursos Mercantiles*), this kind of clause cannot be considered valid.

9.9.2.2 Decennial liability and liability generally for the total or partial collapse of structures

As noted earlier, there is an action for claiming damages and losses caused to the affected party.

On the other hand, there are types of insurance that can cover decennial liability in case of a total or partial collapse. In this regard, it is important to see if the collapse was caused by negligence and/or due to a *force majeure* event.

9.9.2.3 Dispute resolution

It is common for parties to agree on multi-tier dispute resolution, where they are required to try to reach an agreement in a negotiation phase. If an agreement is not reached, then the parties shall attempt mediation, and in the case that mediation does not achieve an agreement, then the parties can attend to local courts or arbitration.

9.9.2.4 Limitation periods

The parties can agree on a limitation of the periods for dispute resolutions. Indeed, it is common to see clauses stating that if the parties do not reach an agreement in the negotiation procedure within 30 days, the controversy will be referred to mediation or arbitration.

Such clauses are completely valid. However, the parties cannot withdraw any period for any procedure act/phase. Any agreement in that regard will be invalid and can even jeopardise the validity of the procedure.

If the dispute is filed in a local court, the limitation period cannot be changed, nor agreed on.

9.10 Summary of applicable legislation if the Site/Country is in Mexico

9.10.1 Operation of a construction contract

Registration/licencing of Contractors and subcontractors	*Federal Labour Law* (*Ley Federal del Trabajo*)
Labour	*Federal Labour Law* (*Ley Federal del Trabajo*)
Planning	There are different planning regulations at federal and local levels, which require licences in order to develop a project
Environment	*General Law for the Equilibrium and Protection of the Environment*
Local procurement	Each State has its own legislation for construction projects. Thus, Contractors should be aware of the legislation depending on the State of the project site
Public procurement of federal projects	*Public Works and Related Services Law*
Building and construction permits, execution of construction work, standard of construction work	The permits required will depend on the State where the project is going to be built. In general, an Environment Impact Statement is required; also the use of the land and general permission for construction are the most common requirements
Health and safety	*Obligatory Rules of Social Security for the Construction Workers by Work or Time* (*Reglamento del Seguro Social Obligatorio para los Trabajadores de la Construcción por Obra o Tiempo Determinado*) *NOM-031-STPS-2011 Construction – Safety and Health Conditions at Work Regulation* (*Construcción – Condiciones de seguridad y salud en el trabajo*)
Insurance	*Law of the Insurance Contract*
Statutory rights that coexist with contractual rights	*Federal Civil Code* Article 1949
Liability for defective work	The right to claim for defective works vary State by State, but in general defective works can be claimed in the following year from the date of the delivery

9.10.2 Termination of a construction contract

Bankruptcy, insolvency, liquidation	*Bankruptcy Law* (*Ley de Concursos Mercantiles*)

9.11 Applicable law if the 'seat' of the dispute determination is Mexico

9.11.1 Dispute resolution

As mentioned earlier, construction projects are considered 'commercial' due to the nature of the works, as well as the parties participating in the projects. In this regard, the applicable legislation is the *Commercial Code*, and where this is silent on an issue, the *Civil Code* will supplementarily apply.

It is worth noting that in Mexico, whether the commercial subject is federal or local, the claimant can file its lawsuit in either federal or local courts at its own discretion unless expressly agreed otherwise in the contract.

Also, it is important to mention that the *Commercial Code* has substantive and procedural parts. Where there is no special regulation, the *Civil Code* and the *Procedural Civil Code*, respectively, will apply supplementarily.

9.11.2 Limitation periods

The limitation period will depend on the action to be filed.

As a general rule, the action must be filed within ten years. However, there are specific rules for some other actions. For example, in a call for the bond against the bonding company, the period is 180 days from the date when the obligation was executable.

9.11.3 Arbitration

Arbitration follows the rules of the action intended to file. That is, the substance of the dispute is according to the contract and to the law applicable to the substance of the contract and/or the applicable law.

With regards to the procedural rules, the parties are free to agree on institutional rules and/or to prepare their own.

Arbitration is regulated in the *Commercial Code*, which is based on the *UNCITRAL Model Law*.

9.12 Summary of applicable legislation if the 'seat' of the dispute determination is Mexico

Dispute resolution	*Commercial Code* *Civil Code* *Procedural Civil Code*
Arbitration	*Commercial Code*

9.13 Issues that a court or arbitrator may construe differently than expected from the words of the Contract because of local law or custom

There are various topics where there is no unified judicial criterion. For example, some judges state that the period to call for a bond from the bonding company starts from the date when the breach was known, and some other judges have interpreted that such a period starts from the date of the resolution (cancellation) of the contract.

Another relevant topic is punitive damages, which is not an explored concept under Mexican law, and its application is reserved for very exemplary cases.[21]

9.14 Additional references for Mexico

9.14.1 Books

Roberto Hernandez Garcia, *Derecho de la Construcción en México: Perspectivas y retos [Construction Law in Mexico: Perspectives and Challenges]* (Bosch, 2020).

21 For example, the *Mayan Palace* case (amparo number 30/2013).

CHAPTER 10

Applying FIDIC Contracts in Peru

Jaime Gray, Jonnathan Bravo and Guillermo Alarcón

CONTENTS

10.1	Outline of Peru's legal environment	233
	10.1.1 The constitutional structure of Peru	233
	10.1.2 The legal system in Peru	233
	10.1.3 The court system in Peru	234
10.2	The construction industry in Peru	234
	10.2.1 Overview	234
	10.2.2 Structure	235
	10.2.3 Licensing/registration	236
	10.2.4 Labour relations	237
	10.2.5 Safety culture	237
	10.2.6 Modular construction using factory fabricated components	238
	10.2.7 Technology/innovation/BIM	238
	10.2.8 Government/private sector procurement	238
	10.2.8.1 Government procurement	238
	10.2.8.2 Private sector procurement	239
	10.2.9 Insurance requirements	240
	10.2.10 Common forms of contract	240
	10.2.11 Dispute resolution	241
	10.2.12 Current challenges	242
	10.2.13 Unique features of the construction industry in Peru	243
10.3	The impact of COVID-19 in Peru	243
	10.3.1 The impact of COVID-19 on the execution of construction projects in Peru	243
	10.3.2 The impact of COVID-19 on the operation of construction contracts in Peru	244
10.4	Peruvian governing law of the contract	245
	10.4.1 Constraints on the governing law of a construction contract	245
	10.4.2 Formal requirements for a construction contract	246
10.5	What Special Provisions in the Particular Conditions are necessary for consistency with applicable laws in Peru?	248
	10.5.1 FIDIC General Conditions are incompatible or inconsistent with Peruvian governing law of the contract	248
	10.5.1.1 Implied terms	248

DOI: 10.4324/9781003201250-10

10.5.1.2 Illegality of time-bar clauses 248
10.5.1.3 Fitness for purpose versus reasonable skill and care 248
10.5.1.4 Delay Damages – penalties and liquidated damages 249
10.5.1.5 Limitation period for liability 250
10.5.1.6 Illegality of a contractual waiver of liability 251
10.5.2 FIDIC General Conditions are incompatible or inconsistent with the law of the Site/Country 251
10.5.3 FIDIC General Conditions are incompatible or inconsistent with the relevant laws on dispute determination in Peru 251
10.6 What Special Provisions in the Particular Conditions are desirable for consistency with applicable laws in Peru? 252
10.6.1 Local arbitration under the Peruvian Arbitration Act 252
10.6.2 DAAB in public construction contracts 252
10.6.3 Good faith during the performance of the contract 252
10.7 Summary of applicable legislation for Peruvian governing law of the contract 252
10.7.1 Entry into a construction contract 252
10.7.2 Termination of a construction contract 252
10.7.3 Dispute resolution 253
10.8 Summary of applicable legislation if the Site/Country is in Peru 253
10.8.1 Operation of a construction contract 253
10.8.2 Termination of a construction contract 255
10.8.3 Dispute resolution 255
10.9 Applicable legislation if the 'seat' of the dispute determination is in Peru 255
10.10 Issues that a court or arbitrator may construe differently than expected from the words of the Contract because of local law or custom 255
10.10.1 Determination by the Engineer 255
10.10.2 Delay Damages 256
10.11 Additional references for Peru 256
10.11.1 Books 256
10.11.2 Journals 256
10.11.3 Internet 256

10.1 Outline of Peru's legal environment

10.1.1 The constitutional structure of Peru

Peru is a presidential representative democratic republic divided at central and regional government levels and provincial municipalities across the country, operating under the 1993 Peruvian *Constitution*. Since the early 1990s, the country has embarked on a series of reforms of which fiscal consolidation, trade openness, exchange rate flexibility, financial liberalisation, higher reliance on market signals and prudent monetary policy, including a strong build-up of reserves, have been key components largely due to the 1993 *Constitution*.

Those reforms have led to several statutes that try to attract foreign investments into Peru. Just as an example, the *Public Procurement Law*[1] deals with the possibility for private companies to compete under a basic scheme of design-bid-build to contract services, goods or works with the Peruvian Government. The *Public–Private Partnership Law*[2] deals with the possibility for private companies to invest and build big infrastructure projects to later recover the investment on a long-term basis by operating the infrastructure under the PPP scheme in many kinds of modalities: build, own, transfer (**BOT**); build, own, operate, transfer (**BOOT**); design, build, operate, transfer (**DBOT**); and design, construct, manage, finance (**DCMF**). The *Works for Taxes Law*[3] deals with the implementation of priority public infrastructure projects by allowing companies to fund and implement public projects to later recover the total amount of investment from its third category income tax.

Such statutes have been possible thanks to the written 1993 *Constitution*, which is the maximum law that governs all other laws, regulations and rules in Peru. It comprises 206 articles in six chapters. These articles cover rules about the people and society, the State and the Nation, the economic regime, the State's structure, constitutional guarantees and the reform of the *Constitution*. The 1993 *Constitution* recognises a free market economy and the parties' freedom of contract and regulates arbitration as an alternative method to resolve disputes where the Peruvian Government is involved. It regulates the basic three powers: legislative (there is a Parliament that passes laws), judicial (there are civil, commercial, criminal and other courts where judges decide cases) and executive (which deals with the general guidelines in economic, political and social issues).

10.1.2 The legal system in Peru

The Peruvian legal system is a civil law system based – regrettably – on different European civil codes (the *French Civil Code* – sometimes even the Napoleonic Code – the *Italian Civil Code*, the *German Civil Code* and the *Spanish Civil Code*); therefore, there is a continuous confusion on the use of its rules (although sometimes not appreciated in practice). The *Peruvian Civil Code* is applicable to all legal relationships between private parties and serves as supplemental law in case of a lack of regulation regarding any matter.

1 TUO approved by the Supreme Decree No 082-2019-EF.
2 Approved by the Legislative Decree No 1362.
3 TUO Approved by the Supreme Decree No 294-2018-EF.

In cases where the Peruvian Government or any of its public entities participate in a relationship with private parties (people or companies), there is a basic law that applies: the *General Administrative Procedure Law*.[4] In all other cases, there are specific statutes that apply to specific legal relationships. Those statues can be approved and published by the Parliament or by the President of Peru, depending on the subject matter. For example, there is also a specific law that applies to companies: the *General Law for Companies*.[5] There is also a specific law for contracting with the Peruvian Government: the *Public Procurement Law*.[6]

10.1.3 The court system in Peru

The 1993 *Constitution* guarantees the independence of the judiciary (hierarchical system of courts). The highest court in Peru is the 16-member Supreme Court. Superior Courts, sitting in the departmental capitals, hear appeals from the Provincial Courts of first instance, which are divided into civil, criminal, labour, family, commercial and special chambers. Additionally, the Constitutional Tribunal is the highest body that oversees matters of constitutionality.

On the other hand, regarding ADR methods, arbitration is available in Peru and recognised as such under the 1993 *Constitution*. Domestic arbitrations (arbitrations not involving an international party) are governed by the *Arbitration Act*. Non-fundamental rights or disputes not excluded by law can be decided by arbitrators. International and investment arbitration is supported in Peru too.

Peru is a signatory to the *United Nations 1958 Convention on the Recognition and Enforcement of Foreign Arbitral Awards* (*New York Convention*). Other ADR methods used in Peru are conciliation, introduced by law as a mandatory part of the pre-trial process but voluntary for arbitration; negotiation allowed by the *Peruvian Civil Code* and typically included in contracts as the first step to resolve disputes; and Dispute Adjudication Boards (DAB), recently incorporated under the new *Public Procurement Law* and the *Public–Private Partnership Law*.

10.2 The construction industry in Peru

10.2.1 Overview

According to the Instituto Nacional de Estadística e Informática (National Institute of Statistics and Information Technology) (**INEI**),[7] the contribution to GDP from the construction industry for 2007–18 averaged US$1.975 billion, reaching an all-time high of US$2.711 billion in the fourth quarter of 2014 and a record low of US$1.067 billion in the first quarter of 2007. In the last quarter of 2018, the GDP from construction increased to US$2.312 billion.

Construction works in Peru are often affected by unpredictable situations due to factors such as climate or soil conditions, with the result that few, if any, will be completed

4 TUO approved by the Supreme Decree No 004-2019-JUS.
5 Approved by the Law No 26887.
6 TUO approved by the Supreme Decree No 082-2019-EF.
7 Visit: http://m.inei.gob.pe/estadisticas/indice-tematico/construccicn-11154/.

as planned. Technical variations are common practice in Peru – not only at the owner's demand, but also because of poor engineering.

The Peruvian market in the construction sector is composed of many construction companies. They cover the full range of project types, with some companies trying to participate in all of them. The main types of projects in the construction sector are the following: residential buildings, buildings for offices, oil and gas, mining, hydroelectric plants, road works and ports.

The main national and foreign construction companies are the following:

- CUMBRA
- CBI Peruana SAC
- STRACON
- JJC Contratistas Generales SA
- Cosapi SA
- Abengoa SA
- OHL
- HV Contratistas SA
- Ingenieros Civiles y Contratistas Generales – ICCGSA
- Mota-Engil Peru
- Constructora Andrade Gutiérrez SA
- EnergoprojektNiskogradnja SA
- Skanska
- Camargo e Correa
- Queiroz Galvao
- OAS
- OHL
- FCC
- DRAGADOS
- Salini Impregilo
- Ansaldo
- HITACHI
- San José Perú SAC

10.2.2 Structure

In the Peruvian construction industry, as in most of the construction industries around the world, there are a number of participants in a construction project that are not always aligned to work together. Depending on the type of project, the project delivery system chosen and the risks assigned, the participants (or their roles) may change. In this regard, there will be a client (sometimes wrongly called 'employer'), a Contractor, Subcontractors, vendors, suppliers, designers, consultants, supervisors, a construction manager, a management contractor, a project management officer (**PMO**) and a financer, among others.

In recent years there has been increased interest in using a PMO for the execution of construction projects. This interest came, first, under Government to Government Agreements by which a foreign Government offers the Peruvian Government the experience, expertise and transfer of knowledge to implement, execute and conclude construction and/or infrastructure projects. (At the time of writing, the UK, South Korea and France have a Government to Government Agreement with Peru and some construction projects are under execution.)

However, the success of the Panamerican and Parapanamerican Games Lima 2019 using a PMO composed of UK companies has drawn the attention of the Peruvian Government, which recently enacted a new law that purports to regulate the role of the PMO (which is called 'Asistencia Técnica Especializada' [Specialised Technical Assistance]). It can be found in the *Ley que Aprueba Procedimiento para la Contratación del Servicio de Asistencia Técnica Especializada para la Gestión de Inversiones* (Law That Approves the Procedure for Contracting the Services of Specialised Technical Assistance) *Supreme Decree No 236-2020-EF* (Peru). It is quite clear that those are the first steps for the Peruvian Government in the long road of implementing real PMOs inside each Ministry and public entity with an infrastructure office.

Regarding Subcontractors, they normally have a direct relationship with the Contractor and have no relationship with either the owner or the financiers. Their rights are not specifically regulated in the *Peruvian Civil Code* but the same rules of this body of law which apply to Contractors in construction contracts will also apply to Subcontractors. Regarding obligations, it is worth mentioning that the *Peruvian Civil Code* establishes that both the Contractor and the Subcontractor are severally and jointly liable before the owner for the part of the Works executed by the Subcontractor.

10.2.3 Licensing/registration

A construction licence is generally necessary for each and every construction project. However, a licence can only be granted for projects for which a declaration of urban status has been obtained, under which the Municipality establishes that public services are available for the future users of the project. This declaration of urban status is required for projects to be built in urban areas or urban expansion areas. These two authorisations are an owner's responsibility, but the owner could agree with the Contractor that procuring these authorisations will be the responsibility of the Contractor.

However, in these cases, the owner will remain liable under the law before the Municipality and third parties as the one responsible for obtaining these authorisations. Also, depending on the type of construction project and its specific location, other prerequisites for obtaining the construction licence may be applicable, such as a certificate of non-existence of archaeological remains, an environmental impact assessment, etc. Again, the owner is responsible for obtaining these licences, but the owner could agree with the Contractor that it will be the responsibility of the Contractor to obtain them.

In addition to these licences or authorisations, other licences may be required which relate to the activities of the Contractor, such as authorisations for the use of explosives, the improvement of roads to transport components, the use of bridges, etc. Such licences or authorisations are naturally the responsibility of the Contractor and are regulated by the law.

On the other hand, pursuant to Article 3 of the *Ley que Autoriza a los Colegios de Arquitectos del Perú y al Colegio de Ingenieros del Perú para Supervisar a los Profesionales de Arquitectura e Ingeniería* (Law That Authorises Peruvian Architecture Bars and Peruvian Engineering Bar to Supervise Professionals of Architecture and

Engineering) *Law No 16053* (Peru), the licence of engineers and architects can be obtained only through universities. To practice in engineering and architecture it is essential to register the licences obtained at the universities in the Engineering Bar and Architecture Bar. Additionally, Article 1 of the *Ley que Complementa la Ley No 16053* (Law That Complements Law No 16053) *Law No 28858* (Peru) includes a list of requirements to practice in engineering and architecture as well as the main activities for each profession.

On the other hand, for a Contractor to legally participate in public construction contracts with the Peruvian Government (any public entity) it must be registered in the Registro Nacional de Proveedores (National Registry for Contractors). The Registry reviews the type of company and evaluates financial and economic balances, technical experience and capacity and sanctions applied to the company, among other main issues.

10.2.4 Labour relations

There is usually an agreement between the Contractor and its personnel, but not between the Employer and the same personnel. Owners and Contractors almost always include a clause which stipulates that the Employer has no relationship with the Contractor's personnel. As a consequence of this, the Contractor is responsible for the dependent personnel's actions during the construction works.

Unions used to have enough power to make the Peruvian Government enact specific laws and regulations in favour of construction workers; however, it started to change in the last ten years due to economic instability. From time to time, unions enter negotiations with contractors and usually, they agree on common terms. Despite that, there are some strikes, typically, in Peru's Provinces and regions, but they are not common these days.

One of the typical contract provisions related to personnel is the Contractor's payroll obligations and all other labour obligations imposed under the law. In addition, it is mandatory by law that all personnel have complementary risk insurance to cover all risks during construction work. There is a specific provision related to this in construction contracts.

It is also common to include a provision that states that, in the case of changes to the personnel without prior approval of the owner, the Contractor will be obliged to pay liquidated damages. To avoid incurring such penalties, the replacement personnel must have the same skills and qualifications as those who are being replaced. Confidentiality stipulations are typical, and the Contractor's personnel must comply with them.

10.2.5 Safety culture

The *Ley de Seguridad y Salud en el Trabajo* (Health and Safety at Work Law) *Law No 29783* (Peru) requires employers to develop an action plan for the prevention of workplace accidents. Employers are liable for all the economic costs related to workplace accidents or injuries. In addition, all employers must notify authorities of fatal accidents within 24 hours and must keep records of work-related accidents and risks.

Companies that have a workforce of more than 20 employees must establish an Occupational Health and Safety Committee. Employers must also maintain a safe and healthy work environment and provide employees with adequate protective gear.

Employers are also obliged to provide workers with information concerning workplace risks, as well as with occupational safety and health training

10.2.6 Modular construction using factory fabricated components

This is more typical in the construction of multi-family housing buildings and office buildings where companies share one or more floors. Contractors tend to use modular structures made of concrete to speed up the erection of buildings and secure them against earthquakes. Some modular structures are used in social buildings too. For example, some local and international organisations help homeless people and families with no access to bank loans by building modular apartments or houses made of different kinds of materials (usually less expensive than concrete).

10.2.7 Technology/innovation/BIM

The use of methodologies like building information modelling (BIM) has increased since its first appearance in Peru in the early 2010s. Boosted by public initiatives like the implementation plan and roadmap of the BIM Peru plan from the Ministry of Economy and Finance (**MEF**), private developments in BIM have been consolidated and have become more widely used in the construction industry.

There are nevertheless some opportunities in the application of BIM since the market has not yet fully developed to apply 5D, 6D or further dimensions that BIM offers. Some of the more sophisticated owners and Contractors have developed and now use the virtual design and construction (**VDC**) methodology based on 'building' the project twice.

There have been very successful projects where the virtual model, with all the disciplines consolidated and compatibilised, resulted in the construction phase being free of ambiguity and design defects. This methodology has reduced the unnecessary allocation of resources and lessened variability through collaborative work in integrated concurrent engineering (**ICE**) sessions on the joint use of technological tools (such as BIM) and lean philosophies.

On the other hand, the Peruvian Government is working on a national protocol on BIM and some laws that potentially will regulate the obligation to use BIM for public construction projects. In this regard, the interest and knowledge about BIM are increasing more and more in Peru.

10.2.8 Government/private sector procurement

10.2.8.1 Government procurement

Recent Presidents have applied different mechanisms to close the infrastructure gap. Infrastructure works under PPPs, Works for Taxes and Public Procurement Law have traditionally been utilised with some success along with other minor public investment regimes. However, there has been a sense of national disappointment and resistance to these so-called traditional regimes since they are prone to project management issues, delays, defective designs and even abandoned works. Moreover, due to political scandals such as 'Lava Jato' (car wash), involving Brazilian and local construction companies and the 'Construction Club', in which the largest and most important Peruvian construction companies have been implicated, the public has lost confidence in the construction sector.

In response to the aforementioned circumstances, starting in 2019, the Government set up a process to adapt Peruvian legislation to the best infrastructure procurement and construction practices. As a first step, the Peruvian Government published the National Plan of Infrastructure for Competitiveness (the **National Plan**) following a seven-month joint collaborative effort between the public and private sectors, the Inter-American Development Bank and the UK government. The plan's objective is to provide certainty about infrastructure priorities and funding in the short (five years) and long (20 years) terms.

The National Plan established a strategy based on the country's economic potential, regardless of political and economic cycles. The plan focuses on best practices in terms of prioritising existing projects and those that are presently only ideas or are in the preliminary phases. Following the experience of the Pan American Games Lima 2019, an event which was staged with the technical advice of a UK PMO, the plan focuses on the need for a very clear purpose, objectives, work execution timeframes and financing schedules.

In January 2020, the Peruvian Government published *Urgency Decree No 021-2020* (the **Decree**) which creates a new public procurement regime. This regime, parallel to the regimes of Public Procurement, PPP and Public Works Tax Deduction, creates special projects that benefit from more favourable treatment than those regimes for the execution of public investments. The *Decree* establishes that each special project may maintain a PMO within the framework of state-to-state agreements, which must follow guidelines established by the MEF.

In addition, the *Decree* includes conditions to sign resource management agreements with international organisations and the implementation of the collaborative methodology of digital modelling of information for construction (BIM). Special projects are now authorised to apply contractual models of international standard use, such as the New Engineering Contract (**NEC**), and the contracts of the International Federation of Consulting Engineers (FIDIC) and Engineering Advancement Association of Japan (**ENAA**), among others, and they are exempt from applying public procurement law and regulations.

The regulations and guidelines in the *Decree* confirm the approach of the Peruvian Government, which is to place emphasis on the definition stage of a project. Risk allocation principles and the analysis of what delivery model should be applied in a project are now assessed by a competent and experienced private adviser. It seems, however, that the success of this approach depends on the existence of well-prepared public officials in local, regional, and national government entities, trained in international best practices and standards in the areas of project definition and delivery-model analysis.

10.2.8.2 Private sector procurement

For the last five years, Peruvian owners have been investing in more competent in-house project management offices; the use of best practices in construction procurement and project management; and more regular evaluation and utilisation of international contract forms for their projects, such as the FIDIC contracts.

Sectors like mining, oil and gas, housing and commercial construction explore project delivery systems other than the traditional construct-only or design-build. There has been a sharp increase in the evaluation of collaboration in construction projects since the success of the Pan American Games Lima 2019 special project by using the Managing Contractor delivery system, with some degree of collaboration between the parties. Currently, there is a trend towards evaluating more collaborative contracts to establish a win-win relationship between owners and Contractors.

For this purpose, owners are being advised on collaborative agreements, alliances, integrated project delivery (**IPD**) contracts and the risks as well as the pros and cons of fully collaborative contracts and construction contracts with collaborative tools. The differences between a contract in which the risks are not allocated but shared between the parties and a construction contract with collaborative tools with a transparent risk allocation but with some collaborative project management between the parties are not yet fully understood.

Some international contract forms like the Framework Alliance Contract (**FAC-1**), the Project Partnering Contract (**PPC 2000**) and the IPD collaborative approach have been introduced to the market by international users. Nevertheless, the market is still reluctant to apply one of these to its projects.

The early Contractor involvement (**ECI**) delivery system is now in widespread use in the construction market, mainly by traditional owners, in construct-only delivery systems. Owners have identified benefits in the early evaluation of inconsistencies and constructability issues by the Contractor or possible future Contractor in the pre-construction phase, while the designer is developing the scope and details of the project. Nonetheless, owners are still reluctant to enter into long-term agreements with Contractors to construct the project once the pre-construction phase and the design are completed. Owners keep the right to decide whether to complete the execution of the Works with the Contractor of the pre-construction phase or with another Contractor after a bidding process.

10.2.9 Insurance requirements

In Peru, employers and Contractors must obtain life and health insurance for their employees. This insurance is called SCTR. Insurance programmes are not normally implemented in Peru, but parties are entitled to obtain these and other types of insurance abroad, as Peruvian law relating to banking and insurance allows Peruvians to take out insurance internationally.

Parties usually include civil liability and Contractor all-risks insurance in construction contracts. These may not cover the design risk, however. Design risk should be covered by a specific insurance clause, but this is not commonly found even in high-value contracts. More sophisticated insurance is required in complex projects where international companies or public entities supported by international PMOs are involved.

10.2.10 Common forms of contract

There are no specific standard construction forms in Peru; most contracts are drawn up for specific cases. Nevertheless, FIDIC contracts are becoming more frequent, including the FIDIC Red Book, FIDIC Pink Book, FIDIC Yellow Book, FIDIC Silver Book, FIDIC Blue Book and FIDIC Emerald Book, 1999 and 2017 versions.

In addition, there is growing interest in other standard forms of contracts, such as the NEC contracts. NEC3 was first used in Peru for the construction of the infrastructure for the Pan American Games Lima 2019. NEC3 is also being used for the Reconstruction with Changes Project – known as *Reconstrucción con Cambios* in Spanish – a project with many packages to rebuild schools, hospitals, roads and other works in the north of Peru.

Currently, by the effect of *Emergency Decree No 021-2020*, its *Regulations* and the Operational Guidelines for the Implementation of the Public Investment Execution Model through Special Public Investment Projects, approved by *Directorial Resolution 009-2020-EF/63.01*, the use of FIDIC, NEC, FAC-1, PPC 2000 and others are now part of the assessment by the PMOs when recommending the most suitable delivery system and contract form to a project to public entities created under the Decree. Under these 'Special Projects of Public Investment' (*Proyectos Especiales de Inversión Pública* or **PEIP**), Peru is gradually introducing the regular use of not only international contract forms but also best practices in project delivery.

Notwithstanding that the use of international forms of contract is not applicable under the regular *Public Procurement Law*, in 2022 the Ministry of Economics and Finance of Peru has engaged in consultancy contracts with experts in public procurement of innovative solutions and experts in the use of international construction forms of contract. These have the objective of introducing both best practices and contract forms in the medium term. It is expected that the use of international contract forms will increase in the coming five years.

Finally, the Peruvian Government has contracted an international law firm to work on a standard contract for PPP projects exclusively, hence, this will be probably the first standard form for infrastructure projects for the Peruvian construction industry.

10.2.11 Dispute resolution

In addition to the ordinary justice system managed by the State, mediation, negotiation, arbitral tribunals, *Juntas de Resolución de Disputas* and Dispute Boards are commonly used to settle and adjudicate disputes in Peru.

Mediation is not commonly used in public contracts despite the fact that it could help settle controversies by considering parties' arguments to find out the common points of view. In private contracts, its use depends on the complexity and value of the contract. Regarding negotiation, this is frequently used for resolving controversies and is usually the first step in contracts prior to arbitration. A term is generally negotiated and if the controversy cannot be settled, one of the parties can submit the dispute to arbitration.

This kind of clause allows parties to attempt to solve controversies within the negotiation process, helping to reduce the number of disputes and, in some cases, to avoid arbitration. Nonetheless, in public contracts, negotiation is unofficially prohibited since even though it is not prohibited by the law, public officials are constantly under the scrutiny of the National General Comptroller (*Contraloría General de la República*) with the threat of being prosecuted for embezzlement of the public treasury.

Arbitration is very common for companies in the private and public sectors. Under the latter, Peruvian public agencies are required by law to settle their controversies through arbitration, in accordance with the *Public Procurement Law*. Arbitration is regulated by *Legislative Decree 1071*. Peru has one of the most up-to-date practices in arbitration in the world. The rules have been designed to be neutral, to generate an independent environment and, especially, to encourage investment in Peru.

In addition, arbitration law has changed many traditional views on how to manage arbitral stages to be faster and more flexible, efficient and economic by distancing itself as far as possible from the Peruvian *Code of Civil Procedures*. Since construction is a risky activity with many opposing interests between the Contractor and the Employer in most cases, controversies in construction frequently arise, which makes construction arbitration frequent in Peru.

The main institutions related to arbitration are the Chamber of Commerce of Lima Arbitration Centre, the Arbitration Centre of the Pontificia Universidad Católica del Perú, the International Chamber of Commerce and the American Chamber of Commerce Arbitration Centre. The first and the second of these already have Dispute Board rules and are prepared to manage that kind of procedure. Investment arbitrations before the International Centre for Settlement of Investment Disputes (**CIADI**) are also very common in Peru.

The use of Dispute Boards has been increasing in the last eight years because of their benefits in settling differences before they become controversies. Their project-focused approach to resolving controversies by the members of the panels has been confirmed by Contractors and Public Agencies in the field with projects like the Pan American Games Lima 2019 and the Reconstruction with Changes Projects. In Peru, Dispute Boards have been useful to ensure the completion of the works on time and within the budget.

Beliefs that Dispute Boards were a 'new method' and their use as an arbitration-like mechanism have been reducing with time, and now there are more sophisticated companies and public agencies which benefit from Dispute Boards. Generally, Peruvian construction projects choose standing Dispute Boards, implemented at the very beginning of the contract. The Dispute Board can and must cooperate with the parties to tackle problems together, encouraging frequent meetings with the parties, going to the worksite and 'getting its shoes dirty'. Furthermore, the *Procurement Law* has provisions that allow Peruvian Government institutions to settle controversies through *Juntas de Resolución de Disputas* which is a Dispute Board–inspired ADR, which typically resolves controversies much faster than the state judicial system does, but with limitations to resolve matters regarding Variations and nullity of the contract.

10.2.12 Current challenges

The environment and its protection have been a major topic for discussion in Peru in recent years. Politicians recognise that Peru has an incredibly diverse environment that needs to be protected. Accordingly, they recognise the obligation to include policies on environmental protection and conservation in their action plans.

At the end of 2018, the Peruvian Congress and the President approved the *Ley que Regula el Plástico de un Solo Uso y los Recipientes o Envases Descartables* (Single-Use Plastic and Disposable Containers Law) *Ley No 30884* (Peru), which deals with the adverse impact of single-use plastic, plastic marine waste, disposable containers and other polluting elements on human health and the environment. However, there is still more to do according to Peruvian experts.

There are, of course, other laws that regulate the environment in Peru; some examples of these are the *Ley General del Ambiente* (General Environmental Law) (Peru) *Ley No 28611*, the *Ley General de Aguas* (General Water Law) (Peru) *Ley No 17752* and the *Ley de los Recursos Hídricos* (Water Resources Law) (Peru) *Ley No 29338*. All these laws must be applied in every sector, whether it be mining, agriculture or the construction sector. Constructors must comply with environmental regulations as they are directly liable for violating the laws. The sanctions are usually severe.

10.2.13 Unique features of the construction industry in Peru

Many of the key issues in construction contracts are a consequence of bad translations from the original language into Spanish. FIDIC forms are used in Peru both in public and private works. However, translations are frequently not as good as they should be.

It leads to another issue: as translations are often bad, there are frequently conflicts in the wording of some clauses with the *Peruvian Civil Code*. Almost invariably, the key issues surrounding construction contracts involve a conflict of contractual or legal interpretation.

Another factor leading to construction contract problems is the lack of knowledge among professionals about the construction sector and its nature. Lawyers, architects and engineers sometimes wrongly assume things to be true: for example, it is not true that extensions of time must always be compensated; it is not true that Contractors are always responsible for the different Site conditions; and it is not true that a lump sum contract implies an unchangeable price (as it depends on whether there are Variations).

10.3 The impact of COVID-19 in Peru

10.3.1 The impact of COVID-19 on the execution of construction projects in Peru

The Peruvian construction market was hit hard at the very beginning of the COVID-19 crisis, due to the restrictions imposed by the Peruvian Government on 15 March 2020, especially the mandatory curfew. These restrictions forced many infrastructure project activities to be suspended and impeded the commencement of new projects. According to the *Instituto Peruano de Economía*, the Peruvian construction market plunged by 90.4% in April 2020, even more drastically than the global GDP (–39.9%).

Since then, the Peruvian construction market has been recovering gradually, as the restrictions imposed by the Peruvian Government were lifted. In August 2020, the Peruvian construction market reached –6.5%, a dramatic increase since April's plunge, according to the *Instituto Peruano de Economía*.

The Peruvian construction market has steadily rallied since then, supported by mining and infrastructure construction projects and investments from some regional governments, especially those of Ancash, Ica, Piura and Tacna.

Regarding the impact of the pandemic and government decrees which imposed restrictions on the execution of works and compliance with new health, security and safety protocols, we observe that the construction sector has adapted slowly but successfully to the new conditions.

The first measure taken by the Peruvian Government on 15 March 2020 was to order a mandatory curfew which meant, for the construction industry, a lockdown of construction sites. This was adopted and complied with by all companies in the construction industry as they understood that it was a *force majeure* situation; therefore, it will be compensated or – in any case – delays will not be considered as a contractual breach.

After some months, the Peruvian Government ordered the progressive restart of construction activities but under some specific conditions: limited working hours, the use of face masks and other protection tools for COVID-19, physical distancing, cleaning and disinfection, record keeping and implementation of a plan to avoid or mitigate COVID-19 infections, among others related to health and safety of people on site and people working at the main offices.

There was constant supervision about compliance with such measures and companies could not restart construction activities unless they had a Resolution from the Ministry of Health approving the plan previously prepared by the company.

Other constraints that impacted engineering and construction projects were the border closures ordered by the Peruvian Government, prohibitions to travel from Lima to other regions and *vice versa*, compulsory quarantine on arrival (when some travels were allowed), etc. Eventually, the Peruvian Government granted some loans and tax benefits to companies (including consulting and construction companies) so that they could afford some of the compensations generated by such measures.

10.3.2 The impact of COVID-19 on the operation of construction contracts in Peru

Parties have modified most of their contracts to recognise the impact of the new regulations' requirements, such as time and costs. Some Employers now include specific clauses regarding changes in the health, safety and environment regulations, retaining the right to suspend or terminate the Contract, reducing the price or recognising overruns in favour of the Contractor by reimbursable mechanisms.

All the impacts generated because of the measures ordered by the Peruvian Government were considered consequences of a *force majeure* situation in both public and private construction projects. According to the *Peruvian Civil Code*, a *force majeure* event is considered a non-attributable cause which *may* allow a Contractor to seek an EOT and/or compensation. There is no specific regulation in the *Civil Code* regarding the recognition of an EOT and/or compensation for delays; therefore, it will depend on the contractual provisions included by the Parties. If there are no contractual provisions, a Contractor will need to prove that such delay is caused by the Employer.

However, since the start of the pandemic, no new mandatory measures were treated as a *force majeure* event because it was considered that everybody knew about the pandemic and its potential impacts on the price and time of engineering and construction projects.

Regarding all arbitral procedures in the course of the pandemic, they were not stopped nor suspended because private institutions (and eventually public entities) implemented new measures and rules. Therefore, it was possible for parties to initiate or continue an arbitration procedure using virtual tools to send information to the arbitral tribunals or to participate in arbitral audiences and meetings.

10.4 Peruvian governing law of the contract

The applicable law depends on whether it is a public contract (executed between a private company and the State, through public agencies) or a private contract (executed between private entities).

Law No 30225, the *Public Procurement Law*, regulates the contracts formalised and executed with the Public Administration, as the general regime. It establishes the rules for public officers through the project life cycle, the planning, selection process and execution of the phases for the procurement of goods, services, general consultancy, consultancy for design and supervision and works. Although Peru has 24 Regions, the *Public Procurement Law* is applicable in the entire country by all the different levels of Government, from Municipalities to Ministers.

In addition, Peru has 15 other public procurement regimes which coexist with the general regime. We have referred above to *Emergency Decree No 021-2020* which establishes the Special Projects of Public Investment and exempts them from the scope of application of the general regime. There is also a special regime for concessions under *Legislative Decree No 1224* governed by Proinversión, a specialised technical body, attached to the Ministry of Economy and Finance.

On the other hand, in accordance with the *Constitution* and the *Civil Code*, when the contract is between private parties, they are free to agree on its terms and conditions. There are specific limitations to this freedom of contract for the parties, which are the violations of the public order and imperative regulations (public interest rules). The *Civil Code* includes the Works Contract as part of the Services Contracts and regulates a few rules which apply to any kind of works, not only engineering and construction ones. Some of the rules refer to conditions of lump-sum and unit price payment options; rights and obligations of the Employer and the Contractor; matters of allocation of design risk; completion and acceptance of the Works; and responsibility of the Contractor for defects before and after completion.

10.4.1 Constraints on the governing law of a construction contract

Peruvian legislation recognises the parties' freedom to choose the law governing their contract. In fact, this is something recognised as such in the 1993 *Constitution*:

> Article 62. The freedom to contract guarantees that the parties can agree validly according to the regulations in force at the time of the contract. The contractual terms cannot be modified by laws or other provisions of any kind. The conflicts arising from contractual relationships are resolved only in the arbitral or judicial jurisdiction, according to the mechanisms provided in the contract or contemplated in the law.[8]

On the other hand, it is important to remember that the Peruvian *Civil Code* is composed of 'books' that look more like 'chapters', where there are regulations regarding different situations (family law, property, obligations, contracts and public registry, among others).

8 1993 Peruvian Constitution: Artículo 62: 'La libertad de contratar garantiza que las partes pueden pactar válidamente según las normas vigentes al tiempo del contrato. Los términos contractuales no pueden ser modificados por leyes u otras disposiciones de cualquier clase. Los conflictos derivados de la relación contractual sólo se solucionan en la vía arbitral o en la judicial, según los mecanismos de protección previstos en el contrato o contemplados en la ley' (free translation).

One of the books of the *Peruvian Civil Code* is about private international law and regulates jurisdiction, competence and, most importantly, the law applicable to situations where the governing law is not clear. Article 2095 of the *Peruvian Civil Code* establishes the following:

> The contractual obligations are governed by the law expressly chosen by the parties and, failing that, by the law of the place of compliance. However, if they must be fulfilled in different countries, the contractual obligations are governed by the law of the main obligation and, in case such law cannot be determined, by the law of the place of the conclusion of the contract. If the place of compliance is not expressly determined or does not result unequivocally from the nature of the obligation, the law of the place of performance shall apply.[9]

Hence, parties are allowed to choose freely the law governing their contract, and the *Peruvian Civil Code* regulates the governing law in situations where there is not an agreement or where the contract must be complied with in different countries. For local construction contracts, it is common for parties to choose Peruvian law as the law governing their contract. Even in large infrastructure projects or construction works where a party is a consortium formed by international companies, it is common to choose Peruvian law.

However, it is also true that, in these kinds of projects, parties tend to agree on international arbitration as the mechanism to resolve their disputes, and the seat of the arbitration may be a country different from Peru.

If such is the case, Article 5 of the *Peruvian Arbitration Act* recognises such arbitration as international, and parties must comply with the law governing the arbitration:

> Article 5. The arbitration shall have an international character when any of the following circumstances occurs:
>
> [...]
>
> b. If the place of arbitration, determined in the arbitration agreement or pursuant to it, is located outside the State in which the parties have their domiciles.[10]

10.4.2 Formal requirements for a construction contract

According to the *Peruvian Civil Code*, there are two basic requirements for any contract to be valid:

a) *Agreement between parties*: There must be an offer and acceptance given by the future parties. It is deemed to be a contract when the acceptance is known by the offeror. It is deemed to be known by the party when the acceptance gets to the address of the offeror

9 Peruvian Civil Code: Artículo 2095: 'Las obligaciones contractuales se rigen por la ley expresamente elegida por las partes y, en su defecto, por la ley del lugar de su cumplimiento. Empero, si deben cumplirse en países distintos, se rigen por la ley de la obligación principal y, en caso de no poder ser determinadas ésta, por la ley del lugar de celebración. Si el lugar del cumplimiento no está expresamente determinado o no resulta inequívocamente de la naturaleza de la obligación, se aplica la ley del lugar de celebración' (free translation).

10 Peruvian Arbitration Act: Artículo 5: 'El arbitraje tendrá carácter internacional cuando en él concurra alguna de las siguientes circunstancias:

> b. Si el lugar del arbitraje, determinado en el convenio arbitral o con arreglo a éste, está situado fuera del Estado en que las partes tienen sus domicilios' (free translation).

b) *Intent to create, regulate, modify or extinguish a 'patrimonial' legal relationship*: Unlike common law, in the Peruvian legislation parties shall have the intention to create not merely a legal relationship but a 'patrimonial' one. This definition has always been discussed in our jurisdiction. However, the basic notion is that the legal relationship must be related to an economic exchange of something. It does not mean that there must be a consideration (as in the common law); it means that the exchange must be capable of being considered economically

   There cannot be an exchange of something not valuable in economic terms.
   In this regard, for example, a donation is considered a contract pursuant to the *Peruvian Civil Code*. Even if there is no consideration given by one of the parties, there is an economic exchange of something (which is donated).

Regarding construction contracts, there are two basic requirements to be valid as such:

a) *Determined work*: Pursuant to Article 1771 of the *Peruvian Civil Code*, in a construction contract, the Contractor is obliged to execute a determined work in favour of the owner. It means that the work shall be previously specified in the plans and specifications (either given by the owner or prepared by the Contractor). In any case, the work shall be technically determined
b) *Price*: The same article states that, in a construction contract, the owner is obliged to pay to the Contractor a price in exchange for the determined work. The price shall be paid according to the proceedings stated in the contract. If, for any reason, the parties did not include a price in the contract (which is rare), the owner still is obliged to pay a reasonable price considering the works performed by the Contractor. Article 1362 of the *Peruvian Civil Code*[11] regarding good faith during the execution of the contract supports such an idea

Hence, for construction contracts in Peru, there must be consideration (payment of a price for determined work), agreement (offer and acceptance) and intention of the parties to create a 'patrimonial' legal relationship (in the terms explained before). As it is always about construction work, it is considered an economic exchange of value. There is no need to prepare a formal contract with a public notary; therefore, a construction contract is valid and enforceable if parties agree on the terms on a napkin or in a formal Word document.

Such lack of formality to create a construction contract allows parties to commence the Works even with simple documents such as orders to commence, letters of intent or memoranda of understanding. Although it is not in standard use for large infrastructure projects or for public works under the *Public Procurement Act* (there is a specific but simple model of construction contract for public works), there is still some use of such documents in the construction industry, mainly for small works.

11 Peruvian Civil Code: Article 1362: 'The contracts must be negotiated, concluded and performed according to the rules of good faith and common intention of the parties' (free translation); Artículo 1362: 'Los contratos deben negociarse, celebrarse y ejecutarse según las reglas de la buena fe y común intención de las partes'.

10.5 What Special Provisions in the Particular Conditions are necessary for consistency with applicable laws in Peru?

10.5.1 FIDIC General Conditions are incompatible or inconsistent with Peruvian governing law of the contract

10.5.1.1 Implied terms

The FIDIC Contracts are based primarily on common law, and the general theory of implied terms applies in some of their clauses. However, if FIDIC Contracts are used in Peru, there is a different set of rules regarding implied terms, which shall be expressly included as such in the *Peruvian Civil Code.* Hence, the FIDIC General Conditions will be incompatible in Peru regarding the implied terms generally understood in the common law. There must be a Special Provision in the Particular Conditions stating expressly that the implied terms will be the ones applied according to the Peruvian legislation.

10.5.1.2 Illegality of time-bar clauses

According to Article 2004 of the *Peruvian Civil Code,*[12] time-bar clauses cannot be part of an agreement; they can only be set by the law. Therefore, there has been a lot of discussion regarding the time-bar clauses included in the FIDIC contracts because some scholars argue that they go against this rule (typically sub-clause 20.2.1 of the FIDIC Red Book 2017). Others believe that, in fact, they are not the kind of time-bar clauses stated in Article 2004. For more information about this last opinion, we recommend reading 'La fatalidad de los reclamos en los contratos de construcción FIDIC: a propósito de los Dispute Boards' by Jaime Gray and Jonnathan Bravo.[13]

In any case, parties must be aware of it. In an arbitration, it is possible that the counterparty claims for the nullity of such clauses and, consequently, extensions of time and additional costs – initially not granted by the Employer – can be granted by the arbitral tribunal. On the other hand, it is not possible to include in the Particular Conditions a clause stating that Parties expressly agree on the application of time-bar clauses, because Article 2004 is considered an *imperative rule* and, hence, cannot be changed by agreement.

10.5.1.3 Fitness for purpose versus reasonable skill and care

There is a big discussion in Peru regarding the nature of obligations to complete with a certain result and obligations to apply the means when performing a contract. Traditionally, in civil law jurisdictions, there is a difference between those two kinds of obligations. However, some scholars have argued that nowadays – especially in complex industries – all contracts have obligations to obtain a result and obligations to apply the means at the same time.

In construction contracts, for example, it is obvious that the Contractor shall perform the Works to deliver a complete project to the Employer (obtaining a specific result: the Works), but it is also true that the Contractor is obliged to use its experience, skills and

12 Peruvian *Civil Code*: Article 2004: 'Time-bars can only be fixed by the law, without admitting an agreement to the contrary' (free translation); Artículo 2004: 'Los plazos de caducidad los fija la ley sin admitir pacto contrario'.

13 Gray, Jaime and Bravo, Jonnathan. 'La fatalidad de los reclamos en los contratos de construcción FIDIC: a propósito de los Dispute Boards' in *Dispute Boards en Latinoamérica: Experiencias y Retos* (1st edn Estudio Mario Castillo Freyre: Lima, Peru 2014) 33.

care when performing such Works. Such an obligation does not serve to obtain a result; it is a continuous duty to apply reasonable skills and care.

In Peru, Article 1771 of the *Civil Code*[14] is clear on the nature of a construction contract: there is an obligation to obtain a certain result, and such obligation must be complied with by the Contractor. Nevertheless, the topic gets more difficult in Peru when there is an engineering contract. Considering that a 'construction contract' in Peru implies an obligation to obtain a certain result, an engineering contract may be considered a construction contract too. Why is that? Because the designer/engineer needs to deliver a certain result to the Employer, too, basically the provision of technical documents. In this case, such documents are the result.

It may sound confusing, odd and even stupid, but the current legislation is not clear when considering the nature of construction contracts, engineering contracts and supervising contracts, among others. Considering that the FIDIC Red Book is mainly for the execution of Works, it is considered a construction contract with an obligation for the Contractor to obtain a certain result. There is no need to imply a term of fitness for purpose; Article 1771 makes it clear.

However, for the FIDIC Yellow and Silver Books, where the Contractor also prepares the design and engineering of the works, it is recommended to include in the Particular Conditions a clause stating which kind of obligation is handed over to the Contractor regarding the design. Parties should make it clear that the Works will be fit for their intended purpose following the philosophy of such contracts. If not, there is a risk of considering the design part as a reasonable skill and care obligation, which makes the Contractor neither responsible nor liable for the results of the Works related to such design.

Also, it is important to incorporate into the Particular Conditions not only the purposes of the Employer for the project but also the precise meaning and scope of liability of a fitness-for-purpose obligation. We have to bear in mind that, under the terms of FIDIC contracts (based on common law), such duty implies the highest professional standard (including, for example, the duty to correct a wrong Employer Requirement if necessary or agreed) while in Peru, it is not necessarily like that: it implies a general standard to obtain a result.

10.5.1.4 Delay Damages – penalties and liquidated damages

In Peru, there is no such legal term as 'liquidated damages'. Considering the doctrine and current case law of the common law (especially in the UK), liquidated damages are not regulated in Peru. However, there is a term for Delay Damages when Parties agree to them in the contract. In Spanish, the term is *penalidades*, and although it may sound and seem similar to 'penalties', they are not the kind of penalties discussed in the common-law jurisdictions.

Our *penalidades* basically mean that both Parties have agreed on a specific sum (or percentage or any mathematical calculation) which will be paid by the Contractor in case of delays caused by its fault. There is no legal cap for such *penalidades*; however, the Contractor can initiate legal action in the courts to reduce the sum if the judge considers it

14 *Peruvian Civil Code*: Article 1771: 'In a construction contract the Contractor is obliged to perform a determined work and the owner to pay the price'; Artículo 1771: 'Por el contrato de obra el contratista se obliga a hacer una obra determinada y el comitente a pagarle una retribución'.

'manifestly excessive'. The *penalidades* work as a restitution for the Delay Damages, and it is not necessary to prove such damages; proof of non-compliance is enough.

Therefore, in the Particular Conditions, it is necessary to include a clause stating that wherever the Contract includes 'liquidated damages', 'penalties' or 'Delay Damages', they must be considered *penalidades* according to Article 1341 of the *Peruvian Civil Code*.[15]

10.5.1.5 Limitation period for liability

In Peru, there is a legal limitation period for liability, but the period depends on whether the construction works are private or public. Under Article 1784 of the *Peruvian Civil Code*,[16] for private construction contracts, the limitation period is five years, counting from the acceptance of the Works and considering the following:

a) If the Works are destroyed, totally or partially, or
b) If the Works have evident danger of ruin, or
c) If the Works have serious defects due to construction deficiencies, or
d) If the materials are of poor quality when supplied by the Contractor, or
e) If there are defects related to the soil when plans and specifications were prepared by the Contractor

Under Article 40 of the *Public Procurement Act*, for public construction contracts, the limitation period cannot be less than seven years, counting from the reception of the Works (totally or partially). In this case, the period of liability includes any kind of error, bad quality or deficiency of the Works. Considering the wording of this article, it could be more than seven years, in which case, the public entity in charge of the project is the one who should specify the period during the bid process.

15 *Peruvian Civil Code*: Article 1341: 'The agreement by which it is agreed that, in case of non-compliance, one of the contracting parties is obliged to pay a *penalidad*, it has the effect of limiting the compensation to this benefit and of returning the price paid, if any; unless compensation for subsequent damage has been agreed by the parties. In this last case, the debtor must pay the full *penalidad*, but this is computed as part of the damages of they were greater' (Artículo 1341: 'El pacto por el que se acuerda que, en caso de incumplimiento, uno de los contratantes queda obligado al pago de una penalidad, tiene el efecto de limitar el resarcimiento a esta prestación y a que se devuelva la contraprestación, si la hubiere; salvo que se haya estipulado la indemnización del daño ulterior. En este último caso, el deudor deberá pagar el integro de la penalidad, pero ésta se computa como parte de los daños y perjuicios si fueran mayores').

16 *Peruvian Civil Code*: Article 1784: 'If in the course of five years from its acceptance the work is destroyed, totally or partially, or it has evident danger of ruin or serious defects due construction deficiencies, the contractor is liable before the owner or his heirs, provided that the contractor notify the owner in writing of a certain date within six months of the discovery. Any other agreement is null. The contractor is also liable, in the cases indicated in the previous paragraph, for the poor quality of the materials or for defects of the soil, if it had supplied the first ones or elaborated the studies, plans and other specifications necessary for the execution of the work. The period for filing the action is one year counting from the day following the notice referred to in the first paragraph' (Artículo 1784: 'Si en el curso de los cinco años desde su aceptación la obra se destruye, total o parcialmente, o bien presenta evidente peligro de ruina o graves defectos por vicio de la construcción, el contratista es responsable ante el comitente o sus herederos, siempre que se le avise por escrito de fecha cierta dentro de los seis meses siguientes al descubrimiento. Todo pacto distinto es nulo. El contratista es también responsable, en los casos indicados en el párrafo anterior, por la mala calidad de los materiales o por defecto del suelo, si es que hubiera suministrado los primeros o elaborado los estudios, planos y demás documentos necesarios para la ejecución de la obra. El plazo para interponer la acción es de un año computado desde el día siguiente al aviso a que se refiere el primer párrafo').

Consequently, in the Particular Conditions of the FIDIC Contracts, there should be a clause stating the limitation period of liability according to such rules and considering if the nature of the Works is private or public.

On the other hand, we recommend clarifying in the Particular Conditions of the FIDIC Contracts that the Defects Notification Period included in clause 11 of the General Conditions is a timeframe of *responsibility* different from the ones regulated under Article 1784 of the *Peruvian Civil Code* and Article 40 of the *Public Procurement Act* (which are periods of liability, not responsibility).

The Defects Notification Period is a period in which the Contractor is obliged to execute all work required to remedy defects or damage. It has been duly paid by the Employer as part of the Contract Price and even could be considered as a Variation if the work is attributable to any cause other than the ones listed in sub-clause 11.2 of the General Conditions.

10.5.1.6 Illegality of a contractual waiver of liability

Provisions relating to the extinguishing of the Employer's liability will not apply in Peru. Article 1328 of the *Peruvian Civil Code* expressly prohibits any contractual waiver of liability in case of gross negligence or fraud:

> Article 1328. Is null any stipulation that excludes or limits the liability for gross negligence or fraud of the debtor or their third parties.[17]

On the other hand, regarding liabilities arising from errors or defects in construction projects that employ new design methods and techniques such as BIM and new collaborative project delivery systems, it is recommended that Parties clearly establish in the Particular Conditions the scope of work or services and the specific liability each of them should bear. For more information about this, see 'Liabilities for design defects in a collaborative, integrated digital age' by Jaime Gray and Jonnathan Bravo.[18]

10.5.2 FIDIC General Conditions are incompatible or inconsistent with the law of the Site/Country

If the Site is in Peru, professionals shall keep in mind the topics described in the previous section (10.5.1).

10.5.3 FIDIC General Conditions are incompatible or inconsistent with the relevant laws on dispute determination in Peru

No Special Provisions in the Particular Conditions are necessary for consistency with the relevant laws on dispute determination in Peru.

17 *Peruvian Civil Code*: Artículo 1328: 'Es nula toda estipulación que excluya o limite la responsabilidad por dolo o culpa inexcusable del deudor o de los terceros de quien éste se valga' (free translation).

18 Jaime Gray and Jonnathan Bravo, 'Liabilities for design defects in a collaborative, integrated digital age' [2013] 8.4 *Construction Law International*, 19.

10.6 What Special Provisions in the Particular Conditions are desirable for consistency with applicable laws in Peru?

10.6.1 Local arbitration under the Peruvian Arbitration Act

When using FIDIC contracts in Peru, it is important to ask the Parties whether or not they want to resolve their disputes under international arbitration and under the rules of arbitration of the International Chamber of Commerce. Normally, even for large infrastructure projects, parties prefer local arbitration under the rules of arbitration of specific local arbitration centres. If this is the case, clause 21.6 of the General Conditions should be reviewed under the terms of the *Peruvian Arbitration Act* and the interests of the local parties.

10.6.2 DAAB in public construction contracts

Dispute Boards have been introduced in the new *Public Procurement Act* for public construction works as a new mechanism to resolve disputes only if the Parties agree on such terms. However, the DAB regulated in the legislation is not as complex as the clauses included in the FIDIC contracts (from sub-clause 21.1 to 21.4 in the 2017 FIDIC Red Book). Therefore, such clauses should be reviewed to determine whether it is appropriate to maintain or change them in light of the current legislation for public construction contracts.

10.6.3 Good faith during the performance of the contract

It is desirable to include a provision in the Particular Conditions regarding the application of good faith during the performance of the Contract pursuant to Article 1362 of the *Peruvian Civil Code*. Even if the governing law of the contract is Peruvian law, it is better to expressly include such obligations for both Parties. Hence, clause 2 and clause 4.1 should be reviewed.

10.7 Summary of applicable legislation for Peruvian governing law of the contract

10.7.1 Entry into a construction contract

Contracts generally	*Peruvian Civil Code* (from Article 1351 to Article 1528)
Construction contracts	*Peruvian Civil Code* (from Article 1771 to Article 1789)

10.7.2 Termination of a construction contract

Frustration	*Peruvian Civil Code* (Articles 1428, 1429, 1430 and 1440)
Bankruptcy, insolvency, liquidation	*General Law of the Bankruptcy System* (Law No 27809)

Guarantees under forms of Security (Tender Security, Demand Guarantee, Surety Bond, Advance Payment Guarantee, Retention Money Guarantee, Payment Guarantee by Employer)	*Law of Securities* (Law No 27287) *Public Procurement Act* (*Supreme Decree No 082-2019-EF*) and its *Regulation* (*Supreme Decree No 344-2018-EF*)

10.7.3 Dispute resolution

Limitation periods	*Peruvian Civil Code* (Article 2001) *Public Procurement Act* (*Supreme Decree No 082-2019-EF*) and its *Regulation* (*Supreme Decree No 344-2018-EF*) *Arbitration Act* (*Legislative Decree No 1071*)
Liability	*Peruvian Civil Code* (from Article 1314 to Article 1332 and Articles 1784 and 1785) *Public Procurement Act* (*Supreme Decree No 082-2019-EF*), Article 40
Adjudication	*Public Procurement Act* (*Supreme Decree No 082-2019-EF)* and its *Regulation* (*Supreme Decree No 344-2018-EF*) *Public–Private Partnership Law* (Legislative Decree No 1362) and its *Regulation*
Arbitration	*Arbitration Act* (Legislative Decree No 1071) *Public Procurement Act* (*Supreme Decree No 082-2019-EF*) and its *Regulation* (*Supreme Decree No 344-2018-EF*) regarding arbitration in public construction contracts

10.8 Summary of applicable legislation if the Site/Country is in Peru

10.8.1 Operation of a construction contract

Registration and administration of professionals – Engineers, Architects	*Architects and Engineers Law* (*Law No 16053*)
	Public Procurement Act (*Supreme Decree No 082-2019-EF*) and its *Regulation* (*Supreme Decree No 344-2018-EF*) *National Building Regulation*
Registration/licencing of Contractors Subcontractors	*Public Procurement Act* (Supreme Decree No 082-2019-EF) and its *Regulation* (*Supreme Decree No 344-2018-EF*) *Peruvian Civil Code* (Article 1772) *Public Procurement Act* (*Supreme Decree No 082-2019-EF*) and its *Regulation* (*Supreme Decree No 344-2018-EF*)

(*Continued*)

(Continued)

Labour	*Law for the Promotion of Private Investment in Construction* (*Legislative Decree No 727*) *Law for the Creation of the National Registry of Civil Construction Workers* (*Supreme Decree No 005-2013-TR*)
Copyright	*Copyright Act* (*Legislative Decree No 822*) *Criminal Code* (from Article 216 to Article 225)
The product being produced from the Works	*Law of Integral Management of Solid Waste* (*Legislative Decree No 1278*)
First Nation people's land rights	*Law of Native Communities and Agrarian Development of the Jungle* (*Law Decree No 22175*)
Planning	*Regulation of Territorial Conditioning and Sustainable Urban Development* (*Supreme Decree No 022-2016-VIVIENDA*)
Work affecting adjacent property to the Site	*Peruvian Civil Code* (Book of Property)
Heritage	*General Law of the National Cultural Heritage* (Law No 28296) and its *Regulation* (Supreme Decree No 011-2006-ED) *Criminal Code* (from Article 226 to Article 231)
Environment	*General Law of the Environment* (Law No 28611) *Law of the National System of Environmental Assessment and Control* (*Law No 29325*) *Criminal Code* (from Article 304 to Article 314-D)
Building and construction permits, Execution of construction work, Standard of construction work	*Peruvian Civil Code* (from Article 1771 to Article 1789) *Public Procurement Act* (Supreme Decree No 082-2019-EF) and its *Regulation* (Supreme Decree No 344-2018-EF) *National Building Regulation*
Health and safety	*Occupational Health and Safety Law* (29783) *National Building Regulation*
Calibration of testing apparatus, equipment and instruments	*National Building Regulation*
Ownership of Plant and Materials	*Peruvian Civil Code* (from Article 1771 to Article 1789)
Insurance	*Insurance Contract Law* (Law No 29946)
Statutory rights that coexist with contractual rights	*Peruvian Civil Code* (from Article 1771 to Article 1789) *Public Procurement Act* (*Supreme Decree No 082-2019-EF*) and its *Regulation* (*Supreme Decree No 344-2018-EF*) *National Building Regulation*
Liability for defective work	*Peruvian Civil Code* (from Article 1771 to Article 1789) *Public Procurement Act* (*Supreme Decree No 082-2019-EF*) and its *Regulation* (*Supreme Decree No 344-2018-EF*)
Liability for nuisance	*General Law of the Environment* (Law No 28611) *General Law of Health* (*Law No 26842*), Article 105

10.8.2 Termination of a construction contract

Bankruptcy, insolvency, liquidation	*General Law of the Bankruptcy System* (Law No 27809)
Decennial liability and liability generally for the total or partial collapse of structures	*Peruvian Civil Code* (from Article 1314 to Article 1332 and Articles 1784 and 1785)
	Public Procurement Act (*Supreme Decree No 082-2019-EF*) Article 40

10.8.3 Dispute resolution

Dispute before a local board/ Adjudication	*Public Procurement Act* (*Supreme Decree No 082-2019-EF*) and its *Regulation* (*Supreme Decree No 344-2018-EF*) *Public–Private Partnership Law* (*Legislative Decree No 1362*) and its *Regulation*
Limitation periods	*Peruvian Civil Code* (Article 2001) *Public Procurement Act* (*Supreme Decree No 082-2019-EF*) and its *Regulation* (*Supreme Decree No 344-2018-EF*) *Arbitration Act* (*Legislative Decree No 1071*)

10.9 Applicable legislation if the 'seat' of the dispute determination is in Peru

Dispute resolution	*Arbitration Act* (*Legislative Decree No 1071*) *Public Procurement Act* (*Supreme Decree No 082-2019-EF*) and its *Regulation* (*Supreme Decree No 344-2018-EF*) *Public–Private Partnership Law* (*Legislative Decree No 1362*)
Limitation periods	*Peruvian Civil Code* (Article 2001) *Public Procurement Act* (*Supreme Decree No 082-2019-EF*) and its *Regulation* (*Supreme Decree No 344-2018-EF*) *Arbitration Act* (*Legislative Decree No 1071*)
Adjudication	*Public Procurement Act* (*Supreme Decree No 082-2019-EF*) and its *Regulation* (*Supreme Decree No 344-2018-EF*) *Public–Private Partnership Law* (*Legislative Decree No 1362*)
Arbitration	*Arbitration Act* (*Legislative Decree No 1071*)

10.10 Issues that a court or arbitrator may construe differently than expected from the words of the Contract because of local law or custom

10.10.1 Determination by the Engineer

Sub-clause 3.7 of the FIDIC Red Book (as an example only) states that when carrying out his/her duties under such sub-clause, the Engineer shall act neutrally between the Parties and shall not be deemed to act for the Employer.

However, it is a fact – also included in the Contract – that the Engineer is appointed by the Employer. Although sub-clause 3.7 differentiates between the activities of the Engineer as representative of the Employer and duties carried out neutrally when determining any matter or claim, in Peru an arbitrator or judge may understand that such duty (determination of any matter or claim) is neither possible nor legal because of bias and lack of independence.

It is quite difficult for arbitrators or judges in Peru (especially if they do not have experience or have not studied FIDIC Contracts) to understand the philosophy of these kinds of contracts. Even if the Parties made it clear by agreement that the Engineer shall act neutrally, arbitrators and judges may consider it illogical, and any determination made by the Engineer may be deemed null.

10.10.2 Delay Damages

As stated earlier, in Peru, there are no such terms as 'liquidated damages', 'penalties' or 'Delay Damages', at least not as concepts brought by the common law when preparing the FIDIC contracts. Hence, arbitrators and judges may understand clause 8.8 of the FIDIC Red Book (as an example) as a clause of *penalidades* pursuant to Article 1341 of the *Peruvian Civil Code*. This construction has the effects explained in section 10.3.1.

10.11 Additional references for Peru

10.11.1 Books

Jaime Gray and Jonnathan Bravo, 'La fatalidad de los reclamos en los contratos de construcción FIDIC: A propósito de los Dispute Boards', in *Dispute Boards en Latinoamérica: Experiencias y Retos* (1st edn, Estudio Mario Castillo Freyre, 2014) 33.

10.11.2 Journals

Jaime Gray and Jonnathan Bravo, 'Liabilities for Design Defects in a Collaborative, Integrated Digital Age', (2013) Vol. 8 No 4 *Construction Law International* 19.

10.11.3 Internet

All Peruvian legislation: https://spijweb.minjus.gob.pe

CHAPTER 11

Applying FIDIC Contracts in the United States of America

Joseph F Moore

CONTENTS

11.1	Outline of the legal environment in the United States of America	259
	11.1.1 The constitutional structure of the United States of America	259
	11.1.2 The legal system in the United States of America	259
	11.1.3 The court system in the United States of America	259
11.2	The construction industry in the United States of America	260
	11.2.1 Overview	260
	11.2.2 Structure	260
	11.2.3 Licensing/registration	261
	11.2.4 Labour relations	262
	11.2.5 Safety culture	262
	11.2.6 Modular construction using factory-fabricated components	263
	11.2.7 Technology/innovation/BIM	263
	11.2.8 Government/private sector procurement	264
	11.2.9 Insurance requirements	264
	11.2.10 Common forms of contract	264
	11.2.11 Dispute resolution	265
11.3	The impact of COVID-19 in the United States of America	265
	11.3.1 The impact of COVID-19 on the execution of construction projects in the United States of America	265
	11.3.2 The impact of COVID-19 on the operation of construction contracts in the United States of America	266
11.4	United States of America governing law of the contract	267
	11.4.1 Constraints on the governing law of a construction contract	267
	11.4.1.1 Anti-indemnity statutes	267
	11.4.1.2 Paid-if-paid versus paid-when-paid	268
	11.4.1.3 No damage for delay	268
	11.4.1.4 Limitation of liability provisions	268
	11.4.1.5 Consequential damage waivers	268
	11.4.2 Formal requirements for a construction contract	268
11.5	What Special Provisions in the Particular Conditions are necessary for consistency with applicable laws in the United States of America?	269
	11.5.1 FIDIC General Conditions are incompatible or inconsistent with the United States of America governing law of the contract	269

DOI: 10.4324/9781003201250-11

11.6 Applicable legislation if the law of the United States of America governs the contract 270
11.7 Applicable legislation if the Site is in the United States of America 271
11.8 Applicable legislation if the 'seat' of the dispute determination is the United States of America 272
11.9 Issues that a court or arbitrator may construe differently than expected from the words of the Contract because of local law or custom 272

11.1 Outline of the legal environment in the United States of America

11.1.1 The constitutional structure of the United States of America

The United States of America is a nation governed through a system of federalism and the concept of a national republic. As such, powers are shared amongst the Federal Government and the Governments of the 50 States. Each of the 50 States and the nation of the United States have their own constitutions. The *Constitution of the United States* identifies which powers are reserved at the national level. Those powers not reserved at the national level are typically within the jurisdiction of each State. Although there are common concepts applied throughout the *State Constitutions*, each of the *State Constitutions* is a separate and independent document. Residents of a particular State are entitled to the protections afforded by the *Constitution* of the State in which they reside plus those afforded by the *Constitution of the United States.*

11.1.2 The legal system in the United States of America

The legal system in the United States is generally viewed as a common law system; however, that generalisation varies in degree from State to State. Law in the United States is derived from case law and precedent, but it is also based upon legislation, statutes, regulations and local ordinances. Generally, laws are enacted by the legislative bodies and are codified as statutes. Such statutes govern a wide variety of civil, criminal and commercial activities. To the extent that activities are not subject to an applicable statute, common law principles developed through court precedence apply. In addition to codified laws and court-developed common law, the various administrative bodies in the United States develop regulations which are also applicable to a wide variety of civil and commercial activities.

11.1.3 The court system in the United States of America

The court system in the United States is also separated into a federal system and the systems of the various States. Additionally, both the Federal Government and the many State jurisdictions have administrative courts that are intended to address disputes associated with specific administrative regulations and procedures. The Federal Courts of the United States operate as a tiered system. The tiers are comprised of the trial court, the first court of appeal and the ultimate court of appeal. In the Federal Court system, the trial court is called the District Court, the first court of appeal is called the Circuit Court and the ultimate court of appeal is called the Supreme Court. The District Court is the court of initial determination for all matters. The District Court is the initial finder of fact and law and considers the evidence before the court. The District Court then applies the applicable law to the evidence and issues judgment accordingly. Generally, a jury serves as the finder of fact in the District Court and the judge serves as the finder of law. The jury listens to the evidence which is typically presented through live testimony and then makes a finding as to the facts of the matter. The judge rules on what law is applicable to the matter, and the jury, with the judge's guidance, renders judgment by applying the law to the findings of fact. Despite this general rule, in construction disputes, the parties often waive their right to a jury and the judge operates as both the finder of law and the finder of fact. If a party is not satisfied with the judgment from the District Court, it may appeal the matter to the Circuit Court. Generally, the Circuit Court only reviews matters for errors of law and does not review the underlying facts of the matter. If the Circuit Court finds that an error of law has been made, it remands the matter back to the District Court for the District Court to conduct the proceeding based on the Circuit Court's order. The Supreme Court is the ultimate court in the land. If a party disputes the ruling of the Circuit Court, it may petition the Supreme Court for a review of the matter. Supreme Court review is rarely granted, and when it is granted, it typically focuses on unsettled issues involving the interpretation of the *Constitution of the United States*.

The Federal Court system is comprised of 94 District Courts. These District Courts are organised geographically into 12 regional circuits. The Circuit Court for each of these regional circuits acts as the court of appeal for matters arising from the District Courts in its circuit. In addition to the 12 regional circuits, there is a 13th circuit which contains the Court of Appeals for the Federal Circuit. The Federal Circuit Court of Appeals has special jurisdiction over US federal cases involving matters such as patents, trademarks and government contracts.

In addition to the federal court system, each of the 50 states has its own system of courts, which generally mirror the three-tiered federal system. Like the federal system, the State courts have a lower-level trial court, a court of appeal and an ultimate court of appeal. The specific names of each of these courts vary from State to State. For example, in some states, the Superior Court is the trial court, whereas in other states the Superior Court is the ultimate Court of Appeal. As with the Federal Court system, the trial court is the court that determines the facts of the matter, and the courts of appeal are reserved primarily for disputes regarding the interpretation of law.

11.2 The construction industry in the United States of America

11.2.1 Overview

The construction industry is a major contributor to the economy of the United States. According to the Association of General Contractors, the construction industry has more than 754,000 employers and over 7.6 million employees. The construction industry is estimated to have an annual value of US$1.4 trillion.[1]

The construction industry touches almost every aspect of life in the United States. Projects range from residential projects to the construction of factories and manufacturing facilities, power generation, waste treatment, water systems, transportation, technology and defence. Additionally, many of the universities in the United States have departments that focus on construction technology and practices.

11.2.2 Structure

The construction industry in the United States is comprised of companies of varying sizes. The largest of these generate annual revenues exceeding US$14 billion a year and employ tens of thousands of people. On the other side of the spectrum are contractors that are sole

1 Association of General Contractors, www.agc.org/learn/construction-data (accessed 12 August 2022).

proprietors and employ very few people, if any. Generally, construction contracting firms specialise in particular trades. Most projects involved a general contractor and several subcontractors. The general contractors are typically experts in building construction or heavy civil construction, and the subcontractors generally hold expertise in speciality services, such as electrical installation, plumbing, heating ventilation and air conditioning, concrete work, excavation, masonry and the like. It is not uncommon for general contractors to act primarily as managers of various subcontractors. In these relationships, the general contractors typically employ very little labour themselves; rather they rely on the subcontractors to provide the specialty labour needed to construct the project.

The construction market in the United States has attracted a number of international companies. The international companies are primarily involved in large infrastructure projects such as roads, bridges, tunnels, sanitary facilities, industrial complexes, power generation facilities and so on. Many international firms also have branches in the United States that focus on large building construction. The majority of smaller projects are constructed by local contractors and not those with a national footprint or an international presence.

Most work in the United States is performed on a design/bid/build basis. In this methodology, the design team is hired by the project owner and performs its services directly for the owner. The project owner then places the completed design for bid, and the contractor that is awarded the construction has an independent contract with the project owner as well. The design/bid/build approach is not by any means the only construction procurement methodology employed in the United States. Design/build procurements, construction management at risk procurements, turnkey procurements, integrated project delivery and numerous other procurement methodologies are also employed regularly throughout the United States.

Similar to contractors in the United States, design professional firms come in varying sizes and disciplines. Design firms range from large multinational companies with revenues of more than a billion dollars a year to small sole proprietors. Larger projects attract international firms as well as domestic firms, whereas smaller projects are typically performed by smaller regional firms.

The same general structure applies to trade subcontractors and design sub-consultants. Larger projects tend to attract larger firms of speciality consultants and designers, whereas smaller projects tend to be performed by local companies.

11.2.3 Licensing/registration

Licensing requirements for contractors and design professionals vary from State to State and jurisdiction to jurisdiction. Many States require all contractors to pass examinations and hold licenses prior to performing any construction work. Other States, however, do not require contractors to be licensed. In those States that do require licensing, many have legislation designed to discourage the unlicensed performance of construction. Many States have disgorgement statutes that allow owners to avoid paying for work performed by unlicensed contractors. In those States where licensing is required, the licensing regime is typically overseen by a regulatory body that examines contractor qualifications and manages the contractor review and disciplinary system. Interestingly, oftentimes on projects performed solely within the jurisdiction of the Federal Government, licensing is not required.

contractor's insurance premium. As a result, contractors are motivated to keep safety violations to a minimum, which has led to an entire industry focused on workplace safety. This in turn has fostered a safety-first culture on most construction projects in the United States.

11.2.6 Modular construction using factory-fabricated components

Modular construction has been employed in the United States for decades. Historically, modular construction was used to provide inexpensive housing, agricultural shelters and shelters for light industry. In recent years, modular construction has experienced significant growth in interest. This increase has been motivated by the technology industry and seeks to find technology-driven solutions that will allow for high-quality modular construction that can be employed on a wide variety of projects. The expectation is that modular construction and factory-fabricated components will lead to significant cost savings when compared to traditional construction methodology. Fabricating construction components and modular building sections in a factory where much of the work can be performed by machines will reduce the labour costs associated with construction. In recent years several technology companies have focused their attention on disrupting the construction industry using centrally fabricated components. Efforts in this area have yet to have a significant impact on the construction industry, but the general expectation is that such an impact will be felt in the years to come.

11.2.7 Technology/innovation/BIM

In the United States, those in the construction industry are constantly evaluating and adopting innovative technologies. Many companies and universities maintain research and development departments focused on the construction industry. These research and development efforts result in a continuous betterment of construction materials, procedures and approaches. In the past, such innovations resulted in materials such as higher-strength concrete; better functioning waterproofing systems; more efficient heating and cooling systems; less expensive water distribution systems; more durable asphalt paving; more energy efficient electrical distribution and lighting systems; and the list goes on. More recently, innovations and technology are focusing attention on mechanised construction activities. Technologies such as GPS, LIDAR[2] and robotics are being employed to develop automated construction procedures.

One of the largest shifts in recent years is the adoption of building information modelling or BIM. BIM takes various forms, but simply stated is the modelling of a construction project in the virtual space of a computer prior to the construction of the project itself. The model can then be used to develop construction drawings and other resources related to the construction project. In recent years, there has been a transition from the use of paper drawings on projects to the almost exclusive use of computer media. It is expected that these technological advances will continue in the future.

2 Light detection and ranging.

11.2.8 Government/private sector procurement

Construction in the United States can be divided into two large categories, the first being projects constructed for government entities and the second being projects constructed for private owners. Both the Federal Government and the individual States have legislation that governs the procurement of public works contracts. Such legislation is often referred to as the 'competitive bidding rules' and is aimed at removing favouritism and graft from public contracting. This legislation typically requires that construction projects be competitively bid, which entails the simultaneous submission of pricing and bid data. In such instances, contractual terms are typically dictated by the public project owner with no ability for the contractor to negotiate.

Conversely, private construction projects are typically not subject to competitive bidding requirements. Although specific owners may choose a competitive bidding approach, such an approach is typically not mandated by law. Accordingly, in the private sector, it is more common to have negotiated contract terms and varying types of procurement methods, such as guaranteed maximum price procurements, design/build procurements and other approaches.

Because of the restrictive nature of public contracting, the rules of contractual interpretation and the laws related to public work contracting often differ from those associated with private construction projects. Case law and statutes often make distinctions between private and public contracting in determining how to apply equitable principles for cost overruns.

11.2.9 Insurance requirements

Insurance on construction projects in the United States is typically a function of risk assessment and contractual requirements. Generally, individual States require all construction employers to maintain workers' compensation insurance. Other than that, however, there generally is not a statutory mandate to carry specific types of insurance. Rather the companies and the project owner evaluate the levels of insurance and types of insurance that are needed.

Parties may carry a wide variety of insurances on construction projects. Some of the most common are commercial general liability policies; errors and omissions or professional liability policies; property policies, often referred to as builders' risk policies; pollution liability policies; and, with the advent of BIM, cyber and data liability coverage.

On larger projects, owners often purchase project-specific insurance to cover all risks on the project through a specific program. These programs are commonly referred to as Owner Controlled Insurance Programs or OCIPs.

11.2.10 Common forms of contract

There are several form contracts used in the United States construction industry; the applicable form is typically chosen based on the type of project or the type of owner. For example, contracts with the Federal Government are structured around the *Federal Acquisition Regulations*, often referred to as the *FAR*. Similarly, projects performed for large public owners, such as State Departments of Transportation or large Municipalities, often employ forms that they have developed internally by the agency over the years.

In the private sector, there are a number of industry groups that have published forms that are widely used throughout the country. For example, the American Institute of Architects has developed a suite of forms that are well-suited for building construction and facilities projects. The Design-Build Institute of America has developed a suite of forms that are well suited for design/build projects specifically related to facilities construction. ConsensusDocs publishes a suite of forms that are applicable to a variety of project types, and the Engineers Joint Contract Documents Committee publishes a suite of forms developed for infrastructure projects. Notwithstanding the large variety of form contracts, it is not uncommon for projects to use bespoke agreements or to borrow concepts from the various form contracts to develop a contract specifically suited for a given project.

11.2.11 Dispute resolution

In the United States, the default form for the resolution of construction disputes is litigation in the trial courts. Despite this default, there typically is an understanding that arbitration is the most desirable approach for the resolution of construction disputes. Given this, most of the form contracts and many bespoke contracts provide provisions mandating arbitration.

Construction arbitration in the United States is usually administered through an agency such as the American Arbitration Association or JAMS. *Ad hoc* arbitrations in the United States construction industry are rare.

Another popular dispute-resolution mechanism is mediation. In fact, most contracts mandate mediation as a condition precedent to the initiation of legal action. Similarly, most trial courts mandate some form of mediation prior to the actual trial of the dispute.

Historically, Dispute Boards have not been as prevalent in the US construction industry as in other parts of the world; however, this has changed in recent years. It is now not uncommon for large infrastructure projects and public works projects to have provisions providing for the initial review and determination of disputes via a Dispute Board. Such Dispute Boards often act as the initial decision-maker and define a *status quo* that is later subject to challenge in the courts or in arbitration.

11.3 The impact of COVID-19 in the United States of America

11.3.1 The impact of COVID-19 on the execution of construction projects in the United States of America

The impact of COVID-19 on the construction industry in the United States varied across the country depending on the type of construction being performed. Industry-wide impacts included supply chain disruption and impacts on labour efficiency and productivity.

Much of the construction materials used in the United States are manufactured abroad. As COVID-19 rippled through the world, it impacted the production and shipping of construction materials. COVID-19 also impacted the operation of the various seaports through which construction materials flow. Throughout the COVID-19 pandemic, delays were encountered related to crucial materials such as steel, electrical conductors, aggregates, gypsum wallboard, plumbing materials, air handling units, cabinetry, flooring materials and the like. These delays occurred within the country of manufacture and at the seaports of the United States. Oftentimes materials were held at sea for extended periods of time while the ports addressed labour shortages and other disruptions. These supply chain disruptions filtered through the construction industry and delayed progress on the vast majority of projects.

The construction industry was also affected by the mandates imposed by Federal, State and Local Governments within the United States. Many of the regulations and guidance issued by government entities in the United States came from the individual Counties within each State. There were overarching federal mandates combined with state mandates, but the institution of applicable rules by and large was determined by the local Counties and Cities. Some Counties adopted regulations that prohibited all construction work, whereas many others viewed certain types of construction as indispensable activities and allowed that particular work to progress provided adequate safety measures were employed. Other Counties drew distinctions between construction projects on essential facilities as opposed to those on facilities deemed nonessential. For instance, a number of Counties and Municipalities throughout the United States allowed construction to progress on transportation projects, hospitals, power distribution and generation facilities and water treatment facilities, while at the same time not allowing construction to progress on residential remodel projects or new residential or commercial construction.

Initially, the varying mandates from the varying Counties and Municipalities created much confusion throughout the industry. Ultimately, the construction industry was one of the first industries to allow all work to resume provided adequate safety measures were employed. This in turn had the effect of allowing major construction projects to move forward and provided some stability to those in the construction industry.

Once construction activities were allowed to resume, the safety measures employed included the wearing of face masks, provisions for adequate ventilation and adequate and reasonable distancing procedures. Many employers and projects also mandated routine testing as well as active monitoring and response programs in the event COVID-19 was discovered.

Depending on the requirements of the local jurisdiction, many employers were required to establish detailed tracking and registration programs. Additionally, protocols were implemented to mitigate the spread of COVID-19 upon the discovery of an infection. These protocols included disinfection requirements, quarantine requirements and screening requirements depending on the applicable regulations and best practices.

The Federal Government of the United States of America implemented a program of loans for businesses impacted by COVID. Many construction businesses availed themselves of the loan programs to ease the economic impacts of the pandemic. The loan programs were structured such that loans would be forgiven upon a demonstration that the money was used to offset COVID-related impacts.

11.3.2 The impact of COVID-19 on the operation of construction contracts in the United States of America

The long-term impact of the COVID-19 pandemic on the operation of construction contracts within the United States remains to be determined. The initial local mandates and regulations have by and large been repealed; however, some lingering health and safety requirements remain in place and will undoubtedly be adopted as normal work conditions going forward. Additionally, the majority of contracts entered into after the rise of the COVID-19 pandemic include provisions specifically addressing responsibility for costs associated with pandemic events. Similarly, recent contracting practices have had a greater focus on provisions related to supply chain disruption and labour shortages and inefficiencies.

Many of the issues related to contractual interpretation and responsibility for COVID-19 impacts are currently being reviewed in the various courts and forums of arbitration. Given the structure of the United States and its Federal Government, numerous State Governments and countless Local Governments, no universal legal requirements have been adopted to address COVID-19-related contracting issues. What will likely happen is that the issues will be addressed through various court proceedings and, depending on where the common law ultimately resides, such rules may then be modified by the State or Federal legislatures.

It should be noted that COVID-19 impacted the dispute resolution forums typically employed by the construction industry. For example, many of the trial courts suspended operations for civil disputes, and many arbitration proceedings were held in abeyance. Similarly, as the pandemic progressed, many State Courts and arbitration proceedings adopted mechanisms to conduct proceedings remotely and via video testimony. It is expected that the use of remote video testimony will continue to be prevalent in such proceedings.

11.4 United States of America governing law of the contract

11.4.1 Constraints on the governing law of a construction contract

In the United States, the laws typically applicable to construction contracts are the laws of the State in which the work is performed. This general rule can be modified by the parties by defining in the contract which law is to apply. Similarly, for contracts performed for the Federal Government, it is typically federal contracting law that applies as opposed to the law of any specific State. Additionally, various contractual requirements and contracting constraints may apply depending on the laws of the State and whether the contract is being performed for a public entity or a private entity. Even amongst private entities, there is the potential for statutory contracting constraints. For example, many States require contracts with residential homeowners to include certain provisions that a commercial owner contract would not.

11.4.1.1 Anti-indemnity statutes

As a general rule, parties are free to contract as they desire provided the contract does not have an illegal purpose. That said, when it comes to construction contracts, many States have statutes and laws that regulate the types of provisions that may be included. For example, indemnity provisions are common in construction contracts in the United States of America. Typically, indemnity provisions flow in favour of the upstream contracting party –the general contractor indemnifies the owner, the subcontractors indemnify the general contractor, the sub-subcontractors indemnify the subcontractors, and so on. Oftentimes these indemnities are broad and include requirements that the indemnifying party protect the indemnitee from events beyond the indemnifying party's control. Several States have enacted what are known as 'anti-indemnity statutes' aimed at preventing such broad sweeping indemnity provisions. These anti-indemnity statutes vary from State to State. Some prohibit one party from being indemnified for its sole negligence. Others prohibit parties from extending indemnity for anything but their own negligence. These constraints act to invalidate contractual indemnity provisions that violate the terms of the statute. It should also be noted that many States require that indemnity language be emphasised in the contract for it to be enforceable. Some of these States prescribe the typeface and font size required to have an enforceable indemnity agreement.

11.4.1.2 Paid-if-paid versus paid-when-paid

Another constraint on contracting addresses the obligation and timing of payment to subcontractors. The issue is often referred to as 'paid-if-paid versus paid-when-paid'. A paid-if-paid clause implies that the owner's payment of the general contractor is a condition precedent to the general contractor's obligation to pay the subcontractor. However, a paid-when-paid clause does not make payment to the subcontractor dependent upon payment from the owner but rather implies that general contractors must pay subcontractors within a reasonable time. Each State has its own laws regarding the enforcement and interpretation of paid-if-paid provisions. In many States, paid-if-paid clauses are void and unenforceable or are interpreted as paid-when-paid clauses.

11.4.1.3 No damage for delay

Oftentimes, owners insist on provisions that require the Contractors to waive their delay damages. As with many other contractual provisions, each of the 50 States has varying laws on whether such waivers of delay damages are enforceable. Many States provide that such waivers are enforceable, whereas other States hold that they are invalid as a matter of public policy. Still other States will invalidate such waivers in public contracts but allow them in the private setting.

11.4.1.4 Limitation of liability provisions

The majority of the States in the United States enforce limitation of liability provisions in contracts. Even still, some States require that such limitations be emphasised through specific typeface and font size, whereas others will evaluate whether the provision acts as an unenforceable waiver of delay damages or an unenforceable waiver of consequential damages.

11.4.1.5 Consequential damage waivers

Many States have case law that recognises the validity of consequential damage waivers. That said, a large number of States do not have law on point, and courts evaluating such waivers focus on whether or not such clauses lead to inequitable or unconscionable results.

11.4.2 Formal requirements for a construction contract

Whether there are formal requirements for a construction contract is dependent upon the law of the State that applies to the agreement. Some States require that the construction contract contain the licence number of the Contractor. Other States require that contracts for residential remodel projects provide a lump sum price for the work to be performed. Still other States require that contracts for public works projects contain specific clauses such as liquidated damage provisions or provisions for performance bonds. Generally, across the entire United States, the *Statute of Frauds* requires that contracts with performance periods exceeding one year be in writing. Additionally, when public works projects are funded by the Federal Government, either in whole or in part, contracting regulations usually require the local public entity to include various federal contracting requirements and provisions such as those related to workplace safety and prevailing wages.

11.5 What Special Provisions in the Particular Conditions are necessary for consistency with applicable laws in the United States of America?

The majority of the jurisdictions within the United States believe in the strict interpretation of contracts and in the parties' rights to contract as they please. As such, courts will typically give deference to the intent of the parties as captured by the express language of the contract. In order to analyse the need for modification to the FIDIC General Conditions through the addition of specific language in the Special Provisions, one must consider the types of situations where FIDIC contracts could conceivably be used. It is not likely that FIDIC documents would ever be used on a project constructed by the Federal Government. This is because Federal Government projects are mandated to use the *Federal Acquisition Regulations* and its contracting forms. Similarly, it is not likely that FIDIC documents would ever be used for public works projects sponsored by State or local Municipalities. Again, these public entities have statutorily defined competitive bidding requirements and have developed their own forms for use on such projects. Where FIDIC contracts could potentially be used in the United States is on projects with private owners that are not funded by State, Federal or Local Governments. As discussed herein, and with the exception of projects for residential homeowners, parties are generally free to dictate the terms of the contract in private transactions.

A review of the FIDIC General Conditions in the context of non-residential private construction indicates that very few, if any, modifications are needed or desirable. For example, the indemnity provisions provided in the FIDIC General Conditions do not run afoul of any anti-indemnity statutes. Similarly, the damage waivers and liability limits contained in the FIDIC documents are consistent with those provisions typically used within the United States. Additionally, the liquidated damage provisions of the FIDIC General Conditions are not drafted as a penalty, and therefore generally comply with the general rule throughout the United States.

However, although additional contractual provisions or modifications of the existing FIDIC provisions are not necessarily required to meet legal mandates, significant editing of the FIDIC documents would be needed for them to conform to the language and terms typically used within the construction industry of the United States. This topic is discussed in the next section.

11.5.1 FIDIC General Conditions are incompatible or inconsistent with the United States of America governing law of the contract

The FIDIC documents are rarely if ever used in the United States. As a general proposition, there is no specific term in the FIDIC General Conditions that would offend the common law as it relates to contracting practices within the United States. Similarly, it would be difficult to find any specific provision of the FIDIC General Conditions that is inconsistent with any statutory requirements in the various States as they would relate to private non-residential construction contracting.

The primary incompatibility between the FIDIC General Conditions and the contracting practices within the United States of America is found in the form of the English language and terms used in the FIDIC documents. The FIDIC General Conditions adopt a form of the English language and terms that are used within the United Kingdom and the Commonwealth countries, whereas construction contracts in the United States of America are based almost exclusively on the form of English used in the United States of America.

This distinction renders the adoption of the FIDIC General Conditions within the United States of America very difficult. Examples of language differences are found throughout the FIDIC documents.

In the United States, the entity that owns the project and hires the general contractor is referred to as the 'Owner'. In the FIDIC documents, this entity is referred to as the 'Employer'. In the United States, an employer is one that hires employees, not one that hires general contractors.

Similarly, in the United States the term 'Schedule' or 'Project Schedule' is used to refer to the document that defines the timing and sequencing of the construction of the project. The FIDIC documents use the word 'Programme', which is a spelling of the word that does not exist in American English.

In the United States the term 'Change Order' is used to increase or decrease the scope of work. FIDIC uses the term 'Variation'. The FIDIC documents use the word 'Tender' to refer to the American term 'bid'.

The documents contain many other instances of inconsistencies between the terms used in the United States and those used in the FIDIC General Conditions. The extent of these differences is not trivial and, were such documents to be used in the construction industry of the United States, they would undoubtedly lead to confusion, misinterpretations and ambiguities.

Those building the project would need to abandon terms they had used their entire careers in exchange for new and confusing language. Similarly, courts and arbitral tribunals would first need to reconcile the differences in terminology and language before fully understanding the complexities of the actual dispute. For the FIDIC General Conditions to be effective documents in the American construction industry, their terms and definitions would need to be reconciled with common American usage.

11.6 Applicable legislation if the law of the United States of America governs the contract

As discussed, in the United States the law typically applicable to construction contracts is that of the State in which the project is located, unless the parties agree otherwise. As also discussed, there is great variety between the States as to certain aspects of construction contracting such as licensing, competitive bidding and public procurement. There are also variances between the States with respect to how their courts have applied common law principles. Notwithstanding these variances, efforts have been made to document the common themes and similarities among the laws of the various States. The *Second Restatement of Contracts* is a good example of this type of effort. Although the *Second Restatement* is not applicable to any one State, it provides a useful reference to practitioners who seek to gain a general understanding of the principles behind contract law in the United States.

Additionally, efforts have been made by legal scholars, through the Uniform Law Commission, to develop *Uniform Acts* applying to most bodies of law. In many instances States have adopted the *Uniform Acts* as their legislation which leads to the harmonisation of certain principles across the majority of jurisdictions. By way of example, the *Uniform Commercial Code* defines a set of uniform standards to apply to transactions related to the sale of goods. Additionally, the *Uniform Arbitration Act* provides guidelines specific to arbitration proceedings that can be adopted by the States. Practitioners are advised to not follow any specific *Uniform Act* or *Restatement*, but to review the laws of the State holding jurisdiction. Even still, the *Uniform Acts* and the *Restatements* are useful resources for those attempting to understand the general legal framework of the United States.

Notwithstanding the fact that applicable law varies from State to State, for contracts and projects that touch the United States, there are a number of broad federal rules and laws that may be applicable.

One such set of laws is commonly referred to as the *Foreign Corrupt Practices Act* or the ***FCPA***. The *FCPA* prohibits any business or individual with connections to the United States from acting to corruptly influence a foreign official. Although not focused on domestic corruption, those involved in international construction who have connections to the United States need to be aware of the prohibitions of the *FCPA*. Put simply, the *FCPA* prohibits the granting of anything of value to officials of a foreign government in exchange for preferential treatment.

Another set of federal laws that is applicable to government contracting is the *False Claims Act*. The *False Claims Act* prohibits individuals and businesses from overcharging government entities. A party that knowingly overcharges the Federal Government in an open negotiation, or submits false pricing information or false pricing support, risks violating the *Act*. This applies whether the project is located within the United Sates or internationally. The *Act* contains several civil penalties and also provides for the potential of criminal exposure. In general, the *Act* prescribes fines for each violation but also allows for the recovery of treble damages. Treble damages are equal to three times the amount of the damage caused to the Government by the false representation. It should be noted that the federal *False Claims Act* applies to all contracts that are funded through federal sources. In addition to the *Federal False Claims Act*, many States and larger Municipalities have also enacted false claims laws which function in the same manner as the Federal *Act*.

11.7 Applicable legislation if the Site is in the United States of America

There are also specific laws that may apply if the Site of the project is physically located within the United States. The general rule applies, which is that the law of the State is the law that governs the contract unless the parties agree otherwise. That said, there are instances where the law of the State of the project location supersedes any agreement to the contrary.

One such instance is found with respect to the law of mechanics liens. Throughout the United States, those who contribute labour or materials to a work of improvement are entitled to place a lien on the property if they are not paid. The rules applicable to such liens vary from State to State. In some States, the right to a lien is constitutionally protected;

in other States, the right to a lien is a function of statute. In some States, the right to a lien cannot be waived, and in others, it can. Typically, enforcement of such a lien is accomplished through an action to foreclose upon the property. These actions must necessarily be brought in the local courts and are typically not subject to arbitration. Each jurisdiction has its own requirements regarding the form of the lien and what is necessary to perfect the lien in order to maintain a foreclosure action. Such laws apply to the Site irrespective of any agreement to the contrary.

Additionally, there are many other laws and regulations that apply to a project based on the State in which the project is located. These include workplace safety regulations, such as State OSHA requirements, prevailing wage requirements for government projects, state and local environmental and air quality regulations, business license requirements, labour practices and laws related to the protection of civil rights.

11.8 Applicable legislation if the 'seat' of the dispute determination is the United States of America

If the seat of an arbitration is defined to be within the United States, the arbitration will either be subject to the provisions of the *Federal Arbitration Act* or the arbitration legislation adopted by the State in which the seat is located. In the United States, parties are generally free to determine the seat of the arbitration through contractual agreement. The statutes governing arbitration vary from State to State. A majority of States have adopted modified versions of the *Uniform Arbitration Act* or the *Revised Uniform Arbitration Act*, which are based in part upon language from the ***UNCITRAL Model Law*** and the *New York Convention*. Those States that have not adopted the *Uniform Act* have adopted similar legislation.

Parties to arbitration provisions should be aware of the applicable legislation prior to defining the seat of the arbitration. This is important because some States have requirements that impact the selection of counsel and enforceability. For example, some States require parties arbitrating within their borders to retain counsel licensed by its State, whereas other States do not require an association with local counsel.

In determining the seat of the arbitration, parties are also advised to review statutory limitation periods and periods of repose applicable to the State. Limitation periods vary from State to State as do periods of repose. For example, some States require that actions on written contracts be brought within four years of the breach of that contract, whereas other States have enacted a six-year limitation period for breaches of written contracts. Similarly, many States have varying limitation periods with respect to breaches of warranties and other typical claims for relief in construction disputes. With respect to construction defects, some States impose a ten-year outside limit for latent defects and a four-year period for patent defects. Still other States have a shortened limitation period for actions arising from professional negligence.

11.9 Issues that a court or arbitrator may construe differently than expected from the words of the Contract because of local law or custom

As discussed earlier, were the FIDIC documents to be used in the United States, they would most likely be used in the private contracting setting. As also discussed, courts will typically give deference to the intent of the parties as expressed in the language of the contract. Provided the language and terminology incompatibilities were rectified, there are very few provisions within the FIDIC General Conditions that a typical construction arbitrator or court would construe differently than written. However, there are a few overarching concepts throughout the American legal system that could impact the interpretation of the standard FIDIC language.

For example, the vast majority of the jurisdictions within the United States imply a covenant of good faith and fair dealing in all contractual relationships. To the extent a party to a construction contract breached this implied covenant of good faith and fair dealing, a court or arbitrator may be inclined to address the breach through an unanticipated interpretation of the FIDIC language.

Similarly, the courts of the United States tend to avoid forfeitures based on technicalities. To the extent there are deadlines within the FIDIC General Conditions that result in a waiver or forfeiture of claims if not met, there is a possibility that a court or arbitral tribunal would find a way to avoid such forfeiture by finding substantial compliance with the notice requirements or by ignoring the requirements as an inequitable.

Also, with regard to liquidated damages, the general rule in the United States is that contractual penalties are not enforceable. For a liquidated damage provision to be enforced, it must represent a reasonable estimate of the damage to be incurred. To the extent liquidated damage is excessive and does not reflect the actual damage, a court or arbitral tribunal may be inclined to find the liquidated damage to be an unenforceable penalty.

CHAPTER 12

Applying FIDIC Contracts in Uruguay

Dr José Luis Echevarría Petit

CONTENTS

12.1	Outline of Uruguay's legal environment		277
	12.1.1	General information	277
	12.1.2	The constitutional structure of Uruguay	277
	12.1.3	The legal system in Uruguay	278
		12.1.3.1 Free movement	278
		12.1.3.2 Foreign investment protection treaties	278
		12.1.3.3 Inter-American Anti-Corruption Convention	278
	12.1.4	The court system in Uruguay	279
12.2	The construction industry in Uruguay		279
	12.2.1	Overview	279
	12.2.2	Structure	280
	12.2.3	Contractors, formal aspects	280
	12.2.4	Subcontracting	280
	12.2.5	Registration	281
	12.2.6	Labour relations	282
		12.2.6.1 Construction workforce	282
		12.2.6.2 Other employees	282
	12.2.7	Safety	283
	12.2.8	Modular construction	283
	12.2.9	Innovation and BIM	283
	12.2.10	Public procurement	284
		12.2.10.1 Procurement regulation	284
		12.2.10.2 General procurement principles	284
	12.2.11	Public procurement process	285
		12.2.11.1 Procurement processes set out by TOCAF	285
		12.2.11.2 E-procurement	286
		12.2.11.3 Preferences for local products and services	286
	12.2.12	Best practices regarding procurement	286
		12.2.12.1 Public access	286
		12.2.12.2 Centralisation and standardisation	287
	12.2.13	Challenge of decisions made during the procurement process	287

DOI: 10.4324/9781003201250-12

12.2.14 Insurance 287
12.2.14.1 Accident and occupational sickness 287
12.2.14.2 Construction all risks 288
12.2.14.3 Civil liability insurance 288
12.2.14.4 Other bonds 288
12.2.15 Common forms of contract 288
12.2.16 Dispute resolution 288
12.2.16.1 Arbitration in Uruguay 289
12.2.16.2 Main reasons for the adoption of arbitration as ADR 290
12.2.17 Current challenges 290
12.2.18 Unique features of the construction industry in Uruguay 290
12.3 The impact of COVID-19 in Uruguay 291
12.3.1 The impact of COVID-19 on the execution of construction projects Uruguay 291
12.3.2 The impact of COVID-19 on the operation of construction contracts in Uruguay 291
12.4 Uruguyan governing law of the contract 292
12.4.1 Constraints on the governing law of a construction contract 292
12.4.2 Formal requirements for a construction contract 292
12.5 What Special Provisions in the Particular Conditions are necessary for consistency with applicable laws in Uruguay? 293
12.5.1 FIDIC General Conditions are incompatible or inconsistent with Uruguyan governing law of the contract 293
12.5.1.1 Liability of the Contractor 293
12.5.1.2 Termination due to insolvency 293
12.5.1.3 Summary 293
12.5.2 FIDIC General Conditions are incompatible or inconsistent with the law of the Site/Country 293
12.5.3 FIDIC General Conditions are incompatible or inconsistent with the relevant laws on dispute determination in Uruguay 294
12.6 What Special Provisions in the Particular Conditions are desirable for consistency with applicable laws in Uruguay? 294
12.6.1 Damages 294
12.6.2 Other provisions 295
12.7 Summary of applicable legislation for Uruguyan governing law of the contract 295
12.7.1 Entry into a construction contract 295
12.7.2 Operation of a construction contract 295
12.7.3 Termination of a construction contract 295
12.7.4 Dispute resolution 296
12.8 Summary of applicable legislation if the Site/Country is in Uruguay 296
12.8.1 Operation of a construction contract 296
12.8.2 Termination of a construction contract 297
12.8.3 Dispute resolution 297

12.9 Applicable legislation if the 'seat' of the dispute determination is Uruguay 297
12.9.1 Arbitration regulation 297
12.9.1.1 Matters that can be solved by arbitration 297
12.9.1.2 Recognition of arbitral awards 298
12.9.1.3 The arbitration clause 298
12.9.1.4 Arbitral commitment 298
12.9.1.5 Freedom to choose the tribunal 299
12.9.1.6 Kompetenz Kompetenz 299
12.9.1.7 Freedom of arbitral procedure 299
12.9.1.8 Default procedure 299
12.9.1.9 Chamber of Commerce Arbitration Court procedure 299
12.9.1.10 Award 300
12.9.1.11 Challenges to the arbitral award 300
12.9.1.12 Award enforcement 300
12.9.2 Investment protection arbitration 301
12.9.3 Enforcement of international arbitral awards 301
12.9.4 Other alternative dispute resolution methods 302
12.9.4.1 Conciliation 302
12.9.4.2 Mediation 302
12.9.4.3 Dispute Boards 303
12.9.4.4 Expert determination 303
12.10 Summary of applicable legislation if the 'seat' of the dispute determination is Uruguay 303
12.11 Issues that a court or arbitrator may construe differently than expected from the words of the Contract because of local law or custom 303
12.12 Additional references for Uruguay 304
12.12.1 Legislation 304
12.12.2 Court decisions 304

12.1 Outline of Uruguay's legal environment

12.1.1 General information

Uruguay is located between the Uruguay River, the River Plate and the Atlantic Ocean and has 500 km of coastline. Its neighbouring countries are Brazil to the north and north-east and Argentina to the west across the Uruguay River and the River Plate. Its total area is 177,000 square km and it has a population of just over 3.3 million people. Uruguay's GDP is approximately 50 billion US dollars.

Uruguay is a founder of the economic and trade bloc **Mercosur** together with Argentina, Brazil and Paraguay, with around 295 million inhabitants.

The new Government that took office in 2020 has been very active in procuring the waiver of the other Mercosur partners to undertake commercial agreements with third parties, with strong opposition by Argentina and at times a shy nod from Brazil.

12.1.2 The constitutional structure of Uruguay

Uruguay is a unitary Republic and has a *Constitution* that can only be modified after a national and obligatory public consultation. Uruguay's first *Constitution* was approved in 1830, and the last modification was passed and voted on in 1997.

The Country is a Republic, with an elected President who appoints all Ministers, forming the executive power, legislative power and judicial power.

Legislative power is formed by two chambers: Representatives, with 99 members, and Senators, with 31 members. The elected Vice President is the president of the Chamber of Senators. All members are elected by obligatory vote. Senators are elected nationwide and Representatives by the 19 local districts called ***Departamentos***.

The judicial power is presided over by a Supreme Court of Justice with five members, and below this Supreme Court, there are Appeal Courts for different matters (civil, labour, family, criminal, etc.). The third-, fourth- and fifth-level authorities are individual judges of the different matters.

Besides those three powers, there are three other institutions that are independent, and these are the Administrative Tribunal (competent for confirming or declaring the nullity of administrative decisions when challenged), the Accounting Tribunal (competent to declare the rightfulness of all expenditures of the State) and the Electoral Court (that has competence on all electoral matters).

Besides the organisation of the State, the *Constitution* has broad recognition and protection of human rights.

There are basically two levels of government: Central Government and Local Government.

Local districts are called *Departamentos* and are governed by an executive elected authority called ***Intendente*** and a legislative body called ***Junta Departamental***. There is also a third level of government in certain cities, called ***Alcaldes***.

The country is formed of 19 *Departamentos*, one of which is Montevideo, in which the capital of the country is located. Even though these *Departamentos* are not Provinces or States as in federal countries, they have their own legislative and executive powers within the limits of their territory.

Besides this 'political territorial decentralisation', there is also service provision decentralisation, in the form of national utilities that provide electric power, clean water, petroleum, telecommunication services and so on.

As part of public policy in the early nineteenth century, many state-owned corporations were created to provide certain services to the population. These public Companies of the State became very important players within the market as they were granted monopolies.

12.1.3 The legal system in Uruguay

Uruguay's legal framework is a civil law one, with Roman law roots, and a *Civil Code* with remote origins in the Napoleonic *Civil Code*.

First-level rules are stated in the *Constitution*. The *Constitution* and all modifications to it have to be approved by the Parliament and ratified by a national election in which voting (in favour of or against the modification) is obligatory for all citizens over 18 years old.

Second-level rules are laws passed by the Parliament, formed by two elected chambers: 31 Senators (one of which is the Vice President of the Republic) that are elected nationally, and 99 Representatives (called ***Diputados***) that are elected by *Departamentos*.

Executive power is exercised by the President of the Republic who appoints its Ministers. Laws are generally complemented by decrees of executive power that state all necessary details to make those laws applicable.

As noted earlier, there are 19 local territories called *Departamentos* that have an executive authority called *Intendente* and a deliberative power called *Junta Departamental*. At this local level, the *Juntas Departamentales* pass laws that are applicable in their own jurisdiction, and those local laws are complemented by local decrees (binding within their own district) of the *Intendente*.

12.1.3.1 Free movement

Uruguay has traditionally been friendly to foreign investors and has never been in default with its creditors. Capital moves freely into and out of the country and the exchange of foreign currency is free. Most of the important bid calls are international and are open to foreign companies and individuals.

The requirements regarding residence are very easy to comply with as immigration policies are flexible.

12.1.3.2 Foreign investment protection treaties

Uruguay is a signatory to several bilateral treaties to foster and protect foreign investment. It has signed treaties with a myriad of countries as discussed later.

12.1.3.3 Inter-American Anti-Corruption Convention

Another important feature of the country is its low level of corruption. This is one of the most distinctive characteristics of the country, more so if compared to other countries in South America.

Uruguay has signed and ratified the *Inter-American Convention against Corruption* signed in 1996 in Venezuela (ratified in Uruguay by *Law No 17.008* 25 September 1998). This *Convention* sets out certain requirements such as the declaration of income, assets and debts of public servants, adequate public collection procedures and anti-bribery controls. It also defines some crimes and establishes extradition procedures.

12.1.4 The court system in Uruguay

Judicial power is national and is formed by a Supreme Court of Justice with five members. At the second level, there are Appeal Courts for different matters (labour, family, civil and commercial, criminal, etc.) that sit in Montevideo (Uruguay's capital); at the third level, individual judges hear different matters sitting in Montevideo and in other cities in the rest of the country, and at the fourth level local individual judges are located throughout the country.

In addition to the judicial power, there are two constitutional courts with specialised jurisdiction: the Elections Court, that is, the court for matters regarding elections, and the Administrative Tribunal which has specific jurisdiction to confirm or declare null all administrative decisions (all decisions that are not jurisdictional holdings or laws). Both courts are independent of the judicial power but exercise jurisdictional competence.

There is no obligatory precedent for the judges, they are not bound by prior holdings of higher courts. That said, it is clear that higher courts' holdings have influence in lower courts, and Appeal Courts and the Supreme Court of Justice set the trends that are then followed by lower courts and judges.

12.2 The construction industry in Uruguay

12.2.1 Overview

The last decade was an interesting one for infrastructure in Uruguay, and everything suggests that the industry will be busy for the years to come. Public–Private Partnerships in highways, trains and schools have been successful, and there has been a very strong development of clean energy (wind, photovoltaic and biomass). Multi-billion dollar foreign direct investments have arrived in the country with two pulp plants operating, one called Montes del Plata, formed by Stora Enso and Arauco, the second by UPM and a third plant (UPM II) being constructed.

This infrastructure growth, the appearance of new foreign companies, and the participation of international and local institutional lenders have boosted the sophistication of construction contracts, construction loans and the like. Despite that growing sophistication, no standard international construction contract such as FIDIC's is being consistently used.

Before the PPP law was passed in 2011, most contracts were normal construction contracts, and no international structure or format was used to draft their clauses. In these contracts, the Employer provided the design and the private sector Contractor submitted a quotation to build the design. This was also the most common contract in public procurement.

On the other hand, economic infrastructure had the alternative to be contracted as concessions under *Law 15.637* passed on 29 September 1984. That said, projects susceptible to being contracted under concession contracts were not numerous, mainly some busy highways, airports and ports.

The PPP law in 2011 brought new life to social infrastructure. Since then, design-build, design-finance-build, design-finance-build-operate and design-finance-build-operate-maintain contracts have become more common. PPP contracts on highways, penitentiaries, rail and schools became common, and project finance by SPVs[1] became a standard form of funding such contracts.

Installation of very important industrial plants (especially cellulose pulp) and energy projects also brought new contracts: plant design-build, power purchase agreements, etc. Management contracting is currently used for big industrial projects, such as the pulp plants of Montes del Plata and UPM.

12.2.2 Structure

Most contractors in Uruguay are share corporations, and many of them are family businesses. Many contractors are small to medium in size, but there are some companies of considerable size. The biggest national company (though owned by foreign investors) has an annual turnover of US$ 275 million.

There are certain specialisations among the construction companies, and it was usual to have a clear difference between general construction companies and construction companies specialised in roads and bridges. This has been changing recently with some traditional companies venturing into new sectors of construction.

Both local and international contractors have to register in the Commercial Register, the Register of Providers of the State and the Register of Construction and Consulting Companies of the Register of the Ministry of Public Works. International companies may register themselves via a subsidiary (wholly owned Uruguayan corporation) or a branch of the same foreign juridical entity.

12.2.3 Contractors, formal aspects

Before the new development of new contracts, Contractors of public works just built given designs and were paid according to monthly work certification and an advance payment. Given that simple contracting structure, companies were not sophisticated in terms of finance, and project finance was very unusual. This scene obviously changed with the new contracts that became common within PPP, Power Purchase Agreements and concession structures.

Construction contracts can be oral (not necessarily written) according to law, though construction, concession, PPP, EPC and finance contracts are written (both public and private).

12.2.4 Subcontracting

Subcontracting part of the scope of contracts is usual, and major contractors use subcontractors to subcontract electrical, water, electronic and other works.

1 An **SPV** is a Special Purpose Venture: a company specifically formed to enter into a PPP contract with the Government to finance and manage construction and operations of a public facility.

Some contracts oblige the Contractor to inform the Employer of the name of Subcontractors and other contracts oblige the Contractor to obtain the prior consent of the Employer to subcontract.

It is absolutely clear that the liability of the Contractor to the Employer does not vary, and that subcontracting is the Contractor's responsibility. There is ample experience of foreign companies subcontracting local ones and vice versa.

Any employer that uses subcontractors, intermediaries or labour suppliers is severally liable for the labour obligations of these subcontractors towards the hired employees as well as to pay the social security payments not made by the subcontractor. This applies also to the accident insurance premiums for work and occupational disease.

This liability shall be subsidiary when the employer proves diligence and requires the subcontractor documents related to the work history statement, a certificate that evidences regular payment status of social security, a certificate from State Insurance Bank that proves the existence of the accident insurance occupational disease insurance, worksheets and paystubs.

However, the modest size of subcontractors and their lack of capital means that often, the principal Contractor ends up paying, even though it only has subsidiary liability. Much care and attention must be taken to require the relevant guarantees from Subcontractors.

12.2.5 Registration

Uruguay recognises foreign companies and permits them to work in the country. Foreign companies have to fulfil some requirements that are not complicated. Many international construction companies have contracts with the public administration and have branches in Uruguay.

Foreign construction companies have to register in Uruguay (as a branch or subsidiary), and to work with the public administration, they have to register in the National Provider's Register and the Register of Construction Companies of the Ministry of Transport and Public Works. This Register not only verifies the good standing and background of the companies but also determines the annual construction capability of the registered companies. This capability index is called **VECA**. When a construction company participates in a bid process called by any public authority, it has to show the Register's certificate stating that the amount of the contract is within the company's VECA.

Registration of foreign companies in the register of the Ministry of Public Works has two possible paths. If the project is funded by foreign loans, the foreign company registers with minimum requirements and undertakes the obligation to make a full registration if awarded the contract. If the project is funded by government funds or based on users' payments, then the registration is far more complex.

Major requirements for full registration are audited financial statements of the last three fiscal years, certificates of completion of all works included as background, the decision of the relevant body of a company to create a subsidiary or branch in the Country, appointing a representative and providing the branch or subsidiary with capital.

12.2.6 Labour relations

Construction companies typically have two kinds of labour contracts.

12.2.6.1 Construction workforce

To begin with construction workers, companies usually hire employees for the duration of a certain work or contract. This ensures that, when the construction ends, there is no obligation to pay a severance package to the employees hired for such work.

If an employee is fired during that term, the company has to pay a severance package. There is discussion regarding the amount of that severance package when there is a term agreed with the employee. One position is that the severance package is tariffed, equal to the total income of the employee in one month multiplied by the number of years working for the company with a maximum of six, and the other position is that the construction company has to pay all salaries until the end of the term.

Employees have the right to 20 working days of annual leave (counted from Monday to Saturday), an additional amount equal to the annual leave during holidays and a thirteenth salary called ***Aguinaldo***.

In the construction sector, the employer pays the salaries of the construction employees, and the owner of the property (Employer) is the one that supports social security payments, which are 77% of the amount paid by the Contractor as salaries. For this reason, quotations in response to public and private tenders expressly state that in addition to the price to be paid to the Contractor, the Employer shall have to pay a maximum amount of social security obligations. Usually, the Contract states that if the amount payable is below that maximum amount, the Employer obtains the benefit, and if payments are over the forecast maximum amount, the excess is paid by the Contractor.

These social security payments by the Employer cover annual leave, additional holiday payment and thirteenth salary, and are therefore not borne by the Contractor.

12.2.6.2 Other employees

Other employees (for instance the administrative payroll of the Contractor) are hired on indefinite term contracts and have the right to annual leave, additional holiday payment and the thirteenth salary paid by the Company.

Social security payments payable by the Company are 13.125%, but in this case, the employer must pay the annual leave, the additional holiday payment and the thirteenth salary.

Monthly salaries to be taken as a basis for the severance package includes one-twelfth of the annual leave, the additional holiday payment and the thirteenth salary.

Salaries are adjusted by salary councils which are negotiation units formed by government, employees and employers that agree on the salary increase and other aspects of the working conditions. Salary councils usually agree on a term of one or two years, and after the agreement, the increases are every six months.

Labour legal actions can be filed within a year following the day on which the working relationship was terminated.

Labour credits and benefits expire after five years, counted from the date on which they are payable.

12.2.7 Safety

Construction has a specific *Decree* regarding safety.

Safety culture is omnipresent in construction. Companies have the obligation to have a safety and health committee formed by delegates of the employees and the employer. Under Uruguayan law, whatever the provisions set forth in the Contract, all Contractors shall respect the labour laws and safety and health rules that are mainly set forth by *Decrees* of the executive power and are binding nationwide.

A law passed by the Parliament in the previous government that is questioned on the grounds of being unconstitutional and therefore invalid states the criminal liability of employers when a breach of the safety rules endangers personnel. Criminal law academics argue that 'danger crimes' are unacceptable, but in fact, when accidents happen, even if there is a huge discussion around the matter, there is a risk of being held liable under this law.

As noted earlier, social security rules regarding construction differ from those of other sectors and safety regulations in construction are set forth in a specific *Decree.*

Enforcement of safety measures has been a challenge and a very important risk for construction companies. However, the participation of specialists in labour safety and the appearance of cell phones with photographic capabilities has made it easy to detect breaches, provide evidence beyond doubt and apply proper penalties.

12.2.8 Modular construction

Modular construction via factory-fabricated components is being used increasingly.

Pre-stressed concrete, steel framing, and other types of methods such as PIR[2] panels, etc. are used in the country for housing, while many of the PPP schools and sports infrastructures use a majority of steel components.

Pre-stressed steel is also used in some important infrastructures such as the new rail and road access to the Port of Montevideo, highway bridges, etc.

12.2.9 Innovation and BIM

Incorporation of new types of contracts and especially the evolution of project finance in construction projects has resulted in an increase in the use of technology and innovation. Public–Private Partnerships, with the obligation of long-term maintenance and operation have fostered innovation at all levels.

In a recent visit to many of the PPP projects made by the author as the sole member of the Surveillance Committee of three infrastructure funds managed by CAF Asset Management, it was made clear that traditional construction thinking was put to the test by this new procurement system and has determined the interest of the companies in searching for technologies to save interventions that cost time and money.

Innovation in the construction of schools, technological centres and sports facilities is very clear and apparent, and results in a huge impact on small communities that now have access to top-notch infrastructure.

In less sophisticated sectors, such as brownfield highway construction, innovation found its way as a means of avoiding frequent interventions in repair and maintenance.

2 Polyisocyanurate – a thermoset plastic, closed cell rigid insulation with great thermal efficiency.

During the said visit, construction companies had the opportunity to show how the obligation to operate and maintain the infrastructure led them to acquire new technology that improves the quality and avoids common pitfalls of traditional construction.

On the other hand, sectors with old and ageing infrastructure such as railways are being built with cutting-edge technology sleepers, top technical rail welding technology and installation.

That said, the 2020 poll on Building Information Modelling (BIM) showed that Uruguayan companies are not perceiving BIM as necessary or positive. We will see the evolution of this technology in the years to come.

12.2.10 Public procurement

12.2.10.1 Procurement regulation

Public procurement is ruled by a number of laws passed by Parliament that were condensed and organised by a *Decree* of the executive power to create a 'refunded text'. It is important to point out that all those rules regarding public procurement are passed by law notwithstanding being included in a refunded text because laws are far more stable and not subject to unforeseeable changes by the executive power. That 'refunded text' (*texto ordenado* in Spanish) contains (besides the accounting rules) the ones referring to procurement processes. This refunded text is called ***TOCAF*** (*Texto Ordenado de Contabilidad y Administración Financiera*).

The laws contained in the refunded text go back to the 1990 decade in which the government of the day set a general strategy to diminish bureaucracy, facilitate the application of the law and assure its consistency. Unfortunately, three subsequent five-year terms of left-wing bureaucratic governments regressed a long way back in that sense, until a liberal coalition took office at the beginning of 2020, with the intention of reviving the strategy.

Despite the fact that the debate as to whether the administration should be allowed to contract directly had long been resolved, the left-wing governments stated numerous exceptions to the principle that makes it obligatory for public administrations to procure by means of public bid procedures.

The new law passed by the liberal coalition reduces the exceptions to public bids or other competitive processes (such as auctions, multiple award frame contracts and others) but does not apply the restriction principles to all entities using public money (leaving outside of this obligation private law state-owned corporations and public trusts). According to that general 'restriction principle', Central and Local Governments and all state-owned companies must procure contracts using public bids (with some exceptions). Even though the procurement process used by default is called a ***Licitación Pública*** or public bid, there are certain cases in which less complicated processes set by law can be used.

12.2.10.2 General procurement principles

Procurement is a sequence of events that take place in order to take an administrative decision.[3]

The reason for a particularly complex procurement process resides in the important amounts of taxpayers' money involved in procurement, and the risk of corruption.

3 Juan Pablo Cajarville, *Administrative Law* (FCU, 2007) 142.

Uruguay is ranked at first level in Latin America for its very low corruption, and the carefully designed procurement policy partly explains such success.

The procurement process in Uruguay has two main objectives that are close but not the same: the first is to determine the best offer among the different bidders' proposals, and the second is to award the contract to the winning bidder. This process is carried out by the administrative authorities of the different levels of government and by the state-owned corporations. As a result of this 'administrative nature', procurement is ruled by some general principles applicable to all administrative processes and by some specific principles only applicable to procurement processes.

The general principles have different origins, some set by written rules (constitutional, legal or administrative) and some considered inherent to humankind or derived from the republican organisation of the State. These last ones are recognised by the Uruguayan *Constitution*. They are not created by written rule, but instead are deemed pre-existing, showing the clear jus-naturalist inspiration of our legal system.

The most important general principles, applicable to any administrative process are:

- Rule of law
- Impartial and equal treatment
- Due process
- Good faith, and
- Motivation of administrative decisions

In particular, the most important principles that rule all procurement processes are:

- Equal treatment
- Strict application of the terms of reference, and
- Competition

Due to the principle of competition, direct contracting is an exception to the general rule of public bids, even though, as explained later, there are many exceptions to that rule.

12.2.11 Public procurement process

12.2.11.1 Procurement processes set out by TOCAF

The procurement processes are explicitly defined and described by law:

- Public bid
- Abbreviated bid
- Multiple award frame contracts
- Direct contracting, and
- Auction

All the exceptions to the public bid rule set out in Article 33 of *TOCAF* allow the competent authority to contract directly or use any other procedure that it may consider convenient, so some special procedures can be followed under these exceptions. There are also some special procedures created for the procurement of official vehicles or medicines and food. A special law refers to private initiatives for infrastructure.

12.2.11.2 E-procurement

The first law regarding the legal value of electronic documents was passed in 1988. This *Law No 16.002* (25 November 1988) gave full legal status to all documents transmitted electronically between state agencies. Following this Law, *Decree 500/991* (27 September 1991) which regulates administrative procedure, stated in Article 14 that, to facilitate the transparency of information, the administration would link all its IT equipment to allow individuals to access any information held on databases.

In 1998 Parliament passed *Law 16.736*. This law stated that any administrative procedure or activity performed electronically had the same legal value as those performed traditionally. Also in 1998, the executive power issued *Decree 65/998* (10 March 1998) that regulates electronic administrative procedure. New legislation and decrees have been passed since then, and the current ones in operation are *Law No 18.600* passed on (21 September 2009) and its *Decree No 276/2013* (9 September 2013). E-procurement must comply with the e-procedure rules and obviously, all substantial rules of *TOCAF* regarding procurement.

All procurement processes referred to in this chapter can be performed by electronic means and in fact, many state agencies and state-owned corporations are following e-procurement processes. One of the first state agencies to use e-procurement was the Electric Energy state-owned corporation in 1994.

12.2.11.3 Preferences for local products and services

Local products and services (and the ones from Mercosur countries) have preference over foreign products of the same nature and quality with a margin set out by law. The preference is 8%. Those preferences have to be clearly detailed in the different bids.

To be considered, the product must have a certificate of origin issued by the Chamber of Industries. According to Mercosur Agreement, the preference applies to any products with a certificate of origin issued by any country within the block.

12.2.12 Best practices regarding procurement

12.2.12.1 Public access

Some practices promote full public access to information on how procurement is being managed by the government, contributing to transparency and fair competition. One of the developments in this sense is the creation of the website www.comprasestatales.gub.uy. This website has links to the centralised procurement units (food and medicines) and contains all relevant legislation, manuals, information on courses and workshops and information on all procurement calls including statistics.

Any procurement process, either public bid, short bid, auction or direct contracting, must be posted to make it public. All awards must be posted on the website. There is a browser to search by type of call, date and calling agency.

With this information, some relevant questions can be answered:

- Which procurement processes are taking place?
- Is the government using the correct procedure?

- Is the state buying at competitive prices?
- Which providers were awarded, and why?
- What are the different agencies buying and how much are they spending?

Besides this information, standard terms of reference for the procurement of goods, services and works are currently under preparation and will soon be available on the website. The website is intended to be a tool for both the public and private sectors to facilitate procurement.

12.2.12.2 Centralisation and standardisation

Centralisation and standardisation are proving to be best practices for procurement. Uruguay has standardised terms of reference in the past, and some new standard terms of reference that are applicable to certain contracts are currently in the pipeline.

Centralisation is also on the increase. A general procurement agency was implemented as a result of the budget execution law passed in October 2008 and though it changed names, remains the centralising agency for some areas of procurement. This agency, now called the Regulatory Agency on Procurement (ARCE for its name in Spanish) is part of the Presidency of the Republic. Its main objective is to centralise areas of procurement of goods and services for all state agencies, thus taking advantage of the huge weight of the State to obtain better contracting conditions.

The agency has organised and managed a general database of contractors and suppliers and an electronic payment system; issued catalogues; disclosed prices of products purchased by the government; provided training in procurement to different agencies; and issued quality assessments on products and services.

12.2.13 Challenge of decisions made during the procurement process

According to the *Constitution*, administrative decisions can be challenged before the administration by means of administrative challenges called ***recursos administrativos***, and if the final decision of the administration is still considered illegal, it can be challenged before Administrative Court by a legal action called an ***Acción de Nulidad*** or nullity action.

There is no need to give a bond or warranty to file an administrative claim or legal action, as is necessary in some other countries.

Challenges have no suspensive effect, except for the ones against decisions taken within procurement procedures; these suspend the process until the decision of the challenges or a decision to waive the suspensive effects under the responsibility of the resolving authority.

12.2.14 Insurance

12.2.14.1 Accident and occupational sickness

The only compulsory insurance set by law refers to the coverage of employees' occupational sicknesses and labour accidents. This insurance is under the monopoly of the State Insurance Bank and is part of the obligatory social security payments made by the owner of the property where the construction is taking place.

When an employee suffers an accident or professional sickness and is insured by the employer, there is no liability for the latter, as long as there is no gross negligence or wilful conduct.

12.2.14.2 Construction all risks

Another typical insurance policy in construction is the construction all risks (CAR).

The *Civil Code* states that when the Contractor provides work and supplies, it also bears the risk of destruction of the Works until preliminary acceptance by the contracting party, the time when the infrastructure is passed to the owner.

12.2.14.3 Civil liability insurance

In most construction contracts, civil liability coverage is also requested. This insurance covers all claims of third parties based on the civil liability of the Contractor, and, in most cases, the insurance covers legal advice for the Contractor in such claims. Civil liability insurance does not cover claims for damage caused by vehicles or machinery of the Contractor; this is usually covered by specific insurance policies.

12.2.14.4 Other bonds

As elsewhere, bid bonds that assure the maintenance of the offer during the required term are obligatory in most public tenders, and performance bonds are also very common in the sector.

The issuance of performance bonds is standard. They are usually issued for 5% of the contract price. These bonds are usually issued by the State Insurance Bank for most local small to mid-size contracts, though in many cases a first-demand bank guarantee is required.

In addition, bonds that cover the advance payments are also an everyday requirement in construction.

12.2.15 Common forms of contract

The most common contracts in Uruguay are simple construction contracts, with advance payments and design provided by the Employer. Many of them are based on a turnkey model.

Besides this common type of contract, there are many projects that use a design-build model, thus assigning the design risk to the Contractor.

PPP and concession models are also used for specific projects, in which the infrastructure is associated with a certain usage charge (economic infrastructure). These models are generally used for important projects and are usually funded by project finance.

On the other hand, industrial plant turnkey projects were used for the installation of pulp plants of Stora Enso, and for both plants of UPM, one of which is currently being constructed.

12.2.16 Dispute resolution

Uruguay a few years passed ago a law on international commercial arbitration that mainly follows the *UNCITRAL Model Law*. That international commercial arbitration law does not apply to domestic arbitration, which is ruled by the *General Procedure Code*.

The construction sector is in dire need of flexible and agile dispute avoidance and resolution methods to solve differences between developers, contractors and subcontractors. No alternative dispute avoidance or resolution method is banned in Uruguay, so they are all applicable to a wide range of matters and they are used in construction contracts.

It should also be noted that arbitration is included as the binding method for dispute resolution under the new *Public–Private Partnerships Law* passed in 2011 and its regulatory *Decree* approved in 2012. Even after years of performance, fortunately, no PPP contract has needed arbitration to solve disputes, though this may change in the future.

12.2.16.1 Arbitration in Uruguay

The Uruguayan *General Procedure Code* has a specific chapter regarding arbitration, which states the freedom to choose arbitration for all matters that are disposable for individuals and not forbidden by law. There are very few matters that fall outside of this freedom to choose arbitration, and those are mostly criminal and family law matters. Arbitral awards can only be challenged for nullity on four specific grounds, as will be described, giving arbitration a great deal of stability and certainty. Arbitration can be institutional or *ad hoc*, either based on law or on equity.

Arbitration is not a new phenomenon in Uruguay as it was the necessary dispute resolution method for matters related to corporations in the *Commercial Code*, a rule that was binding for many decades. For more than a hundred years, all aspects referred to commercial corporations had to be solved by means of arbitration, becoming a widely used alternative dispute resolution method in Uruguay. This obligation to go to arbitration to solve corporate matters was derogated and corporate disputes are mainly solved by the State judges and courts.

Uruguayan tradition in favour of arbitration is longstanding, and made its way to the *Constitution*, which in Article 6 states: 'In the international treaties that the Republic signs, it will propose that all difference that may arise between the parties shall be decided by arbitration of other pacific means'.

Uruguay has ratified a list of important treaties and conventions regarding arbitration and this tendency was fortified in recent years with the growth of direct foreign investment. Foreign investment meant a new boost for arbitration as the main alternative dispute resolution method. As noted earlier, the treaties signed by Uruguay with many countries worldwide set arbitration for dispute resolution between the nationals of those countries and the Uruguayan State.

Furthermore, the *Industrial Promotion Law* passed by Parliament in 1998 states that any dispute arising from the application or interpretation of the law between a foreign investor and the Uruguayan State can be submitted to arbitration based on law. This shows a clear and wide acceptance of arbitration, but also a clear decision of the Uruguayan State to take part in arbitration in certain disputes with individuals, giving national and foreign individuals more certainty of fair and equal treatment, which is very important in public infrastructure. In fact, many public construction contracts contain arbitration clauses, with all the advantages that this method has against the traditional jurisdictional suits against the Administration.

The Uruguayan Chamber of Commerce has organised a Court of Arbitration and has a wide list of arbitrators (that the author is part of), some of whom were appointed by the chambers of different industries, thus giving the parties the chance to appoint specialised arbitrators suggested by the different chambers. Under the rules of the Chamber, each party appoints an arbitrator (these can be part of the list or not), and both arbitrators appointed by the parties appoint the President of the Tribunal from the list of arbitrators of the Court. If no agreement is met, the arbitrator is nominated by a State court.

12.2.16.2 Main reasons for the adoption of arbitration as ADR

The use of arbitration is growing worldwide due to several factors, and Uruguay has been part of this trend. One of the main reasons for arbitration being a preferred dispute resolution method is the lack of a specialised jurisdiction for certain sectors.

This is the case in construction. Despite being a civil law matter, construction has its own special features and uses that should be considered while discussing and deciding disputes arising among the parties to a contract. Multiple technical aspects have important incidence in construction disputes, many of them not familiar to civil judges.

Another important reason for arbitration is the agility of the process, due to its final and not appealable decision, in addition to the capability of the parties to choose a short procedure, taking less time to arrive at the final arbitral award.

An important advantage of arbitration is that parties are able to decide by mutual agreement the term within which the award shall be issued. This gives parties the key to short and agile procedures.

Confidentiality is another feature that has been very much appreciated by disputing parties to construction contracts. This factor is very important in Uruguayan institutional arbitration, and the Chamber of Commerce Arbitration Court has very strict confidentiality clauses in its arbitration rules. Section VI of such rules contains Articles 46 to 49 that provide for confidentiality about the existence of the arbitration, the information disclosed during arbitration, the award, etc.

As noted, arbitration is increasingly being used by Uruguayan construction parties to solve their differences and disputes.

12.2.17 Current challenges

One of the main challenges for arbitration is that the cost of state justice is very low, compared to the cost of an arbitral process.

Another challenge that was addressed by the Directive Council of the Arbitration Court of the Chamber of Commerce is the foreseeability of the costs. This is a very important issue, key for the lawyers who draft the contract and suggest the dispute resolution method to the client.

The author, as a member of the Board of the Centre of Arbitration of the Chamber of Commerce, an arbitrator and an arbitration lawyer, has raised this issue, which is currently being addressed by the creation of a 'cost calculator' for the Centre's website.

12.2.18 Unique features of the construction industry in Uruguay

The construction industry in Uruguay was, until recent years, mainly formed by small to medium family businesses and many international companies that compete with them. The introduction of more complex contracts that need a project finance approach has sophisticated the companies and improved their corporate governance, attracting outside investors to participate in their capital. That said, as these more complex financial and construction arrangements are quite recent, the growth process is now taking place and will probably gain pace in the future years.

There are some preferences for local production that are stated by law. This preference is extended to Mercosur products. Local products are the ones that have at least 30% of national components that mean a change in the Import Tariff Nomenclature (**Nadi** for the name in Spanish: *Nomenclatura Arancelaria de Importación*) position.

As projects increase their size and complexity, with projects ranging from energy projects to Public–Private Partnerships, companies are on a steep learning curve, becoming more technically and financially sophisticated and entering into joint ventures that also help to professionalise management and corporate governance.

12.3 The impact of COVID-19 in Uruguay

12.3.1 The impact of COVID-19 on the execution of construction projects Uruguay

The COVID-19 pandemic, with its different waves, had a strong impact in Uruguay as it happened worldwide, but the Government focused on minimising the economic impact. This approach was known as 'responsible freedom', thus not applying a lockdown to all activities as was applied in other countries, such as Argentina.

Of course, it had multiple consequences. One of the most visible ones was the implementation of the 'home office' where this mode was feasible, which is not the case in construction.

In the case of the construction sector, the Government called the Construction Union and the Construction Chamber to discuss a protocol for the recommencement of activities that were only paralysed for one month. These parties entered into an agreement to restart construction activity by 13 April 2020, with a very strict health protocol including:

- Minimum distance (1 metre) between workers
- Use of masks
- Sanitary measures (disinfection) of changing rooms
- Rules for eating rooms
- COVID outbreak early alarms
- Transportation measures (disinfection, masks, number of users, etc.)

The protocol proved to be very solid and permitted continuous activity during the pandemic. As the policy avoided lockdown, the protocol was effective and the vaccination was very fast, the pandemic had very little impact on construction contracts. It affected the procurement of foreign materials, but in most cases, did not affect the critical path.

12.3.2 The impact of COVID-19 on the operation of construction contracts in Uruguay

As the impact of COVID-19 was mitigated by the measures described earlier, no general rule such as a law or *Decree* was passed regarding the operation of construction contracts in Uruguay.

As the situation was absolutely general and of public knowledge and in some cases made impossible the performance as agreed in the Contract, if the parties did not agree on a way to prevent a conflict, the judges would determine whether it was a case of *force majeure* or not. As discussed earlier, Uruguay is a civil law country, and *force majeure* is abstractly defined, so the judges are the competent authority to determine in each particular case whether *force majeure* (or even hardship) has happened and if the obligated party is totally or partially unable to perform as agreed.

Submitting such cases to arbitration or state jurisdiction would have resulted in worse consequences for all parties in terms of costs, time and effort than entering into a negotiation and settling the difference.

Another relevant aspect was that the consequences of the pandemic were rapidly mitigated by the agreement between the Government, the construction companies and the unions, so delays were not so important.

Due to the foregoing, the general solution was that the parties of construction contracts negotiated for themselves how to mitigate the consequences.

12.4 Uruguyan governing law of the contract

12.4.1 Constraints on the governing law of a construction contract

Election of the applicable law in Uruguay is only feasible when the contract is international, according to the definition of the law from February 2021, when a new international private law was passed by the Parliament.

In accordance with this law, a contract is international when the parties have their locations in different countries or when the performance of the contract has a relevant relationship with two or more countries. If a contract is international, the parties can choose the law of a foreign state or a set of rules generally accepted (for example UNIDROIT, UNCITRAL, etc.).

Choice of law is not possible in domestic contracts.

12.4.2 Formal requirements for a construction contract

Under the *Uruguayan Civil Code*, the general rule is that contracts do not have to follow any formality to be valid. In general, a contract doesn't have to be in writing to be valid, and there is no other general formality.

Although that's the general rule, there are certain exceptions: some contracts have to be agreed upon in written form, and some have to be executed in a public document before a Notary Public. This is the case, for instance, for buy/sell agreements on real estate.

According to the general rule, construction contracts can be executed orally, though this is not usual at all.

When a construction contract is the result of a public call by the Government, the contract becomes valid when the offer of the Contractor is accepted, approved by the Accounting Tribunal and notified to the awarded party. In this case, the terms of the contract are those of the call and of the offer. However, after the offer is awarded, a written contract is signed by the Government and the Contractor.

In some cases, a pro forma contract is part of the terms of reference, and therefore there is little room for discussions on the wording of the contract. When that is not the case, the parties discuss the terms after the acceptance of the offer.

On the other hand, it must be pointed out that the *Civil Code* states that when a Contractor is obliged to perform the Works and provide the materials for a lump sum, any modification to the scope, the term and the price of the contract shall be in written form, whatever the form of the modified original contract.

12.5 What Special Provisions in the Particular Conditions are necessary for consistency with applicable laws in Uruguay?

12.5.1 FIDIC General Conditions are incompatible or inconsistent with Uruguyan governing law of the contract

12.5.1.1 Liability of the Contractor

Liability of the Contractor is set in the *Civil Code* and is a public order rule that cannot be modified by mutual agreement of the parties. Under Article 1844 of the *Civil Code*, the Architect, the Engineer and the Contractor are responsible for:

- Ten years for the stability and suitability of the construction plus liability for defects due to the ground, the materials, the calculations or the deficient direction of the works (**decennial liability**)
- Five years for all defects except those in the details (mostly aesthetic)
- Two years for defects in details and issues with the finish

12.5.1.2 Termination due to insolvency

Uruguay has a specific law that rules insolvency and the reorganisation procedures due to such a condition. That specific law prohibits clauses that state that the insolvency of one party is a cause for termination of the contract. For that reason, clauses that make insolvency of one party a cause for termination (for example sub-clauses 15.2.1[g] and 16.2.1[i] of the Yellow Book and sub-clauses 15.2.1[g] and 16.2.1[h] of the Silver Book) are not valid under Uruguayan law.

In such cases, the person appointed by the judge or the creditors to follow the reorganisation procedure has to evaluate the situation and decide whether to continue with the contract or not.

12.5.1.3 Summary

FIDIC contracts are a very useful tool and they can be used in Uruguay with practically no restriction, and with very small adjustments by Special Provisions in the Particular Conditions. They could represent a huge step forward for the construction sector, both private and public, and a very significant advance in terms of conflict avoidance.

12.5.2 FIDIC General Conditions are incompatible or inconsistent with the law of the Site/Country

One of the key aspects of the application of FIDIC contracts is the compatibility of such rules with the law of the Country in which the Contract is performed. This aspect has a lot to do with what the internal laws of the Site country are that are considered to be public order.

In general, Uruguayan legislation is applicable in the absence of provisions agreed upon by the Parties and included in the Contract. This is the concretion of the principle of freedom of contract, or, as denominated in Uruguay, of the 'autonomy of the parties' will'.

There are very few 'public order' rules under the law regarding construction in Uruguay. The most relevant of such public order rules are decennial liability and the need to state in writing any modification of a 'turnkey contract' as explained earlier.

There are therefore no incompatibilities because the FIDIC General Conditions do not contradict those public order rules.

12.5.3 FIDIC General Conditions are incompatible or inconsistent with the relevant laws on dispute determination in Uruguay

The FIDIC General Conditions are absolutely compatible with the relevant Uruguayan laws on dispute determination.

Arbitration is unanimously admitted for construction contracts, and there is no discussion as to whether the State can be bound by an arbitration clause. In Public–Private Partnerships arbitration clauses are obligatory under the *Law of PPP*.

However, there are no rules regarding Dispute Adjudication Boards, as they have not yet been introduced to the country.

The author of this chapter gave a lecture on DABs at a Congress organised by the Administrative Tribunal in 2020, showing that the recommendations of DAB will become the most important piece of evidence for the Tribunal to decide on the validity or not of a certain administrative decision taken by the authority that is part of a construction contract.

The Administrative Tribunal, as explained before, has the competence to confirm or to declare null an administrative decision and to decide whether the decision is contrary to a law, a decree, a contract or the General Principles (human rights or republican rights). Nothing will be more illustrative for the Administrative Tribunal than a recommendation of a DAB to help the Tribunal decide whether the decision of the authority contradicts what is stated in the contract.

During that presentation, the author also stressed that a DAB will help avoid discussions and lawsuits on collateral aspects that are not material matters affecting the dispute. As an arbitrator and an arbitration lawyer, the author has been involved in many cases in which parties have introduced irrelevant matters that only confuse and draw the Tribunal's attention to what is not central to the discussion.

If a DAB helps to solve those collateral and less relevant issues during the life of a contract, they will not interfere with the really significant things that need to be discussed in a final arbitration.

12.6 What Special Provisions in the Particular Conditions are desirable for consistency with applicable laws in Uruguay?

12.6.1 Damages

FIDIC contracts (sub-clause 1.15 of the Red and Yellow Books and sub-clause 1.14 of the Silver Book) consider loss of profit as an indirect damage, and this differs from what the *Uruguayan Civil Code* states on the matter.

There is a coincidence in that only direct damages can be claimed, but the difference is that under Uruguayan law, loss of profit is not considered indirect as it is in FIDIC contracts.

Is this an obstacle to applying a FIDIC definition on the issue? The answer is no. As with most of the rules set out in the *Civil Code* regarding contracts, they are applicable only where the Parties have not chosen another way to rule the matter.

The signature on a FIDIC contract with this definition of damages is valid and binding and it could be also customised to allow to a certain extent a loss of profit as claimable damage also.

12.6.2 Other provisions

It must be stressed that the absence of local regulation on DABs does not affect the freedom of the Parties to agree on having such a body during the life of the Contract. The challenge is to draft it correctly and to give the recommendations relevance and a binding nature if not challenged by any Party. It is yet to be discussed whether a recommendation not challenged that becomes a decision binding on the Parties can be enforced as a decision of an arbitral tribunal. This aspect should be solved by local and international laws.

12.7 Summary of applicable legislation for Uruguyan governing law of the contract

12.7.1 Entry into a construction contract

Contracts generally	*Civil Code*, Articles 1247 and following
Construction contracts	*Civil Code*, Articles 1831 to 1855

12.7.2 Operation of a construction contract

Force majeure	*Civil Code*, Article 1343
Hardship	There is no law regarding hardship, but it is unanimously accepted that the economic balance of the contract (only public contracts with administrations) shall be maintained
Guarantees under forms of Security (Tender Security, Demand Guarantee, Surety Bond, Advance Payment Guarantee, Retention Money Guarantee, Payment Guarantee by Employer)	Tender Security: *TOCAF*, Article 64 Performance Bond: *TOCAF*, Article 64

12.7.3 Termination of a construction contract

Bankruptcy, insolvency, liquidation	Insolvency cannot be a cause of termination under *18.387 Law of Insolvency (Ley de Concursos)* that rules insolvency

(*Continued*)

(Continued)

12.7.4 Dispute resolution

Limitation periods	Claims under construction contracts can be filed within a period of ten years after the occurrence of a defect (which can appear within ten years from completion). If a defect appears in year ten, then the claim shall be filed within ten years from such date: Article 1216 of the *Civil Code*, with the wording given by *Law 19.889*
Liability	*Civil Code*, Article 1844
Adjudication	No law passed yet on Dispute Adjudication Boards
Arbitration	International arbitration – *International Commercial Arbitration: Law 19.636* passed on 26 July 2018 Domestic arbitration – *General Procedure Code*, Article 475 and following

12.8 Summary of applicable legislation if the Site/Country is in Uruguay

12.8.1 Operation of a construction contract

Registration and administration of professionals – Engineers, Architects	Foreign Engineers and Architects have to validate their degrees in Uruguay according to the rules of the University of the Republic (Resolution of 15 September 2020)
Registration/licencing of Contractors and subcontractors	*Decree 208/009* of 4 May 2009
Use of liens/assignment of debts	*Civil Code*, Articles 1757 to 1766
Labour	A myriad of laws and decrees
Design/moral rights	*Law 9739 Law of Author's rights* (*Ley de Derechos de Autor*)
Copyright	*Law 9739 Law of Author's rights* (*Ley de Derechos de Autor*)
The product being produced from the Works	*Law 9739 Law of Author's rights* (*Ley de Derechos de Autor*)
First Nation people's land rights	No law passed on this matter
Planning	No law passed on this matter
Heritage	*Civil Code*, Articles 776 to 1187
Environment	*Law 17.28 Law of Environment* (*Ley de Medio Ambiente*)
Local procurement	*Civil Code*, Articles 1688 and following *Commercial Code*, Articles 513 and following
Public procurement	*TOCAF* (*Decree 150/012* of May 11, 2012)

Building and construction permits, Execution of construction work, Standard of construction work	Construction permits are within the competence of each *Departamento* so there are 19 different *Regulations* on this matter
Health and safety	Different laws cover the health and safety matters of the different sectors. Construction health and safety rules are unified by *Decree 125/014* of 7 May 2014
Insurance	*Commercial Code*, Articles 634 to 699
Liability for defective work	Decennial liability: *Civil Code*, Article 1844
Liability for nuisance	Each *Departamento* has rules on this matter

12.8.2 Termination of a construction contract

Bankruptcy, insolvency, liquidation	Insolvency cannot be a cause of termination: *Law 18.387 Law of Insolvency* (*Ley de Concursos*)
Decennial liability and liability generally for the total or partial collapse of structures	*Civil Code*, Article 1844

12.8.3 Dispute resolution

Limitation periods	Claims under construction contracts can be filed within a period of ten years after the occurrence of a defect (which can appear within ten years from completion). If a defect appears in year ten, then the claim shall be filed within ten years from such date: Article 1216 of the *Civil Code*, with the wording given by *Law 19.889*

12.9 Applicable legislation if the 'seat' of the dispute determination is Uruguay

12.9.1 Arbitration regulation

Legal regulation of domestic (between two parties with their domicile in Uruguay) arbitration is contained in the *General Procedure Code.*

12.9.1.1 Matters that can be solved by arbitration

There is a wide scope of application of alternative dispute resolution methods in Uruguay. This acceptance is consistent with the historical trend to accept arbitration in dispute resolution between countries and for disputes between individuals or corporations regarding certain commercial matters.

Only a few matters cannot be decided by arbitration: family matters and all criminal law matters (although the civil claims arising from criminal acts can be submitted to arbitration).

Under Article 472 of the *General Procedure Code*, any particular or collective dispute can be subject to arbitration.

12.9.1.2 Recognition of arbitral awards

The *General Procedure Code* states that law recognises *de jure* all arbitral awards either issued by *ad hoc* or institutional tribunals. This means that the State gives validity to all arbitral awards, and therefore, once an arbitral award is issued, there is no need for homologation or approval by the judicial power.

General *de jure* recognition shows the low level of intervention of the State jurisdiction over arbitration, which is critical when deciding applicable law and the seat of arbitration. Uruguay has a very liberal approach to arbitration, demonstrated by this low intervention in arbitration.

12.9.1.3 The arbitration clause

When parties of a certain contract wish to submit all their disputes to arbitration, an arbitration clause shall be included in writing in the contract.

This written form is ***ad solemnitatem***,[4] so the absence of a written clause means the nullity of the agreement to submit eventual cases to arbitration. Thus, if no written arbitration clause is included in the contract, there is no way to cause the other party to be bound by arbitration. The written form is also required by the *International Commercial Arbitration Law*, but not with such formality, accepting email exchanges and other ways to agree on arbitration.

The inclusion of the written clause entitles a party to oblige a resisting party to go to arbitration. The *General Procedure Code* has a provision stating that a judge can sign the arbitration commitment on behalf of the resisting party. Once the commitment is signed by the judge and the other party, arbitration can be started, and any further absences of the resisting party have negative effects on it.

It must be stressed that even in cases where there is no arbitration clause in a contract, parties can voluntarily agree to submit their disputes to arbitration. In other words, the inclusion of a written clause is essential to force a resisting party, but the absence of the clause is not an obstacle for parties willing to submit their differences to arbitration, despite not having agreed on that matter at contract execution.

12.9.1.4 Arbitral commitment

Once one party decides to submit a dispute to arbitration, it has to notify the arbitral institution (or the arbitrator appointed) and the other party of its intention to submit the difference to arbitration. Once the notice is given, both parties must sign an arbitral commitment.

This commitment is the key document of domestic arbitration (not required in international arbitration) and it must be executed before a Notary Public or a judge in a hearing.

The arbitral commitment contains the appointment of the arbitrators, all the issues that the arbitrators have to decide, the procedure to be followed, the decision of whether the arbitration will be founded in law or in equity and the time to issue the award.

---

4 A civil law expression that means 'for solemnity' and consists of a formal requirement imposed by law for a legal act to be valid.

12.9.1.5 Freedom to choose the tribunal

Parties can choose to submit their differences either to institutional arbitration or to an *ad hoc* tribunal. There is no provision in law in that respect, and both kinds are used in contracts.

Notwithstanding the freedom to choose, there is a strong trend to adopt the Chamber of Commerce institutional arbitration in most contracts setting arbitration as the dispute resolution method.

12.9.1.6 Kompetenz Kompetenz

The principle under which the arbitral tribunal has the competence to decide whether or not it is competent in each particular case is practically universal in international arbitral regulations and Uruguay is no exception.

This principle is set forth in the *International Commercial Arbitration Law* and in Article 26 of the Chamber of Commerce's arbitration rules. This is paramount when the validity of the contract or of the particular arbitration clause is challenged for nullity by one party.

12.9.1.7 Freedom of arbitral procedure

Article 477 of the *General Procedure Code* states that the parties shall determine in the arbitral commitment the procedure to be followed in the arbitration. This means that the parties have the freedom to determine which is the most suitable procedure for them, providing that said procedure fulfils the requirements of fair and due process.

12.9.1.8 Default procedure

The *General Procedure Code* sets a default procedure for the case of the silence of the parties regarding the procedure. In such a case, the 'ordinary procedure' set forth in the *Code* must be followed by the tribunal. This ordinary process has basically three phases:

- Written phase, in which the plaintiff files its claim including all documents that it intends to use as evidence, the names of all witnesses, the information that is required from public or private third parties and any other evidence that it wishes to bring to the arbitration. Once filed and notified to the defendant, it has 30 calendar days to file its defence, including, as in the claim, all the evidence
- Oral phase, comprising a preliminary hearing in which the tribunal tries to help the parties to settle their disputes. If a settlement is not reached, the parties ratify their positions, and the tribunal details the issues to be solved and the evidence to be produced. If all evidence cannot be examined in the preliminary hearing, a second hearing is held. After all the evidence is produced, each party makes its final submissions
- Award issuance phase, in which the tribunal studies all the evidence and issues the award

12.9.1.9 Chamber of Commerce Arbitration Court procedure

This procedure is very similar to the one described before but contains the confidentiality clause explained in section 12.2.16, which is not included in the *General Procedure Code*.

This rule of the Chamber of Commerce allows the parties to introduce particular variations to suit their needs.

12.9.1.10 Award

One very important aspect contained in the *General Procedure Code* refers to the term for the tribunal to issue the award. That term is set by the parties in the arbitral commitment and can be set in business or calendar days. The arbitral tribunal must issue the award within the term. This is paramount because the consequence of the award being issued outside that period is nullity.

12.9.1.11 Challenges to the arbitral award

The *General Procedure Code* has set a very narrow path to challenge arbitration awards, which provides a great deal of stability to arbitration. Under this regulation, the award can only be challenged on the grounds of nullity, and this can only be based on four possible cases:

- Award issued after the expiry of the term set by the parties in the commitment
- Award on matters not included in the arbitration commitment (***extra petita***)
- Award that does not decide matters included in the arbitration commitment
- Refusal of the tribunal to receive certain evidence that was essential for ruling the case

This is a closed list that admits no extension, so no other cause of nullity is admitted. Only the first and the last cause of nullity affects the whole award, while the other two just affect parts of the award, especially the parts with the *extra petita* or the issues not decided. As noted earlier, this restrictive list provides arbitral awards certainty and stability.

Nullity challenges are decided by a civil Appeal Court, composed of three judges.

Jurisprudence on challenges to arbitral awards filed by losing parties is very reassuring because Appeal Courts competent on such challenges have ruled against most of those challenges, charging the losing party (plaintiff of the challenge) with all expenses, thus discouraging such challenges when they are not founded in one of the cases of nullity set forth by law.

12.9.1.12 Award enforcement

Under the *General Procedure Code*, when arbitral awards are not complied with by the parties voluntarily, they can be enforced before the tribunal that would have been competent to decide the case if the arbitration clause was not included by the parties.

The procedure of enforcing domestic awards is the same that must be followed to enforce a decision of a State judge or tribunal and is set forth in Articles 372 to 376 of the *General Procedure Code*. Enforcement starts with the presentation of the award before the State judge that would have been competent if the case was submitted to state jurisdiction. The judge orders the defeated party to comply with the award. If the party does not comply, the judge issues a seizure injunction and enforces the award, with all costs payable by the resisting party.

12.9.2 Investment protection arbitration

In addition to the international conventions ratified by Uruguay regarding international arbitration, the country has signed a number of international agreements for foreign investment protection, setting arbitration as the dispute resolution method.

The countries with which Uruguay has investment protection treaties are the following:

Albania	Australia	Austria	Armenia
Barbados	Belorussia	Belgium	Bolivia
Bulgaria	Canada	Chile	China
Costa Rica	Croatia	Cuba	Czech Republic
Ecuador	Egypt	El Salvador	European Union
Finland	France	Great Britain	Germany
Greece	Holland	Hungary	India
Indonesia	Israel	Italy	Korea
Lebanon	Latvia	Lithuania	Luxembourg
Malaysia	Mauritius	Mexico	Morocco
Nicaragua	Panama	Paraguay	Peru
Poland	Portugal	Qatar	Rumania
Saudi Arabia	San Marino	Slovenia	South Africa
Spain	Sweden	Switzerland	Thailand
Turkey	USA	Venezuela	Vietnam

These treaties allow nationals of the aforementioned countries to go to an international court of arbitration and file a claim against Uruguay if the investor is treated unfairly or with discrimination, breaching the obligation of the State under the protection treaty.

12.9.3 Enforcement of international arbitral awards

Domestic arbitral awards are enforced by the tribunals of the State as explained earlier.

Enforcement of foreign arbitral awards, according to the *General Procedure Code*, shall be implemented following the treaties signed by Uruguay applicable to the case, or following the procedure set by law for the enforcement of foreign judicial decisions.

To enforce foreign awards under the *General Procedure Code* when no other procedure is set by the treaties signed by Uruguay and the country of origin of the award, a petition must be filed before the Supreme Court of Justice, which will notify the party against which it will be enforced, giving 20 days to file its defence. The resolution is final and is not appealable. If the decision of the Supreme Court is to enforce the award, the interested party must follow the same procedure explained for domestic awards.

Uruguay has ratified many international conventions on arbitration. Among many others, the country has ratified:

- *New York Convention on the Recognition and Enforcement of Foreign Arbitral Awards*
- *Inter-American Convention on International Commercial Arbitration* (Panama 1975)

- *Inter-American Convention on the Extraterritorial Validity of Foreign Judgments and Arbitral Awards* (Montevideo, 1979)
- *Protocol on Cooperation and Jurisdictional Assistance in Civil, Commercial, Labor and Administrative Matters* (Mercosur, Las Leñas, Argentina)

Having ratified international conventions that ensure the validity and enforcement of foreign judgments and arbitral awards, Uruguay allows parties to agree upon a foreign institutional or *ad hoc* arbitration to decide differences between construction parties. This helps create a very positive and secure environment for foreign construction companies to develop projects in Uruguay.

12.9.4 Other alternative dispute resolution methods

There is no rule forbidding alternative dispute resolution methods in Uruguay, therefore, mediation, conciliation, Dispute Boards, expert determination and other procedures are accepted in Uruguay.

12.9.4.1 Conciliation

This method is a type of mediation in which a specialised judge helps the parties to settle their differences, without having the competence to decide the case if such an agreement is not reached. Conciliation is the most common way of dispute resolution besides the jurisdictional suit.

Conciliation is obligatory as a preliminary procedure, and any prospective plaintiff must follow it before filing any lawsuit. Conciliation is conducted by special judges that do not have the competence to decide on the case. The judges help the parties settle the difference, even proposing settlement alternatives.

As noted, those judges do not have the competence to rule the case, so if there is no settlement, a minute stating that the conciliation was unsuccessful is issued, and that document must be attached to any claim filed before the competent judge to rule on the case.

An important feature of conciliation is that all arguments made during the hearing are not included in the minute and therefore, expressions of the parties on the particular case cannot be used against the parties in the suit if the conciliation is not successful (without prejudice).

12.9.4.2 Mediation

Another alternative dispute resolution method used in Uruguay is mediation. Mediation differs from conciliation in the individual helping the parties, who is not a judge but a mediator, and in the way this individual helps the parties. In mediation the mediator does not usually propose ways to settle the dispute but simply helps the parties to discover their own interests and assists them to find a way to negotiate a solution for their dispute with each other.

The Uruguayan Chamber of Commerce has a list of mediators (of which the author is one). To be included on that list, each interested individual has to follow a certain program and participate in mediation in countries in which mediation is obligatory, for example, Argentina.

Mediation is sometimes included as a preliminary phase of dispute resolution. It is usual to find clauses that state that the parties shall try to settle their differences amicably within a certain term, and if this negotiation does not succeed, then they should file for mediation. Only when this method proves to be unsuccessful shall arbitration take place.

12.9.4.3 Dispute Boards

Though Dispute Boards are admitted under Uruguayan Law on disposable matters (the same as arbitration, conciliation and mediation), this is not a method usually found in Uruguay. There is no regulation or provision in Uruguayan law regarding this method that has proved very useful in many parts of the world.

12.9.4.4 Expert determination

This alternative dispute resolution method (which the author uses to include in most construction contracts) is rarely used in Uruguay. Expert determination has been shown to the author to be a best practice in construction contracts.

This method has proved to be the best way to distance the parties from many insubstantial differences that tend to complicate the relationships between them, avoiding the escalation of conflict. Many technical aspects of a contract can be solved by expert determination in a very clear and agile fashion. Some of those technical aspects that can be solved by expert determination are very common disputes, for example, quality of materials, craftsmanship quality, certification of work, preliminary acceptance and final acceptance of works, etc.

This very fast way of solving everyday differences also works as a desirable incentive for good faith during the execution of the contract – more so when the cost is paid by the losing party. Another advantage of this method is its agility, which avoids unfair situations persisting over time, therefore avoiding negative consequences to both parties.

The difficulty in finding an expert who has the confidence of both parties is worth the effort in the long run, often avoiding the submission of disputes to arbitration.

12.10 Summary of applicable legislation if the 'seat' of the dispute determination is Uruguay

Dispute resolution	*General Procedure Code*
Limitation periods	The ones fixed in the contract, and in absence of such clause, ten years (*Civil Code*)
Arbitration	International arbitration – *International Commercial Arbitration: Law 19.636* passed on 26 July 2018 Domestic arbitration – *General Procedure Code*, Article 475 and following

12.11 Issues that a court or arbitrator may construe differently than expected from the words of the Contract because of local law or custom

According to the principle of freedom of contract, only public order rules may be considered against contract rules, and as said, they are extremely few, for example, decennial liability and written form for modification of turnkey contracts.

12.12 Additional references for Uruguay

12.12.1 Legislation

Civil Code: www.impo.com.uy/bases/codigo-civil/16603-1994
Commercial Code: www.impo.com.uy/bases/codigo-comercio
General Procedure Code: www.impo.com.uy/bases/codigo-general-proceso/15982-1988
TOCAF: www.comprasestatales.gub.uy/ManualesDeUsuarios/manual-procedimiento-compras/TOCAF.html
Environment Law: www.impo.com.uy/bases/leyes/17283-2000
Insolvency Law: www.impo.com.uy/bases/leyes/18387-2008
Author's rights: www.impo.com.uy/bases/leyes/9739-1937
International Commercial Arbitration: www.impo.com.uy/bases/leyes-originales/19636-2018

12.12.2 Court decisions

Judicial Power decisions: http://bjn.poderjudicial.gub.uy/

GLOSSARY

Term	Meaning	Defined in section
1977 Red Book	**FIDIC**[1] Conditions of Contract for Works of Civil Engineering Construction – Third Edition 1977.	**1.3.1**
1987 Red Book	**FIDIC** Conditions of Contract for Works of Civil Engineering Construction – Fourth Edition 1987.	**1.3.1**
1987 Yellow Book	**FIDIC** Conditions of Contract for Electrical and Mechanical Works – Third Edition 1987.	**1.3.1**
1995 Orange Book	**FIDIC** Conditions of Contract for Design-Build and Turnkey – First Edition 1995.	**1.3.1**
1999 Red Book	**FIDIC** Conditions of Contract for Construction – First Edition 1999.	**1.3.1**
1999 Silver Book	**FIDIC** Conditions of Contract for EPC/ Turnkey Projects – First Edition 1999.	**1.3.1**
1999 Yellow Book	**FIDIC** Conditions of Contract for Plant and Design-Build – First Edition 1999.	**1.3.1**
2017 Red Book	**FIDIC** Conditions of Contract for Construction – Second Edition 2017.	**1.3.1**
2017 Silver Book	**FIDIC** Conditions of Contract for EPC/ Turnkey Projects – Second Edition 2017.	**1.3.1**
2017 Yellow Book	**FIDIC** Conditions of Contract for Plant and Design-Build – Second Edition 2017.	**1.3.1**
Abrahamson Principles	Principles of fair and balanced risk allocation, articulated in Max W Abrahamson, 'Risk Management' (1983) *International Construction Law Review* 241, 244.	**2.4**
Accepted Contract Amount	**FIDIC** definition (**Red,**[2] **Pink, Yellow,**[3] **Gold** and **Emerald Books**).	**FIDIC GCs**
Acción de Nulidad	Nullity action (Uruguay).	**12.2.13**
ad solemnitatem	A civil law expression that means 'for solemnity' and consists of a formal requirement imposed by law for a legal act to be valid.	**12.9.1.3**

(*Continued*)

1 Terms in bold in the Meaning column are defined elsewhere in the Glossary.
2 Red Book refers to the 1999 Red Book and the 2017 Red Book.
3 Yellow Book refers to the 1999 Yellow Book and the 2017 Yellow Book.

(Continued)

Term	Meaning	Defined in section
adhesion contract	A contract in which its essential clauses are imposed or are drafted by one party, by a third person especially for a party or as a result of its instructions, the other party having only the possibility to accept the contract as such.	
ADR	Alternative dispute resolution – alternative to resolution by litigation in court.	
Advance Payment Certificate	**FIDIC** definition (**2017 Red, 2017 Yellow** and **Emerald Books**).	**FIDIC GCs**
Advance Payment Guarantee	**FIDIC** definition (**2017 Red, 2017 Yellow, 2017 Silver**[4] and **Emerald Books**).	**FIDIC GCs**
Aguinaldo	Thirteenth salary (Uruguay).	**12.2.6.1**
Alcades	The third level of government in certain cities (Uruguay).	**12.1.3**
amiable compositeur	The power given by parties to an arbitrator to decide a dispute equitably or ***ex aequo et bono*** without strict regard to the rules of law that would otherwise apply.	
Appendix to Tender	**FIDIC** definition (**1987 Red, 1999 Red** and **1999 Yellow Books**).	**FIDIC GCs**
ART	Technical Responsibility Annotation (Brazil).	**5.2.3**
Bank	**FIDIC** definition (**Pink Book**).	**FIDIC GCs**
Base Date	**FIDIC** definition (**Red, Pink, Yellow, Silver, Gold** and **Emerald Books**).	**FIDIC GCs**
Bill of Quantities	**FIDIC** definition (**Red, Pink** and **Emerald Books**).	**FIDIC GCs**
BIM	Building information modelling or building information management.	**6.2.5**
BIT	Bilateral investment treaty.	**4.2.11**
Blue-Green Book	**FIDIC** Form of Contract for Dredging and Reclamation Works – First Edition 2006, Second Edition 2016.	**1.3.1**
BoQ	**Bill of Quantities**.	
Borrower	**FIDIC** definition (**Pink Book**).	**FIDIC GCs**
BOOT	Build, own, operate, transfer.	**10.1.1**
BOT	Build, operate and transfer.	**7.2.10**
CABOCO	Cámara Boliviana de la Construcción (Bolivia)	**4.2.2**
CADECOCRUZ	Cámara de la Construcción de Santa Cruz (Bolivia).	**4.2.2**
CAM Santiago	Santiago Chamber of Commerce (Chile).	**7.2.11**

4 Silver Book refers to the 1999 Silver Book and the 2017 Silver Book.

Term	Meaning	Defined in section
CAR	Construction all risks insurance policy.	**7.2.9**
CAU	Regional Councils for Architecture and Urbanism (Brazil).	**5.2.3**
causa	A lawful cause required for the existence of a contract in a civil law system.	
CC	*Chilean Civil Code.*	**7.1.2**
CCA	Canadian Construction Association.	**6.2.9**
CChC	Chilean Chamber of Construction.	**7.2.2**
CCQ	Commission de la construction du Québec (Canada).	**6.2.2**
CFPO Act	*Corruption of Foreign Public Officials Act* (Canada).	**6.2.7**
CIADI	International Centre for Settlement of Investment Disputes.	**10.2.11**
CIB	Canada Infrastructure Bank.	**6.2.1.1**
CIPA	Accident Prevention Commission (*Comissão Interna de Prevenção de Acidentes*) (Brazil).	**5.2.5**
Civil Code	*Civil Code of Quebec* (Canada).	**6.1.2**
civil law	A system of law in which the laws are codified in a large number of general rules and principles.	**1.1.2**
Claim	**FIDIC** definition (**2017 Red, 2017 Yellow, 2017 Silver** and **Emerald Books**).	**FIDIC GCs**
Commencement Date	**FIDIC** definition (**Red, Pink, Yellow, Silver, Gold** and **Emerald Books**).	**FIDIC GCs**
common law	The body of law developed by judges from around the 11th century in England, and later exported to its various colonies such as Canada, the USA, Australia, Fiji, Hong Kong, India, Malaysia and Singapore.	**1.1.2**
Completion Schedule	**FIDIC** definition (**Emerald Book**).	**FIDIC GCs**
Compliance Verification System	**FIDIC** definition (**2017 Red, 2017 Yellow, 2017 Silver** and **Emerald Books**).	**FIDIC GCs**
Conditions of Contract	**FIDIC** definition (**2017 Red, 2017 Yellow, 2017 Silver** and **Emerald Books**).	**FIDIC GCs**
Contract	The construction contract being referred to.	**1.1.1**
Contract	**FIDIC** definition (**Red, Pink, Yellow, Silver, Gold** and **Emerald Books**).	**FIDIC GCs**
Contract Agreement	**FIDIC** definition (**Red, Pink, Yellow, Silver, Gold** and **Emerald Books**).	**FIDIC GCs**
Contract Data	**FIDIC** definition (**2017 Red, Pink, 2017 Yellow, 2017 Silver, Gold** and **Emerald Books**).	**FIDIC GCs**

(Continued)

(Continued)

Term	Meaning	Defined in section
contract of adhesion	See **adhesion contract**.	
Contract Participants	All the persons referred to in a **FIDIC Contract**.	**2.4**
Contract Price	**FIDIC** definition (**Red, Pink, Yellow, Silver, Gold** and **Emerald Books**).	**FIDIC GCs**
Contract Risk Management Plan	**FIDIC** definition (**Emerald Book**).	**FIDIC GCs**
Contract Risk Register	**FIDIC** definition (**Emerald Book**).	**FIDIC GCs**
Contracting Authority	The government authority that contracts with a special-purpose entity (**Project Co**) in a **P3** (**PPP**) (Canada).	**6.2.1.2**
Contractor	The party to a construction contract (the **Contract**) who carries out the work.	**1.1.1**
Contractor	**FIDIC** definition (**Red, Pink, Yellow, Silver, Gold** and **Emerald Books**).	**FIDIC GCs**
Contractor's Documents	**FIDIC** definition (**Red, Pink, Yellow, Silver, Gold** and **Emerald Books**).	**FIDIC GCs**
Contractor's Equipment	**FIDIC** definition (**Red, Pink, Yellow, Silver, Gold** and **Emerald Books**).	**FIDIC GCs**
Contractor's Key Equipment	**FIDIC** definition (**Emerald Book**).	**FIDIC GCs**
Contractor's Key Personnel	**FIDIC** definition (**Emerald Book**).	**FIDIC GCs**
Contractor's Personnel	**FIDIC** definition (**Red, Pink, Yellow, Silver, Gold** and **Emerald Books**).	**FIDIC GCs**
Contractor's Proposal	**FIDIC** definition (**Yellow, Gold** and **Emerald Books**).	**FIDIC GCs**
Contractor's Representative	**FIDIC** definition (**Red, Pink, Yellow, Silver, Gold** and **Emerald Books**).	**FIDIC GCs**
Cost	**FIDIC** definition (**Red, Pink, Yellow, Silver, Gold** and **Emerald Books**).	**FIDIC GCs**
Cost Plus Profit	**FIDIC** definition (**2017 Red, 2017 Yellow, 2017 Silver, Gold** and **Emerald Books**).	**FIDIC GCs**
Country	**FIDIC** definition (**Red, Pink, Yellow, Silver, Gold** and **Emerald Books**).	**FIDIC GCs**
CPE	*Constitucion Politica del Estado 2009* (Bolivia)	**4.1.1**
CREA	*Conselho Regional de Engenharia, Arquitetura e Agronomia* (Regional Council of Engineering, Architecture and Agronomy) (Brazil).	**5.2.3**
curial law	The law governing the existence and operation of the arbitral tribunal, generally the law of the 'seat' of arbitration. Also known as the ***lex arbitrii***.	**1.5.5**
DAAB	**Dispute Avoidance/Adjudication Board**.	**FIDIC GCs**

Term	Meaning	Defined in section
DAAB Agreement	**FIDIC** definition (**2017 Red, 2017 Yellow, 2017 Silver** and **Emerald Books**).	**FIDIC GCs**
DAB	**FIDIC** definition (**1999 Red, 1999 Yellow, 1999 Silver** and **Gold Books**).	**FIDIC GCs**
Date of Completion	**FIDIC** definition (**Red, Yellow, Silver** and **Emerald Books**).	**FIDIC GCs**
day	**FIDIC** definition (**Red, Pink, Yellow, Silver, Gold** and **Emerald Books**).	**FIDIC GCs**
Daywork Schedule	**FIDIC** definition (**Red, Pink, 2017 Yellow, 2017 Silver** and **Emerald Books**).	**FIDIC GCs**
DB	**Dispute Board. FIDIC** definition (**Pink Book**).	**FIDIC GCs**
DBFM	Design, build, finance and maintain.	**6.2.1.2**
DBOT	Design, build, operate, transfer.	**10.1.1**
DCMF	Design, construct, manage, finance.	**10.1.1**
decennial liability	Liability of the Architect, Engineer and Contractor for a period of ten years for the stability and suitability of the construction and for defects due to the ground, the materials, the calculations or the deficient direction of the works (Uruguay).	**12.5.1.1**
Decree	*Urgency Decree No 021-2020* creating a new public procurement regime (Peru).	**10.2.8.1**
Defects Notification Period	**FIDIC** definition (**Red, Pink, Yellow, Silver** and **Emerald Books**).	**FIDIC GCs**
Delay Damages	**FIDIC** definition (**2017 Red, 2017 Yellow, 2017 Silver** and **Emerald Books**).	**FIDIC GCs**
Departamento	Local district (Uruguay).	**12.1.2**
design	All plans, drawings, sketches, instructions and descriptions that determine the way the **Works** (or parts of it) are to be constructed. Design includes the writing or selection of specifications as well as the production of plans and drawings and any element of choice on the part of the designer, such as requirements as to materials or working methods.	
design contract	A contract for the preparation of a **design** to be constructed under a construction contract.	
Diputados	The members of the Chamber of Representatives elected by the ***Departamentos*** (Uruguay).	**12.1.3**

(Continued)

(Continued)

Term	Meaning	Defined in section
Dispute	**FIDIC** definition (**2017 Red, 2017 Yellow, 2017 Silver, Gold** and **Emerald Books**).	**FIDIC GCs**
Dispute Avoidance/ Adjudication Board	**FIDIC** definition (**2017 Red, 2017 Yellow, 2017 Silver** and **Emerald Books**).	**FIDIC GCs**
Dispute Adjudication Board	A **Dispute Board** that provides a provisionally binding decision on a dispute referred to it; if neither party issues a notice of dissatisfaction within a defined time, the decision becomes final and binding.	
Dispute Board	A panel of one or three suitably qualified and experienced independent persons appointed under the **Contract** to provide a determination of a dispute referred to it. A Dispute Board may be a **Dispute Avoidance/Adjudication Board (DAAB)**, a **Dispute Adjudication Board (DAB)**, a **Dispute Review Board (DRB)** or a **Dispute Resolution Board (DRB)**.	
DNP	**Defects Notification Period**. **FIDIC** definition (**2017 Red, 2017 Yellow, 2017 Silver** and **Emerald Books**).	**FIDIC GCs**
doctrine of separability	The generally recognised principle of the law of international arbitration that an arbitration agreement incorporated in a contract is treated for legal purposes as a separate and independent agreement for the purpose of determining its validity or enforceability.	**1.5.6**
Drawings	**FIDIC** definition (**Red** and **Pink Books**).	**FIDIC GCs**
ECI	Early Contractor involvement.	**10.2.8.2**
Emerald Book	**FIDIC** Conditions of Contract for Underground Works, First Edition 2019.	**1.3.1**
Employer	The party to a construction contract for whom the work is done. Also referred to as the Principal or sometimes the Owner or Client.	**1.1.1**
Employer	**FIDIC** definition (**Red, Pink, Yellow, Silver, Gold** and **Emerald Books**).	**FIDIC GCs**

Term	Meaning	Defined in section
Employer's Equipment	**FIDIC** definition (**Red, Pink, Yellow, Silver, Gold** and **Emerald Books**).	**FIDIC GCs**
Employer's Personnel	**FIDIC** definition (**Red, Pink, Yellow, Silver, Gold** and **Emerald Books**).	**FIDIC GCs**
Employer's Representative	**FIDIC** definition (**2017 Silver** and **Gold Books**).	**FIDIC GCs**
Employer's Requirements	**FIDIC** definition (**Yellow, Silver, Gold** and **Emerald Books**).	**FIDIC GCs**
Employer-Supplied Materials	**FIDIC** definition (**2017 Red, 2017 Yellow, 2017 Silver** and **Emerald Books**).	**FIDIC GCs**
ENAA	Engineering Advancement Association of Japan.	**10.2.8.1**
Engineer	**FIDIC** definition (**Red, Pink, Yellow** and **Emerald Books**).	**FIDIC GCs**
Engineer's Representative	**FIDIC** definition (**1987 Red, 2017 Red, 2017 Yellow** and **Emerald Books**).	**FIDIC GCs**
EOT	Extension of time.	
EPC contract	Engineer, procure and construct contract. A construction contract (also referred to as a turnkey contract) in which the **Contractor** takes total responsibility for the engineering (**design**), procurement and construction and provides a fully equipped facility ready for operation (at the 'turn of the key').	**1.1.1**
EPCM contract	Engineer, procure and construction management contract. A construction contract in which the **Contractor**, as Construction Manager, designs, procures and manages the construction as agent of the **Employer**.	**1.1.1**
EPI	Personal protective equipment (*Equipamentos de Proteção Individual*) (Brazil).	**5.2.5**
EQ	Emploi-Québec (Canada).	**6.2.2**
Excavation	**FIDIC** definition (**Emerald Book**).	**FIDIC GCs**
Exceptional Event	**FIDIC** definition (**2017 Red, 2017 Yellow, 2017 Silver, Gold** and **Emerald Books**).	**FIDIC GCs**
Extension of Time or **EOT**	**FIDIC** definition (**2017 Red, 2017 Yellow, 2017 Silver** and **Emerald Books**).	**FIDIC GCs**

(*Continued*)

(Continued)

Term	Meaning	Defined in section
ex aequo et bono	Latin for 'according to the right and good' or 'from equity and conscience'. An arbitrator authorised to act *ex aqueo et bono* has the power to dispense with strict consideration of the law and consider solely what they consider to be fair and equitable in the circumstances.	**9.7.2.8**
extra petita	A Latin expression that means a judge or arbitral tribunal is prohibited from issuing a decision of a different nature to the one requested.	**12.9.1.11**
FAC-1	Framework Alliance Contract.	**10.2.8.2**
FIDIC	International Federation of Consulting Engineers (Fédération Internationale des Ingénieurs-Conseils).	**1.3.1**
FIDIC	**FIDIC** definition (**Red, Pink, Yellow, Silver, Gold** and **Emerald Books**).	**FIDIC GCs**
FIDIC Golden Principles	The essential features of a **FIDIC** Contract that make the risk/reward allocation fair and balanced.	**2.1**
Final Payment Certificate or **FPC**	**FIDIC** definition (**Red, Pink, Yellow** and **Emerald Books**).	**FIDIC GCs**
Final Statement	**FIDIC** definition (**Red, Pink, Yellow, Silver** and **Emerald Books**).	**FIDIC GCs**
force majeure	In civil law, *force majeure* applies to situations where the performance of a contract is substantially impossible, not merely something different from what was originally contemplated by the parties. In civil law systems, *force majeure* operates independently of party agreement, which means that it will protect an obligee even if the contract does not contain a *force majeure* clause. Since in civil law the liability is based on fault, the party will not be liable in case of *force majeure*.[5]	
Force Majeure	**FIDIC** definition (**1999 Red, Pink, 1999 Yellow** and **1999 Silver Books**).	**FIDIC GCs**
Foreign Currency	**FIDIC** definition (**Red, Pink, Yellow, Silver, Gold** and **Emerald Books**).	**FIDIC GCs**
Fund	The Canada Community-Building Fund.	**6.2.1.1**
FUNDEMPRESA	Fundación para el Desarrollo Empresarial (Bolivia).	**4.2.3**

5 Pepovic, Casalev, 'Civil Law and Common Law: Two Different Paths Leading to the Same Goal' 42 (2001) 32(3) *Victoria University of Wellington Law Review* 817. www.victoria.ac.nz/__data/assets/pdf_file/0008/830780/Pejovic.pdf (accessed 15 July 2018).

Term	Meaning	Defined in section
GBR	**Geotechnical Baseline Report**.	**FIDIC GCs**
GCs	**General Conditions. FIDIC** definition (**Emerald Book**).	**FIDIC GCs**
GDP	Gross domestic product.	
GDPC	Gross domestic product of construction.	**4.2.1**
GDR	**Geotechnical Data Report**.	**FIDIC GCs**
General Conditions	**FIDIC** definition (**2017 Red, 2017 Yellow, 2017 Silver** and **Emerald Books**).	**FIDIC GCs**
General Conditions	**FIDIC** definition (**Red, Yellow, Silver** and **Emerald Books**).	**FIDIC GCs**
Geotechnical Baseline Report or **GBR**	**FIDIC** definition (**Emerald Book**).	**FIDIC GCs**
Geotechnical Data Report or **GDR**	**FIDIC** definition (**Emerald Book**).	**FIDIC GCs**
GNP	Gross national product.	
Gold Book	**FIDIC** Conditions of Contract for Design, Build and Operatre Projects – First Edition, 2008.	**1.3.1**
Goods	**FIDIC** definition (**Red, Pink, Yellow, Silver, Gold** and **Emerald Books**).	**FIDIC GCs**
governing law of the contract	The law that governs the **Parties'** contractual relations. Also known as the **proper law of the contract**.	**1.1.6**
GPs	**FIDIC Golden Principles**.	**2.1**
Green Book	**FIDIC** Short Form of Contract – First Edition, 1999.	**1.3.1**
Hague Principles	*Principles on Choice of Law in International Commercial Contracts* (2015) published by the Hague Conference on Private International Law.	**3.2.1**
Head Contract	A contract for construction of a facility between the owner or user of the facility (**Employer**) and a contractor (**Contractor**) who takes responsibility for construction of the complete **Works** in accordance with the requirements of the **Contract**. The **Contractor** generally employs one or more **Subcontractors** to execute some (but not all) of the **Works**.	**1.1.1**
ICC	International Chamber of Commerce.	**7.2.11**
ICE	Institution of Civil Engineers.	**4.2.5**
ICE	Integrated concurrent engineering (Peru).	**10.2.7**
ICSID	International Centre for Settlement of Investment Disputes.	**4.2.11**

(*Continued*)

(Continued)

Term	Meaning	Defined in section
IMSS	*Instituto Mexicano del Seguro Social* – the Mexican Institute of Social Security.	**9.2.4**
***in rem* claim**	A claim *in rem* literally means 'against the thing'. It is taken directly against property and it can be brought even though the owner has no personal liability.	**1.5.5**
INEI	National Institute of Statistics and Information Technology (Peru).	**10.2.1**
Intendente	The executive elected authority that governs a ***Departamento*** (Uruguay).	**12.1.3**
Interim Payment Certificate or **IPC**	**FIDIC** definition (**Red, Pink, Yellow, Gold** and **Emerald Books**).	**FIDIC GCs**
international construction contract	An international construction contract is a contract for the provision of goods and services in which: (a) The parties to the Contract have, at the time of the conclusion of their agreement, their places of business in different legal jurisdictions, or (b) One of the following places is situated outside the legal jurisdiction in which the parties have their places of business: (i) The Site, or (ii) Any place where a substantial part of the obligations for the Works is to be performed.	**1.1.7**
IP	Intellectual property.	
IPD	Integrated project delivery.	**10.2.8.2**
ipso facto	By the fact itself (Latin).	
ipso jure	By the operation of the law itself (Latin).	
JICA	Japan International Cooperation Agency.	**1.3.2**
Joint Venture or **JV**	**FIDIC** definition (**2017 Red, 2017 Yellow, 2017 Silver** and **Emerald Books**).	**FIDIC GCs**
Junta Departamental	The legislative body in a ***Departamento*** (Uruguay).	**12.1.3**
JV Undertaking	**FIDIC** definition (**2017 Red, 2017 Yellow, 2017 Silver** and **Emerald Books**)	**FIDIC GCs**
law of the forum	The law of the place in which court or arbitral proceedings are conducted.	**1.5.5**
Laws	**FIDIC** definition (**2017 Red, Pink, 2017 Yellow, 2017 Silver, Gold** and **Emerald Books**).	**FIDIC GCs**

Term	Meaning	Defined in section
LDs	Liquidated damages.	
Letter of Acceptance	**FIDIC** definition (**Red, Pink, Yellow, Gold** and **Emerald Books**).	**FIDIC GCs**
Letter of Tender	**FIDIC** definition (**Red, Pink, Yellow, Gold** and **Emerald Books**).	**FIDIC GCs**
lex arbitrii	The law governing the existence and operation of the arbitral tribunal, generally the law of the 'seat' of arbitration. Also known as the **curial law**.	**1.5.6**
lex fori	See **law of the forum**.	
lex loci rei sitae	A Latin phrase meaning law of the place where the property is situated.	**1.5.5**
Licitación Pública	Public bid (Uruguay).	**12.2.10.1**
Lining	**FIDIC** definition (**Emerald Book**).	**FIDIC GCs**
Local Currency	**FIDIC** definition (**Red, Pink, Yellow, Silver, Gold and Emerald Books**).	**FIDIC GCs**
mandatory law or **mandatory rules of law**	Provisions of a statute which the parties to a contract may not derogate from.	**1.5**
Materials	**FIDIC** definition (**Red, Pink, Yellow, Silver, Gold** and **Emerald Books**).	**FIDIC GCs**
MDB	Multilateral Development Bank.	**1.3.2**
MEF	Ministry of Economy and Finance (Peru).	**10.2.7**
Mercosur	An economic and political block of South American countries founded in 1991 currently comprising Argentina, Brazil, Paraguay and Uruguay.	**12.1.1**
Milestone	**FIDIC** definition (**Emerald Book**).	**FIDIC GCs**
Milestone Certificate	**FIDIC** definition (**Emerald Book**).	**FIDIC GCs**
MOP	Ministry of Public Works (Chile).	**7.2.3**
Model Law	*1985 UNCITRAL Model Law on International Commercial Arbitration.*	**Annexure to Chapter 1**
month	**FIDIC** definition (**2017 Red, 2017 Yellow, 2017 Silver** and **Emerald Books**).	**FIDIC GCs**
multas	Penalty (Spanish).	**7.5.2**
mutatis mutandis	Notwithstanding differences between two things being compared because of their different situations, the basic point remains the same (Latin).	
Nadi	Import Tariff Nomenclature (*Nomenclatura Arancelaria de Importación* in Spanish) (Uruguay).	**12.2.18**
National Plan	National Plan of Infrastructure for Competitiveness (Peru).	**10.2.8.1**
NEC	New Engineering Contract.	**10.2.8.1**

(*Continued*)

(Continued)

Term	Meaning	Defined in section
New York Convention	*United Nations 1958 New York Convention on the Recognition and Enforcement of Foreign Arbitral Awards.*	1.8.1
No-objection	**FIDIC** definition (**2017 Red, 2017 Yellow, 2017 Silver** and **Emerald Books**).	FIDIC GCs
NOD	**Notice of Dissatisfaction**.	FIDIC GCs
non-mandatory law or **non-mandatory rules of law**	Provisions of a statute which the parties can opt out of by appropriate agreement otherwise in their contract.	1.5
Notice	**FIDIC** definition (**2017 Red, 2017 Yellow, 2017 Silver, Gold** and **Emerald Books**).	FIDIC GCs
Notice of Dissatisfaction or **NOD**	**FIDIC** definition (**2017 Red, Pink, 2017 Yellow, 2017 Silver and Emerald Books**).	FIDIC GCs
ODACC	Ontario Dispute Adjudication for Construction Contracts (Canada).	6.2.10
OECD	Organization for Economic Co-operation and Development.	6.2.7
ordre public	Public policy (French).	3.2.1
OSHA	Occupational Safety and Health Administration (USA).	11.2.5
P3	Public Private Partnership.	6.2.1.2
pacta sunt servanda	A Latin phrase that means that agreements are to be kept.	1.1.5
Part	**FIDIC** definition (**2017 Red, 2017 Yellow** and **Emerald Books**).	FIDIC GCs
Particular Conditions	**FIDIC** definition (**2017 Red, 2017 Yellow, 2017 Silver** and **Emerald Books**).	FIDIC GCs
Party	**FIDIC** definition (**Red, Pink, Yellow, Silver, Gold** and **Emerald Books**).	FIDIC GCs
Payment Certificate	**FIDIC** definition (**Red, Pink, Yellow** and **Emerald Books**).	FIDIC GCs
PCs	**Particular Conditions**.	2.3
PEIP	Special Projects of Public Investment (Peru).	10.2.10
pena enorme	Huge penalty (Spanish).	7.5.2
penalidades	**Delay Damages** when Parties agree to them in the contract (Peru).	10.5.1.4
Performance Certificate	**FIDIC** definition (**Red, Pink, Yellow, Silver** and **Emerald Books**).	FIDIC GCs
Performance Damages	**FIDIC** definition (**2017 Yellow, 2017 Silver Emerald Books**).	FIDIC GCs
Performance Guarantees	**FIDIC** definition (**1999 Silver Book**).	FIDIC GCs
Performance Security	**FIDIC** definition (**Red, Pink, Yellow, Silver, Gold** and **Emerald Books**).	FIDIC GCs

Term	Meaning	Defined in section
Permanent Works	**FIDIC** definition (**Red, Pink, Yellow, Silver, Gold** and **Emerald Books**).	**FIDIC GCs**
PFI	Private Finance Initiative.	
Pink Book	**FIDIC** Conditions of Contract for Construction MDB Harmonised Edition for Building and Engineering Works Designed by the Employer (MDB Harmonised Edition 2010).	**1.3.1**
Plan	The Investing in Canada Plan in which the Government of Canada committed 180 billion Canadian dollars over 12 years to infrastructure investment.	**6.2.1.1**
Plant	**FIDIC** definition (**Red, Pink, Yellow, Silver, Gold** and **Emerald Books**).	**FIDIC GCs**
PMO	Project management officer (Peru).	**10.2.2**
PPC 2000	Project Partnering Contract.	**10.2.8.2**
PPE	Personal protective equipment.	**1.6.6**
PPI	Programme of Investment Partnerships (Brazil).	**5.2.1**
PPP	Public–Private Partnership.	**7.2.2**
Program	The Investing in Canada Infrastructure Program.	**6.2.1.1**
Programme	**FIDIC** definition (**2017 Red, 2017 Yellow, 2017 Silver and Emerald Books**).	**FIDIC GCs**
ProjectCo	The special purpose entity that contracts with a government authority in a **P3** (**PPP**).	**6.2.1.2**
proper law of the contract	The law that governs the **Parties'** contractual relations. Also known as the **governing law of the contract**.	**1.1.6**
Provisional Sum	**FIDIC** definition (Red, Pink, Yellow, Silver, Gold and **Emerald Books**).	**FIDIC GCs**
public policy	Public policy is largely concerned with the potential for manifest unfairness or injustice within a given situation. Courts may disregard or refuse to give effect to contractual obligations which, whilst not directly contrary to any express or implied statutory prohibition, nevertheless contravene 'the policy of the law' as discerned from a consideration of the scope and purpose of the particular statute.	**1.1.4**
Quality Management or **QM System**	**FIDIC** definition (**Emerald Book**).	**FIDIC GCs**

(Continued)

(Continued)

Term	Meaning	Defined in section
QM System	**FIDIC** definition (**2017 Red, 2017 Yellow** and **2017 Silver Books**).	**FIDIC GCs**
rainbow suite	The construction contracts published by **FIDIC**: **Red Book** **Pink Book** **Yellow Book** **Silver Book**	**1.3.1**
RB	Régie du bâtiment du Québec (Canada).	**6.2.2**
rebus sic stantibus	The civil law doctrine or rules relating to changed circumstances.	**1.2.3**
recepción definitiva	Final acceptance (Spanish).	**7.5.3**
recepción provisoria	Provisional acceptance (Spanish).	**7.5.3**
recursos administrativos	Administrative challenge (Uruguay).	**12.2.13**
Red Book	**FIDIC** Conditions of Contract for Construction for Building and Engineering Works Designed by the Employer – First Edition 1999 and Second Edition 2017.	**1.3.1**
Retention Money	**FIDIC** definition (**Red, Pink, Yellow, Silver, Gold** and **Emerald Books**).	**FIDIC GCs**
RENCA	National Register for Environmental Consultants (Bolivia).	**4.2.3**
RENTRAA	National Register for Refrigeration and Air-Conditioning Work (Bolivia).	**4.2.3**
REPSE	*Registro de Prestadoras de Servicios Especializados y Obras Especializadas* – Special Services Provider or Specialized Works Registry (Mexico).	**9.2.4**
Review	**FIDIC** definition (**2017 Red, 2017 Yellow, 2017 Silver** and **Emerald Books**).	**FIDIC GCs**
RFA	Request for approval.	
RFI	Request for information.	
RFP	Request for proposal.	
RFQ	Request for qualifications (Canada).	**6.2.6**
RMBS	Residential mortgage-backed securities.	**8.2.8**
Rome I	*Convention on the Law Applicable to Contractual Obligations. Regulation (EC) No 593/2008* of the European Parliament and of the Council of 17 June 2008 on the law applicable to contractual obligations.	**1.1.4**
SBD	Standard Bidding Document.	**1.3.2**

Term	Meaning	Defined in section
Schedules	**FIDIC** definition (**Red, Pink, Yellow, 2017 Silver, Gold** and **Emerald Books**).	**FIDIC GCs**
Schedule of Baselines	**FIDIC** definition (**Emerald Book**).	**FIDIC GCs**
Schedule of Contractor's Key Equipment	**FIDIC** definition (**Emerald Book**).	**FIDIC GCs**
Schedule of Guarantees	**FIDIC** definition (**1999 Yellow Book**).	**FIDIC GCs**
Schedule of Payments	**FIDIC** definition (**Red, Yellow, Silver, Gold** and **Emerald Books**).	**FIDIC GCs**
Schedule of Performance Guarantees	**FIDIC** definition (**2017 Yellow, 2017 Silver** and **Emerald Books**).	**FIDIC GCs**
Schedule of Rates and Prices	**FIDIC** definition (**2017 Yellow, 2017 Silver** and **Emerald Books**).	**FIDIC GCs**
Schedule, Payment Currencies	**FIDIC** definition (**Pink Book**).	**FIDIC GCs**
Section	**FIDIC** definition (**Red, Pink, Yellow, Silver, Gold** and **Emerald Books**).	**FIDIC GCs**
SESMET	Specialised Work Safety and Medicine Services (*Serviços Especializados em Engenharia de Segurança e em Medicina do Trabalho*) (Brazil).	**5.2.5**
Site	**FIDIC** definition (**Red, Pink, Yellow, Silver, Gold** and **Emerald Books**).	**FIDIC GCs**
Silver Book	**FIDIC** Conditions of Contract for EPC/ Turnkey Projects – First Edition 1999, Second Edition 2017.	**1.3.1**
SME	Small to medium enterprise.	
Special Provisions	**FIDIC** definition (**2017 Red, 2017 Yellow, 2017 Silver** and **Emerald Books**).	**FIDIC GCs**
Specification	**FIDIC** definition (**Red, Pink** and **Yellow Books**).	**FIDIC GCs**
SPV	Special Purpose Vehicle. A company specifically formed to enter into a **PPP** contract with the Government to finance and manage construction and operations of a public facility.	**12.2.1**
stare decisis	'The decision stands' (Latin). The doctrine under which a common law court is required to follow previous decisions unless they are inconsistent with a higher court's decision or determined to be wrong in law.	**1.1.2**
stare decisis et non quieta movere	'To stand decided and not to move peacefully' (Latin) (Canada).	**6.1.6**
Statement	**FIDIC** definition (**Red, Pink, Yellow, Silver, Gold** and **Emerald Books**).	**FIDIC GCs**

(*Continued*)

(Continued)

Term	Meaning	Defined in section
Subcontractor	**FIDIC** definition (**Red, Pink, Yellow, Silver, Gold** and **Emerald Books**).	**FIDIC GCs**
Taking-Over Certificate	**FIDIC** definition (**Red, Pink, Yellow, Silver** and **Emerald Books**).	**FIDIC GCs**
Temporary Works	**FIDIC** definition (**Red, Pink, Yellow, Silver** and **Emerald Books**).	**FIDIC GCs**
Tender	**FIDIC** definition (**Red, Pink, Yellow, Silver, Gold** and **Emerald Books**).	**FIDIC GCs**
Tests after Completion	**FIDIC** definition (**Red, Pink, Yellow, Silver** and **Emerald Books**).	**FIDIC GCs**
Tests on Completion	**FIDIC** definition (**Red, Pink, Yellow, Silver** and **Emerald Books**).	**FIDIC GCs**
TG15	**FIDIC** Task Group 15, responsible for articulating the **FIDIC Golden Principles**.	**2.3**
Time for Completion	**FIDIC** definition (**Red, Pink, Yellow, Silver** and **Emerald Books**).	**FIDIC GCs**
TOCAF	*Texto Ordenado de Contabilidad y Administración Financiera* – Textbook of the Accountability and Financial Administration Ordinance (Uruguay).	**12.2.10.1**
UNCITRAL	United Nations Commission on International Trade Law.	**1.5.6**
UNCITRAL Model Law	*UNCITRAL Model Law on International Commercial Arbitration* 1985 with Amendments as adopted in 2006.	**1.5.6**
Underground Works	**FIDIC** definition (**Emerald Book**).	**FIDIC GCs**
Unforeseeable	**FIDIC** definition (**Red, Pink, Yellow, Silver, Gold** and **Emerald Books**).	**FIDIC GCs**
UNIDROIT	International Institute for the Unification of Private Law.	
USMCA	The United States–Mexico–Canada Agreement that regulates trade in North America.	**9.2.1**
Variation	**FIDIC** definition (**Red, Pink, Yellow, Silver, Gold** and **Emerald Books**).	**FIDIC GCs**
VDC	Virtual design and construction.	**10.2.7**
VECA	Construction capability index (Uruguay).	**12.2.5**
Works	**FIDIC** definition (**Red, Pink, Yellow, Silver, Gold** and **Emerald Books**).	**FIDIC GCs**
writing	**FIDIC** definition (**1987 Red Book**).	**FIDIC GCs**
WSIB	The Workplace Safety and Insurance Board in Ontario (Canada).	**6.2.4**
WTO	World Trade Organization – the only global international organisation dealing with the rules of trade between nations.[6]	**1.8.2**

6 www.wto.org/english/thewto_e/thewto_e.htm (accessed 9 November 2020).

Term	Meaning	Defined in section
WTO GPA	**WTO** Agreement on Government Procurement.	**1.8.2**
year	**FIDIC** definition (**Red, Yellow, Silver, Gold** and **Emerald Books**).	**FIDIC GCs**
Yellow Book	**FIDIC** Conditions of Contract for Plant and Design-Build for Electrical and Mechanical Plant and for Building and Engineering Works, designed by the Contractor – First Edition 1999, Second Edition 2017.	**1.3.1**

INDEX

Abrahamson Principles 12–13, 50
alternative dispute resolution (ADR) 148–149, 171, 197, 289, 297, 302–303
  see also dispute resolution
amiable compositeur (natural justice) 306
anti-corruption measures
  Canada 146–147
anti-trust/corruption laws 25
applicable law
  governing law of the contract 24
  impact of laws 33–34
  intersection of local laws with governing law of the contract 25
  laws applicable to arbitration of dispute 26
  laws applicable to execution of construction project 25
  laws with extra-territorial reach 25
  mandatory law 21
  non-mandatory law 21
  Particular Conditions *see* Particular Conditions
  Yellow Book 2017 provisions on 21–24
  see also governing law of the contract
applicable legislation
  Bolivia 78, 100–103
  Brazil 123–126
  Canada 156–159
  Chile 181–184
  Ecuador 201–206
  Mexico 225, 228–229
  Peru 252–255
  United States 270–272
  Uruguay 295–303
arbitration
  applicable law 26, 224, 229
  Bolivia 88–89
  Brazil 114–115
  Canada 149
  Chile 170–171, 184
  Ecuador 197–198
  Mexico 216, 224, 227, 229
  Peru 234, 241–242, 246, 252
  United States of America 265, 267, 272
  Uruguay 288–290, 294, 297–303
  see also enforcement of foreign judgments; UNCITRAL Model Law on International Commercial Arbitration 1985

bankruptcy 30, 97, 200, 211, 224, 227
  Bolivia 97
  Brazil 127
  Ecuador 200
  Mexico 224
  Peru 252, 255
  Uruguay 295, 297
banks
  multilateral development banks 17–18
  performance bank guarantees 196
behaviour *see* conduct
best practice, promotion of 12–13
bids *see* tenders
Bilateral Investment Treaty (BIT) 89
BIM *see* building information modeling system
Blue-Green Book 16, 43
Bolivia
  applicable legislation 78, 100–103
  arbitration 88–89
  bankruptcy 97
  Bilateral Investment Treaty (BIT) 89
  building information modeling system 85–86
  challenges 90
  civil law 78
  common forms of contract 88
  constitutional structures 77–78
  construction industry overviews 80–90
  contract liquidation 97
  court systems 79–80
  COVID-19 90–93
  current challenges for construction industry 90
  damages 94, 95, 97, 99

defects 94, 95
delays, damages/penalties for 99
Dispute Boards 89, 90
dispute resolution 88–90, 102–103
entry into contract 100
exceptional events (*Force Majeure*) 96
extension of time clauses 95
FIDIC General Conditions 94–98
good faith 99
governing law of the contract 93–94
health and safety 102
innovation 85–86
insolvency 97
insurance 87–88, 97
labour relations 83–84
legal system in 78
licensing/registration 82–83
liens 101
limitation periods 99
liquidation 97
modular construction 85
moral rights 101
Particular Conditions 94–99
procurement 86–87
Public Private Partnership (PPP) 86
safety culture 84–85
Special Provisions 94–99
Subcontractors 97
surplus Materials 97
Temporary Works, sale of 97
termination 96, 97, 100, 102, 103
variations 95
wreckage, sale of 97, 102
Brazil
applicable legislation 123–126
arbitration 114–115
bankruptcy 127
building information modeling system 112
challenges 115
civil law 107, 119
common forms of contract 114
constitutional structures 107
construction industry overviews 108–116
contract liquidation 127
court systems 107–108
COVID-19 116–119
current challenges for construction industry 115
damages 120
defects 121
delays, damages/penalties for 117
Dispute Adjudication Board 122
Dispute Avoidance and Adjudication Board 121
Dispute Boards 114, 122
dispute resolution 114–115, 124, 126
entry into contract 123
exceptional events (*Force Majeure*) 117, 118
extension of time clauses 117
FIDIC General Conditions 120–122
governing law of the contract 119–121, 123–124
government procurement 112–114
gross negligence 122–123
hardship 127–128
health and safety 110, 125
innovation 112
insolvency 127
labour laws 110
labour relations 110
legal system 107
licensing of professionals 109–110
liens 124
limitation of liability 123
liquidation 127
local law and custom 126–128
modular construction 111
Particular Conditions 120–123
Program of Investment Partnerships (PPI) 108
Public Private Partnership (PPP) 108
safety culture 110–111
Temporary Works, sale of 125
termination 121–127
third parties 122
UNCITRAL Model Law 114
variations 126–127
wreckage, sale of 125
breach of contract
damages for 9, 172
building information modeling system (BIM)
Bolivia 85–86
Brazil 112
Canada 144
Chile 168
Mexico 214
Peru 238
United States of America 263
Uruguay 283–284

Canada
anti-corruption measures 146–147
applicable legislation 156–159
arbitration 149
building information modeling system 144
civil law 132
common forms of contract 147–148
common law 132, 133, 137
constitutional structures 131
construction industry overviews 137–149

Construction lien legislation 133–134
contract forms in common use 148
contract liquidation 157
Contracting Authority 139
court systems 135–137
COVID-19 149–152
damages 147
Dispute Avoidance and Adjudication Board 155, 156
Dispute Boards 149
dispute resolution 148–149, 157, 158
entry into contract 157
exceptional events (*Force Majeure*) 147, 150, 151
FIDIC General Conditions 153–156
frustrated contracts 157
governing law of the contract 152–153
health and safety 143, 144, 158
Indigenous peoples 132–133
innovation 144–145
insurance 147
labour relations 142–143
legal system 132
licensing of professionals 140–142
liens 133, 134, 157
local law and custom 159
moral rights 158
Particular Conditions 153–156
private law 133
procurement 145–146
public law 133
Public Private Partnership (PPP) 139
safety culture 143–144
technology and innovation 144–145
termination 158

Chile
applicable legislation 181–184
arbitration 170–171, 184
building information modeling system 168
challenges 171
civil law 164
common forms of contract 170
common law 175, 176, 178
constitutional structures 164
construction industry overviews 165–171
contract liquidation 182
court systems 164–165
COVID-19 172–174
current challenges for construction industry 171
damages 169, 177–178
defects 179
delays, damages/penalties for 177–178
Dispute Avoidance and Adjudication Board 176
Dispute Boards 171
dispute resolution 170–171, 182–184
entry into contract 181
exceptional events (*Force Majeure*) 172–174
extension of time clauses 173
FIDIC General Conditions 181
good faith 176–177
governing law of the contract 175, 181–182
government procurement 168–169
health and safety 172, 182, 183
insurance 169
labour relations 167
legal system 164
licensing of Contractors 166–167
liens 183
limitation periods 180, 181
local law and custom 184
modular construction 168
moral rights 183
multas 178
Particular Conditions 176–181
pena enorme 178
Public Private Partnership (PPP) 166
safety culture 167–168
Temporary Works, sale of 183
termination 179–180, 183
third parties 169, 184
UNCITRAL Model Law 184
wreckage, sale of 183

choice of law *see* applicable law

civil law
Bolivia 78
Brazil 107, 119
Canada 132
Chile 164
differences to common law 5–6
Ecuador 188
freedom of contract 8
Mexico 210
Peru 233
public policy (*ordre public*) 8
system of 5
Uruguay 278

commercial contracts and construction contracts distinguished 3

common forms of contract
Bolivia 88
Brazil 114
Canada 147–148

common law
Canada 132, 133, 137
Chile 175, 176, 178
differences to civil law 5–6
Peru 247–249
system of 5

United States of America 259, 267, 269–270
conduct
reckless misconduct 122
consequential loss or damage *see* indirect or consequential loss or damage
constitutional structures
Bolivia 77–78
Brazil 107
Canada 131
Chile 164
Ecuador 188
Mexico 210
Peru 233
United States of America 259
Uruguay 277–278
construction contracts
choice of law (proper law) 9–11
civil law 5–6
common law 5–8
contract law 6
definition 3
distinction from other commercial contracts 3
entry *see* entry into contract
freedom of contract 6–9
frustration *see* frustrated contracts
international construction contracts 11
legal systems 5–6
operation *see* operation of contract
overview 3–5
pacta sunt servanda 9
termination *see* termination of contracts
uniqueness 5
variations *see* Variations
see also FIDIC contracts
construction industry overviews
Bolivia 80–90
Brazil 108–116
Canada 137–149
Chile 165–171
Ecuador 189–198
Mexico 211–218
Peru 234–243
United States of America 260–265
Uruguay 279–291
see also current challenges for construction industry
contract agreements 18
Contract Data *see* Particular Conditions
contract forms in common use
Canada 148
Ecuador 197
Peru 239–241
see also construction contracts; FIDIC contracts
contract liquidation
Bolivia 97
Brazil 127
Canada 157
Chile 182
Ecuador 203
Mexico 224, 227
Peru 252, 255
Uruguay 295
Contract Participants 48–50
Contractor's Equipment, sale of 97
Contractors
claims 12, 14, 31, 47, 120, 123, 151
foreign 115, 166, 235, 281
indemnities by 267–268
licensing requirements 261
limitation of liability 268
obligations in EPC Silver Book 61, 95
registration/licensing 261–262
sale of equipment by Employer 97
see also licensing of Contractors
Corpus Iuris Civilis 5
corruption *see* anti-corruption laws
court proceedings 9, 25, 79, 165, 267
court systems
Bolivia 79–80
Brazil 107–108
Canada 135–137
Chile 164–165
Ecuador 189
Mexico 210–211
Peru 234
United States of America 259–260
Uruguay 279
COVID-19
Bolivia 90–93
Brazil 116–119
Canada 149–152
Chile 172–174
claims arising under FIDIC contracts 31–33
dispute resolution 33
economic measures 31
Ecuador 198–200
execution of construction projects 29–30
government responses 26–28
impact on construction 28–29
Mexico 218–220
operation of construction contracts 30–31
Peru 243–244
United States of America 265–267
Uruguay 291–292
curial law (*lex arbitrii*) 26, 58–59
current challenges for construction industry
Bolivia 90
Brazil 115

Chile 171
Ecuador 198
Mexico 218
Peru 242–243
Uruguay 290

DAAB *see* Dispute Avoidance and Adjudication Board
DAB *see* Dispute Adjudication Board
damage, indirect or consequential 66
damages
Bolivia 94, 95, 97, 99
Brazil 120
breach of contract 9, 172
Canada 147
Chile 169, 177–178
delays, for 117, 177–178, 249–250
Ecuador 196
liquidated damages 60, 147, 177, 178, 237, 249–250, 256, 273
Mexico 215, 219, 227
Peru 249–250, 256
United States of America 268–269, 271, 273
Uruguay 294–295
Data, Contract *see* Particular Conditions
deed 152
defects
Bolivia 94, 95
Brazil 121
Chile 179
Ecuador 196
liability 5, 179, 251, 293
Mexico 223
notification periods 19, 49, 67, 70, 179, 251
Peru 238, 245, 250–251
United States of America 272
Uruguay 293
delayed payments, financing charges in 72
delays, damages/penalties for
Bolivia 99
Brazil 117
Chile 177–178
Peru 249–250, 256
design
obligations 22, 24
regulations 176
rights 101, 124, 158, 183, 204, 226, 296
risk 240, 245, 288
Dispute Adjudication Board (DAB)
arbitration 51–52
Brazil 122
Mexico 217
Peru 234, 252
Uruguay 294
Dispute Avoidance and Adjudication Board (DAAB)
arbitration 51–52
Brazil 121
Canada 155, 156
Chile 176
failure to appoint members 24
Mexico 216
Peru 252
Dispute Boards
Bolivia 89, 90
Brazil 114, 122
Canada 149
Chile 171
Mexico 217, 222
Peru 241, 242, 252
United States of America 265
Uruguay 303
dispute resolution
alternative 148–149, 171, 197, 289, 297, 302–303
applicable law 33
Bolivia 88–90, 102–103
Brazil 114–115, 124, 126
Canada 148–149, 157, 158
Chile 170–171, 182–184
COVID-19-related claims 33
Ecuador 197–198, 204, 206
Mexico 216–218, 225, 227, 229
Peru 241–242, 253, 255
United States of America 265
Uruguay 288–291
see also arbitration; enforcement of foreign judgments
doctrine of separability 26

Ecuador
applicable legislation 201–206
arbitration 197–198
bankruptcy 200
challenges 198
civil law 188
constitutional structures 188
construction industry overviews 189–198
contract forms in common use 197
contract liquidation 203
court systems 189
COVID-19 198–200
current challenges for construction industry 198
damages 196
defects 196
dispute resolution 197–198, 204, 206
employment 192–194
entry into contract 203

exceptional events (*Force Majeure*) 199, 200
FIDIC General Conditions 201
governing law of the contract 200–204
health and safety 205
innovation 195
insurance 196
labour relations 191
licensing of Contractors 191
liens 204
local law and custom 206
modular construction 195
moral rights 204
Particular Conditions 201
procurement 195–196
Public Private Partnership (PPP) 190, 197
safety culture 194–195
Temporary Works, sale of 205
termination 193–194, 201, 203, 205, 206
third parties 196
unique features of the construction industry 198
wreckage, sale of 205
Emerald Book 16
Golden Principles 20–21, 47–48, 53–54
Employers
FIDIC Conditions of Contract 15, 16, 43
Particular Conditions as to preferences 55
payment of Subcontractors by 155
sale of Contractor's Equipment, surplus material, wreckage and Temporary Works 97, 102, 125, 183, 205, 226
Special Provisions necessary or desirable for preferences of 62, 66–69
termination by 123, 180
Engineers
decisions as final and binding 122
dissatisfaction with determinations of 121
exercise of duties 49
instructions by 63, 65
qualifications 82, 97
role of 49, 52
entry into contract
Bolivia 100
Brazil 123
Canada 157
Chile 181
Ecuador 203
Mexico 222–223, 225
Peru 252
Uruguay 295
EPC contract 88, 176
EPCM contract 4, 15
equipment
sale of 97, 102, 125, 183, 205, 226
testing apparatus, equipment and instruments, calibration of 125, 183, 254
ex aequo et bono 224
exceptional events (*Force Majeure*) 24, 31, 32
Bolivia 96
Brazil 117, 118
Canada 147, 150, 151
Chile 172–174
Ecuador 199, 200
Mexico 215, 219, 223
Peru 244
Uruguay 292
extension of time (EOT) clauses
Bolivia 95
Brazil 117
Chile 173
Peru 244
extra-territoriality, applicable law and 25

fair and balanced contracts
Golden Principles 45–47
FIDIC contracts
aims of book 38–39
contract agreement 18
contract documents 18, 19
General Conditions 20
JICA usage *see* Japan International Cooperation Agency
MDB use of 17–18
order of precedence of documents 66
overview 15–17
Particular Conditions *see* Particular Conditions
rainbow suite 19
Special Provisions 19–20
subcontracts 16
underground Works *see* Emerald Book
FIDIC General Conditions 17, 18, 20, 45, 69
Bolivia 94–98
Brazil 120–122
Canada 153–156
Chile 181
Ecuador 201
Mexico 221–222
Peru 248–251
United States of America 269–273
Uruguay 293–294
FIDIC Golden Principles *see* Golden Principles
financing charges in delayed payments 72
force majeure see exceptional events
foreign judgments *see* enforcement of foreign judgments
freedom of contract 6–9
frustrated contracts
Canada 157

General Conditions *see* FIDIC General Conditions
Gold Book 16, 43
Golden Principles (GPs)
consistency with 51–53
drafting contract documents 51–53
fair and balanced contracts 45–47
overview 20–21, 45, 47–49
purpose of 39
reasons for 49–51
risk allocation 45–49, 50
use of 53
good faith 13–14
Bolivia 99
Chile 176–177
Peru 252
governing law of the contract
Bolivia 93–94
Brazil 119–121, 123–124
Canada 152–153
Chile 175, 181–182
Ecuador 200–204
Mexico 220–225
Peru 245–248, 252–253
United States 267–270
Uruguay 292–293, 295–296
government procurement *see* procurement
Green Book 16, 43, 313
gross negligence
Brazil 122–123
Peru 251
ground risks, allocation of 95
guarantees *see* performance bank guarantees

Hague Convention on Choice of Court Agreements 119
Hague Principles 56–58, 313
hardship 31
Brazil 127–128
Mexico 223
Uruguay 295
Head Contract 3, 313
health and safety 96
Bolivia 102
Brazil 110, 125
Canada 143, 144, 158
Chile 172, 182, 183
Ecuador 205
Mexico 226, 228
Peru 237–238, 254
Uruguay 283, 297

ICSID Convention 38, 89, 313
implied terms
Peru 248
in rem claim 25, 313
income tax 233
indirect or consequential loss or damage 66
innovation
Bolivia 85–86
Brazil 112
Canada 144–145
Ecuador 195
Mexico 214
Peru 238
United States 263
Uruguay 283–284
insolvency
Bolivia 97
Brazil 127
Mexico 224, 227
Uruguay 293
insurance
Bolivia 87–88, 97
Canada 147
Chile 169
Ecuador 196
Mexico 215
Peru 240
provided by contractor 24
United States 264
Uruguay 287–288
intellectual property 211, 226
international construction contracts 11, 314
international conventions and agreements, country accessions to 34–38
interpretation *see* contract interpretation under local law and custom
ipso facto 314

Japan International Cooperation Agency (JICA) 18, 314
Checklist for One Sided Contracts 15
documents, availability of 18, 48
FIDIC Golden Principles, and 48
JICA *see* Japan International Cooperation Agency
joint and several liability 65

labour laws 23, 30
Brazil 110
Mexico 213
Uruguay 283
law of the forum 25, 56–57, 314
legal system
Bolivia 78
Brazil 107
Canada 132
legal systems *see* civil law; common law
legislation *see* applicable legislation

lex arbitrii (curial law) 26, 58–59, 315
lex constructionis 11–15
  concept 11–12
  principles of 13–14
  promotion of best practice for successful projects 12–13
lex fori 25, 57, 315
lex loci rei sitae 25, 315
liability
  contractual 196
  decennial 102, 125, 158, 183, 205, 227, 255, 293, 297, 309
  defects 5, 102, 125, 158, 183, 205, 228, 254, 297
  insurance 288
  limitations of 66, 99, 250–251, 268
  nuisance, for 102, 125, 183, 205, 227, 254, 297
  see also limitation periods; proportionate liability
licensing of Contractors
  Chile 166–167
  Ecuador 191
  Peru 236–237
  United States 261–262
licensing of professionals
  Brazil 109–110
  Canada 140–142
  Mexico 212, 225
  United States 261–262
licensing/registration
  Bolivia 82–83
liens
  Bolivia 101
  Brazil 124
  Canada 133, 134, 157
  Chile 183
  Ecuador 204
  Mexico 226
  Uruguay 296
limitation of liability
  Brazil 123
  United States 268
limitation periods
  Bolivia 99
  Chile 180, 181
  Mexico 224, 227, 229
  Peru 250–251
liquidated damages 315
  Peru 249–250
  United States 273
liquidation
  Bolivia 97
  Brazil 127
  Mexico 224, 227
local labour *see* labour laws
local law and custom
  Brazil 126–128
  Canada 159
  Chile 184
  contract interpretation (*see* contract interpretation under local law and custom)
  Ecuador 206
  Mexico 229–230
loss, indirect or consequential 66
lump sum contracts 95

mandatory law 21, 33, 47, 56, 59–60, 315
Materials
  ownership of 23, 67, 97
  surplus Materials, sale of 97
MDBs *see* multilateral development banks
Mercosur 286
Mexico
  applicable legislation 225, 228–229
  arbitration 216, 224, 227, 229
  bankruptcy 224
  building information modeling system 214
  challenges 218
  civil law 210
  common forms of contract 215–216
  constitutional structures 210
  construction industry overview 211–218
  contract liquidation 224, 227
  court systems 210–211
  COVID-19 218–220
  current challenges for construction industry 218
  damages 215, 219, 227
  defects 223
  Dispute Adjudication Board 217
  Dispute Avoidance and Adjudication Board 216
  Dispute Boards 217, 222
  dispute resolution 216–218, 225, 227, 229
  entry into contract 222–223, 225
  exceptional events (*Force Majeure*) 215, 219, 223
  FIDIC General Conditions 221–222
  governing law of the contract 220–225
  hardship 223
  health and safety 226, 228
  innovation 214
  insolvency 224, 227
  insurance 215
  labour laws 213
  labour relations 213
  legal environment 210–211
  legal system 210
  licensing of professionals 212, 225

liens 226
limitation periods 224, 227, 229
liquidation 224, 227
local law and custom 229–230
modular construction 213–214
moral rights 226
Particular Conditions 221–222
procurement 214–215
residential mortgage backed securities (RMBS) 195
safety culture 213
Subcontractors 225
termination 223–225, 227
UNCITRAL Model Law 229
USMCA 212
misrepresentation
United States 271
Model Law 26, 114, 184, 229, 272, 288, 315
moral rights
Bolivia 101
Brazil 124
Canada 158
Chile 183
Ecuador 204
Mexico 226
Uruguay 296
multilateral development banks (MDBs)
FIDIC contracts usage 17
standard bidding documents 17

natural justice (*amiable compositeur*) 306
negligence *see* gross negligence
New Engineering Contract (NEC) 239
New York Convention 15, 34–35, 114, 115, 234, 272, 316
non-mandatory law 21, 33, 56, 316
notices of claim 120–121, 180–181

operation of contract 30–31, 33
Bolivia 91–93, 100
Brazil 117–119, 124–125
Canada 150–152, 157–158
Chile 173–174, 181, 183
Ecuador 199–200, 203, 204–205
Mexico 219–220, 223, 225–227, 228
Peru 244, 253
United States 266–267
Uruguay 291–292, 295, 296–297
Orange Book 1995 16, 42, 43, 305
ordre public 8, 56–57, 316

pacta sunt servanda 9, 316
Particular Conditions
agreement to arbitrate, governing law as to 58–59
choice of law 58
Contract Data 19
format of 69–70
General Conditions and 20
governing law of the contract 24, 56–58
Part A – Contract Data 19, 55
Part B – Special Provisions 19, 55–56
preparation of 56–59
reasons for 47
Special Provisions 19, 59–61
Particular Conditions, desirable Special Provisions in 62–69
Bolivia 98–99
Brazil 122–123
Canada 156
Chile 181
Ecuador 201
Mexico 222
Peru 252
Uruguay 294–295
Particular Conditions, necessary Special Provisions in 62–69
Bolivia 94–98
Brazil 120–122
Canada 153–156
Chile 176–181
Ecuador 201
Mexico 221–222
Peru 248–251
United States 269–270
Uruguay 293–294
Payment Legislation 155
payments
certainty and promptness of 15
for variations 95
security of 4
performance security 316
pena enorme 178
penaldides 249
Peru
applicable legislation 252–255
arbitration 234, 241–242, 246, 252
bankruptcy 252, 255
building information modeling system 238
challenges 242–243
civil law 233
common forms of contract 240–241
common law 247–249
constitutional structures 233
construction industry overviews 234–243
contract forms in common use 239–241
contract liquidation 252, 255
court systems 234
COVID-19 243–244

current challenges for construction industry 242–243
damages 249–250, 256
defects 238, 245, 250–251
delays, damages/penalties for 249–250, 256
Dispute Adjudication Board 234, 252
Dispute Avoidance and Adjudication Board 252
Dispute Boards 241, 242, 252
dispute resolution 241–242, 253, 255
entry into contract 252
exceptional events *(Force Majeure)* 244
extension of time clauses 244
FIDIC General Conditions 248–251
good faith 252
governing law of the contract 245–248, 252–253
gross negligence 251
health and safety 237–238, 254
implied terms 248
innovation 238
insurance 240
integrated project delivery (IPD) 240
labour relations 237
legal system 233–234
licensing of Contractors 236–237
limitation periods 250–251
liquidated damages 249–250
modular construction 238
New Engineering Contract (NEC) 239
Particular Conditions 248–252
penaldides 249
procurement 238–240
project management officer 235
Project Partnering Contract (PPC 2000) 240
safety culture 237–238
termination 252, 255
third parties 236, 251
unique features of the construction industry 243
variations 235, 251
virtual design and construction (VDC) 238
Pink Book 16–18, 317
Plant
Contractor's Equipment, sale of 97, 226
ownership of 23, 97
PPP *see* Public Private Partnership
price *see* costs
private law 133
procurement
Brazil 112–114
Canada 145–146
procurement, private
Bolivia 86–87
Ecuador 195–196
Mexico 214–215
Peru 238–240
United States 264
procurement, public
Bolivia 101
Brazil 112–113
Ecuador 205
Mexico 214, 222
Peru 239
Uruguay 284–285, 285–286
professionals *see* licensing of professionals
project requirements, Particular Conditions 64–65
proper law *see* choice of law
proper law of the contract 9–11, 317
public law 133
public policy (*ordre public*)
civil law 8
freedom of contract 6–9
mandatory law 21, 57
proper law of the Contract 10
Public Private Partnership (PPP) 15, 317
Bolivia 86
Brazil 108
Canada 139
Chile 166
Ecuador 190, 197
public procurement *see* procurement, public
public–private partnership (PPP) 86

rainbow suite 16, 17, 19
rebus sic stantibus 13, 318
recepción definitiva 179
recepción provisoria 178
reception 178, 179, 250
reckless misconduct 122
recursos administrativos 287
Red Book 1977 16, 305
Red Book 1987 16, 42, 305
Red Book 1999 16, 17, 51, 305
Red Book 2017 16, 18, 19, 248, 305
request for qualifications (RFQ) 145
Retention Money 318
risk
Golden Principles 20, 45–50
ground risks, allocation of 95
JICA 18, 47
Rome I 8, 57–58, 318

safety *see* health and safety
scope of work, variation of *see* Variations
security of payment 4
separability *see* doctrine of separability
Silver Book 1999 16, 51, 305

Silver Book 2017 16, 305
  order of precedence of documents 19
Special Provisions *see* Particular Conditions
stamp duty 18
standard bidding documents 17
stare decisis 5, 319
statute of limitations *see* limitation periods
Subcontractors
  Bolivia 97
  Mexico 225
surplus Materials, sale of
  Bolivia 97

taxation
  income tax 64
  stamp duty 18
Temporary Works, sale of
  Bolivia 97
  Brazil 125
  Chile 183
  Ecuador 205
tenders 17, 19, 22, 45, 46, 50, 55, 58, 69, 88, 100, 113, 124, 145, 146, 157, 159, 173, 182, 203, 215, 225, 253, 270, 282, 288, 295
termination
  Bolivia 96, 97, 100, 102, 103
  Brazil 121–127
  Canada 158
  Chile 179–180, 183
  Ecuador 193–194, 201, 203, 205, 206
  Mexico 223–225, 227
  Peru 252, 255
  Uruguay 293, 295, 297
testing apparatus, equipment and instruments, calibration of 125, 183, 254
third parties
  Brazil 122
  Chile 169, 184
  Ecuador 196
  Peru 236, 251
  Uruguay 277, 288, 299
time
  extension of time (EOT) clauses 31, 32, 95, 117, 173, 244
time bars 51, 61, 248

UNCITRAL Model Law on International Commercial Arbitration 1985 (UNCITRAL Model Law)
  applicable laws as to arbitration 26
  Brazil 114
  Chile 184
  Mexico 229
  United States of America 272
  Uruguay 288, 292
underground works 16, 41, 192
unfair contract terms 61
UNIDROIT 8, 9, 14, 58, 292
United States of America
  applicable legislation 270–272
  arbitration 265, 267, 272
  building information modeling system 263
  common forms of contract 264–265
  common law 259, 267, 269–270
  constitutional structures 259
  court systems 259–260
  COVID-19 265–267
  damages 268–269, 271, 273
  defects 272
  Dispute Boards 265
  dispute resolution 265
  FIDIC General Conditions 269–273
  governing law of the contract 267–270
  innovation 263
  insurance 264
  labour relations 262
  legal system 259
  licensing of Contractors 261–262
  licensing of professionals 261–262
  limitation of liability 268
  liquidated damages 273
  modular construction 263
  Particular Conditions 269–270
  procurement 264
  safety culture 262–263
  UNCITRAL Model Law 272
  variations 270
Uruguay
  ad solemnitatem 298
  applicable legislation 295–303
  arbitration 288–290, 294, 297–303
  bankruptcy 295, 297
  building information modeling system 283–284
  challenges 290
  civil law 278
  constitutional structures 277–278
  construction capability index 281
  construction industry overviews 279–291
  contract liquidation 295
  contractors 280
  court systems 279
  COVID-19 291–292
  current challenges for construction industry 290
  damages 294–295
  defects 293
  Dispute Adjudication Board 294
  Dispute Boards 303
  dispute resolution 288–291

entry into contract 295
exceptional events *(Force Majeure)* 292
extra petita 300
FIDIC General Conditions 293–294
governing law of the contract 292–293, 295–296
hardship 295
health and safety 297
innovation 283–284
insolvency 293
insurance 287–288
labour laws 283
labour relations 282
legal system 278–279
liens 296
modular construction 283
moral rights 296
Particular Conditions 293–295
registration 281
safety culture 283
SPV 280
subcontracting 280–281
termination 293, 295, 297
third parties 277, 288, 299
UNCITRAL Model Law 288, 292
unique features of the construction industry 290–291

Variations
  Bolivia 95
  Brazil 126–127
  Employers' duty to pay for changes 61
  payments 95
  Peru 235, 251
  United States of America 270
  valuation of Variations 61
virtual design and construction (VDC) 238

worker and workplace safety *see* health and safety
wreckage, sale of
  Bolivia 97, 102
  Brazil 125
  Chile 183
  Ecuador 205
WTO Agreement on Government Procurement, country accessions to 35–38
WTO GPA 35

Yellow Book 1987 16, 42
Yellow Book 1999 16, 51
Yellow Book 2017 16, 19, 20–21, 24, 55, 70, 96
  applicable law 19–20
  Contract Data 70
  order of precedence of documents 19